heck for abbreviations that should be spelled out (232-233)

se adverb form to modify verbs and other modifiers (45-47)

heck agreement of subject and verb, pronoun and antecedent (17-22, 32-35)

heck for omission or misuse of apostrophe (247)

heck for words that should be capitalized (251-252)

trengthen sequence of ideas; show relevance of detail (149ff., 207ff.)

se semicolon or period between independent clauses (267)

heck for awkward, inaccurate, inappropriate wording (104-118)

evelop your point more fully—support, explain, illustrate (168-170)

heck dictionary for syllabication of the word (231)

ewrite the sentence to indicate what the modifier modifies (51)

heck form or adequacy of documentation (290ff.)

heck for unemphatic, anticlimactic diction or organization (398, 464)

o not punctuate as a sentence—lacks an independent clause (~~580~~) 258

ut items joined by "and," "but," "or" in same grammatical category (64)

heck standing of debatable usage in glossary (361ff.)

heck for unsatisfactory forms or constructions (1ff.)

heck for unidiomatic, un-English expression (81)

ewrite the sentence to make it clearer or more natural (137-141)

heck for faulty or unnecessary capitalization (251-252)

hift modifier into more appropriate position or rewrite sentence (50)

heck for omission or misuse of punctuation (254ff.)

reak up into paragraphs that reflect organization (149ff.)

void confusing or unnecessary paragraph break (149ff.)

heck reference of pronouns (32-35)

void unnecessary or awkward repetition (143)

heck faulty predication, incomplete or mixed construction (55, 56, 59)

heck for inadequate or inappropriate subordination (125, 140)

heck for shift in time or use of pronouns, shift to passive (68-72)

xpression is too slangy for its context (95)

heck for spelling errors (234ff.)

se appropriate tense of verb (25-27, 68)

trengthen transition from point to point (152, 207-211)

emove deadwood (106, 137)

orrect obvious error

orrect obvious omission

se punctuation mark indicated (see reference chart, 254)

# CONCISE
# ENGLISH
# HANDBOOK

# CONCISE ENGLISH HANDBOOK

## THIRD EDITION

HANS P. GUTH
SAN JOSE STATE COLLEGE

*Wadsworth Publishing Company, Inc.*
*Belmont, California*

2 3 4 5 6 7 8 9 10   74 73 72 71 70

HANS P. GUTH
CONCISE ENGLISH HANDBOOK, THIRD EDITION

*L.C. Cat. Card No.: 77–99036
Printed in the United States of America*

# PREFACE

The *Concise English Handbook* makes available the handbook sections of *Words and Ideas* for use as a compact guide to written English. The aim is to provide useful information in a clearly organized and succinctly worded form. Improvements in the current Third Edition are designed to help the book attain more fully its original goals: to focus clearly on essentials; to provide a common-sense approach to usage; to set realistic standards for college writing; and to provide materials that the student finds accessible, intelligible, and relevant to his needs.

As in earlier editions, the chapter on grammar presents essential terminology and describes basic features of standard written English. The chapters on diction and sentence style concentrate on accurate, effective, and economical use of language. The chapters on the paragraph, the whole theme, and the research paper present essential principles of composition and rhetoric. Chapters 6 and 7 offer a concise review of mechanics; the glossaries provide brief discussions of points of usage and definitions of grammatical terms.

In this new Third Edition, two chapters have been extensively reorganized: the updated and simplified chapter on diction; and the streamlined chapter on sentence style, stressing a positive approach to sentence building. Throughout, there is more extensive use of literary sample sentences and sample passages, with new illustrations drawn from the best contemporary and earlier writers. The research paper chapter includes a new sample paper on a literary subject, "The Furor over Ibsen."

A book such as this must attempt to mobilize a latent consensus among people who teach, write, and write about, educated English. In preparing the present version, I have again profited greatly from the example and advice of interested colleagues. My special thanks are due to Wayne Harsh, University of California, Davis; Arthur Williams, University of Massachusetts; James Bashore, Bowling Green State University; John Nichol, University of Southern California; Wilbur Huck, Idaho State University; Bruce Anawalt, Washington State University; and J. J. Lamberts, Arizona State University.

Hans Guth

# CONTENTS

## CHAPTER 2/Diction    74

# CHAPTER 7/Punctuation 255

# 1

# GRAMMAR

When a child begins to talk, he learns not only to name things but also to work the names of things into complicated patterns. Soon he is able to say "Suzie won't give me my ball back" or "Johnny says there isn't any Santa Claus." He has evidently mastered the major principles of **grammar**; that is, *the system by which words combine into larger units to convey ideas and information.*

## G 1   Grammar and Usage

*The study of grammar can help a writer make appropriate use of the resources of the language.*

The student in high school and college must learn to adapt the grammatical patterns he learned as a child to changing needs. The language that the educated adult uses in serious conversation and in writing differs to some extent from the language he uses when not on his best behavior. A student learns early that often he should say "is not" rather than "ain't," "can hardly wait" rather than "can't hardly wait," and "this kind of car" rather than "these kind of cars."

Differences such as these are called differences in **usage**. The study of usage investigates *choices among alternative words, word forms, and constructions.* An effective writer has learned to make the choices that will prove acceptable to his readers.

## G 1a    Standard and Nonstandard

*Serious writing employs the kind of English that enjoys social and cultural prestige.* **Standard** usage is the language of education, journalism, and other white-collar occupations. You will use it in your written work except when you record or deliberately imitate **nonstandard** speech. Nonstandard speakers have usually had relatively little formal education. Their jobs often require little reading of instructions and little writing of reports. They may have few dealings with teachers, lawyers, and other presumably highly literate persons.

Here are some of the distinctive forms and constructions of nonstandard English:

| | |
|---|---|
| **Verb Forms:** | he *don't*, you *was*, I *says; knowed, growed;* I *seen* him |
| **Pronoun Forms:** | *hisself, theirself; this here* book, *that there* car; *them* boys |
| **Connectives:** | *without* you pay the rent; *on account of* he was sick; *being as* she couldn't come |
| **Double Negatives:** | we *don't* have *no* time;  a little rain *never* hurt *no* one |

(See the Glossary of Usage for *as, being as, couple,* double comparative, double negative, *all the farther, hadn't ought to, learn, used to could, without.*)

## G 1b    Formal and Informal

*Different kinds of standard English are appropriate to different occasions.* Relatively **informal** usages are found primarily in casual conversation, but also in writing designed to sound chatty or familiar. Relatively **formal** usages are characteristic of the language of scholarly studies, books on serious subjects, articles in serious magazines. Though more characteristic of written than of spoken English, these usages are also found in formal lectures, speeches, and discussions.

Here are some grammatical features of informal English:[1]

[1] For a discussion of formal and informal diction, see D 3.

| | |
|---|---|
| **Contractions:** | *don't, doesn't, isn't, won't, can't; I'm, you've, they're* |
| **Conversational Tags:** | *well, . . . ; why, . . . ; now, . . .* |
| **Pronoun Forms:** | it's *me*, that's *him; who* did you invite |
| **Pronoun Reference:** | everybody took *theirs*; somebody left *their* gloves |
| **Intensifiers:** | *so* glad, *such* a surprise; *real* miserable, *awful* fast |

The line between informal and formal English is not easy to draw. It is a matter not only of forms and constructions but also of word choice, sentence style, and organization. The difference is often a matter of degree, with some expressions sounding more easygoing than others. At one extreme, the term **colloquial**, used in this book mainly in reference to word choice, describes the *usages most clearly suggestive of informal, improvised speech.* At the other extreme is usage so punctiliously formal as to be stilted or affected. As used in this book, the term *formal* describes usage generally appropriate to the discussion of serious issues.

Most college writing requires a knowledge of formal usage. Even if you are content to have your writing sound casual and relaxed, you have to be able to use a more formal style when the situation clearly demands it.

(See the Glossary of Usage on *apt/liable, between/among, blame on, can* and *may, cannot help but, couple of, different than, due to, each other/one another, get hit, it's me, less/fewer, like I said, most everybody,* possessive with verbal noun, preposition at the end of a sentence, *providing, reason is because, shall/will,* split infinitive, *these kind* and *those kind, used to/didn't use to, where at, you* with indefinite reference.)

## Exercises

**A**. How successful are the following attempts to reproduce in writing the characteristic forms and constructions of *nonstandard speech*? Which features of nonstandard usage do you recognize?

**1.** I be dog iffen there wadden more folks there. Coming by wagon and foot and car, they was. Brother Slynum, he was standing at the entrance in his preaching suit just a-waving and helloing to everybody. The women was in their print dresses and sunbonnets. The men folks, too, was in their Sunday-go-to-meeting clothes. That ere tent with the sign painted over the door, "Welcome! All Day Singing and Dinner on the Ground," it was sagging in the wind. Outen front was the tables where everybody was putting the victuals: salads, cakes, cornbread, preserves, puddins, and Lord knows what all. At the far end of the table over a stone-built stove they was frying the catfish.

It was a jump-rope day. The spring was all stretched out on the pastures beyond, pretty and a little shy maybe, like a lazy gal waiting for her feller. With buttercups for freckles. But that ere spring didn't have nothing on me, I had more freckles than ere was buttercups. Yep. Mama said I swollered a dollar and it broke out in pennies. But she was just spoofing. I hadden never seen a dollar.—Clancy Carlile, "The Animal Fair," *New Campus Writing*

**2**. Well, anyway, they come over to help us celebrate the Golden Wedding and it was pretty crimpy weather and the furnace don't seem to heat up no more like it used to and Mother made the remark that she hoped this winter wouldn't be as cold as the last, referring to the winter previous. So Edie said if she was us, and nothing to keep us home, she certainly wouldn't spend no more winters up here and why didn't we just shut off the water and close up the house and go down to Tampa, Florida? You know we was there four winters ago and staid five weeks, but it cost us over three hundred and fifty dollars for hotel bill alone. So Mother said we wasn't going no place to be robbed. So my son-in-law spoke up and said that Tampa wasn't the only place in the South, and besides we didn't have to stop at no high price hotel but could rent us a couple rooms and board out somewheres, and he had heard that St. Petersburg, Florida, was *the* spot and if we said the word he would write down there and make inquiries.—Ring W. Lardner, "The Golden Honeymoon," *How to Write Short Stories*

**B**. Study recent columns by a columnist using a deliberately informal or humorous style. Report on his use of distinctive grammatical features of *informal English.*

# G 2   Grammatical Analysis

*Grammar is the study of how words work together in a sentence.*

Words convey only vague and tentative meanings as long as they are loosely strung together. G.I.s and tourists abroad can carry on a rudimentary conversation with foreigners after picking up a few isolated words. A foreign visitor to the United States can make some headway by taking individual words from a dictionary. But he will not be speaking English until he can work words into meaningful patterns like the following:

| Actor | Action Verb | Target | |
|---|---|---|---|
| The agent | scrutinized | my passport. | |
| **Sender** | **Action Verb** | **Address** | **Missive** |
| The travel bureau | sent | me | a brochure. |
| **Person** | **Linking Verb** | **Label** | |
| Maurice | looked | disappointed. | |
| **Actor** | **Action Verb** | **Target** | **Label** |
| Maurice | called | the trip | a disaster. |

## G 2a   Grammatical Devices

*English employs several kinds of grammatical devices to give precise meaning to a succession of words.* In the typical written sentence, inflections, word order, and function words combine to help the reader select among the possible meanings of words and work those words into a meaningful sequence.

(1) **Inflections** are *changes in the form of a word that correspond to differences in grammatical relationships.* Inflections signal the differences in meaning between the sentences in each of the following pairs:

Stop*s* annoy*ed* our passenger.
Stop annoy*ing* our passenger.

The physician studi*ed* burns.
The physician*'s* study burn*ed*.

The endings spelled *s, ed,* and *ing* are the inflections most frequently used in English.

NOTE: Some languages, such as Latin and German, rely heavily on inflections. Originally, English was close to German in number and importance of inflected forms. Through the centuries, however, English has shed many of these. Modern English relies primarily on other grammatical devices.

(2) A second major grammatical device is **word order**. In English, *different arrangements of words in a sentence produce different meanings.* Compare the sentences in the following pairs:

> *Gentlemen* prefer *blondes.*
> *Blondes* prefer *gentlemen.*
>
> A *tramp* called *the mayor a liar.*
> A *liar* called *the mayor a tramp.*
> *The mayor* called *a tramp a liar.*
>
> He ate *only* the steak.
> He ate the *only* steak.

(3) A third major grammatical device is the use of *words whose main function is to clarify relationships among other words.* Many modern grammarians group these words together as **function words**. Function words account for the differences in meaning in the following pairs:

> George set *a* poor example.
> George set *the* poor *an* example.
>
> He left the lady his estate.
> He left *with* the lady *for* his estate.
>
> The nurse neglected the patient.
> The nurse *was* neglected *by* the patient.

## G 2b    Basic Sentence Elements

*The most important of the basic grammatical categories are those required to make up the various typical sentence patterns.* In analyzing sentences, grammarians assign words to basic categories, or **parts of speech**, according to the functions they perform. The same word may serve different functions, and belong to different grammatical categories, in different sentences. The word *light* performs a different function in each of the following:

> Turn off the *light*.
> Let's *light* a candle.
> She had *light* hair.
> The water was *light* blue.

(1) *The basic model of the English sentence consists of only two major elements.* A complete sentence normally has at least a **subject** and a **predicate**:

| Subject | Predicate |
|---------|-----------|
| The boy | reads. |
| A car | stopped. |
| Dogs | bark. |

The most important part of the subject is usually a **noun**: *car, student, bulldog, college, education.* Characteristically, nouns name or classify things, places, people, animals, concepts. The housewife looking up entries in the Sears Roebuck catalog, the chemist giving names to new plastics, the businessman naming new products—all rely on the naming function of the noun.

Here are the most important features of nouns:

• They occur in typical noun positions: "*Dogs* bark," "I like *dogs*," and "for my *dogs*."

• Their appearance is often signaled by noun markers such as *a, an,* and *the* (**articles**); *this, these, that,* and *those* (**demonstrative pronouns**); or *my, our,* and *your* (**possessive pronouns**). Modern grammars group these noun markers together as **determiners.**

• They typically add the inflectional *-s* to refer to more than one (plural): *boys, dogs, cars, ideas, preparations.* But note irregular plurals like *children* and *oxen;* unmarked plurals like *deer, sheep, offspring;* and nouns normally occurring only in the singular: *chaos, courage, rice.*

- They often show noun-forming endings (**suffixes**) like *-acy, -age, -ance, -dom, -ness, -hood: literacy, bondage, importance, wisdom, happiness, brotherhood.*

- The place of nouns may be taken by **noun equivalents** or noun substitutes, such as the **personal pronouns**:

| | |
|---|---|
| *He* | reads. |
| *It* | stopped. |
| *They* | bark. |

The predicate, the second major part of a simple sentence, normally makes some kind of assertion concerning the subject. (Sometimes the predicate asks a question about the subject.) The most important word, or group of words, in the predicate is the **verb**: *reads, stopped, has left, will return, is reprimanded, has been elected.* The verb signals the performance of an action, the occurrence of an event, or the presence of a condition. A noun may *name* an action: *theft, movement, investigation.* A verb refers to present, future, past, possible, or hypothetical performance: *steals, has moved, may investigate.*

Here are the most important features of verbs:

- They occur in typical verb positions: "Let's *eat*," "*Eat* your cereal," and "Big fishes *eat* little fishes."

- In the present tense, most verbs add the inflectional *-s* when *he, she,* or *it* could substitute for the subject (third person singular): "He eat*s*," "She write*s*," "It surprise*s* me." Many verbs have a separate inflected form for past tense: *eat–ate, sing–sang, ask–asked, investigate–investigated.*

- Typical verb-forming suffixes are *-ize* and *-en*: organ*ize*, redd*en*, sharp*en*.

- In verb forms consisting of several words, a limited number of **auxiliaries** occur. If there are several auxiliaries, they typically appear in the following order: first, a modal, if any (*will/would, shall/should, can/could, may/might*); second, a form of *have*, if any (*has, had*); third, a form of *be*, if only one such form occurs (*is, am, are, was, were, be, been*); fourth, *being*, if two forms of *be* are present. Here are some of the resulting combinations:

| Modal | Have | Be | (Being) | Main Verb |
|-------|------|------|---------|-----------|
| can | | | | happen |
| | has | | | arrived |
| could | have | | | called |
| | | is | | waiting |
| may | | be | | canceled |
| | | is | being | checked |
| will | have | been | | sold |
| | | was | being | rebuilt |
| should | have | been | | revised |

(2) *In several typical sentence patterns, the predicate is completed by one or more complements.* **Complements** become essential parts of the basic structure. An action verb may carry its action across to its target (**direct object**). An action verb like *give, send,* or *write* may carry the pattern first to the destination (**indirect object**) and then proceed to the missive (direct object). A verb like *name, elect,* or *call* may carry the pattern first to a direct object and then pin a label on the direct object. (The second complement is then called an **object complement**.)

| Subject | Action Verb | Complement | Complement |
|---------|-------------|------------|------------|
| The student | reads | a book. | |
| My friend | sent | me | a letter. |
| Fred | called | his roommate | a liar. |

In other sentences, the verb is a **linking verb**, which introduces a description of the subject. A linking verb pins a label on the subject.

| Subject | Linking Verb | Complement |
|---------|-------------|------------|
| Schoogle | is | a mailman. |
| He | may be | your brother. |
| The price | seemed | reasonable. |
| The food | tasted | good. |

The description following the linking verb is often a noun (*mailman, brother*). It may also be an **adjective**, a word that can point out a quality of a noun (see G 2c).

(3) *Several simple transformations rearrange (and sometimes omit or expand) basic sentence elements.* Thus, the **passive** makes the original *object* the subject of a new sentence. The original subject appears after *by* at the end of the pattern, or is omitted altogether. The verb is changed to its passive form, which uses the auxiliary *be* and the past participle (see G 4a). The resulting pattern reverses the more common actor-action sequence. It makes the receiver, the target, or the result of the action the subject of the sentence.[2]

| Subject | Passive Verb | |
|---------|-------------|--|
| The book | was read | (by the student). |
| A letter | has been sent | (by my friend). |

A second transformation changes the verb to the form used in requests or commands (**imperative**) and omits the subject:

| Verb | Complement |
|------|------------|
| Shut | the door. |
| Be | a man. |
| Keep | quiet. |

A third transformation introduces an initial *there* and postpones the subject:

| | Verb | Subject |
|--|------|---------|
| There | is | hope. |
| There | was | no time. |
| There | were | few survivors. |

[2] On the overuse of the passive, see S 3b.

NOTE: In identifying basic sentence elements, you will have to distinguish between verbs and **verbals**. *Verbals are derived from verbs but do not by themselves function as predicates.* The most distinctive and the most important of the verbals are the *to* forms (**infinitives**) and the *-ing* forms (**gerunds** and **present participles**). Infinitives and gerunds often serve as subjects or as complements, taking the place of nouns:

| | | |
|---|---|---|
| *Speeding* | causes | accidents. |
| He | refused | *to pay.* |
| Teachers | discourage | *cheating.* |

These verbals do have some important similarities to verbs. For instance, they are often followed by objects:

| | | |
|---|---|---|
| Studying *grammar* | inspires | me. |
| Fred | refused | to pay *his dues.* |
| Courtesy | forbids | calling *a policeman a cop.* |

The *-ing* forms are called present participles when they function as adjectives (see G 2c).

## G 2c  Modifiers

*The typical sentence contains words (or groups of words) that develop, restrict, or otherwise modify the meaning of the basic sentence elements.* Such **modifiers** can be roughly divided into two main groups: those that modify nouns and those that modify other parts of a sentence.

(1) All of the modifiers italicized in the following examples modify the noun *dog* and thus belong in the first group:

A *shaggy* dog barred my way.
A *big, yellow* dog was chewing the rug.
A dog *wearing a muzzle* emerged from the door.
A *police* dog tracked me down.
A dog *with droopy eyes* dozed in the sun.

Of these modifiers, only the first three (*shaggy, big, yellow*) have the structural and formal characteristics of adjectives. An **adjective** occurs in typical adjective positions: "a *reasonable* price," "The price is *reasonable*," "a very *reasonable* price." Most adjectives have distinctive forms for use in comparisons: *small–smaller–smallest; good–better–best; reasonable–more reasonable–most reasonable.* Typical suffixes serving to derive adjectives from other words are *-ic, -ish, -ive,* and *-ous:* bas*ic*, fool*ish*, expens*ive*, courage*ous*. In traditional grammar, however, any modifier that modifies a noun is said to *function* as an adjective.

(2) The second group of modifiers is illustrated in the following sentences:

The bell rang *twice.*
*Suddenly* the bell rang.
The bell rang *loudly.*
The bell rang *at intervals.*

*Twice, suddenly,* and *loudly* are **adverbs**. Many of these show the distinctive *-ly* ending. *At intervals* is not formally an adverb, but in traditional grammar it is said to serve an adverbial function.

NOTE: Combinations introduced by *with, at, on,* and similar words may modify either nouns or other parts of a sentence.

The girl *from Chicago* disappeared.        (adjective function)
The girl disappeared *from Chicago.*        (adverbial function)

*With, at, on,* and *from* are **prepositions**. They typically relate a noun (or noun equivalent) to the rest of the sentence. Other common prepositions are *about, by, during, in, of, through, to, under, until,* and *without.* A preposition plus the noun it introduces is called a **prepositional phrase**.

## G 2d   Joining Clauses

*When several subject-predicate groups combine, they need to be distinguished from the sentence as a whole.* They are traditionally referred to as **clauses**. The following sentences illustrate different ways of joining one clause to another:

| | | |
|---|---|---|
| My brother proposed to Elvira; | *however,* | she dislikes him. |
| My brother proposed to Elvira, | *but* | she dislikes him. |
| My brother proposed to Elvira, | *though* | she dislikes him. |
| My brother proposed to Elvira, | *who* | dislikes him. |

(1) Clauses are called **independent** when they are *self-sufficient enough to stand by themselves,* to be punctuated as complete sentences. They are still considered independent when they are joined to another independent clause by an adverbial connective or by a coordinating connective.[3] **Adverbial connectives** (often called conjunctive adverbs) are such words as *however, therefore, moreover, nevertheless, besides.* **Coordinating connectives** (often called coordinating conjunctions) are such words as *and, but,* and *for.* A grammatically complete sentence ordinarily contains at least one independent clause. A sentence combining two or more independent clauses is called a **compound sentence**.

(2) Clauses are called **dependent** when they are *subordinated to another clause* by a subordinating connective or by a relative pronoun. **Subordinating connectives** (often called subordinating conjunctions) are words like *if, when, because, though,* and *whereas.* **Relative pronouns** are *who, which,* and *that.* A sentence combining an independent clause with one or more dependent clauses is called a **complex sentence**.

Dependent clauses can be considered as modifiers. Those introduced by subordinating connectives usually, though not always, serve adverbial functions: "The bell rang *when I started to answer.*" Those introduced by relative pronouns usually serve adjective functions: "The bell *that had startled me* had ceased to ring."

(3) A special type of dependent clause, rather than being joined to the main clause, *replaces one of its nouns.* Such a

---

[3] For a full discussion of connectives and their bearing on punctuation, see P 3–4.

clause-within-a-clause is called a **noun clause**:

**Noun:**          *The thief* returned my documents.
**Noun Clause:**   *Whoever stole my wallet* returned my documents.

**Noun:**          He was excited by *the news.*
**Noun Clause:**   He was excited by *what he had heard.*

*That*, frequently used as a relative pronoun, is also used to introduce a noun clause:

Osbert denied *that he had forged the check.*
*That Osbert forged the check* has not been proved.

NOTE: Dependent clauses are often hard to recognize, because one or more elements of the clause may be missing. Especially in informal writing, *whom, which*, and *that* are often omitted. Supplying the missing element in such constructions often facilitates grammatical analysis:

The speaker [*whom*] *we had invited* failed to appear.
The support [*that*] *we received* was inadequate.

After a subordinating connective, the subject and all or part of the verb are often omitted, provided they can be inferred from the context. The resulting clause is sometimes called an **elliptical clause**:

*When* [*you are*] *in doubt*, consult your dictionary.
*When* [*he was*] *questioned*, the suspect readily admitted the theft.

## Exercises

**A.** Take five groups of three or four words each (for example, *boy–follow–dog*). Arrange each group in five different patterns using the grammatical devices described in G 2a. Example: *The boy follows the dog. Dogs followed the boy. Follow the boy's dogs. Follow the dog, boys. Dog the following boys.*

**B.** Collect five groups of words that show the same root taking different suffixes for different parts of speech.

# exercises

EXAMPLES

*red* red*ness* redd*ish* redd*en*
*organ* organ*ism* organ*ic* organ*ize*

**C.** Choose three simple subject-predicate sentences that can be expanded and transformed so as to illustrate several of the sentence types described in G 2b.

EXAMPLE

John called.
John called me.
John called me rude.
I was called by John.
Call a taxi!

**D.** Compose ten simplified sentences illustrating the variations in sentence pattern described in G 2b.

**E.** From your current reading, select ten short sentences (one clause each) in which typical sentence patterns are complicated by modifiers. Underline all basic sentence elements: subjects, verbs, complements.

**F.** From your current reading, select ten sentences that illustrate different ways of joining clauses. Underline the basic elements of each clause.

**G.** Write three *pairs* that each consist of two simple sentences. Then illustrate different ways of working the material in each pair into a more complicated sentence.

EXAMPLE

The guests had departed. Alvin tidied the room.
After the guests had departed, Alvin tidied the room.
Alvin tidied the room, for the guests had departed.
The guests had departed, so Alvin tidied the room.
The guests having departed, Alvin tidied the room.
Alvin tidied the room, the guests having departed.

**H.** In the following sentences, identify the basic elements in each clause. Describe the function and grammatical category of as many other elements as you can. Point out distinctive grammatical features.

 **1.** The water in the bowl was purple, and the goldfish were gulping for air. **2.** Throughout the length of the valley, the river's course widens and narrows by turns. **3.** In recent years, sport parachuting has enjoyed a small boom. **4.** The only means of access was to hack one's way through hundreds of miles of jungle. **5.** He painted with the suppleness of an artist who wanted a deep union with nature. **6.** Many customs were common to both sides of the Rio Grande when the river became a frontier. **7.** Recipes for happiness cannot be exported without being modified. **8.** Uncle Alfred complained that outboard motors had driven off the fish. **9.** Avoiding traffic policemen is easy if they ride in specially marked cars. **10.** Fritz annoyed the neighbors by blowing the bugle his father had brought back from France. **11.** What maintains one vice would bring up two children. (Benjamin Franklin) **12.** When lost in the woods, remember your Indian lore.

**I.** Analyze the following passage, using the terminology provided in G 2. Identify all basic sentence elements. Describe the function and grammatical category of as many other elements as you can. Point out unusual or difficult grammatical features.

The rain began with gusty showers, pauses and downpours; and then gradually it settled to a single tempo, small drops and a steady beat, rain that was gray to see through, rain that cut midday light to evening. And at first the dry earth sucked the moisture down and blackened. For two days the earth drank the rain, until the earth was full. Then puddles formed, and in the low places little lakes formed in the fields. The muddy lakes rose higher, and the steady rain whipped the shining water. At last the mountains were full, and the hillsides spilled into the streams, built them to freshets, and sent them roaring down the canyons into the valleys. The rain beat on steadily. And the streams and the little rivers edged up to the bank sides and worked at willows and tree roots, bent the willows deep in the current, cut out the roots of cottonwoods and brought down the trees. The muddy water whirled along the bank sides and crept up the banks until at last it spilled over, into the fields, into the orchards, into the cotton patches where the black stems stood. Level fields became lakes, broad and gray, and the rain whipped up the surfaces. Then the water poured over the highways, and cars moved slowly, cutting the water ahead, and leaving a boiling muddy wake behind.—John Steinbeck, *The Grapes of Wrath*

# G 3   Agreement

*The subject and its verb agree in number.*

Most nouns and pronouns have one form for references to a single item (**singular**), another form for references to more than one (**plural**). Often, verbs also offer us two choices, one to be used when the subject is singular, the other when the subject is plural: *is/are, was/were, has/have, asks/ask*. When subject and verb are both either singular or plural, they are said to agree in **number**.

| Singular | Plural |
|---|---|
| The boy *goes* home. | The boys *go* home. |
| Love *makes* fools. | Fools *make* love. |
| My girl friend *was* pleased. | My girl friends *were* pleased. |

(See G 5e for agreement of a *pronoun* with its antecedent.)

## G 3a   Irregular Plurals

*Some nouns borrowed from other languages preserve irregular plurals.* Although most English nouns use the familiar -*s* plural (car*s*, building*s*, tree*s*, book*s*, petition*s*), a number of words have difficult, irregular alternative forms.

(1) *Many Greek and Latin words require you to learn irregular plural forms:*

| Singular | Plural | Singular | Plural |
|---|---|---|---|
| crisis | crises | criterion | criteria |
| thesis | theses | phenomenon | phenomena |
| analysis | analyses | medium | media |
| hypothesis | hypotheses | stimulus | stimuli |

NOTE: "Dat*a*" are items of information, and "bacteri*a*" are very small organisms that may cause disease. The singular forms of these two words (*datum* and *bacterium*) are rarely used, with the result that *data* now often occurs as a singular. A boy who graduates from college becomes an "alumn*us*," a

girl an "alumn*a*." Several male graduates would call themselves "alumn*i*," several female graduates "alumn*ae*." (An
"alumn*i* organization," on the other hand, may include *both*
men and women.)

(2) *Many other Greek and Latin words are shedding their original plurals.* According to recent dictionaries and handbooks of
usage, it is becoming both common and acceptable to say
"ind*exes*" rather than "ind*ices*," "curricul*ums*" rather than
"curricul*a*," and "formul*as*" rather than "formul*ae*." Even so,
many scientists, physicians, and teachers who use Greek and
Latin terminology as a matter of daily routine prefer the older
forms.

## G 3b   Confusing Singulars and Plurals

*Check for agreement problems caused by expressions that are
not clearly either singular or plural.*

(1) *Each, neither, either,* and *everyone* (**indefinite pronouns**)
may seem to refer to more than one person or thing, but they
are treated as singulars in formal written English:

> Each of the students *is* going to receive a diploma.
> Either of the plans *sounds* all right.

*A number of* is treated as a plural if it means "several" or
"many":

> A number of people *were* standing in the hallway.

(2) Expressions indicating quantity may be treated as
singulars even when they seem plural in form, provided the
sentence is concerned with *the whole amount* rather than with
the individual units:

> In those days two dollars *was* much money.
> It is the most imperative social truth of our age that about one-
> third of the world is rich and two-thirds of the world *is* poor.—
> C. P. Snow, "On Magnanimity," *Harper's*

(3) Words like *audience, committee, family, group, jury, police,* and *team* may be singular in one sentence and plural in another. We use these **collective nouns** as singulars when we are thinking of the group as a whole; we use them as plurals when we are thinking of the individual members of the group:

**Singular:**   The family *is* a crucial social unit.
**Plural:**     The family *were* seated around the dinner table.

(4) Words ending in *-ics* look like plurals but are often singular. Singular are *aeronautics, mathematics, physics,* and similar words that identify a branch of knowledge or field of study:

Mathematics *is* an indispensable tool of modern science.

*Athletics* is used most often as a plural but may also occur as a singular: "Athletics *are* said [could be "*is* said"] to be good for a boy." Other words ending in *-ics* are singular in some senses and plural in others. We say "Statistics *doesn't* appeal to me" when speaking of the *science* of statistics; we say "Statistics *don't* convince me" when speaking of statistical *data.*

NOTE: Consult a college dictionary when you are not sure whether a given form is to be treated as a singular or as a plural.

## G 3c   Compound Subjects

*Check for agreement problems in clauses that contain more than one subject.* After such a **compound subject**, the verb may appear in the plural form even if each of the subjects is singular when taken by itself:

Tom and Sue *don't* smoke.
Hiking and canoeing *are* fun.

Whereas *and* actually adds one possible subject to another, *or* merely gives us a choice between two possible subjects, each of which may be just one single item. Thus, we say "Both his father and his mother *are* to blame" but "Either his father or his mother *is* to blame."

Note some special difficulties:

(1) *As well as, together with,* and *in addition to* often seem to add one subject to another. Strictly interpreted, however, they merely show that what is said about the subject applies *also* to other things or persons:

Aunt Martha, together with her six children, *is* leaving town.

NOTE: Some writers use the plural form when the singular seems to fight with the overall meaning of such a sentence. However, you will be safer from criticism if you revise the sentence, using *and*:

The president, as well as the deans and department heads, *was* sitting on the platform.
The president, the deans, and the department heads *were* sitting on the platform.

(2) Sometimes even two nouns joined by *and* do not add up to a plural. They may be merely different parts of the *description of a single thing or person:*

Pork and beans *is* not one of my favorite dishes.
My closest friend and associate *was* a cocker spaniel.

(3) In some sentences, an *or*, an *either . . . or*, or a *neither . . . nor* gives the reader a *choice between a singular subject and a plural one*. Make the verb of such a sentence agree with the subject closer to it:

Either laziness or excessive social obligations *have kept* him from his work.
Either excessive social obligations or just plain laziness *has kept* him from his work.

Such a sentence often sounds more natural if the subjects can be changed so that they are *both* singular or *both* plural:

> Too much social life or just plain laziness *has kept* him from his work.

## G 3d   Blind Agreement

*Do not make the verb agree with a word that stands in front of it but is not its subject.* The result would be **blind agreement**.

(1) Agreement errors are common when *a plural noun intervenes between a singular subject and its verb.* Beware of faulty agreement whenever the subject of a sentence is one thing singled out among several, one quality shared by several members of a group, or one action affecting different things or persons:

> Only one of my friends *was* ready [not "*were* ready"] in time.
> The usefulness of his remedies *has been* questioned [not "*have been* questioned"].
> Understanding the opponent's motives *is* important [not "*are* important"].

(2) When for some reason *the subject follows the verb,* do not make the verb agree with a stray noun that stands in front of it:

> Sleeping in the cradle *were* two rosy-cheeked infants.
> (Who was sleeping? The infants *were* sleeping.)
>
> In the very first chapter *occur* several incredible incidents.
> (What occurs? Incidents *occur*.)

## G 3e   Agreement After *There* and *It*

*Check for agreement in sentences starting with "there is," "there are," "it is," and the like.*

(1) *There* is neither a noun nor a pronoun and cannot be the subject of a sentence. After *there*, the verb agrees with the **postponed subject**—that is, with whatever is "there":

| Singular: | There *was* much *work* to be done. |
|---|---|
| Plural: | There *were* scattered *rumblings* of dissent. |

In formal usage, the plural verb is required even when followed by a compound subject of which each part is singular:

> On the crown of the hill, there *are* a miniature plaza, miniature cathedral, and miniature governor's palace. — Arnold J. Toynbee, "The Mayan Mystery," *Atlantic*

(2) *It* is a pronoun and can occur as a subject. After *it*, the verb is *always* singular:

> It's your last chance.
> It *was* the Joneses.

## G 3f   Agreement After *Who, Which,* and *That*

*Check for agreement problems caused by relationships between several clauses.* For instance, *who, which,* and *that* often serve as subjects in **adjective clauses** — that is, dependent clauses that modify a noun or pronoun. The verb following the *who, which,* or *that* agrees with the *word being modified:*

| Singular: | I hate a man who *stares* at me. |
|---|---|
| Plural: | I hate men who *stare* at me. |

NOTE: Formal English requires agreement in combinations like "one of those who know" and "one of those who believe." "Jean is *the only one* of those girls *who goes* to college for an education" means that one girl *goes* to college for an education but that the others don't. "Jean is one of *those girls who go* to college for an education" means that a number of girls *go* to college for an education and that Jean is one of them.

## G 3g   Logical Agreement

*Where meaning requires it, observe agreement in other sentence elements in addition to verbs.* Often, you have to carry through agreement in number from the subject not only to the verb but also to the remainder of the sentence. (See G 5e for agreement of pronoun and antecedent.)

**Illogical:**  Average newspaper *readers* go through their whole *life* knowing a little about everything but nothing well.

**Revised:**  Average newspaper *readers* go through their whole *lives* knowing a little about everything but nothing well.

**Illogical:**  My more studious *friends* are wise like *an owl* and always look up to higher things.

**Revised:**  My more studious *friends* are wise like *owls* and always look up to higher things.

(See the Glossary of Usage on *these kind* and *those kind*.)

## Exercises

**A.** In a college dictionary, look up the plural forms of the following nouns: *antenna, appendix, beau, bureau, cactus, cello, cherub, focus, hippopotamus, nucleus, oasis, stadium, stigma, vertebra, virus.* Check whether the following forms are singular or plural or both: *addenda, agenda, apparatus, candelabra, deer, dice, Saturnalia, series, species, strata.*

**B.** Select appropriate forms, paying special attention to *irregular plurals.*

1. Constant crises *(1)has/(2)have* undermined the confidence of the people in their government.   2. For many of us, prestige is one of the most important *(3)criterion/(4)criteria* of success.   3. Jean and Margaret were the only *(5)alumna/(6)alumnae/(7)alumni* present at the ceremony.   4. The college offers more than twenty *(8)curriculum/(9)curricula.*   5. The mass media of communication *(10)has/(11)have* rapidly increased their influence in recent decades.   6. The *(12)analysis/(13)analyses* of such material takes time.   7. The memoranda he sent out *(14)was/(15)were* often unintelligible.   8. These data *(16)invalidates/(17)invalidate* all previous *(18)hypothesis/(19)hypotheses* concerning the origin of life.

**C.** Check for *agreement problems* in the following sentences. Your instructor may ask you to revise all unsatisfactory sentences.

**1**. Her big mouth, bad temper, and insistence upon revealing the truth to everyone is canceled out by one charming quality.

**2**. Years ago there wasn't the same social and racial problems that young people face today.

**3**. Many girls give up their interest in education and art when they become a wife and mother.

**4**. Learning tolerance and proper respect for people with other views are necessary to civilized living.

**5**. Jane's features and shape was far above average.

**6**. In former times there weren't as many educational opportunities as there are today.

**7**. At one time I thought of college as a place where everyone studies hard and then relax during the week.

**8**. The significance of many of the words used by Shakespeare are hard to understand.

**9**. I am not one of those who believe in the indiscriminate use of force to restore "law and order."

**10**. In college, a girl's ideals and outlook on life broadens.

**D**. Select *appropriate forms*, paying special attention to common sources of faulty agreement.

**1**. In many of my classes the attitude of the students *(1)was/ (2)were* very poor.    **2**. The benefits that the city has derived from its new industries *(3)is/(4)are* negligible.    **3**. Cooking, as well as sewing or cleaning, *(5)has/(6)have* always bored me. **4**. I was raised in a home where smoking and excessive drinking *(7)was/(8)were* not permitted.    **5**. Getting along with one's neighbors *(9)is/(10)are* not always easy.    **6**. The qualities that a girl looks for in a future husband *(11)is/(12)are* determined in part by her family background.    **7**. The World's Fair dazzled everyone who *(13)was/(14)were* there.    **8**. The ability to talk about something other than money and children *(15)is/(16)are* important if a marriage is to last.    **9**. Colleges have to make provision for students who are below average academically but who nevertheless *(17)wants/(18)want* a college education.    **10**. Using words like *dichotomy* and *schizophrenia* *(19)is/(20)are* no sign of superior intelligence.    **11**. She was one of those hostesses who *(21)makes/(22)make* no attempt to entertain the guests.  **12**. His father felt that five dollars *(23)was/(24)were* more than sufficient as a monthly allowance.  **13**. According to the judge, neither of the witnesses *(25)was/(26)were* guilty of perjury.  **14**. We soon realized that our supply of food and fuel *(27)was/(28)were* dangerously low.  **15**. Weapons like the bow and arrow, the spear, or the knife *(29)was/(30)were* among the first major inventions of man.

# G 4  Difficult Verb Forms

*Use verb forms appropriate to serious written English.*

Verb forms like *knowed* and *growed* are among the most distinctive features of nonstandard English; differences like those between "If I *was*" and "If I *were*" help set apart informal from formal standard English. The most important verb forms are those traditionally grouped together to form the system of tenses. The **tenses** of a verb are the various *forms that indicate primarily, though not exclusively, different relationships of events in time:*

**Active**

|  |  | *Progressive* |
|---|---|---|
| *Present* | I ask | (I am asking) |
| *Past* | I asked | (I was asking) |
| *Future* | I shall (will) ask | (I shall be asking) |
| *Perfect* | I have asked | (I have been asking) |
| *Past Perfect* | I had asked | (I had been asking) |
| *Future Perfect* | I shall (will) have asked | (I shall have been asking) |

**Passive**

|  |  |  |
|---|---|---|
| *Present* | I am asked | (I am being asked) |
| *Past* | I was asked | (I was being asked) |
| *Future* | I shall (will) be asked | ___ |
| *Perfect* | I have been asked | ___ |
| *Past Perfect* | I had been asked | ___ |
| *Future Perfect* | I shall (will) have been asked | ___ |

## G  4a    Regular Verbs

*Most English verbs, the regular verbs, have two basic forms* (**principal parts**).

(1)  The first form is the plain form of the verb (*consent, smoke, depart, investigate, organize*). Standing by itself, it can form the **present tense**. This "simple present" may indicate that something is actually happening now, but it often refers to something that is done regularly or habitually, or that will take place in the immediate future:

> We *consent.*
> I *smoke* a pack a day.
> They *depart* tonight.

The plain form can combine with *will* or *shall* in the **future tense**:

> He *will* talk to you later.[4]

The plain form plus *-ing* makes up the present participle, used in the various tenses of the **progressive construction**. The progressive construction normally indicates that at a given time an action or event is in progress:

> We *are considering* your request.
> Her husband *was painting* the house.

(2)  The second basic form of a verb can stand by itself as the **past tense**, which indicates that an action took place in the past and came to an end in the past. To form this "simple past," regular verbs add *-ed* or *-d* to the plain form:

> He *consented.*
> We *asked* him.
> They *investigated* him thoroughly.

Regular verbs make the *-ed* form do double duty as a

[4] See the Glossary of Usage for *shall–will, should–would.*

verbal (past participle) combining with the various forms of *have* to make up the **perfect tenses**. The present perfect ("I *have considered* your request") describes something that may have happened in the fairly recent past and that has a bearing on the present. The past perfect ("I *had considered* his request very carefully") describes something that had already happened when *other* events in the past took place.[5]

## G 4b Irregular Verbs

*Irregular verbs often have not two but three basic forms.* The simple past is often different from the past participle: *run–ran–run; know–knew–known; go–went–gone.* Furthermore, the difference between the simple present and the simple past is not merely a matter of adding a characteristic ending. Instead, there are changes difficult to schematize: *run–ran; know–knew; go–went.*

(1) Pay special attention to verbs whose basic forms are *confusing in spelling or in sound.* Here is a brief list:

| Present | Past | Perfect |
|---------|------|---------|
| begin | began | have begun |
| bend | bent | have bent |
| blow | blew | have blown |
| break | broke | have broken |
| bring | brought | have brought |
| burst | burst | have burst |
| choose | chose | have chosen |
| come | came | have come |
| deal | dealt | have dealt |
| dig | dug | have dug |
| do | did | have done |
| draw | drew | have drawn |
| drink | drank | have drunk |
| drive | drove | have driven |
| eat | ate | have eaten |
| fall | fell | have fallen |
| flee | fled | have fled |

[5] See G 12a for sequence of tenses and shifts in tense.

| Present | Past | Perfect |
|---------|------|---------|
| fly | flew | have flown |
| freeze | froze | have frozen |
| go | went | have gone |
| grow | grew | have grown |
| know | knew | have known |
| lead | led | have led |
| run | ran | have run |
| see | saw | have seen |
| send | sent | have sent |
| sing | sang | have sung |
| speak | spoke | have spoken |
| swim | swam | have swum |
| take | took | have taken |
| throw | threw | have thrown |
| wear | wore | have worn |
| write | wrote | have written |

(2) Sometimes you have a *choice of two acceptable forms:*

They gracefully *dived* (or *dove*) into the pool.
She *dreamed* (or *dreamt*) of a sloe-eyed Arab prince.
He *lighted* (or *lit*) his cigarette.
Your prediction *has proved* (or *has proven*) wrong.
The ship *sank* (or *sunk*) within minutes.
Business *thrived* (or *throve*) as never before.
The sleepers *waked* (or *woke*) refreshed.

(3) In a few cases different forms for the same tense correspond to *differences in context or in meaning.* For instance, it is "The picture was *hung*" but "The prisoners were *hanged*"; "The sun *shone*" but "The boy *shined* my shoes."

NOTE: When in doubt about the basic forms of a verb, consult your dictionary. It lists the basic forms of all irregular verbs in the *choose–chose–chosen, run–ran–run* order.

## G 4c *Lie, Sit,* and *Rise*

*Some verbs have doubles just different enough to be confusing.*
(1) *Lie–lay–lain* indicates that somebody or something

is situated somewhere. The same basic forms are used in the combination *lie down.*

> On hot days the animals *lie* in the shade.
> A letter *lay* on the floor.
> He *should have lain down.*

*Lay–laid–laid* indicates that somebody is placing something somewhere. Use it when you can substitute *place* or *put.*

> I wish I *could lay* my hands on him.
> The weary travelers *laid down* their burdens.
> You *should have laid aside* some money for emergencies.

(2) *Sit–sat–sat* indicates that someone is seated. *Sit down* follows the same scheme.

> Though he told me that he seldom *sat* while at work, he *has sat* for an hour exactly where he *sat down* when he looked for a place to *sit.*

*Set–set–set*, one of the few verbs with only one basic form, belongs with *lay* as a possible substitute for *place* or *put.* You, yourself, *sit,* or *sit down*; you *set,* or *set down,* something else:

> When you *have set* the alarm, *set* it down by the cot I *set* up.

(3) *Rise–rose–risen* means "get up" or "go up." *Raise–raised–raised* refers to lifting something or *making* it go up:

> Since you *rose* this morning, the tax rate *has risen* ten cents.
> Though he *is* always *raising* his prices, he *has* not *raised* the salaries of his employees.

## G 4d    Subjunctive

*One special set of verb forms is disappearing from informal speech and writing but is still often required in formal usage:* "She would call us if she *were* [not "if she *was*"] ill." "We demand that he *answer* [not "that he *answers*"] the question." *Were* and *answer* here represent special forms that make no distinction between singular and plural. These **subjunctive** forms occur in clauses concerned with possibilities rather than with facts:

(1) After *if, as if,* and *as though,* use *were* instead of *was* if the possibility you have in mind is *contrary to fact or highly improbable:*

The bird looked as if it *were* a plane.
If I *were* you, I would try to improve my language habits.
He acts as if his name *were* John D. Rockefeller.

Use *is* or *was* if you are considering a genuine possibility:

If your brother *was* ill, he should have notified you.
It looks as if the plane *is* going to be late.

In borderline cases, make sure that the *if*-clause uses a verb form that corresponds to the point of view adopted in the main clause. Use the ordinary or factual form after *if* when the main clause uses a matter-of-fact form like *will, shall, can,* or *may.* Use the subjunctive form when the main clause uses a form suggesting improbability:

**Factual:**      If she *is* wise, he *will* propose.
**Subjunctive:**  If she *were* wise, he *would* propose.

NOTE: Do not use *would* in the *if*-clause as a kind of poor man's subjunctive: "If he *were* elected [not "*would be* elected"] he would eliminate corruption and graft."

(2) Use subjunctive forms in noun clauses *after verbs indicating that something is desirable or necessary* but has not yet come about. "I wish I *were* [not "I *was*"] a wise old man." Forms like *answer* instead of *answers, go* instead of *goes* or *went,* and *be* instead of *is* or *was* occur after verbs signaling a suggestion, a request, a command, or a resolution:

His wife insists that he *spend* more time at home.

We demand that he *repay* all his debts.

I move that this question *be* referred to one of our innumerable committees.

(3) In some *set phrases* ("*be* that as it may") and *in writing that is distinctly formal or literary in tone*, the subjunctive expresses ordinary conditions or alternatives:

He was determined to go on, *come* what might.

The artist must have faith in the all-importance of art, and particularly in his own form of art, *be* it painting, sculpture, poetry, drama, fiction, or music.—Malcolm Cowley, "Artists, Conscience, and Censors," *Saturday Review*

# Exercises

**A**. Select verb forms appropriate to formal written English.

    **1**. If a teacher *(1)lays/(2)lies* a hand on an unruly student, he is likely to be sued by the student's parents.   **2**. In discussions touching on religious issues, many perplexing questions can be *(3)raised/(4)risen*.   **3**. After the class *(5)sat/(6)set* down, Mrs. Warner wanted to know who had *(7)wrote/(8)written* "The Student's Lament."   **4**. The picture showed two elderly gentlemen *(9)setting/(10)sitting* at a table and playing chess. **5**. While the boys *(11)swam/(12)swum* in the clear, cold water, I *(13)sat/(14)set* in the canoe watching them.   **6**. While *(15)setting/(16)sitting* up a new filing system, we must have *(17)mislaid/(18)mislain* your letter.   **7**. The report has been *(19)laying/(20)lying* on his desk all summer; at least I saw it *(21)lay/(22)lie* there last week.   **8**. When I *(23)saw/(24)seen* the deserted entrance, I *(25)knew/(26)knowed* that the performance had already *(27)began/(28)begun*.   **9**. The Park Department finally *(29)sat up/(30)set up* benches for visitors who might want to *(31)set down/(32)sit down*.   **10**. Satisfied with the conditions *(33)sat/(34)set* by the negotiators, the rebels *(35)laid down/(36)lay down* their arms.

**B**. Select subjunctive forms where appropriate.

    **1**. If there *(1)is/(2)was/(3)were* another war, untold millions would lose their homes or their lives.   **2**. I wish grammar

*(4)was/(5)were* less complicated than it is.  **3**. Washington is often presented as if he *(6)is/(7)was/(8)were* a godlike figure. **4**. It looks as if there *(9)is/(10)were* just enough gasoline to get us back into town.  **5**. The ordinance requires that subdivision signs *(11)are/(12)be* kept smaller than the houses they advertise.  **6**. If the vocationally minded student *(13)was/(14)were/(15)would be* sent to a trade school, high schools could put more emphasis on academic subjects than they do now. **7**. If your record *(16)is/(17)were/(18)would be* as clean as you claim, the commission will gladly grant your request.  **8**. Mariners used to drink rum as if it *(19)is/(20)was/(21)were* water. **9**. No one suggested to Raymond that he *(22)read/(23)reads The Brothers Karamazov* rather than *Treasure Island*.  **10**. These practices would not be tolerated if the founder *(24)is/(25)was/ (26)were/(27)would be* still alive.

**C**. From the current issue of a magazine, select five sentences that illustrate different uses of the subjunctive.

# G 5  Reference of Pronouns

*To make a pronoun stand for the right noun, place the right pronoun in the right position.*

When you use a pronoun like *he, it,* or *this,* be sure that your reader will know who or what *he, it,* or *this* is. A pronoun has to refer clearly to its **antecedent**, the thing or person for which the pronoun is a substitute.

## G 5a  Ambiguous Reference

*Do not let a pronoun point to more than one possible antecedent.* Look at the use of *she* and *her* in the following example: "Mary was friendly to my sister because *she* wanted *her* to be *her* bridesmaid." The reader here has no way of knowing which of the two girls was getting married, and which was going to be a bridesmaid. The sentence is **ambiguous**; it confuses the reader because of an unintended double meaning.

(1) If the substitute could refer to more than one antecedent, you may have to repeat the noun itself: "When Tom was talking to Jim's brother, *Jim's* girl friend smiled at *Jim's*

*brother* from across the street." Preferably, *shuffle the different parts of the sentence* until the pronoun is preceded by only one possible antecedent:

| | |
|---|---|
| **Ambiguous:** | After *Father* brought *Junior* back from the game, we took pictures of *him.* |
| **Clear:** | We took pictures of *Father* after *he* brought *Junior* back from the game. |
| **Clear:** | We took pictures of *Junior* after *Father* brought *him* back from the game. |

(2) The pronouns that most often cause ambiguity have distinctive forms for singular and plural antecedents: the singular *he, she,* or *it,* as against the plural *they.* If a *they* is preceded by two plural nouns, you can sometimes avoid ambiguity by *making one of them singular:*

| | |
|---|---|
| **Ambiguous:** | *Students* like *science teachers* because *they* are realistic and practical. |
| **Clear:** | A *student* usually likes his *science teachers* because *they* are realistic and practical.<br>(*They* can no longer be mistakenly referred to *students.*) |

Similarly, one of two possible singular antecedents might be changed into a plural:

> A *writer* must necessarily talk to his *readers* [better than "to his *reader*"] in simple language if *his* vocabulary is limited.
> (The singular *reader* would leave it doubtful whose vocabulary is assumed to be limited.)

NOTE: The *farther removed* a pronoun is from its antecedent, the greater the danger of ambiguous reference. Do not make a reader go back through several sentences in a paragraph to check what *he, this,* or *they* stands for.

## G 5b   Reference to Modifiers

*Make pronouns refer to one of the basic elements of a sentence rather than to a modifier.* The following sentence would sound absurd: "During the summer, Grandfather worked on a river boat, but in the winter *it* usually froze over." The *it* seems to refer to the boat, but boats do not freeze over. Similarly absurd sentences may result when a pronoun is expected to refer to a **possessive**:

**Ambiguous:**   I reached for the *horse's* bridle, but *it* ran away.
(The bridle seems to be running away.)

**Clear:**   The *horse* ran away after I reached for *its* bridle.
(The possessive has been changed to a pronoun, and the noun put where it is needed to prevent confusion.)

NOTE: Reference to a possessive accounts for the awkwardness of sentences like the following: "In *John Steinbeck's* novel *The Grapes of Wrath,* he describes the plight of the marginal farmer." Better: "In *his* novel . . . *John Steinbeck* describes . . ."

## G 5c   Vague *This* and *Which*

*Avoid ambiguity caused by idea reference.* Vague **idea reference** results when a *this* or *which* refers to the overall idea expressed in the preceding statement: "I knew that Bob was cheating, but the other students were not aware of *this.*" The *this* may refer either to Bob's *cheating* or to the writer's *knowing* it.

**Ambiguous:**   She spent her time getting special help for her English course, *which* her roommates considered unfair.
(What did her roommates consider unfair—the English course, her getting special help, her spending her time this way?)

A vague *this* can be easily supplemented by a noun indicating the idea referred to: "this assumption," "this outrage." A vague *which* is more difficult to improve. Often you will find it easier to do without it:

| Ambiguous: | I have received only one letter, *which* frightens me. |
|---|---|
| Clear: | Receiving only one letter frightened me. |
| Clear: | The letter (the only one I received) frightened me. |

## G 5d    Implied Antecedents

*To make a sentence acceptable in formal English, eliminate indirect reference.*

(1) In informal conversation, we often make a pronoun refer to an antecedent that we have not actually mentioned, though we *expect its identity to be understood.* We say, "In London, *they* have a great deal of fog" without explaining that the *they* means "Londoners" or "the people living in London." We say, "I like *Life* magazine, because *they* print many interesting articles." The implied antecedent of *they* is not the magazine itself but its editors or its publishers.

| Revised: | *Life* magazine prints many interesting articles. |
|---|---|

(2) Avoid the orphaned *it* or *they,* which refers to an *implied idea* in a sentence like the following: "My mother was a teacher; therefore, I have also chosen *it* as my profession." The *it* stands not for "teacher" but for "teaching."

| Revised: | My mother was a teacher; therefore, I have also chosen *teaching* as my profession. |
|---|---|
| Ambiguous: | The prisoner's hands were manacled to a chain around his waist, but *they* were removed at the courtroom door. (What was removed? The prisoner's hands?) |
| Revised: | The prisoner's hands were manacled to a chain around his waist, but *the manacles* were removed at the courtroom door. |

## G 5e    Indefinite Antecedents

*In formal usage, treat indefinite expressions that are singular in form as singular antecedents.*

(1) Treat the **indefinite pronouns**—*everybody* (*everyone*), *somebody* (*someone*), *nobody* (*no one*), *anybody* (*anyone*), *one*—consistently as singular. Informal English typically uses a singular verb after these words but then often switches to a plural pronoun.

**Formal:**   Someone left *his* gloves [not "*their* gloves"].

**Formal:**   After hours everybody does as *he* pleases [not "as *they* please"].

**Formal:**   Nobody should meddle in affairs that are none of *his* business [not "none of *their* business"].

**Formal:**   One must honor *his* (or *one's*) obligations [not "*their* obligations"].

NOTE: *None* started as the equivalent of "no one," but today either singular or plural forms after it are acceptable:

None of the students *has his* books ready [or "*have their* books ready"].

(2) Consistently treat as singulars expressions like *a person, an individual, the typical student,* or *an average American.* These may seem to refer to more than one person but are singular in form.

**Faulty:**    *A person* can never be too careful about *their* use of language.

**Revised:**   *A person* can never be too careful about *his* use of language.

**Faulty:**    *A student* is here in college to study, but *they* are usually poorly prepared for this task.

**Revised:**   *A student* is here in college to study, but *he* is usually poorly prepared for this task.

NOTE: When we use *everybody, a person,* or *none,* we are often thinking of both men and women. However, "Everybody ate *his or her* lunch" would sound clumsy. *His* can do double duty in such cases.

# Exercises

**A.** Check the following sentences for problems in *pronoun reference.* Your instructor may ask you to revise all unsatisfactory sentences.

1. Evelyn was the kind of neighbor who goes out of her way to help someone or make them feel good.

2. Most adults take notice of teen-agers only when they get into trouble, which is true of every generation.

3. Samuel Butler wrote *The Way of All Flesh,* which was published after his death.

4. The average individual respects the wishes of the group because they hate to be considered odd.

5. My father is extremely intelligent, though he does not always express it in a verbal form.

6. Dave would go out of his way to help a person in the minority obtain their rights.

7. If some individual were to ask me what my philosophy of life is, they would get an involved answer.

8. Many people vaguely respect the arts, but for most of them it is not a source of increased awareness or self-realization.

9. One seldom has the satisfaction of converting his opponents to his own point of view.

10. Water spills from a pipe atop the rock formation; it resembles lava coming from an active volcano.

**B.** Of the numbered pronouns in each passage, identify the one that is *vague, ambiguous, or misleading.*

1. No one *(1)who* has ever been at a horse race can forget *(2)his* excitement at seeing *(3)them* come down the home stretch.
2. On the far side of the town, *(4)they* are clearing land for a housing project, *(5)which* is to be completed before next July.
3. When leading newspapers have *(6)their* top correspondents write stories accusing *(7)our* government of being corrupt, steps should be taken to correct *(8)this.*   4. We finally bought Uncle Peter a power lawnmower, but *(9)he* rarely cuts *(10)it* more than once every three or four weeks.   5. Gophers have been eating our geraniums. *(11)This* annoys my father, *(12)who*

has been trying to get rid of *(13)them* for a long time. **6**. A good secretary does not discuss business matters with *(14)her* friends unless *(15)they* are generally known or unless *(16)she* has the permission of *(17)her* employer. **7**. While the little boy's father read *(18)his* newspaper, *(19)he* kept reaching for *(20)it* and crying "Daddy!" **8**. The public often discovers that *(21)it* has been deprived of important information, *(22) which* goes counter to the traditional policy of *(23)our* government. **9**. When Elizabeth came home, *(24)she* told *(25)her* grandmother that the cost of *(26)her* new permanent alone was enough to curl a woman's hair. **10**. *(27)My* history instructor announced to the students in *(28)his* class that *(29) they* would write a paper on the fall of Constantinople. *(30)This* was a major catastrophe.

**C**. Select pronouns appropriate to formal written English.

**1**. Belonging to too many organizations keeps a person away from *(1)his/(2)his or her/(3)their* studies. **2**. A child that has real problems is often too embarrassed to discuss them with *(4)his/(5)their* parents. **3**. Teen-agers often adopt a new fad as a way of expressing *(6)his/(7)their* rebellion against authority. **4**. A newspaper can never satisfy all *(8)its/(9)their* subscribers. **5**. The American public enjoys Westerns because they give *(10)it/(11)them* a chance to escape from humdrum reality. **6**. Participation in student government is good for the students because it develops an understanding of the institution of which *(12)he is/(13)they are* a part. **7**. Sometimes it seems as if nowadays no one has the time to enjoy *(14)himself/ (15)themselves.* **8**. A number of my friends take more interest in playing golf in a gym class than *(16)he does/(17)they do* in solving mathematical problems. **9**. Love stories are popular because love is something that everyone knows or will experience in *(18)his/(19)his or her/(20)their* lifetime. **10**. Much confusion would have been avoided if each one of them had waited for *(21)his/(22)their* turn.

# G 6   Pronoun Forms

*Use pronoun forms in accordance with the conventions of formal written English.*

Pronouns have alternative forms, used depending on the function of the pronoun in the sentence. *I* and *he* are **subject forms**, identifying the person that the predicate says something about. *Me* and *him* are **object forms**, identifying the object of a verb or preposition. Only half a dozen pronouns have a distinct object form: *I–me; we–us; he–him; she–her; they–them; who–whom.*

| Subject | Object | Object of Preposition |
|---------|--------|----------------------|
| *I* congratulated | *him.* | |
| *He* recommended | *me* | to *them.* |
| *They* prejudiced | *her* | against *me.* |

These forms for subject and object, like the possessive of nouns, are isolated survivals of a once elaborate system of inflections indicating grammatical **case**.

A third possible form typically indicates that the object of an action is identical with the performer. *Himself, themselves, myself, ourselves,* and similar forms are **reflexive forms**:

He cut *himself.*
They asked *themselves* what had gone wrong.

They are also used as **intensives** reidentifying something for emphasis:

The dean told me so *himself.*
We should also weigh the testimony of the accused men *themselves.*

## G 6a　Subject and Object Forms

*Use the pronoun forms for subject and object as appropriate in written English.* Formal use of these forms differs to some extent from what we commonly hear in informal and nonstandard speech.

(1) Choose the standard form when a pronoun is *one of several subjects or objects in a clause:*

My brother and *I* [not "*me* and my brother"] were reading comic books.
(Who was reading? *I* was reading.)
She asked my brother and *me* [not "my brother and *I*"] to dry the dishes.
(Whom did she ask? She asked *me.*)

(2) Since nouns have no distinct forms for subject and object, be careful with *pronoun-noun combinations* like *we Americans–us Americans* or *we girls–us girls:*

*We boy scouts* are always eager to help. (*We* are eager.)
He told *us boy scouts* to keep up the good work. (He told *us.*)

(3) Object forms are required *after prepositions* (with *her;* because of *him;* for *me*). Use the object form for a pronoun that is the second or third object in a prepositional phrase:

This kind of thing can happen to you and *me* [not "to you and *I*"].
I knew there was something between you and *her* [not "between you and *she*"].

(4) *As* and *than* are treated as connectives even when most of the clause they presumably introduce is missing. To decide whether they should be followed by the subject form or the object form, *reconstruct the missing clause:*

He is as tall as *I* (am).
I owe you as much as (I owe) *them.*
Her sister was smarter than *she* (was).
I like her better than (I like) *him.*

(5) In formal usage, subject forms are required *after linking verbs,* which introduce not an object of an action but a description of the subject:

The only ones not invited were *she* and a girl with measles.

The need for this use of the subject form seldom arises except after "it is," "it was," "it must be," and so on. (See the Glossary of Usage for *it's me/it is I*.)

NOTE: Formal English avoids the use of the reflexive pronoun as a substitute for the plain subject form or object form:

> My friend and *I* [not "and *myself*"] were the last ones to leave.
> I asked both his wife and *him* [not "and *himself*"] to come over after dinner.

## G 6b   *Who* and *Whom*

Who *and* whom *are easily confused because their function in a sentence is not always obvious.* Furthermore, *who* is increasingly replacing *whom* in speech.

**Spoken:**   Tell me *who you are thinking of.*

**Written:**   It is good for the sanity of all of us to have *someone whom we continue to think of* as Mister even though we address him by his given name.—Philip M. Wagner, "Mencken Remembered," *The American Scholar*

An inappropriate *who* may sound too informal for its context; an inappropriate *whom* may sound ignorant and forced.

(1) When *who* or *whom* occurs *at the beginning of a question,* *who* asks a question about the subject. *He, she, we,* and *they* would be possible answers: *Who* did it? *He* did. *Whom* asks a question about an object. *Him, her, us,* and *them* would be possible answers: *Whom* did you meet? I met *him. Whom* also serves as the object of a preposition: To *whom* should I write? To *him.* The pronoun remains in the object form even if the preposition does not precede the pronoun but follows the verb: *Whom* are you looking *for*? I am looking for *him.*

In more complicated questions it may not be obvious whether a *who* inquires about a subject or about an object. However, the *he*-or-*him* test will always work:

*Who* do you think will win? (I think *he* will win.)
*Whom* did you expect to come? (I expected *him* to come.)

(2) *Who* and *whom* may *introduce dependent clauses.* They may introduce an indirect question or may link a modifier to the noun or pronoun being modified. In order to apply the *he*-or-*him* test to a dependent clause, separate it from the rest of the sentence:

**Subject:**   Ask her / *who* wrote the letter.
        (*He* wrote the letter.)

**Subject:**   We approached the man / *who* was waiting.
        (*He* was waiting.)

**Subject:**   Here is a nickel for / *whoever* gets there first.
        (*He* gets there first.)

**Object:**   *Whom* we should invite / is a difficult question.
        (We should invite *him*.)

**Object:**   She knew my brother, / *whom* I rarely see.
        (I rarely see *him*.)

**Object:**   He knew few people / on *whom* he could rely.
        (He could rely on *them*.)

NOTE: Often a parenthetic comment like *I think, he feels,* or *she thought* is inserted into the dependent clause. The "I think" does not affect the choice of *who* or *whom* if you could enclose it in parentheses without changing the meaning of the clause:

**Subject:**   He introduced us to Mrs. Sweets, / *who* (I think) is his
        mother-in-law.

## G 6c   *Who, Which,* and *That*

*Who* and *whom* refer to persons ("the man *whom* I asked"). *Which* refers to ideas and things ("the car *which* I bought"). A *who, whom,* or *which* introducing a **restrictive modifier** may be replaced by *that* (but *need* not be):

The man *that* I asked liked the car *that* I bought.

A *whom* or a *which* that is the object in a restrictive modifier is often left out:

> The man (*whom*) I asked liked the car (*which*) I bought.

NOTE: *Of which* and *in which* can easily make a sentence awkward. *Whose* is therefore widely used and accepted in reference to ideas and things: "the Shank-Painter Swamp, *whose* expressive name . . . gave it importance in our eyes" (Thoreau).

## G 6d    Possessives with Verbal Nouns

*Formal usage prefers a possessive pronoun before a verbal used as a verbal noun.* A combination of a pronoun and a verbal with the *-ing* ending may express two different relationships. In the sentence "I saw *him returning* from the library," you actually saw *him*. In the sentence "I object to *his using* my toothbrush," you are not objecting to *him* but merely to one of *his* actions. In the first sentence, the object of the verb is *him*, while *returning* is a **present participle** modifying the object. In the second sentence, the object of the verb is *using*, while *his* is a **possessive pronoun** indicating *whose* action the speaker has in mind. The verbal here is a **gerund**, or **verbal noun**.

Use *my, our, his, their* instead of *me, us, him, them* when the object of a verb or of a preposition is not the person himself but one of his actions, traits, or experiences:[6]

> We investigated the chances of *his* being elected.
> There is no excuse for *their* not writing sooner.
> I do not like *your* associating with the neighborhood children.

## Exercises

**A**. Which of the italicized pronoun forms are inappropriate to formal English? Why?

[6] In formal usage, nouns observe a similar distinction, provided they have a distinctive possessive form. See Glossary of Usage under "possessives."

**1**. A teacher should not be condescending just because *he* knows more than *us* students.

**2**. Jack constantly enriched the conversation of my friends and *I* with brilliant comments.

**3**. People *who* are asked to "play *themselves*" in a movie often find that a good actor can portray their type more effectively than *them*.

**4**. My brother and *I* had no respect for the people with *whom* we worked, and soon we had no respect for *ourselves*.

**5**. I am tired of *his* spreading rumors about a rift between the board and *I*.

**B**. Select pronoun forms appropriate to formal written English.

**1**. When my mother punished my sister and *(1)I/(2)me/ (3)myself*, she always seemed to suffer more than *(4)we/(5)us*. **2**. I stopped at Jane's house because I had some letters for her mother and *(6)she/(7)her/(8)herself*. **3**. My parents did not mind *(9)me/(10)my* associating with artists as long as I did not imitate their habits. **4**. Most of *(11)we girls/(12)us girls* were looking for the tall, handsome athletic star with the winning personality. **5**. I recognize the man's face; it was *(13)he/(14)him* who started the riot. **6**. My sister is much better than *(15)I/(16)me/(17)myself* at learning foreign languages. **7**. In discussing contemporary authors, the lecturer objected to *(18)their/(19)them* painting too gloomy a picture of the American scene. **8**. Every year, my father takes my brother and *(20)I/(21)me* camping. **9**. Between you and *(22)I/(23)me*, I would rather have a husband in a Ford than a friend in a Jaguar. **10**. Space navigators need to protect *(24)them/(25)themselves* against the powerful radiation of the sun to prevent *(26)their/(27)them* dying from acute sunburn.

**C**. Explain the choice of *who* or *whom* in the following sentences.

**1**. People who cannot suffer can never grow up, can never discover who they are. (James Baldwin)

**2**. The inhabitants of the coast, whom he called Ichthyophagi or Fisheaters, not only ate fishes raw but gave them to their cattle.

**3**. Grandmother disapproved of John, who she felt lacked some of the qualities of a gentleman.

**4**. He was a man of singular patience and intelligence, who, when our queries struck him, rang as clear as a bell in response. (Thoreau)

**5**. Every reader occasionally encounters a fictional character with whom he can immediately identify.

**D**. Select the pronoun (*who* or *whom*) required by formal usage.

**1**. No matter *(1)who/(2)whom* I meet, I always in the end have to listen to his problems.  **2**. I felt more at ease talking to boys *(3)who/(4)whom* had definite ambitions in life than to those *(5)who/(6)whom* lived from football game to football game.  **3**. As a principal, he knew many parents *(7)who/ (8)whom/(9)which* took only a casual interest in their children's education.  **4**. The man *(10)who/(11)whom* knocked at the door was not the one *(12)who/(13)whom* we expected.  **5**. After the abortive revolt, the prince surrounded himself with subordinates on *(14)who/(15)whom/(16)which* he could rely.  **6**. *(17)Who/(18)whom* she corresponds with and *(19)who/ (20)whom* is allowed to visit her are jealously guarded mysteries.  **7**. *(21)Who/(22)whom* do you think was the girl with *(23)who/(24)whom* I saw him?  **8**. I wonder *(25)who/(26)whom* you expect to believe these fantastic stories.

**E**. From a local newspaper, select ten sentences using *who* or *whom*. Which of them conform to the conventions of formal usage?

# G 7  Forms of Modifiers

*Distinguish between adjectives and adverbs.*

Modifiers may be single words. Such single-word modifiers fall into two main categories. *Beautiful, strange,* and *happy* are **adjectives**. An adjective modifies a noun by identifying it as one of a kind or by pointing out one of its characteristics. *Beautifully, strangely,* and *happily* are **adverbs**. Characteristically an adverb comments on the manner or the circumstances of the action or condition indicated by the verb. (See G 2c.)

## G 7a   Adverb Forms

*Formal English requires a more frequent use of distinctive adverb forms than everyday conversation.* Most adverbs are distinguished from the corresponding adjectives by the *-ly* ending: *bright–brightly, cheerful–cheerfully, considerable–considerably, frequent–frequently, happy–happily, rapid–rapidly, rare–rarely, single–singly.* However, some adverbs, such as *fast, much, thus,* and *well,* have no distinctive ending. Some words ending in *-ly* are not adverbs but adjectives: a *friendly* talk, a *lonely* life, a *leisurely* drive, a *manly* reply.

Use distinctive adverb forms in sentences like the following:

**Adverb:**   In my absence, the town had changed *considerably.*
**Adverb:**   A teacher must be firm if he wants to be taken *seriously.*

Note the following special problems:

(1) *Good* and *bad* used as adverbs are commonly heard in informal speech but are widely considered nonstandard. In formal English, "I don't hear so good" would be "I don't hear *well.*" "I write pretty bad" would be "I write *badly.*"

**Objectionable:**   This morning, the motor was running *good.*
**Formal:**             This morning, the motor was running *well.*

NOTE: The adverb *well,* however, may do double duty as an adjective, in the sense of "healthy," "not ill": "He looks *well*"; "I don't feel *well.*"

(2) Formal usage prefers "talks *loudly*" to "talks loud," "go *slowly*" to "go slow," or "come *quickly*" to "come quick," though both the long form and the short form of these adverbs have long been standard English.

## G 7b   Adjectives with Linking Verbs

*Not every modifier appearing next to a verb is necessarily an adverb.*

(1) Linking verbs link the subject to a description of it, which may be a noun but is often an adjective:

His habits are *expensive.*
Most of the bottles were *empty.*
The speaker seemed *nervous.*

A **predicate adjective**, even though it becomes part of the predicate, points back to the subject. Here are some other verbs that may function as linking verbs and may thus be followed by adjectives:

Genevieve *turned* pale.
The heat *grew* oppressive.
He *became* rich overnight.
Your fears *will prove* silly.
The accused *remained* silent.

Honeysuckle *smells* sweet.
The soup *tasted* flat.
His hands *felt* moist.
Sirens *sound* frightening.
Your friend *looks* ill.

NOTE: Some verbs may function either as ordinary verbs or as linking verbs. In "The waiter appeared hurriedly," *hurriedly* tells us how the man acted. In "The waiter appeared hurried," *hurried* describes the man himself. In "John slowly looked at me," *slowly* describes John's action. In "John looked slow," *slow* describes John.

(2) In some sentences, a verb and its object are followed by a description of the object. The description, called the **object complement**, may be either a noun ("He called me a *genius*") or an adjective ("He called me *lazy*"). Notice the difference between adjective and adverb in the following pairs:

He called the meeting *accidental.*
He called the meeting *accidentally.*

George called his girl friend *eager.*
George called his girl friend *eagerly.*

## G 7c   Adverbs to Modify Modifiers

*In formal usage, use the distinctive adverb form to modify either an adjective or another adverb.* In "a *poorly* informed American," *poorly* is an adverb modifying the adjective *informed*. The man's supply of information is poor, though he himself may be wealthy.

| | |
|---|---|
| **Adverb + Adjective:** | a surprising*ly* beautiful bird |
| | a hopeless*ly* retarded student |
| | an impressive*ly* versatile actor |
| **Adverb + Adverb:** | You sang admirab*ly* well. |
| | He answered surprising*ly* fast. |
| | She worked incredib*ly* hard. |

Many everyday expressions use adjective forms instead of adverb forms as informal **intensifiers**: "He speaks *awful* fast." "Dean Howard is *real* popular." "I am *dreadful* sorry." In formal English, *omit* such intensifiers altogether or use a formal intensifier like *very*. Use *fairly* to replace the informal *pretty* in "pretty old."

# Exercises

**A**. In simplified sample sentences, use each of the following words once as an adjective and once as an adverb: *better, early, fast, hard, just, only, well.*

**B**. Which of these sentences use adjectives and adverbs as required in formal written English? Your instructor may ask you to revise unsatisfactory sentences.

**1**. Because of my father's influence, I will do good in college and make the best of my opportunities for education.

**2**. During the time Judy spent in France, her French improved considerable.

**3**. No matter what dish Carolyn prepared, it tasted flat.

**4**. I read the questions as careful as the time allowed.

**5**. All the girls performed admirably, but Judy did exceptionally well.

**6**. I had to talk fast and furious before the householder could slam the door in my face.

**7.** An experienced cryptographer can decipher a simple code very easy.

**8.** My father didn't do very good in school because he had to work on my grandfather's farm.

**9.** On the night before our departure, everyone felt miserable.

**10.** Women of today want to be treated equal.

**11.** Falling from the slippery roof, he hurt himself badly.

**12.** As the questions continued, the lecturer sounded more and more impatient.

**13.** The characters in many current movies speak and act fairly realistic.

**14.** The interview with the star of the show proved real disappointing.

**15.** Most drivers drive too fast and careless most of the time.

**16.** The director stubbornly insisted on using a real lion.

**17.** A girl should not plan to become a secretary if she does not spell good.

**18.** He easily talked the man into giving us a real bargain.

**19.** The plans looked beautiful on paper, but progress has been awful slow.

**20.** The rescue party unaccountably lost its way.

## G 8    Position of Modifiers

*Place modifiers in such a way as to prevent misunderstanding or unintended double meanings.*

A modifier may modify different things depending on where it occurs. A word like *only*, which serves as both adjective and adverb, may appear almost anywhere in a sentence:

> *Only* I asked the girl for her name.
> I asked *only* the girl for her name.
> I asked the *only* girl for her name.
> I asked the girl for her name *only*.

In each of these sentences, *only* points clearly to what it modifies. But what is the meaning of the following sentence?

I only asked the girl for her name.

In informal English, we often rely on the situation, or on intonation, to make the meaning clear:

*I* only asked the girl for her name.
I only asked the girl *for her name.*

In formal written English, we would have to recast the sentence to make the modifier point unambiguously in the right direction.

## G 8a  Misplaced Modifiers

*Place modifiers so that they point clearly to what they modify.* Notice the changes in meaning that result from changes in the position of modifiers:

| | |
|---|---|
| **Adverb:** | The car *almost* broke down on every trip we took. (It never quite did.) The car broke down on *almost* every trip we took. (It did frequently.) |
| **Prepositional Phrase:** | The man *with the ax* opened the door. The man opened the door *with the ax.* |
| **Verbal:** | Jerry married a wealthy wife *yearning for high social status.* *Yearning for high social status,* Jerry married a wealthy wife. |

**Misplaced modifiers** seem to point to the wrong part of the sentence. Usually you can simply shift the modifier to a more appropriate position, though you may sometimes have to recast the sentence as a whole:

| | |
|---|---|
| **Misplaced:** | He looked at the tree he had felled *with his hands in his pocket.* |

|  |  |
|---|---|
| | (It is hard to fell trees with one's hands in his pocket.) |
| **Revised:** | *With his hands in his pocket,* he looked at the tree he had felled. |

|  |  |
|---|---|
| **Misplaced:** | *Being made of stone,* the builder expected the house to stand for a century. |
| | (They called him Old Stoneface, no doubt.) |
| **Revised:** | Since *the house* was made of stone, the builder expected it to stand for a century. |

|  |  |
|---|---|
| **Misplaced:** | She was a well-proportioned woman dancing for an audience *trying to make a living.* |
| | (But there were no performances for idlers?) |
| **Revised:** | She was a well-proportioned woman *trying to make a living* by dancing for an audience. |

Note the following special problems:

(1) A **squinting modifier** seems to point two ways at once:

|  |  |
|---|---|
| **Squinting:** | I feel *subconsciously* Hamlet wanted to die. |
| | (Are you talking about *your* subconscious feelings—or Hamlet's?) |
| **Revised:** | I feel that Hamlet *subconsciously* wanted to die. |

(2) The reader expects modifiers to point to major sentence elements rather than to possessives like *my* or *your.* "*At the age of ten,* my grandfather died" seems to mean that your grandfather died when he was ten years old. To improve such a sentence, you often need to *spell out the meaning intended by the modifier:*

*When I was ten,* my grandfather died.

## G 8b    Dangling Modifiers

*Make sure that what a verbal (or verbal phrase) modifies actually appears in the sentence.* A sentence containing a verbal or verbal phrase as a modifier can be analyzed as derived from two source sentences sharing *one major element:*

|  |  |
|---|---|
| **First Source:** | *The bride* caught her rival's eye. |

| **Second Source:** | *The bride* was walking down the aisle. |
| **Result:** | *Walking down the aisle,* the bride caught her rival's eye. |

When the two source sentences do *not* share a major element, the verbal may have nothing to hook onto in the combined sentence. It is then left dangling:

| **First Source:** | The house was dark. |
| **Second Source:** | We were coming home late last night. |
| **Dangling:** | The house was dark, *coming home late last night.* (*Who* was coming home? Not the house.) |

Some danglers merely throw the sentence off balance; others make it sound absurd. Revise by bringing back into the sentence what the verbal is supposed to modify:

| **Dangling:** | *To do well in college,* good grades are essential. |
| **Revised:** | To do well in college, *a student* needs good grades. |

| **Dangling:** | Often, *after convincing a girl to finish school,* she is married on the day of her graduation. |
| **Revised:** | Often, after *her friends* have convinced her to finish school, a girl is married on the day of her graduation. |

| **Dangling:** | *Walking down the aisle,* the wedding march began to play. |
| **Revised:** | While *the bride and groom* were walking down the aisle, the organist started to play the wedding march. |

NOTE: Some verbal phrases are not intended to modify any one part of the main sentence. These are called **absolute constructions**. The most common ones are the many generally acceptable expressions that *clarify the attitude or intention of the speaker:*

> *Generally speaking,* traffic is getting worse rather than better.
> He had numerous children—seven, *to be exact.*
> *Considering the location,* the house is not a bad bargain.

Formal English, more frequently than informal English, uses verbals that *carry their own subjects along with them:*

*The air being warm,* we left our coats in the car.
*Escape being impossible,* he prepared for the worst.
*Most of his colleagues having left the room,* the senator decided to omit the last ten pages of his speech.

## Exercises

**A**. Check the following sentences for *confusing or misleading modifiers.* Label each sentence *S* (satisfactory), *DM* (unsatisfactory because of a dangling modifier), or *MM* (unsatisfactory because of a misplaced modifier). If your instructor desires, rewrite unsatisfactory sentences.

**1**. It was very common for a family to commit their children to a prearranged marriage during the time of Shakespeare.

**2**. Being a normal, complex-ridden youth, I was bored by domestic chores and withdrew into a world of books.

**3**. The escaped lion was captured before anyone was clawed or injured by its keepers.

**4**. While walking on the hard concrete, the clicking or dragging of shoes is very evident to the ear.

**5**. Although we are the leading country in the world financially we lack something equally important.

**6**. These magazines clearly appeal to women readers with stories about torrid love affairs.

**7**. Sometimes a student studies only so that he can prove in class the professor is wrong just to be showing off.

**8**. The Nehru look being then in fashion, Fred walked around the campus clad like a diplomat from India.

**9**. Having grown up in a small mining town in West Virginia, most of her life was spent there cooking and cleaning.

**10**. While taking a bath, a radio should never be left plugged into an outlet close to the tub.

**B**. Follow the same instructions as for **A**.

**1**. Stopped by a policeman in a 30-mile zone, George Van Meter was given a ticket for doing 42 mph on his bicycle.

**2**. While riding in pursuit of the bandits, the hero's horse was shot from under him. **3**. Being a high school sophomore, Shakespeare meant very little to me. **4**. Having lived in India for many years, he knew many of the country's problems from first-hand experience. **5**. By assigning question-and-answer problems, students fail to develop the ability to think a problem through by themselves. **6**. The weather being unusually mild, we decided to have supper on the terrace. **7**. As a child, my mother used to tell me stories of handsome princes on white chargers and of lovely princesses asleep in charmed castles. **8**. Its siren wailing frantically, the ambulance skidded into the stalled sedan. **9**. Sharks are a danger when vacationing in tropical waters. **10**. Considering his lack of training, his performance has been truly remarkable. **11**. The author's critics conducted a running argument in a literary magazine, which lasted for several months. **12**. Listening to a live concert, music has a spontaneous quality that no mechanical equipment can reproduce. **13**. To speak a language well, one has to know the overtones as well as the dictionary meanings of words. **14**. The searching party returned to the camp, all efforts to find the missing girl having been unsuccessful. **15**. Sir Malcolm heard the news that an heir had been born with great pleasure.

# G 9   Confused Sentences

*Avoid garbled sentences resulting from hasty writing, inaccurate copying, or careless typing.*

Even when the reader can make out the intended meaning, he will be annoyed at being temporarily tripped up by a defect that the writer should have caught in revision.

## G 9a   Omission and Duplication

*Check your sentences for carelessly omitted or duplicated elements.* Make sure you have transcribed each sentence in full, without omitting minor sentence elements like *a, the, has, be,* or *am*. Make sure you have not awkwardly repeated minor elements, especially connectives like *that* or *when:*

I think *that* because he is ill (*that*) he will not come.
When school starts in the fall (*that is when*) most parents sigh with relief.

Many hastily written sentences lack some essential part:

**Hasty:** After my sister moved to Ohio, her little girl contracted polio, but did not cause paralysis.
(It was not *the girl* that didn't cause paralysis, but the disease.)

**Revised:** After my sister moved to Ohio, her little girl contracted polio, but fortunately *the disease* did not cause paralysis.

## G 9b  Mixed Construction

*A writer should not confuse different ways of expressing the same idea.* The experienced writer will try out various possible constructions and select the one that seems to fit best. The inexperienced writer may plunge ahead, confusing the various possibilities. The result is known as **mixed construction**:

**Mixed:** *Any pretty girl* he ran after her.
**Consistent:** *Whenever he saw a pretty girl,* he ran after her.
**Consistent:** Any pretty girl *caused him* to run after her.

**Mixed:** The department manager *rejected him to be* one of his assistants.
**Consistent:** The department manager *rejected his application.*
**Consistent:** The department manager *did not want him to be* one of his assistants.

To unscramble such sentences, you have to consider the alternatives and limit yourself to one of them. Thus, "In case of emergency should be reported to the head office" yields "*In case of emergency, report* to the head office" and "*Emergencies should be reported* to the head office."

Note some frequent causes of mixed construction:

(1) In informal English, an adverbial clause starting with *because* sometimes appears as the subject of a verb. Formal English requires a noun clause starting with *that.*

**Mixed:** *Because people enjoy watching a light comedy* does not mean that our society is in a state of decay.

**Consistent:** *That people enjoy watching a light comedy* does not mean that our society is in a state of decay.

(2) Confusion of *because* and *because of* is an especially frequent cause of mixed construction. *Because* introduces a clause: "The course was canceled *because not enough students registered*." *Because of* introduces a prepositional phrase: "The course was canceled *because of insufficient enrollment*." Disregard of this distinction produces sentences like this one: "The course was canceled *because of not enough students registered*."

## G 9c Faulty Predication

*The predicate of a sentence should not say something about the subject that does not logically apply to the subject.* For instance, a writer may anticipate in the subject all or part of the assertion contained in the predicate. Suppose you say, "*The choice* of our new home *was selected* by my mother." What was actually selected? Not a choice, but a home.

**Logical:** The choice *was made* by my mother.
**Logical:** *The home* was selected by my mother.

The idea anticipated in the subject may only partly overlap with that expressed in the predicate: "*The price* of our new cabin *was* rather *expensive*." (What was actually expensive? The cabin, not the price. A price can be high, and the expense can be great, but a price cannot be said to be expensive.)

**Faulty:** At the beginning of the year, *the participation* in club activities is always *overcrowded.*
(The meetings—not the participation—are overcrowded, though the fact that many people participate is the reason for the overcrowding.)

**Logical:** At the beginning of the year, *our club meetings* are always overcrowded.

## G 9d  Faulty Equation

*A linking verb should not equate two things that are not logically equal.* In informal English, such equations are often loose and illogical. "His job *is* a mailman" is illogical because a mailman is a person, not a job. Formal English would require "*He* is a mailman" or "His job is *that of* a mailman."

To check for faulty equation in a more complicated sentence, reduce it to a simple Subject–Linking Verb–Complement pattern. Do you obtain a logical "A equals B" statement?

**Faulty:** *A woman* going to college to increase her knowledge is as valid a reason as a man going to college to become a dentist or a lawyer. (A woman is a reason?)

**Revised:** *A woman's* going to college . . .
(Going to college is a reason.)

**Revised:** *For a woman* to go to college . . .
(To go to college is a reason.)

Note the following special problems:

(1) A common type of faulty equation makes a linking verb introduce an **adverbial clause**. Children, for instance, will say, "A zoo is *when you go to look at animals.*" "When you go to look at animals" is not logically a description of a zoo; normally it would indicate *when* an action takes place or a condition occurs.

**Faulty:** Punishment is *when you are told to stand in the corner.*

**Satisfactory:** When you are told to stand in the corner, you are being punished.

**Satisfactory:** One form of punishment is to make the child stand in a corner.

**Satisfactory:** Punishment is a means of keeping children out of mischief.

Sometimes, however, an *is-when* or an *is-where* sentence actually does describe a time or a place:

| | |
|---|---|
| **Satisfactory:** | Tuesday *was when* I saw him last. |
| **Satisfactory:** | Poughkeepsie *is where* I was born. |

(2) Linking verbs often cause faulty equation when they introduce **prepositional phrases** that would normally indicate the circumstances of an action. Use an infinitive (or similar noun equivalent) instead:

> Our only hope *is to convince* your parents [not "*is by convincing* your parents"].
> Their method of selection *was to question* the candidates carefully [not "*was by questioning* the candidates"].

## G 9e   Faulty Appositives

*Make sure that your appositives can be equated with the nouns they modify.* An **appositive** is a noun placed next to another noun to explain or describe it: "John, *a sophomore*, came to see me." Here, John and the sophomore are identical. However, it does not make sense to say, "There was only *one telephone call, a friend* of yours." A friend can *make* a telephone call, but we would not say that he *is* one.

| | |
|---|---|
| **Faulty:** | We have only one *vacancy, a mathematics teacher.* |
| | (A teacher is not a vacancy, and a vacancy is not a teacher.) |
| **Revised:** | We have only one *vacancy,* a *position* for a mathematics teacher. |
| | (What is actually vacant is a *position* for a teacher.) |

# Exercise

In the following sentences, point out all instances of hasty writing, mixed construction, faulty predication, and faulty apposition. Label each sentence *S* (satisfactory) or *U* (unsatisfactory). If your instructor desires, revise unsatisfactory sentences.

**1**. Scientists know how to distill drinking water from salt water, but the cost of such a project is too unprofitable.

**2**. One good example of romantic love triumphing against odds is when there is an interracial marriage.

**3.** *A Moon for the Misbegotten* is the story of Josie, a loud-mouthed country girl living on a Connecticut farm.

**4.** The differences in intellects of college students do not vary to the extremes that they do in high school students.

**5.** Cornelia had always wanted to meet one of the artists of whom she had heard a great deal about.

**6.** In my experience, the older a man is, the more chivalrous and the more gallantry he possesses.

**7.** Nowadays, the idea of love is begun at a very tender age.

**8.** Just because Lisa's father was a general is no reason for her to order everyone around.

**9.** Because little of the pledged money actually came in, the repertory company had to give up its noble experiment.

**10.** My father first met his business partner in the army, for whom he drove a jeep and was his immediate supervisor.

**11.** In modern industrial society, the sponsorship of the fine arts is no longer supported by wealthy aristocratic patrons.

**12.** Amnesia is when a character in a second-rate novel temporarily loses his memory.

**13.** The purpose of the reception was to acquaint old-timers with some of the newcomers to the area.

**14.** A prizefighter is not the kind of profession that offers its devotees economic security.

**15.** In case of new outbreaks of the disease should be reported to the health authorities immediately.

# G 10   Incomplete Constructions

*In formal English, spell out relationships merely implied in various informal constructions.*

Formal written English requires accuracy in a number of relationships that, though common, are less central to the basic structure of a sentence than predication and apposition.

## G 10a    Informal *So* and *Such*

*Statements of degree need to be accurately worked out in formal English. So* and *such* often indicate that something has reached a definite point, producing certain characteristic results:

> She was so frightened *that she was unable to speak.*
> There was such an uproar *that the chairman banged his gavel in vain.*

Informal English often omits the characteristic result. *So* and *such* then function as **intensifiers**: "I am *so* glad." "He is *such* a lovely boy." You can make such sentences generally acceptable in two different ways. You can substitute an intensifier like *very* or *extremely*: "I am *very* glad." You can add a clause giving the characteristic result: "He is such an attractive boy *that all the girls adore him.*"

## G 10b    Incomplete Comparison

*Formal English frowns on incomplete comparisons.* Normally, *more, better,* and *whiter,* the **comparative forms**, establish a comparison between at least two elements:

> *Carpenters* make more money than *teachers.*
> *Half a loaf* is better than *a slice.*

*Most, best,* and *whitest,* the **superlative forms**, establish a comparison within a group of at least three elements.[7]

> The annual classic at Le Mans is the most dangerous *automobile race in Europe.*

Formal English gives a writer less leeway than informal English in letting the reader find out for himself *what is being compared with what.*

---

[7] See the Glossary of Usage for discussion of the double comparative and of the superlative in reference to two.

(1) Most obviously informal are incomplete comparisons resulting from the use of *more* and *the most* as intensifiers: "That girl has *more* luck" (than who or than what?). "I had *the most* wonderful experience" (of the day? of the year? of a lifetime?). "I saw *the most* exciting play" (the most exciting play of the season? the most exciting play ever produced?).

(2) To satisfy demanding readers, state explicitly what is being compared even when the *terms of a comparison can be inferred* from the context:

> After I took a course in Remedial Reading, I read twice as fast *as I had before.*
> When we saw the revised estimate, we realized we would have to spend more money *than we had planned.*

## G 10c  Illogical Comparison

*Avoid comparisons that are absurd or ambiguous.* Some sentences compare things that are not really comparable: "The skin of her cheeks was as soft as a child." Actually, her skin was as soft as a *child's* (skin), or as soft as *that* of a child. Check for logical balance in sentences like the following:

**Illogical:**    *Her personality* was unlike *most other girls* I have known in the past.
**Logical:**    *Her personality* was unlike *that of* most other girls I have known.

**Illogical:**    *The teachings* of Horatio Alger reached a wider audience than *Whitman.*
**Logical:**    The *teachings* of Horatio Alger reached a wider audience *than those of* Whitman.—Saul Bellow, "The Writer as Moralist," *Atlantic*

Some comparisons mention *three items* without making it clear which two are being compared. "Tom liked Dick better than Harry" may mean two different things:

**Clear:**    Tom liked Dick better than Harry *did.*
**Clear:**    Tom liked Dick better than *he liked* Harry.

NOTE: Sometimes the absurdity of an illogical comparison is not immediately obvious: "Their fullback was heavier than *any man on their team.*" Their fullback is part of their team, and he cannot be heavier than *any man* on the team, including himself. He can be heavier than *other* men on the team:

**Logical:**   Their fullback was heavier than *any other man* on their team.

## G 10d   Contraction of Coordinate Elements

*Telescoping of coordinate elements does not work in written English if the forms concerned are merely similar rather than identical.* When several items of the same kind are coordinated by a connective like *and* or *but,* we often omit forms that would cause unnecessary duplication. But such omission may cause truncated sentences.

(1) If one of *several verbs* in a sentence appears in a shortened form, fill in the complete forms first and omit only identical items. In "It *can be done* and *will be done,*" the *be done* after *can* is identical with that after *will.* You can therefore omit it and say: "It *can* and *will be done.*" But formal writing would avoid "It *can* and *has been done.*" The complete forms are *can be done* and *has been done. Been* would have to serve as a substitute for an omitted *be.*

**Incomplete:**   Some men never *have* and never *will master* the fundamentals of punctuation.
**Complete:**   Some men never *have mastered* and never *will master* the fundamentals of punctuation.

**Incomplete:**   The patient *was given* an injection and the instruments *made* ready.
**Complete:**   The patient *was given* an injection, and the instruments *were made* ready.

(2) Unsatisfactory telescoping occurs in *double-barreled comparisons* of the *as-good-if-not-better* type: "My theme is as good if not better than yours." The complete forms would be

*as good as* and *better than,* and *than* cannot substitute for an omitted *as.* Formal English would require "My theme is as good *as,* if not better *than,* yours." Less awkward is shifting the second part of the comparison to the end of the sentence:

My theme is as good as yours, *if not better.*

(3) When you coordinate *several prepositional phrases,* do not omit prepositions that are not identical but merely express a similar relationship:

| | |
|---|---|
| **Unsatisfactory:** | I have great *respect and faith* in him.<br>(Taken up separately, the two phrases would require different prepositions: "respect *for* him" and "faith *in* him.") |
| **Satisfactory:** | I have great *admiration and respect* for him.<br>(Taken up separately, the two prepositions would prove identical: "admiration *for* him" and "respect *for* him.") |

Notice the use of different prepositions in the following examples:

She was jealous *of* but fascinated *by* her rival.
His behavior during the trial adds *to* rather than detracts *from* my admiration for him.

## Exercise

Check the following sentences for incomplete and ambiguous constructions. Point out unsatisfactory comparisons and unsatisfactory contraction. Label each sentence *S* (satisfactory) or *U* (unsatisfactory). If your instructor desires, revise unsatisfactory sentences.

**1**. Women on the whole understand children better than men.
**2**. Roger's stews and sauces were as good as the best restaurant in Paris, if not better. **3**. The light at the intersection of Sixth and Grove will turn green exactly six seconds after the intersection of Wright and Grove. **4**. In this district, teachers have always been and will always be hired on the basis of their

professional competence alone.  **5**. In much of Europe, American films are more popular than any other country. **6**. The discussion grew so heated that David decided to keep his views to himself.   **7**. The English spoken in the farm area where I grew up differs from that spoken on the East Coast or in the South.   **8**. Children seem to like the so-called "adult" Westerns as much as adults do.   **9**. Year after year, American colleges produce more physical education teachers than mathematics.   **10**. The Secretary of State usually attracts more criticism than any member of the President's cabinet.   **11**. Critics of our schools must realize that they can and are doing great harm by indiscriminate attacks.   **12**. Unlike a track coach, a history teacher seldom has a newspaper article written about him when his students do exceptional work.   **13**. Most young children learn a second language more readily than an older person does.   **14**. The impact of American books, magazines, and comics in Great Britain is much greater than British publications in the United States.   **15**. A good background in the liberal arts is excellent preparation for such practical professions as engineers and lawyers.   **16**. The United States has more television sets to the square mile than any other country in the world.   **17**. Mike never has and never will succeed in making his restaurant something more than a place to eat food.   **18**. Many of the legislators lacked the taste—and the capacity—for brilliant political debate. **19**. Unlike America, traveling abroad is a rare luxury in many foreign countries.   **20**. Few of my friends were preoccupied or even interested in making a living.

# G 11   Parallel Structure

*Use parallel grammatical structure for elements serving the same function in a sentence.*

Like a road full of unexpected twists and turns, sentences that lack parallel structure slow down and confuse the reader.

## G 11a   Faulty Parallelism

*Formal English requires consistency in the coordination of elements serving a similar function in a sentence.* Sentence elements joined by *and, or,* and *but* have to be **parallel**; they have

to fit into the same grammatical category. If you put an *and*
after *body*, the reader expects another noun: "body and *chassis*," "body and *soul*." If you put an *and* after *swore*, he expects
another verb: "swore and *affirmed*," "swore and *raved*." The
same principle applies to other elements, including whole
clauses:

**Infinitives:**    Two things that a successful advertisement must ac-
                   complish are *to be noticed* and *to be remembered.*

**Participles:**    I can still see my aunt *striding* into the corral, *cornering*
                   a cow against a fencepost, *balancing* herself on a one-
                   legged milking stool, and *butting* her head into the cow's
                   belly.

**Clauses:**       The young people *who brood* in their rooms, *who forget*
                   to come down to the dining hall, and *who burst out* in fits
                   of irrationality are not worrying about who will win the
                   great game.—Oscar Handlin, "Are the Colleges Killing
                   Education?" *Atlantic*

You can often make elements parallel by *shifting one of
them to a different grammatical category.* For instance, "*ignorant*
and *a miser*" is off balance because it joins an adjective and a
noun. You could change *ignorant* to a noun ("He was an *ignora-
mus* and a miser") or *miser* to an adjective ("He was ignorant
and *miserly*"). But many ideas are not easily shifted from one
grammatical category to another. You may have to consider
several different ways of *shortening, expanding, or rewording a
sentence:*

**Faulty:**      High school students want to be *popular* and *leaders.*
**Parallel:**    High school students want to *be* popular and *become*
                 leaders.

**Faulty:**      My grandfather liked *the country* and *to walk* in the fields.
**Parallel:**    My grandfather liked *to live* in the country and *to walk* in
                 the fields.

**Faulty:**      He told me *of his plans* and *that he was leaving.*
**Parallel:**    He *informed* me of his plans and *told* me that he was leaving.

Look especially for the following sources of faulty parallelism:

(1) Sentences sound awkward when a noun appears in coordination with an adjective as the modifier of *another noun:*

**Faulty:**     The schools must serve *personal and society* needs as they evolve.

**Parallel:**   The schools must serve *personal and social* needs as they evolve.

(2) Lack of parallelism is especially obvious after **correlatives**: *either . . . or, neither . . . nor, not only . . . but also, whether . . . or.*

**Faulty:**     I used to find him either *on the porch* or *dozing* in the living room.

**Parallel:**   I used to find him either *sitting* on the porch or *dozing* in the living room.

**Faulty:**     We wondered whether *to believe* him or *should we try* to verify his story.

**Parallel:**   We wondered whether we should *believe* him or *try* to verify his story.

## G 11b   Faulty Series

*Avoid faulty parallelism in a series of three or more elements.* Often a writer will lead his reader into what looks like a conventional series only to make the last element snap out of the expected pattern:

**Faulty:**     He liked to *swim, relax,* and *everything peaceful.*

**Parallel:**   He liked *swimming, relaxation,* and peaceful *surroundings.*

**Faulty:**     Jim would always *open* doors, *walk* on the side toward the curb, and *helping* whenever needed.

**Parallel:**   Jim would always *open* doors, *walk* on the side toward the curb, and *help* whenever needed.

If the elements in a faulty series are not really parallel in *meaning,* the revision might break up the series altogether:

| | |
|---|---|
| **Faulty:** | Her new friend was *polite, studious,* and *an only child.* |
| **Parallel:** | Her new friend was a *gentleman, a scholar,* and *an only child.* |
| **Broken Up:** | Her new friend, *an only child,* was a gentleman and a scholar. |

## Exercises

**A**. Check the following sentences for parallel structure. Label each sentence *S* (satisfactory), *FS* (unsatisfactory because of a faulty series), or *FP* (unsatisfactory because of other instances of faulty parallelism). If your instructor desires, rewrite unsatisfactory sentences.

1. Teen-agers assert their independence through the way they dress, comb their hair, and their tastes in music.

2. Parents can no longer rely on school and religious influences to set moral standards for their children.

3. O'Neill's last plays are alive with archetypal American experience and anguished family biography.

4. Students come to college to have fun, find a husband or wife, get away from home, and many other ridiculous reasons.

5. At the beginning, the story focuses on whether the old man will capture the large beautiful fish or will the fish elude him.

6. My work consists of planning the day's production, assigning the men to their jobs, and actual supervision of their work.

7. If the states are allowed to allot federal funds for education, and politics being what it is, the neediest school districts will not get much help.

8. My high school teachers never analyzed my essays from the structural and content point of view.

9. If we want mankind to survive, we had best produce men whose lungs thrive on poisoned air, whose bodies can tolerate polluted water, and whose minds resist the psychological effects of overcrowding.

10. Dr. Johnson was gruff, stern, and a man with many peculiarities.

**11**. Foreign exchange students often expect to see rugged, tanned cowboys roaming the prairies and pug-faced gangsters shooting people down in the streets.

**12**. My father thought that young girls should not go to dances, see young men only in the company of a chaperone, and many other old-fashioned prejudices.

**13**. In many gangster movies, the hero deceives the police, moves in the best society, and comes to a bad end only because his mother-in-law shoots him for having slapped her daughter.

**14**. To most readers, the word *home* suggests security and comfort as well as a place to live.

**15**. The success of a television program depends on how well the program has been advertised, the actors taking part, and is it comedy or serious drama.

**B**. Write or collect ten sentences illustrating parallel structure. Devote each sentence to a different type of word or construction.

## G  12    Consistent Point of View

*Do not confuse your readers by unmotivated shifts in tense, reference, or grammatical perspective.*

The need for consistency makes a serious writer guard against confusing shifts in the perspective he adopts toward people and events.

### G  12a    Shifts in Tense

*Be consistent in your use of verb forms that indicate the relationship of events in time.*

(1) Avoid the shift *from the past to the present tense* when something remembered becomes so real that it seems to be happening in front of you. Note the shift in time in the following sentences:

We *disembarked* at noon and fought our way through the jungle in the sultry afternoon heat. Suddenly, there *is* a tiger! I *aim* my rifle and *pull* the trigger! Nothing *happens*—the gun *wasn't* loaded. Luckily, one of my bearers *saved* me from the consequences of my carelessness.

If the writer wants the description to be especially vivid, he should tell *the whole story* as though it were happening now: "We *disembark . . . fight* our way . . . one of them *saves* me." Otherwise, he should describe everything in the past.

(2) Avoid shifts in perspective when two events happen *at different times or during different periods:* "When I *saw* the F on my report card, I *was* terribly disappointed, because I *studied* very hard." If studying hard was a matter of past history by the time the student received his grade, the **sequence of tenses** would be more accurate like this:

I was terribly disappointed, because I *had studied* very hard.

Formed with *have* or *has,* the **present perfect** indicates that something has happened prior to events taking place *now:* "He *has finished* his supper and *is getting* up." Formed with *had*, the **past perfect** indicates that something happened in the relatively distant past, prior to *other* events in the past: "He *had finished* his supper and *was getting* up." A confusing shift results when a writer disregards these relations:

**Shift:** Last March, the Secretary of the Air Force told the committee what *has happened* to air transport in this country.

**Consistent:** Last March, the Secretary of the Air Force told the committee what *had happened* to air transport in this country.
(The secretary could not have told the committee what *has happened* since he testified and up to the present time.)

(3) *Avoid shifts resulting from failure to observe the distinction between direct and indirect quotation.* What the speaker observed at the time he spoke would occur in the present tense in direct quotation: He said, "I *feel* fine." It would occur in the

past tense in indirect quotation: He said that he *felt* fine. What the speaker felt *before* he spoke would occur in the past (or perhaps in the present perfect) when quoted directly: He said, "I *felt* fine." It would occur in the past perfect when quoted indirectly: He said that he *had felt* fine.

Failure to adjust the tenses in indirect quotations can lead to sentences like the following:

> Her husband admitted that he *was* [should be "*had been*"] a confirmed bachelor.
> Mr. Chamberlain said that there *will be* [should be "*would be*"] peace in our time.

NOTE: When *a statement made in the past formulates a general truth* many writers find the present tense plausible:

Galileo said that the earth *moves* and that the sun *is* fixed; the Inquisition said that the earth *is* fixed and the sun *moves*; and Newtonian astronomers, adopting an absolute theory of space, said that both the sun and the earth *move*.—A. N. Whitehead, *Science and the Modern World*

(4) *Avoid inconsistent combinations between forms that indicate differences in attitude toward possible events* (called differences in **mood**). In the following sentences, note the differences between factual reference to a possibility and the **conditional**, which makes the same possibility seem less probable, or contrary to fact. (See also G 4c.)

**Inconsistent:**   If he *comes* to this country, the army *would* draft him.
**Factual:**        If he *comes* to this country, the army *will* draft him.
**Conditional:**    If he *came* to this country, the army *would* draft him.

## G 12b    Shifts in Reference

*Be consistent in the way you refer to yourself and others.* The least ambiguous pronoun you can use to refer to yourself is of course *I, me,* or *my* (**first person singular**). When you do not want to focus attention on yourself, you may use *we, us,* or *our* instead (**first person plural**). This "editorial" we, however, sounds artificial in most student writing, especially in short themes.

Note the following special problems:

(1) When a writer wants to speak directly to his reader, he can call him *you* (**second person singular** and **plural**) and use *we* to refer both to the reader and himself:

> *You* will agree that *we* must do everything in our power.
> As *you* no doubt remember, *we* have witnessed several similar incidents during the past year.

But *you* also appears as an informal equivalent of *one* or *a person*, referring not so much to the reader as to people in general:

**Formal:**    *One* cannot be too careful.
**Informal:**  *You* can't be too careful.

Confusion results when a writer shifts to the indefinite, generalized *you* after he has already identified the person he has in mind in some other way: "I don't want to be a famous actress. *I* would rather lead my own life without people always knowing what *you* are doing." The easiest way to avoid this shift is to use *you* only to mean "you, the reader."

(2) Similar in effect to shifts to *you* are shifts to the **imperative**, the request form of verbs: "*Come* in." "*Put* it down." "*Leave* him alone." Imperatives are most appropriate in directions and exhortations. They startle the reader when they suddenly break into ordinary expository prose:

**Shift:**        High schools *should stop* educating all students at the same rate. *Give* aptitude tests for placement and then *separate* the students accordingly.

**Consistent:**   High schools *should stop* educating all students at the same rate. They *should give* aptitude tests for placement and then *separate* the students accordingly.

## G 12c    Shifts to the Passive

*Avoid shifting to the passive when the person in question is still the active element in the sentence.* Some sentences confuse the reader by shifting from an **active** construction (*"He built* the house") to a **passive** one (*"The house was built* by him"):[8]

| | |
|---|---|
| **Inconsistent:** | He *returned* to the office as soon as *his lunch had been eaten.* (This sounds as though his lunch might have been eaten by somebody else.) |
| **Consistent:** | He *returned* to the office as soon as he *had eaten* his lunch. |

Unsatisfactory shifts to the passive are frequent after an impersonal *one* or *you:*

| | |
|---|---|
| **Inconsistent:** | As *you scan* the area of your backyard, a small patch of uninhabited earth *is located.* |
| **Consistent:** | As *you scan* your backyard, *you locate* a small patch of earth. |

# Exercise

Check the following passages for unnecessary or confusing shifts in perspective. Label each sentence *S* (satisfactory) or *U* (unsatisfactory). If your instructor desires, revise unsatisfactory sentences.

**1.** One of the most important things that I learned from my mother was how to appreciate your friends without being dependent on them.

**2.** When Marilyn walked down the hall, she often pretends not to notice a fellow student getting ready to greet her.

**3.** Now that I am in college I definitely found that I have to study in order to meet competition.

**4.** Suddenly the sky darkens, a breeze springs up, and a premonitory rumble rolls across the lake.

**5.** The boat moved quietly down the river, the girls sang, and mandolins were played by some of the older boys.

[8] For a fuller discussion of the passive, see S 3b.

**6**. Our culture teaches the individual to maintain an even countenance at all times, especially when you are angry.

**7**. Men are not qualified to speak of good if evil has never been examined.

**8**. College should mean a place where one learns things to fit him for his chosen place in life.

**9**. If the club limited its membership, it would have to raise its dues.

**10**. If we believed nothing is sacred, our value system will be lost.

**11**. Millions of people every day rush off to jobs they detest.

**12**. To the early Christians, endurance meant seeing one's loved ones thrown to wild beasts without losing faith in your God.

**13**. You could not help finding Cheryl obnoxious, especially since one could never confront her successfully with a lie in which she had been caught.

**14**. A true gentleman behaves the way he does because courtesy has to him become second nature.

**15**. If a war comes, many small nations would be at the mercy of those countries that have nuclear weapons.

# 2

# DICTION

A good writer knows that in order to study and write in any major field he has to learn its language: the terms for objects and ideas often discussed, for the standards applied, and for the procedures followed. He knows that a student of literature has to become familiar with terms like *monograph, didactic, elegiac,* and *allegory.* He knows that a student of cultural history cannot be content with merely a blurred notion of *metaphysics, asceticism, dogmatism,* or *anthropology.*

In order to use words with confidence, a good writer does more than look for a single basic meaning; he becomes aware of the *different uses* to which a word is put, and the *different effects* it may have on a reader. In its more technical use, *phenomenon* stands for *any* observable fact. But in more popular use, the word often stands for a *rare* or *outstanding* object of observation. *Critical* sometimes means "faultfinding"; but "critical thinking" is sharp and systematic, whether concerned with good points or bad. The effective writer knows how to use words in such a way that they carry the *intended* meaning and produce the *desired* effect.

The effective writer knows that words can work for him, but also *against* him. He is always looking for words that will help him say what he wants to say more clearly, more directly.

He looks for words that are fresh and vigorous rather than stale and tired. Whether merely in odd moments or in systematic studies, he will concern himself frequently with vocabulary and diction; that is, with word resources and word choice.


## D 1   College Dictionaries

*To make the best possible use of your dictionary, familiarize yourself fully with how it provides information.*

Authoritative college dictionaries provide information not only on the full range of meaning of a word but also on its history, implications, and possible limitations. The following dictionaries are widely recommended:

*Webster's New World Dictionary* (NWD) makes a special effort to explain the meanings of words simply and clearly, using "the simplest language consistent with accuracy and fullness." Historical information *precedes* current meanings, so that the reader is given a sense of how a word developed. Lists of idioms provide an excellent guide to how a word is used in characteristic phrases. Throughout, informal and slang uses of words are so labeled.

The *Standard College Dictionary* (SCD) was first published in 1963. Usually, the most *frequent* (rather than the oldest) meaning of a word appears first. Coverage of informal English and slang is excellent and up to date, with authoritative notes on debatable points of usage. Like the NWD, the *Standard College Dictionary* has valuable introductory materials on the history of English and on modern approaches to the study of language.

*Webster's New Collegiate Dictionary*, in its current seventh edition, is published by the G. & C. Merriam Company, whose collection of several million citation slips has been referred to as "the national archives of the language." The *Collegiate* is

| | |
|---|---|
| Vocabulary Entry | **beau·ty** (by$\overline{oo}$'tē), n., pl. -**ties** for 2–6.  **1.** a quality that is present in a thing or person giving intense aesthetic pleasure or deep satisfaction to the senses or the mind.  **2.** an attractive, well-formed girl or woman.  **3.** a beautiful thing, as a work of art, building, etc.  **4.** Often, **beauties**. that which is beautiful in nature or in some natural or artificial environment.  **5.** a particular advantage: *One of the beauties of this medicine is the absence of aftereffects.*  **6.** a person or thing that excels or is remarkable of its kind: *His black eye was a beauty.*  [ME *be(a)ute* < OF *beaute*; r. ME *bealte* < OF, var. of *bellet* < VL *\*bellitāt-* (s. of *\*bellitās* = L *bell(us)* fine + -*itāt-* -ITY]  —**Syn. 1.** loveliness, pulchritude, comeliness, fairness, attractiveness.  **2.** belle.  —**Ant. 1.** ugliness. |
| Pronunciation | |
| Syllabication Dots | |
| | |
| Synonym Lists | |
| Part of Speech and Inflected Forms | **be·gin** (bi gin′), v., **be·gan, be·gun, be·gin·ning.**  —v.i.  **1.** to proceed to perform the first or earliest part of some action; commence or start.  **2.** to come into existence; originate: *The custom began during the Civil War.*  —v.t.  **3.** to proceed to perform the first or earliest part of (some action): *Begin the job tomorrow.*  **4.** to originate; be the originator of: *Civic leaders began the reform movement.*  [ME *beginn(en)*, OE *beginnan* = *be-* BE- + -*ginnan* to begin, perh. orig. to open, akin to YAWN]  —**be·gin′ner**, n. |
| Etymology | |
| | —**Syn. 3.** BEGIN, COMMENCE, INITIATE, START (when followed by noun or gerund) refer to setting into motion or progress something that continues for some time. BEGIN is the common term: *to begin knitting a sweater.* COMMENCE is a more formal word, often suggesting a more prolonged or elaborate beginning: *to commence proceedings in court.* INITIATE implies an active and often ingenious first act in a new field: *to initiate a new procedure.* START means to make a first move or to set out on a course of action: *to start paving a street.*  **4.** inaugurate, initiate.  —**Ant. 1.** end. |
| Synonym Study | |
| Antonym | |
| Usage Note | **bent¹** (bent), adj.  **1.** curved or crooked: *a bent bow; a bent stick.*  **2.** determined, set, or resolved (usually fol. by *on*): *to be bent on buying a new car.* |
| | **be·la·bor** (bi lā′bər), v.t.  **1.** to discuss, work at, or worry about for an unreasonable amount of time: *He kept belaboring the point long after we had agreed.*  **2.** to scorn or ridicule persistently.  **3.** Archaic. to beat vigorously. Also, Brit., |
| Variant Spelling | **be·la′bour.** |
| Hyphenated Entry | **belles-let·tres** (Fr. bel le′tR³), n.pl.  literature regarded as a fine art, esp. as having a purely aesthetic function.  [< F: lit., fine letters]  —**bel·let·rist** (bel le′trist), n.  —**bel·let·ris·tic** (bel′li tris′tik), adj.  —**Syn.** See literature. |
| Word Element | **bene-,** an element occurring in loan words from Latin where it meant "well": *benediction.* [comb. form of bene (adv.) well] |
| Consecutive Definition Numbers | **be·neath** (bi nēth′, -nēth′), adv.  **①** below; in or to a lower place, position, state, or the like.  **②** underneath: *heaven above and the earth beneath.*  —prep.  **③** below; under: *beneath the same roof.*  **④** further down than; underneath; lower in place than: *the first drawer beneath the top one.*  **⑤** inferior in position, rank, power, etc.: *A captain is beneath a major.*  **⑥** unworthy of; below the level or dignity of: *beneath contempt* |
| Example Contexts | **bet·ter¹** (bet′ər), adj., compar. of **good** with **best** as superl.  **1.** of superior quality or excellence: *a better coat.*  **2.** morally superior; more virtuous: *He's no better than a thief!*  **3.** of superior value, use, fitness, desirability, acceptableness, etc.: *a better time for action.*  **4.** larger; greater: *the better part of a lifetime.*  **5.** improved in health; healthier: *Is your mother better?*  —adv., compar. of **well** with **best** as superl.  **6.** in a more excellent way or manner: *to behave better.*  **7.** to a greater degree; more completely or thoroughly: *I probably know him better than anyone else.*  **8.** more: *I walked better than a mile to town.*  **9. better off a.** in better circumstances.  **b.** more fortunate; happier.  **10. go (someone) one better**, to exceed another's effort; be superior to.  **11. had better,** would be wiser or more reasonable to; ought to: *We had better stay indoors today.*  **12. think better of**, to reconsider and decide more favorably or wisely: *She was tempted to make a sarcastic retort, but thought better of it.*  —v.t.  **13.** to make better; improve; increase the good qualities of.  **14.** to improve upon; surpass; exceed: *We have bettered last year's production record.*  **15. better oneself**, to improve one's social standing, financial position, or education.  —n.  **16.** that which has greater excellence: *the better of two choices.*  **17.** Usually, **betters**. those superior to one in wisdom, social position, etc.  **18. for the better**, in a way that is an improvement: *His health changed for the better.*  **19. get the better of a.** to get an advantage over.  **b.** to prevail against.  [ME *bettre*, OE *betera*; c. OHG *bezziro* (G *besser*), Goth *batiza* = *bat-* (akin to BOOT²) + -*iza* comp. suffix]  —**Syn. 13.** amend; advance, promote. See **improve.** |
| Idiomatic Phrases | |

Explanation of Dictionary Entries
(From *Random House Dictionary*)

based on *Webster's Third New International Dictionary,* the most authoritative and comprehensive unabridged dictionary of current American English. Historical information precedes meanings, presented in the order of their development. The Merriam-Webster dictionaries have abandoned the practice of labeling words informal as too arbitrary or subjective. They make only sparing use of the label "slang." Unlike the NWD and the SCD, the *Collegiate* lists names of people and places in separate indexes at the end of the book.

*The American College Dictionary* (ACD) was comparable in coverage and quality to its major competitors and was distinguished for its intelligible definitions. In 1968, the same publisher brought out the college edition of the *Random House Dictionary,* a new work intermediate in coverage between *Webster's Third* and the desk dictionaries. Its college edition, like the SCD, aims especially at students who use the dictionary as a guide to the preferences of conservative teachers. Thus, both informal English and slang are marked; usage notes "recognize the existence of long-established strictures." As in the SCD, the most frequently encountered meanings of a word come first.

In the wording of definitions, the major college dictionaries range from the everyday language of the NWD to the more technical and scholarly style of the NCD. Compare the first two meanings of *peach* in the entries on page 78.

1. a small tree
with lance-shaped leaves, pink flowers, and round,
juicy, orange-yellow fruit, with a fuzzy skin and a
single, rough pit.   2. its fruit.

From *Webster's New World Dictionary*

1. The drupaceous, edible fruit of a tree
(*Prunus persica*) of the rose family, widely cultivated in
many varieties.   2. The tree itself.

From *Standard College Dictionary*

1 a : a low
spreading freely branching Chinese tree (*Prunus persica*) of the
rose family that is cosmopolitan in cultivation in temperate areas
and has lanceolate leaves, sessile usu. pink flowers borne on the
naked twigs in early spring, and a fruit which is a single-seeded
drupe with a hard endocarp, a pulpy white or yellow mesocarp,
and a thin downy epicarp   b : the edible fruit of the peach   2 : a
variable color averaging a moderate yellowish pink

From *Webster's Seventh New Collegiate Dictionary* [1]

## D 1a   Synonyms and Antonyms

*A good dictionary discriminates between the exact meanings of
closely related terms.* Often, it indicates meaning by a **synonym**,
a word that has nearly the same meaning as the word you are
looking up. Thus, your dictionary may give "sad" or "mourn-
ful" as a synonym for *elegiac,* or "instructive" as a synonym for
*didactic.* Often, your dictionary will explain a word by giving
an **antonym**, a word of approximately opposite meaning.
*Desultory,* for instance, is the opposite of "methodical"; *hack-
neyed* is the opposite of "fresh" or "original."

Synonyms are seldom simply interchangeable. Their
areas of meaning overlap, but at the same time there are
subtle differences. *Burn, char, scorch, sear,* and *singe* all refer
to the results of exposure to extreme heat, but whether a
piece of meat is charred or merely seared makes a difference to the person who has it for dinner.

[1] By permission. Copyright, 1963 by G. & C. Merriam Co., Publishers
of the Merriam-Webster Dictionaries.

Here is how a dictionary discriminates between the synonyms
of *pay*:

**syn** PAY, COMPENSATE, REMUNERATE, SATISFY, REIMBURSE, IN-
DEMNIFY, REPAY, RECOMPENSE, REQUITE mean to give money or its
equivalent in return for something. PAY implies the discharge of
an obligation incurred; COMPENSATE implies a making up for
services rendered or help given; REMUNERATE more clearly suggests
paying for services rendered and may extend to payment that is
generous or not contracted for; SATISFY implies paying a person
what is demanded or required by law; REIMBURSE implies a return of
money that has been expended for another's benefit; INDEMNIFY
implies making good a loss suffered through accident, disaster, war-
fare; REPAY stresses paying back an equivalent in kind or amount;
RECOMPENSE suggests due return in amends, friendly repayment,
or reward

From *Webster's Seventh New Collegiate Dictionary*[2]

## D 1b   Denotation and Connotation

*A good dictionary pays attention to the associations of words and
to the attitudes they imply.* Many words **denote**—that is, point
out or refer to—very nearly the same objects or qualities. At
the same time, they **connote**—that is, suggest or imply—different attitudes toward the objects or qualities they point out.
*Cheap* and *inexpensive* both mean relatively low in price or cost.
However, we may call an article "cheap" to suggest that we
consider it shoddy or inferior; we may call it "inexpensive"
to suggest that we consider it a good bargain, valuable in
spite of its low price. *Unwise* and *foolish* both indicate a lack of
wisdom. However, calling a proposal "unwise" suggests a
certain amount of consideration or respect for the person
who made it; "foolish" suggests ridicule and contempt. Similarly, we may call a boy of low intelligence a "slow learner"
or a "dunce," a new history of the United States "ambitious"
or "pretentious."

Here is how a dictionary discriminates between the connotations of synonyms of *plan*:

[2] By permission. Copyright, 1963 by G. & C. Merriam Co., Publishers
of the Merriam-Webster Dictionaries.

**SYN.**—**plan** refers to any detailed method, formulated beforehand, for doing or making something (vacation *plans*); **design** stresses the final outcome of a plan and implies the use of skill or craft, sometimes in an unfavorable sense, in executing or arranging this (it was his *design* to separate us); **project** implies the use of enterprise or imagination in formulating an ambitious or extensive plan (they've begun work on the housing *project*); **scheme,** a less definite term than the preceding, often connotes either an impractical, visionary plan or an underhand intrigue (a *scheme* to embezzle the funds).

From *Webster's New World Dictionary*

## D 1c   Context

*Often a dictionary supplies phrases suggesting the kind of context where a given meaning is appropriate.* The **context** of a word may be another word ("square meal"), a whole sentence or paragraph ("Square your precepts with your practice"), a whole article or book (a treatment of squares in a book on plane geometry), or a situation (a policeman directing a pedestrian to a square).

Here is an entry showing a word used in different contexts:

**apt** (apt), *adj.* **1.** inclined; disposed; given; prone: *too apt to slander others.* **2.** likely: *Am I apt to find him at home?* **3.** unusually intelligent; quick to learn: *an apt pupil.* **4.** suited to the purpose or occasion: *an apt metaphor.*

From *Random House Dictionary*

In an unfamiliar context, familiar words may have a new or different meaning. For instance, an author praising modesty and thrift may describe them as "homely virtues." Looking up the word, you will find that its original meaning, as you might expect, is "associated with the home." Favorable associations of domestic life account for such meanings as "simple," "unpretentious," "intimate"; unfavorable associations account for such meanings as "crude," "unpolished," "ugly." An eighteenth-century writer may talk about the "wit" of a person who does not seem at all "witty" in the sense of cleverly humorous or ironic. *Wit* in this context means general intellectual and imaginative capacity, as in phrases like "half-wit" and "at one's wit's end."

NOTE: Even when the denotation of a word remains fairly stable, its connotations may vary in different contexts. *Academic* basically means "associated with higher learning." "Academic standards," then, may mean standards of responsible and competent scholarship. An "academic argument," on the other hand, may mean an argument that is unrealistic or impractical because, like higher learning, it is removed from the hustle and bustle of economic and political reality.

## D 1d  Grammatical Labels

*A good dictionary gives reliable information about the functions a word can serve in a sentence.* For instance, *human* is usually labeled both as an **adjective** (adj.) and as a **noun** (n.), with some indication that the latter use ("a human" rather than "a human being") is not generally accepted as appropriate to written English. *Annoy* is labeled a **transitive verb** (v.t.); it is incomplete without an object. In other words, we usually annoy somebody or something; we don't just annoy. *Set* also is usually transitive ("*set* the bowl on the table"), but it is labeled **intransitive** (v.i.) when applied to one of the celestial bodies. In other words, the sun doesn't set anybody or anything; it just sets.

## D 1e  Idiom

*A good dictionary lists idiomatic phrases whose meanings may be more than the sum of their parts.* A word often combines with other words in an expression that becomes the habitual way of conveying a certain idea. Such expressions are called **idioms**.

To write idiomatic English, you have to develop an ear for individual phrases and ways of saying things. For instance, we *do* a certain type of work, *hold* a job or position, *follow* a trade, *pursue* an occupation, and *engage in* a line of business. We *replace* an original *with* a copy, but we *substitute* a copy *for* the original. Here is an exceptionally full list of idiomatic phrases using the word *mind:*

**bear in mind,** to remember.
**be in one's right mind,** to be mentally well; be sane.
**be of one mind,** to have the same opinion; agree.
**be of two minds,** to be undecided or irresolute.
**be out of one's mind,**  1. to be mentally ill; be insane.
 2. to be frantic (*with* worry, grief, etc.).
**call to mind,**  1. to remember.  2. to be a reminder of.
**change one's mind,**  1. to change one's opinion.  2. to
 change one's intention, purpose, or wish.
**give a person a piece of one's mind,** to tell a person
 plainly one's disapproval of him; rebuke; scold.
**have a (good** or **great) mind to,** to feel (strongly) inclined or disposed to.
**have half a mind to,** to be somewhat inclined or disposed to.
**have in mind,**  1. to remember.  2. to think of.  3. to
 intend; purpose.
**keep in mind,** to remember.
**keep one's mind on,** to pay attention to.
**know one's mind,** to know one's real thoughts, feelings, desires, or intentions.
**make up one's mind,** to form a definite opinion or decision; resolve.
**meeting of minds,** an agreement.
**never mind,** don't concern yourself; it doesn't matter.
**on one's mind,**  1. occupying one's thoughts.  2. worrying one.
**pass out of mind,** to be forgotten.
**put in mind,** to remind.
**set one's mind on,** to be determined on or determin-
 edly desirous of.
**speak one's mind,** to say plainly what one thinks.
**take one's mind off,** to stop one from thinking about;
 turn one's attention from.
**to one's mind,** in one's opinion.

From *Webster's New World Dictionary*

   A special problem for inexperienced writers is the idiomatic use of **prepositions**. The following list reviews idiomatic
uses of some common prepositions:

abide *by* (a decision)
abstain *from* (voting)
accuse *of* (a crime)
acquiesce *in* (an injustice)
adhere *to* (a promise)
admit *of* (conflicting interpretations)
agree *with* (a person), *to* (a
   proposal), *on* (a course
   of action)
alarmed *at* (the news)

apologize *for* (a mistake)
aspire *to* (distinction)
assent *to* (a proposal)
attend *to* (one's business)
avail oneself *of* (an
   opportunity)
capable *of* (an action)
charge *with* (an offense)
collide *with* (a car)
compatible *with* (recognized
   standards)

comply *with* (a request)
concur *with* (someone), *in* (an opinion)
confide *in* or *to* (someone)
conform *to* (specifications)
deficient *in* (strength)
delight *in* (mischief)
deprive *of* (a privilege)
derived *from* (a source)
die *of* or *from* (a disease)
disappointed *in* (someone's performance)
dissent *from* (a majority opinion)
dissuade *from* (doing something foolish)
divest *of* (responsibility)
find fault *with* (a course)
identical *with* (something looked for)
ignorant *of* (a fact)
inconsistent *with* (sound procedure)
independent *of* (outside help)
indifferent *to* (praise or blame)
infer *from* (evidence)
inferior *to* (a rival product)
insist *on* (accuracy)

interfere *with* (a performance), *in* (someone else's affairs)
jealous *of* (others)
long *for* (recognition)
object *to* (a proposal)
oblivious *of* (warnings)
part *with* (possessions)
partial *to* (flattery)
participate *in* (activities)
persevere *in* (a task)
pertain *to* (a subject)
preferable *to* (an alternative)
prevail *on* (someone to do something)
prevent someone *from* (an action)
refrain *from* (wrongdoing)
rejoice *at* (good news)
required *of* (all members)
resolve *on* (a course of action)
rich *in* (resources)
secede *from* (the Union)
short *of* (cash)
succeed *in* (an attempt)
superior *to* (an alternative)
threaten *with* (legal action)
wait *for* (developments), *on* (a guest)

NOTE: College dictionaries vary in their coverage of idioms. Only an unabridged dictionary giving one or more sample quotations for each possible use of a word can come close to being a complete guide for idiomatic usage.

## Exercises

**A**. Compare *three* of the major college dictionaries by investigating the following:

**1**. Read the definitions of *dada, kitsch,* and *gobbledygook.* Are they clear and informative?

**2**. Study the order of meanings for *coy, nice, operate.* How does the order differ, and why?

**3**. Compare the treatment of synonyms (if any) for *dogmatic, prompt,* and *train* (v.).

**4**. What and where are you told about Dreyfus, Prometheus, Niels Bohr?

**5**. How does the dictionary deal with *Aryan, dago, nigger?*

**B.** Look up the following entries in your dictionary: *apothegm, denouement, farce, flying buttress, hauberk, limerick, machete, solecism, symbiosis, syncopation.* What special fields of interest do they represent? How clear and adequate are the definitions?

**C.** Explain to what extent the synonyms in each of the following groups overlap and how they differ: *agreement–contract–covenant; amateur–dilettante–tyro; apology–excuse–pretext; bearing–behavior–conduct; betray–divulge–reveal; common–ordinary–familiar; correct–discipline–punish; decline–reject–spurn; destiny–doom–lot; dogmatic–doctrinaire–arbitrary; enterprise–project–venture; fad–fashion–vogue; fantastic–imaginary–visionary; flippant–glib–impertinent; mumble–murmur–mutter.*

**D.** Explain the differences in connotation between the words in each of the following pairs: *clever–intelligent; famous–notorious; gaze–ogle; godsend–windfall; juvenile–youngster; lucre–wealth; obedient–obsequious; obstinate–persistent; petty–punctilious; populace–population; regret–remorse; revenge–retribution; revolt–revolution; slender–thin; teenager–adolescent.*

**E.** How does your dictionary distinguish among the changing meanings of each of the following words? Show how context determines your choice of the meaning appropriate in each phrase.

*Bay* leaves, at *bay, bayed* at the moon, *bay* window, bomb *bay,* a breeze from the *bay*

*head* of lettuce, *head* the procession, a *head* of steam, *heads* or tails, over the listeners' *heads,* went to his *head, heads* of government, *head* off complaints, not have a *head* for figures

*let* blood, without *let* or hindrance, *let* go, *let* me see it, *let* us ignore him, rooms to *let* car of recent *make, make* the beds, *make* money, *make* excuses, *makes* my blood boil, *make* a speech, *makes* easy reading, *made* him a sergeant

*repair* a car, *repaired* to the meeting, in good *repair, repair* the damage

*straight* to the point, *straight* alcohol, *straight* party line, the comedian's *straight* man, *straight* hair, thinking *straight*

a *tender* smile, *tender* an apology, legal *tender*

**F.** Each of the italicized words in the following expressions is a familiar word used in an unfamiliar sense. Find the meaning that fits the context.

To write an *abstract* of a speech; an *academic* painting; to write an *apostrophe* to the gods; an *arresting* performance; a monster of fearful *aspect*; to give someone a *civil* answer; an anti*clerical* political party; to give *countenance* to a crime; to wear a characteristic *habit*; to receive *intelligence*; to *justify* a line of type; to cultivate *polite* learning; to make a character stand out in full *relief*; to lie in *state*; to be *transported* with gratitude.

**G.** Check your answers to the following questions by consulting your dictionary: **1.** Is *incompetent* used as a noun? **2.** Which of the following words are used as verbs: *admonition, loan, lord, magistrate, minister, sacrilege, spirit, war?* **3.** Is "superior than" idiomatic English? **4.** Is *smooth* used as an adverb? **5.** Is *entertain* used as an intransitive verb? **6.** Is *very* used as an adjective? **7.** What idiomatic preposition goes with *glory* used as a verb? **8.** Do we always censure somebody or something, or can we just censure, period? **9.** How many different grammatical categories can *ill* belong to? **10.** Are "angry with," "angry at," and "angry about" interchangeable? **11.** Is *animate* used as an adjective? **12.** Is *predominate* used as an adjective?

**H.** Point out and correct unidiomatic use of prepositions:

**1.** To seek a good grade at someone else's expense would be a violation to our standards of conduct. **2.** During the past fifty years, deaths caused by highway accidents have been more numerous than those incurred from two world wars and the war in Korea. **3.** Plans for cost reduction have been put to action by different agencies of the federal government.

4. Several families volunteered to take care for the children of flood victims.   5. Only the prompt help of the neighbors prevented the fire of becoming a major disaster.   6. During the first years of marriage we had to deprive ourselves from many things that other people take for granted.   7. The arrival of the ship to its destination caused general rejoicing.   8. Though I support Mr. Finchley's candidacy, I take exception with some of his statements.   9. We Americans do not hesitate in waving our flag if the occasion arises.   10. The people of this country naturally shun at the thought of having any kind of censorship imposed upon their newspapers.   11. As an instrument of the popular will, the senate suffers from defects inherent to its constitution.   12. A businessman cannot succeed unless he takes heed to the preferences of his customers.

**I.** Study the general scheme, the introductory material, and several sample entries of *one* of the following specialized dictionaries. Report your findings.

> *Bartlett's Familiar Quotations;* Sir William A. Craigie and James R. Hulbert, *A Dictionary of American English on Historical Principles;* H. W. Horwill, *A Dictionary of Modern American Usage;* John S. Kenyon and Thomas A. Knott, *A Pronouncing Dictionary of American English;* Mitford M. Mathews, *A Dictionary of Americanisms;* Eric Partridge, *A Dictionary of Slang and Unconventional English;* Roget's *Thesaurus of English Words and Phrases.*

# D 2   Word History

*Knowledge of the history of a word helps a writer understand its uses, meanings, and associations.*

After giving the spelling, pronunciation, and grammatical category of a word, college dictionaries often summarize its **etymology**; that is, they briefly trace its origin and history. The following sample entry relates the word *lock* to corresponding words in earlier English (ME. = Middle English; AS. = Anglo-Saxon or Old English), in other Germanic languages (G. = German; ON. = Old Norse or Early Scandinavian), and in the hypothetical common parent language of most European languages (IE. = Indo-European):

**lock** (lok), *n.* [ME. *lokke;* AS. *loc,* a bolt, bar, enclosure, prison; akin to G. *loch,* a hole, ON. *lok,* a lid; prob. IE. base *\*leug-,* to bend, seen also in AS. *lucan,* to close (cf. LEEK)],

From *Webster's New World Dictionary*

In addition to tracing words to other languages, the etymologist is concerned with **semantic change**—that is, gradual changes in meaning. The most complete record of such changes is the unabridged *New English Dictionary on Historical Principles,* reissued in 1933 as the *Oxford English Dictionary* (OED). This monumental reference work gives the earliest date a word occurs and then provides quotations tracing its development down through the centuries.

The most extensive changes in vocabulary come about through contacts between cultures. Armed conquest, colonial expansion, international trade, and cultural influences all make possible the absorption of words from other languages. Roughly three fourths of the words in your dictionary were absorbed into English from foreign sources. When the Anglo-Saxon tribes came to England from continental Europe during the period between 450 and 600 A.D., they spoke Germanic dialects, closely related to the dialects from which modern Dutch and German are derived. The American tourist coming to Germany can still easily recognize the German equivalents of *arm, drink, father, fish, hand,* or *house.* However, the basic Germanic vocabulary of **Anglo-Saxon** or **Old English** was enriched and modified by an almost continuous absorption of words from other languages throughout early English history.

## D 2a   Latin and Greek

*The most persistent influences on the English vocabulary were Latin and Greek, the languages of classical antiquity.* Latin had been the language of the Roman empire. It became the official language of the Roman Catholic Church, which established itself in England in the seventh century and remained the supreme spiritual authority until the sixteenth century. English early absorbed Latin words related to the Scriptures and to the doctrines and ritual of the church, such as *altar, candle, chalice, mass, palm, pope, shrine, relic,* and *rule.* Other early borrowings were related to church administration, to the everyday life of monks and clergymen, and to the church-controlled and church-conducted medieval system of education. Many have long since lost all suggestion of foreignness: *beet, cap, circle, cook, fever, lobster, mat, pear, school, silk, sock,* or *turn.*

   Greek was the language of the literature, philosophy, and science of ancient Hellenic culture, flourishing both in Greece proper and in other parts of the Mediterranean world. Either in the original Greek or in Latin translation, this body of knowledge exercised a continuous influence on Christianity and Western civilization during the Middle Ages and Renaissance. Modern philosophical, scientific, and technological terminology draws heavily on Latin and Greek roots. More generally, the language of educated people is saturated with words that are derived from one of the classical languages. Examples of words absorbed either directly from Greek or from Greek through Latin are *anonymous, atmosphere, catastrophe, chaos, climax, crisis, enthusiasm,* and *skeleton.* Examples of words absorbed from Latin are *contempt, gesture, history, incredible, index, individual, intellect, legal, mechanical, picture,* and *rational.*

**Latin and Greek Roots.**   Knowledge of a Latin or Greek root often provides the key to a puzzling word. For instance, the Greek root *phys-* usually refers to the body or to material things, whereas the Greek root *psych-* usually refers to the mind or the soul. This distinction explains *physician* (heals the body) and *psychiatrist* (heals the mind), *physiology* (study of bodily functions) and *psychology* (study of mental functions), *physical* (characteristic of material reality) and *psychic* (going beyond material reality).

Here is a brief list of common Latin and Greek roots. Explain how each root is used in the sample words given for it:

| | | |
|---|---|---|
| auto- | *self* | autocratic, automatic, automobile, autonomy |
| capit- | *head* | capital, decapitate, per capita |
| carn- | *flesh* | carnal, carnivorous, incarnation, carnival |
| chron- | *time* | anachronistic, chronometer, synchronize |
| culp- | *fault* | culpable, culprit, exculpate |
| doc- | *teach* | docile, doctor, doctrine, indoctrinate |
| graph- | *write* | autograph, graphic, geography, orthography |
| hydr- | *water* | dehydrate, hydrant, hydraulic, hydrogen |
| jur- | *swear* | conjure, juror, perjury |
| man- | *hand* | manacle, manicure, manual, manufacture |
| phon- | *sound* | euphony, phonetics, phonograph, symphony |
| terr- | *land* | inter, terrestrial, subterranean |
| urb- | *city* | suburb, urban, urbane |
| verb- | *word* | proverb, verbal, verbiage, verbose |
| vit- | *life* | vitality, vitamin |
| vol- | *wish* | volition, voluntary, volunteer |

**Common Prefixes and Suffixes.** Especially useful is a knowledge of the most common Latin and Greek **prefixes** and **suffixes**—that is, syllables attached at the beginning or at the end of a word to modify its meaning. A common prefix like *sub-*, meaning "below" or "beneath," helps to explain not only *sub-standard* and *subconscious* but *submarine* (below the sea), *sub-lunar* (below the moon—that is, on earth; characteristic of existence on this earth), *subterranean* (beneath the surface, underground). The suffix *-cide* means "killer" or "killing" in *homicide* (of a human being), *suicide* (of oneself), *fratricide* (of a brother), *parricide* (of a parent), and *insecticide* (of insects).

Here is a brief list of Latin and Greek prefixes:

| | | |
|---|---|---|
| bene- | *good* | benediction, benefactor, benefit, benevolent |
| bi- | *two* | bicycle, bilateral, bisect |
| contra- | *against* | contraband, contradict, contravene |
| ex- | *out, out of* | exclude, exhale, expel |
| extra- | *outside* | extraordinary, extravagant, extrovert |
| omni- | *all* | omnipotent, omnipresent, omniscient |
| per- | *through* | percolate, perforate, permeate |
| pre- | *before* | preamble, precedent, prefix |
| poly- | *many* | polygamy, polysyllabic, polytheistic |
| re- | *back* | recall, recede, revoke, retract |
| tele- | *distant* | telegraph, telepathy, telephone, television |
| trans- | *across, beyond* | transatlantic, transmit, transaction, transcend |

## D 2b  French Borrowings

*Over the centuries, thousands of words were absorbed into English from French.* The historical event that most drastically influenced the development of the language was the conquest of England by the French-speaking Normans in the years following 1066. At the beginning of the so-called **Middle English** period, about 1150, the Norman conquerors owned most of the land and controlled the most important offices in state and church. The language of law, administration, and literature was French. When the native English of the conquered people gradually reestablished itself as the language of political and social life, thousands of French words were retained. Many of these words were associated with the political and military role of the aristocratic Norman overlords: *castle, court, glory, mansion, noble, prince, prison, privilege, servant, treason, treasure, war.* But hundreds of other words absorbed into Middle English were everyday words like *avoid, branch, chair, demand, desire, disease, envy, praise, table, uncle.*

NOTE: Many French words passed into English through the hands of English poets who found them in medieval French poetry and romance, both Norman and continental. Some of these words are still used mainly in imaginative literature and preserve a poetic and often old-fashioned flavor. Such words are *chevalier* for "knight," *damsel* for "girl," *fealty* for "loyalty," *paramour* for "sweetheart," *prowess* for "valor," *puissance* for "power" or "strength," *travail* for "toil."

## D 2c    Recently Borrowed Words

*A number of foreign languages have influenced the vocabulary of special fields of interest.* Since the consolidation of **Modern English** (about 1500), numerous words have come into English from French, Italian, Spanish, and various other sources. The leadership of seventeenth- and eighteenth-century France in elegant living, artistic style, and military organization is reflected in words like *apartment, ballet, battalion, cadet, caress, corps, façade, infantry, negligee, patrol.* Italy, which saw the origin of modern opera and symphonic music, provided terms like *cantata, concert, falsetto, sonata, solo, soprano, violin.* From Spain, which pioneered in the discovery and exploitation of new continents, came words like *alligator, banana, cannibal, cocoa, mosquito, Negro, potato, tobacco, tomato,* some of them absorbed into Spanish from New World sources.

Modern English has a number of foreign words in different stages of assimilation. If they are still felt to be foreign, your dictionary puts a special symbol in front of them or labels them "French," "Italian," or whatever is appropriate. A writer may use an occasional foreign word because it sums up the particular flavor of a thing or of an idea more aptly than any possible native equivalent. For instance, the French word *esprit* describes a kind of irreverent wit for which it is hard to find an English name. Do not use foreign phrases merely to impress your reader.

# Exercises

**A**. Find the original meaning of each of the following words: *Attenuate, circumlocution, cornucopia, egregious, metaphysics, philosophy, premise, protract, recalcitrant, translucent.* How does the original meaning help explain the current use of each word?

**B**. Investigate the history of the following words: *bedlam, bowdlerize, bowie knife, carnival, credit, curfew, dollar, emperor, fellow, gerrymander, glamour, gossip, hallmark, Halloween, jeep, kerchief, lynch, picayune, propaganda, thug.*

**C**. Select one of the following words: *boor, cattle, fee, husband, hussy, knave, lewd, meat, villain, virtue.* Report fully on the contrast in nature and extent of its treatment in your own dictionary and in the *Oxford English Dictionary.*

**D**. Explain the meaning of the common element in each of the following groups of words: *anarchy–monarchy–oligarchy; anthropology–misanthrope–philanthropy; antibiotic–biography–biology; audio-visual–audition–inaudible; biennial–centennial–perennial; centipede–century–percent; cosmic–cosmopolitan–microcosm; describe–prescribe–proscribe; effrontery–frontispiece–confrontation; eugenics–eulogy–euphonious; heterogeneous–homogeneous; insect–intersection–section; magnify–magnificent–magnitude; portable–portage–transport; precedent–procedure–secede.*

**E**. Indicate the basic meaning of each Latin and Greek prefix used in the following words: *anesthetic, ambivalent, antedate, antipathy, circumvent, concord, disunity, hypersensitive, international, introvert, malpractice, multimillionaire, neofascist, postgraduate, prelude, pseudoscientific, retroactive, semitropical, synchronize, ultramodern, unilateral.*

**F**. Find out from which languages the following words were derived: *bandana, boomerang, brunette, caviar, chocolate, crescendo, cynic, focus, hurricane, Mumbo Jumbo, pretzel, pundit, skin, snoop, vaudeville.*

**G**. What are the meanings of the following expressions? How many of them does your dictionary consider foreign rather than English? *Ad hoc, aficionado, auto-da-fe, blitz, corpus delicti, coup de grace, cum laude, de jure, enfant terrible, ersatz, eureka, fait accompli, hara-kiri, hoi polloi, laissez faire, non sequitur, pax Romana, quod erat demonstrandum, tour de force, Zeitgeist.*

# D 3   Varieties of Usage

*Some words are appropriate only to certain situations or limited to specific uses.*

No matter what dictionary you buy, you should study the introductory notes and find out the significance of the various symbols and abbreviations used. The most important abbreviations are the **restrictive labels**. They indicate that a word is used only under certain circumstances and that it can be out of place when used without attention to its limitations. In the following dictionary entry, six of the nine principal meanings of *brass* are preceded by restrictive labels:

**brass** (bras, bräs), *n.* **1.** any of various metal alloys consisting mainly of copper and zinc. **2.** an article made of such an alloy. **3.** [*Mach.*] a partial lining of soft metal for a bearing.     —— Subject Label
**4.** *Music.* **a.** an instrument of the trumpet or horn family. **b.** such instruments collectively. **5.** [*Brit.*] **a.** a memorial tablet or plaque incised with an effigy, coat of arms,     —— Geographic Label
or the like. **b.** *Slang.* money. **6.** *Furniture.* any piece of ornamental or functional hardware. **7.** *U.S. Slang.* **a.** high-ranking military officers. **b.** any very important officials.
**8.** [*Informal*] excessive assurance; impudence; effrontery.     —— Usage Label
—*adj.* **9.** of or pertaining to brass. [ME *bras*, OE *bræs*; c. OFris *bres* copper, MLG *bras* metal] —**brass′ish,** *adj.*

From *Random House Dictionary*

Usage labels can help you develop your sense of what words are generally acceptable in written English. They provide a guide when roughly synonymous choices have different associations. One choice may suggest the non-standard folk speech of factory and barracks ("nohow"); the other may suggest the standard English of school and office ("not at all"). One choice may suggest an informal variety of standard English ("gimmick"); the other may suggest a formal variety ("device"). College dictionaries differ sharply in their use of restrictive labels to indicate varieties of usage. Compare the practice followed in your own dictionary with the description of usage labels in the following section.

## D 3a    Nonstandard Words

*Some words suggest nonstandard speech rather than educated usage.* Many words are appropriate to almost any occasion. A hand can be appropriately called a "hand" at any time and at any place. Other words are limited in their usefulness because of the associations they suggest. For instance, words like *anywheres* and *nohow* are either not noted in your dictionary at all or labeled illiterate, **nonstandard**, or vulgate. Like non-standard grammatical patterns, they are often associated with low social standing or a lack of formal education. (See G 1a.)

## D 3b    Informal Words

*Some words suggest informal conversation rather than systematic exposition or argument.* Some dictionaries label such words **colloquial**. The word does *not* mean "local" but "characteristic of informal speech." People use colloquial language when at ease and with their friends; as a result, it tends to sound relaxed and folksy. But the man who is most comfortable in a robe and slippers puts on a tie and a business suit when going to the office on Monday morning. Similarly, a writer has to be able to use formal language in formal situations. In particular, he has to guard against sudden shifts from the tone of the lecture hall to that of the snack bar around the corner.

| Informal | Formal | Informal | Formal |
|----------|--------|----------|--------|
| boss | superior | kid | child |
| brainy | intelligent | mean | ill-natured |
| bug | germ | skimpy | meager |
| faze | disconcert | sloppy | untidy |
| flunk | fail | snoop | pry |
| folks | relatives | snooze | nap |
| hunch | premonition | splurge | spend lavishly |
| job | position | stump | baffle |

Other familiar words are generally acceptable in one sense but colloquial in another. Colloquial are *alibi* in the sense of "excuse," *aggravate* in the sense of "annoy," *funny* in the sense of "strange," and *mad* in the sense of "angry."

Informal language uses qualifiers like *kind of* hard, *sort of* easy, *a lot, lots;* abbreviated forms like *ad, bike, exam, gym, phone.* It uses many **phrasal verbs**, verbs that combine a short basic verb with one or more prepositions: *check up on, chip in, come up with, cut out* (noise), *get across* (a point), *take in* (a show), *take up with* (a person). Informal English usually contains a liberal sprinkling of catch-all words like *nice, cute, awful, wonderful,* or *terrible.* It is fond of **figurative expressions** like *have a ball, polish the apple, shoot the breeze, hit the road.*

Used with discretion, colloquial expressions can set a casual, leisurely tone:

There was a broad streak of mischief in Mencken. He was forever *cooking up* imaginary organizations, having *fake* handbills printed, inventing exercises in pure nonsense.—Philip M. Wagner, "Mencken Remembered," *The American Scholar*

To reject the book because of the immaturity of the author and the *bugs* in the logic is to throw away a bottle of good wine because it contains bits of the cork.—E. B. White, "A Slight Sound at Evening," *Yale Review*

But more often, colloquialisms suggest a put-on folksiness, the public-relations heartiness of some advertisers and some political candidates (Uncle Sam from a billboard: "My folks mostly drive Ford V-8s"). Many college teachers require the student to keep expository writing free from a colloquial tinge.

## D 3c    Slang

*Slang is appropriate only in the most informal kinds of writing or when deliberately used for special effects.* Slang has typically adolescent qualities: a disregard for convention, a lack of restraint, a tendency to regard people and accepted social attitudes with condescension or contempt. Much slang is merely faddish: New slang expressions are born overnight, repeated over and over, and then forgotten. Different high schools, colleges, and professions develop their own special varieties of slang, which change from year to year. As a result, much slang is unintelligible to outsiders.

Slang often has a vigor missing in more pedestrian diction. The figurative expressions it substitutes for less imaginative formal terms are often apt: *blow-hard, gumshoe, highbrow, rubberneck, sawbones, whirlybird.* Often a striking slang expression has no very satisfactory formal equivalent: *eyewash, runaround, stuffed shirt.* Many slang terms appeal to the user's love of the grotesque: *beat one's brains out, blow one's top, chew the fat, fly off the handle, hit the ceiling, kick the bucket, lay an egg.*

Slang is the major resource of many a humorous writer:

> Despite that great wellspring of love and pity I have for the afflicted and the misbegotten, and those who have been *just plain took,* I find it hard to get worked up over the plight of those *gaffers* who play golf on the city's links. Little boys lurk in the brush, and when one of the superbly conditioned athletes knocks a *nifty* their way, they keep the ball. Then, if things haven't changed since my day, they sell the balls to other superbly conditioned athletes, who then *scream like banshees* when the golf-ball connoisseurs *steal 'em* again. Since grabbing the little thieves by the scruff of their necks and *beating the bejabbers out of them* would obviously be in violation of their civil rights, we must look elsewhere for a solution.

Unfortunately, the humor in slang tends to be crude. Calling a person "fatso" or "skinny" or "bonehead" may be funny, but it also suggests a lack of tact or respect. The extravagant and contemptuous elements in slang make many readers interpret all slang expressions as signs of bad taste and bad manners.

## D 3d    Fancy Words

*When writing formal English, avoid words that are pompous, affected, or stilted.* Students whose writing has been criticized as slangy or colloquial sometimes have difficulty finding middle ground. Trying to avoid excessive informality, they may go to the opposite extreme:

**Stilted:** I sincerely believe that the government should *divulge* more on the subject of socialism and its *cohorts*, because its *impetus* has reached a frightening *momentum*.

Do not imitate writers who habitually prefer the fancy word to the plain word, the elegant flourish to the blunt phrase.

Dictionaries do not usually distinguish between plain and fancy words. Some of the latter may carry the label *poetic* or *literary*, indicating that they are most appropriate in poetry, in fiction, in imaginative description. Here is a brief list of words that can make your writing seem affected (see also D 6b):

| Fancy | Plain | Fancy | Plain |
|-------|-------|-------|-------|
| adumbrate | hint | nuptials | wedding |
| ameliorate | improve | obsequies | funeral |
| asseverate | assert | pachyderm | elephant |
| astound | amaze | potentate | ruler |
| betrothal | engagement | presage | predict |
| commence | begin | pulchritude | beauty |
| concomitant | result | purchase | buy |
| demise | death | quaff | drink |
| diurnal | daily | residence | home |
| emolument | pay, reward | tome | volume |
| eschew | avoid | vernal | springlike |
| gelid | cold | vista | view |

NOTE: Whether a word sounds natural or affected depends on its use. A word appropriate in a stylized social note may sound artificial in a personal letter. Contemporary expository prose, on the whole, avoids both "fine writing" and the strained joviality of a deliberately colloquial style in favor of simple, unpretentious language.

# Exercises

**A**. Which of the following expressions would you expect to carry restrictive labels? Check your answers with the help of your dictionary. *Bookworm, Chinaman, go Dutch, grease monkey, guttersnipe, guzzle, hubbub, highfalutin, jalopy, mob, moniker, mooch, moonshiner, persnickety, rake-off, ritzy, schoolmarm, shyster, victuals, walkie-talkie, windbag, wallop, Yankee.*

**B**. Check the standing of the following *abbreviations.* Which does your dictionary list without a restrictive label? *Ad-lib, auto, bus* (for "omnibus"), *doc, econ, IQ, lab, math, photo, plane* (for "airplane"), *prof, snafu, TV, ump* (for "umpire"), *VIP.*

**C**. Arrange the expressions in each group in order *from the most formal to the most informal.* Be prepared to defend your decisions. (Your instructor may ask you to check your own judgments against those of your dictionary.)

    **1**. live it up, live on little, live up to a promise

    **2**. dress up for a party, dress down an offender, dress a wound

    **3**. dream up a scheme, a cherished dream, dreamboat

    **4**. tear up the bill, tear into someone, that tears it

    **5**. hook up the microphone, got him off the hook, did it on his own hook

    **6**. crack a book, his voice cracked, crack down on crime

    **7**. have a go at it, go through with it, go for blondes

    **8**. skip town, skip a grade, children skipping down the path

    **9**. deal cards, make a deal, big deal!

    **10**. sweat shirt, sweat out a decision, no sweat

**D**. Point out *colloquialisms and slang expressions* and comment on their appropriateness. If your instructor desires, rewrite the sentences, avoiding all expressions that are not appropriate to formal written English.

    **1**. Uncle Amos was a spendthrift in his youth, but he changed after he married a penny-wise wife.    **2**. My family was on the move all through my early childhood, but we finally located in the state of New York.    **3**. Psychologists have discovered that many young people get a kick out of cutting up in front of a group. **4**. Our unlimited material resources will avail us nothing unless we keep alive the gumption that comes down to us from colonial farmers. **5**. When the refugees were told that the train was going to leave in ten minutes, there was a mad rush to the station. **6**. Parents only confuse a child by bawling him out every time he commits a minor mistake. **7**. I prefer being blown to pieces by an atomic bomb to being brained with a club. **8**. Sent to size up our new allies, he found most of them in good shape. **9**. The concert was scheduled to start at eight o'clock, but unfortunately the soloist did not show up. **10**. Guests who crash a party must not be surprised if the host gives them a cold shoulder. **11**. In view of the late hour, we decided we better shove off and get some shuteye. **12**. My education was rather lopsided; it never came to grips with the problems that really interested me. **13**. It is too bad that we should run out of gas only a couple of miles from home. **14**. When Lovelace fails to suggest a definite date for the wedding, Clarissa begins to suspect that he is only pulling her leg. **15**. Modern medicine has found ways of licking many dread diseases.

**E**. Observe the language used by your fellow students, friends, or acquaintances to find *six current slang expressions* not listed in your dictionary. Define them, explain their use, and indicate what, if anything, they reveal about the speaker's attitude.

**F**. Study the writing of a columnist who makes frequent use of colloquialisms or of slang. Examine and describe his attitude toward his material and toward his readers.

**G**. Compare the use of usage labels for the following words in *three college dictionaries: batty, corny, fuddy-duddy, gimmick, gyp, shoo-in, snazzy, splendiferous, swap, yak.*

**H**. Study the treatment of usage in *three* of the following specialized dictionaries: H. W. Fowler, *A Dictionary of Modern English Usage* (or one of its modern adaptations); Bergen Evans and Cornelia Evans, *A Dictionary of Contemporary American Usage;* Margaret M. Bryant, ed., *Current American Usage;* Wilson Follett, *Modern American Usage;* Lester V. Berrey and Melvin Van Den Bark, *American Thesaurus of Slang;* H. Wentworth and S. B. Flexner, *Dictionary of American Slang.* For fruitful comparison, select several expressions treated in at least two of the books you have chosen.

# D 4   Words in Limited Use

*Some words have only regional currency; others are no
longer in general use.*

Dictionaries use restrictive labels to show that a word is
not current throughout the English-speaking world, or not
current at this time, or familiar mainly to specialists in a
limited field.

## D 4a   Regional Labels

*Dictionaries use geographic labels to indicate words in use
mainly in one region.* During the centuries before travel, books,
and finally radio and television exercised their standardizing
influence, languages gradually developed regional varieties.
Here are the types of regional variation that you are likely to
encounter:

(1) *Vocabulary differs somewhat from one English-speaking
country to another.* Students of British English notice **Americanisms**
brought into the language through American movies
and television programs. American travelers in England
notice the British uses of *tram, lorry, lift, torch, wireless, fortnight.*
Here is a passage with many British terms:

A scale or two adhered to the *fishmonger's* marble slab; the *pastrycook's*
glass shelves showed a range of interesting crumbs; the *fruiterer*
filled a long-standing void with fans of cardboard bananas and a
"Dig for Victory" placard; the *greengrocer's* crates had been emptied
of all but earth by those who had somehow failed to dig hard
enough. . . . In the *confectioner's* windows the ribbons bleached on
dummy boxes of chocolate among fly-blown cut-outs of pre-war
blondes. *Newsagents* without newspapers gave out in angry red
chalk that they had no matches either.—Elizabeth Bowen, *The Heat
of the Day*

(2) *Like most European languages, British English varies greatly from area to area.* Such regional varieties within a country are called **dialects**. Students of English literature usually encounter some dialect writing. For instance, a poet to whom a pretty girl is a "bonny lass," a church a "kirk," and a land-owner a "laird" is using one of the dialects of Scotland and Northern England rather than standard British English.

(3) *American speech shows some regional differences.* These are now being recorded in linguistic atlases. By and large, the constant intermingling of settlers from many areas, and the rapid growth of mass media of communication, have kept these American dialects from drifting very far apart. Here are some of the words that your dictionary is likely to mark as dialectal: *dogie, poke* (bag), *reckon* (suppose), *tote* (carry), *you all.*

Dialect differences are exploited by comedians and comic-strip writers for comic effects. Dramatists and novelists reproduce dialectal differences to give a down-to-earth quality to the conversation of their characters. You yourself may at times experiment with dialect expressions when striving for local color or a quaint, folksy touch.

## D 4b Obsolete and Archaic

*Dictionaries label words no longer in common use.* Some words, or meanings of words, have gone out of use altogether. They are called **obsolete**. Examples of obsolete meanings are *coy* (quiet), *curious* (careful), *nice* (foolish). Some words or meanings are no longer in common use but still occur in special contexts. Such words and meanings are called **archaic**. The King James version of the Bible and the vocabulary of religious devotion preserve many archaisms that were in common use in seventeenth-century England: *thou* and *thee, brethren, kine* (cattle).

In the following dictionary entry, five of the numbered meanings of *brave* are labeled obsolete:

**brave** (brāv) *adj.* **brav·er, brav·est  1.** Having or showing courage; intrepid; courageous.  **2.** Making a fine display; elegant; showy.  **3.** *Obs.* Excellent.  — *v.* **braved, brav·ing** *v.t.*  **1.** To meet or face with courage and fortitude: to *brave* danger.  **2.** To defy; challenge: to *brave* the heavens.  **3.** *Obs.* To make splendid.  — *v.i.*  **4.** *Obs.* To boast.  — *n.*  **1.** A man of courage.  **2.** A North American Indian warrior.  **3.** *Obs.* A bully; bravo.  **4.** *Obs.* A boast or defiance.

From *Standard College Dictionary*

Here are some archaisms familiar to readers of poetry and historical fiction:

| | | | |
|---|---|---|---|
| *anon* | (at once) | *fere* | (companion) |
| *brand* | (sword) | *forsooth* | (truly) |
| *childe* | (aristocratic youth) | *methinks* | (it seems) |
| *erst* | (formerly) | *rood* | (cross) |
| *fain* | (glad or gladly) | *sprite* | (ghost) |

NOTE: Some words have an old-fashioned flavor even though they may not be labeled archaic in your dictionary. *Albeit* (although), *lief* (gladly), and *threescore* (sixty) would sound quaint in a paper written by a college student.

## D 4c   Neologisms

*A writer should be cautious in using words that have recently come into the language.* Lexicographers, who at one time resisted the introduction of new words, now compete in their coverage of **neologisms**, or newly coined expressions. Many new words serve a need and rapidly become generally accepted: *bookmobile, cybernetics, astronaut, supersonic, transistor.* But many other coined words make conservative readers squirm.

Inexperienced writers sometimes coin words *inadvertently* by way of analogy: *vanishment* (analogous to "banishment"); *neglectfulness* (analogous to "bashfulness"). Much awkward, inexact prose suffers from improvisations like *cowardness* (cowardice) and *unpainful* (painless).

Journalists and advertisers are constantly inventing terms designed to dazzle their customers. The most popular type is the combination of two familiar words, as in *beautility* (beautiful utility) or *modelovely* (lovely model). Some of these are entertaining, like *Time's phenomoppet* (phenomenal moppet), but many are neither humorous nor ingenious.

Many new words are part of an impersonal *bureaucratic jargon* that lacks the life and color of real human language. Memos and reports often use words made up, by people with tin ears, on the model of *escapee, personalize, finalize, socioeconomic.* (See D 6b.)

## D 4d    Subject Labels

*Dictionaries label technical terms that are not likely to be familiar to laymen.* Labels like *Law, Naut.* (nautical), or *Mach.* (machinery) are called subject labels. The **technical terminology** or, on a less formal level, the **shoptalk** of a trade or profession makes possible precise and rapid communication among its members but requires careful definition or explanation in writing addressed to the general reader. The math student will have no difficulty with *set, natural number, integer, rational number,* and *number sentence.* But the layman would want them explained.

NOTE: Some words associated with a specific field have acquired unfavorable associations. *Contact* for "get in touch with," *deal* for "transaction," *feature* for "exhibit" or "offer for sale," and *proposition* for "proposal" are words used primarily by salesmen. Even when used in a noncommercial context, they may carry overtones of the hard sell. *Personnel, domicile,* and *dependents* are used primarily by public officials and administrators. When used in a nonofficial situation, such words suggest impersonality and red tape.

# Exercises

**A**. Investigate the regional or dialect uses of the following words. Where necessary, consult an unabridged dictionary: *bannocks, bloke, bonnet, boot, cant (v.), complected, coulee, cove, dogie, goober, petrol, power, pram, quid, rant, trolley, tube.*

**B**. E. B. White, in an article on Maine speech, discussed the following expressions among others: *tunk* a wedge, *soft* weather, *dozy* wood, people *from away*, a *snug* pasture, *gunkhole, nooning*. Write a paper in which you discuss a number of expressions that you associate with a specific region. For instance, investigate dialect features that set your own native speech apart from that of the region where you now live.

**C**. Which of the following words (or which of their uses) are archaic? Which are obsolete? *Bower, cark, costermonger, favor, gentle, goodman, hackney, perpend (v.), thorpe, yestreen, ywis.*

**D**. Read a scene from a play by Shakespeare or by one of his contemporaries. Compile a list of ten words or meanings that have become obsolete, archaic, or old-fashioned. Check in an unabridged dictionary words not listed in your own.

**E**. Discuss the use of newly coined words in current advertising. Show which of these you think may eventually become standard English and explain why.

**F**. What special fields of interest do the following technical terms represent? Which of the terms would you expect the average high school graduate to know? *A priori, barbican, bend sinister, brochure, calorie, camshaft, crochet, de facto, denouement, epistemology, graupel, hole in one, lien, plinth, solstice, sonata, sprit, symbiosis, tachistoscope, thyroid, transubstantiation, umlaut, valence, venireman, ventricle.*

**G**. A student investigating Post Office shoptalk discussed the following terms: *swing room, star route, merry-go-round, Tour Three, fat stock, confetti, shedders, scheme man, nixie clerk*. Investigate and report on Post Office shoptalk in your area. Are any of the same terms in use? Are any of the terms recorded in general or specialized dictionaries? *Or* conduct a similar investigation of shoptalk in one of the following areas: railroading, trucking, flying.

# D 5 Exactness

*An effective writer uses the exact words needed to convey the intended meaning.*

Effective writing is clear, exact, concise. The effective writer uses exactly the right words — and no more — for his intended purpose.

## D 5a Accurate Words

*An effective writer employs accurate words and exact shades of meaning.* Hastily written words often express the intended meaning almost but not quite. Thus, an editorial may start like this: "Only by widespread voting will the desires of the nation be executed on the administrative and legislative levels of our government." There are several inexact expressions here: Orders are "executed," but desires are "realized," "fulfilled," or "complied with." They would be fulfilled not *by* voting but perhaps as a result of it. The main divisions of the United States government are not really "levels" of which one could be more elevated than another, but collateral branches, each with more or less clearly defined and independent authority.

Similar instances of hit-or-miss diction are common in student papers that are merely a hasty first draft rather than a carefully revised final version:

**Hasty:** *The news* about widespread corruption was first *exposed* by the local press.

**Revised:** The news about widespread corruption first *appeared* in the local press.

(Evildoers or shortcomings are "exposed," but news about evildoers is "printed," "presented," or "reported.")

Check your papers specifically for the following kinds of inaccurate diction:

(1) Watch out for words easily *confused* because closely related in sound or meaning.

The work was sheer *trudgery* [should be *drudgery*].
Similar choices *affront* every student [should be *confront*].
He grew up in a *staple* environment [should be *stable*].

(2) Watch out for *garbled idioms:*

| | |
|---|---|
| **Garbled:** | Unemployment *played* an important *factor.* |
| **Should Be:** | Unemployment *played* an important *role.* |
| **Garbled:** | Many young people have *lost their appeal* for fraternities. |
| **Should Be:** | Fraternities have *lost their appeal* for many people. |

(3) Watch out for words with the wrong *connotation:*

| | |
|---|---|
| **Inexact:** | Life in the suburbs *subjects* a family to the beauties of nature. |
| | (The connotations of *subject* are unfavorable; it implies that we are exposed to something unwillingly.) |
| **Revised:** | Life in the suburbs *brings* a family *closer* to the beauties of nature. |

## D 5b    Redundancy

*Avoid wordiness.* As a rule, a finished paper is the better for some vigorous pruning. Try to substitute one word that gives your meaning exactly for two words that give it blurrily. The most easily spotted kind of wordiness is **redundancy**, or unnecessary duplication. The phrase *basic fundamentals* is redundant because *basis* and *foundation* mean nearly the same thing. *Important essentials* is redundant because something could not be essential and unimportant at the same time.

In the following sentences one or the other way of expressing the same idea should be omitted:

We left *in the morning* at about six o'clock *a.m.*
*As a rule*, the weather was *usually* warm.
There is more to it than *seems apparent.*
I was given the *choice* of *choosing* whether I wanted to go.
*Physically*, he has not grown much in *height.*
*In my opinion, I think* you are right.

Here are some sources of wordiness other than direct duplication:

(1) *All-purpose nouns* like *situation, angle, factor, aspect, line,* or *element* are often mere padding. (See also D 6b.)

**Padded:** When I first came to Smith College, *there was a situation where* some students lived in better housing than others.
**Concise:** When I first came to Smith College, some students lived in better housing than others.

**Padded:** Another *aspect* that needs to be considered is the consumer relations *angle*.
**Concise:** We should also consider consumer relations.

(2) *Roundabout transitions* sometimes take the place of *for example, however,* and *therefore:*

**Wordy:** *In considering this situation we must also take into account the fact that* other students do not feel this way.
**Economical:** Others, *however,* do not feel this way.

**Wordy:** *Taking these factors into consideration, we must conclude that* your request is unjustified.
**Economical:** *Therefore,* your request seems to us unjustified.

(3) Introductory phrases like *the fact that* or *the question whether* can often be trimmed without loss. (See also S 3a on deadwood in sentences.)

**Wordy:** *The question of whether* churches should unite agitates people of many denominations.
**Economical:** Whether churches should unite agitates people of many denominations.

NOTE: Colloquial English uses many phrases that show a weakening of etymological meanings. *Continue* means "go on," *refer* means "point back," *eliminate* means "take out." *Continue on, refer back,* and *eliminate out* would be considered redundant in formal situations.

## Exercises

**A.** Make sure you can distinguish between the confusing words in the following pairs: *antic–antique; biography–bibliography; clique–cliché; connive–conspire; difference–deference; ethical–ethnic; feudalism–fatalism; gentle–genteel; literal–literary–literate; manners–mannerisms; sensible–sensitive; specie–species; unfaithful–infidel; venal–venial.*

**B**. Write down a *more exact word* for the word italicized in each sentence.

    **1**. The town's income *relies* heavily on the logging and fishing industries.

    **2**. Civil disobedience *contorts* the issues because it keeps everyone from discussing the problem in a calm, adult manner.

    **3**. A good listener can listen to his teachers and retain the knowledge they have *expelled.*

    **4**. The most despised task *bestowed* upon the motorist is the changing of a flat tire.

    **5**. The dog went bounding down the steps, emitting *whelps* at every leap.

    **6**. Our next *fiascle* took place in Hollywood.

    **7**. The March of Dimes was organized to help those *inflicted* with infantile paralysis.

    **8**. The chairman *contributed* the low attendance to inadequate publicity.

    **9**. The voters can hardly be *credible* enough to believe some of the things they are told.

    **10**. Sick people no longer can pay for their hospital costs without a tremendous *drain* being put on their families.

  **C**. Point out and correct examples of *inaccurate or unidiomatic diction.*

    **1**. He felt that a hands-off policy was the best one for the government to play.  **2**. A teacher has to be able to handle emotionally disturbed children without bias or ill-favored feelings.  **3**. Few people accomplish the asset of ignoring gossip circulated about them by thoughtless persons.  **4**. The United States lost much of the prestige that other countries used to have for her.  **5**. The support we received from our parent organization has aided greatly to our success.  **6**. The situation has become drastic and requires immediate action. **7**. Nations armed with nuclear weapons will be a constant fear to their less powerful neighbors.  **8**. In his speech, the mayor suggested several ways of helping the traffic problem. **9**. The administration, in exposing the apathy of Congress, has done a great deed to the country.  **10**. If we accept your theory, our whole concept of democracy will have to make a drastic change.    **11**. If the new city hall is to serve the whole community, it should be centralized in the city.    **12**. In an emergency, some drivers become a panic and freeze to the wheel.    **13**. Most of our objections to the behavior of other people fall under the generalization of prejudice.    **14**. Competence alone should be the judge whether a teacher should be allowed to teach or not.    **15**. Pearl Buck explains how her early environment cultivated her toward a love of learning.

**D**. Point out and correct examples of *wordiness*.

**1**. Mormons fleeing persecution founded the beginning of our community.

**2**. In due time, a new fad will eventually replace this current craze.

**3**. Some of today's popular music seems to revert back to music popular thirty years ago.

**4**. The weatherman said that at times there would be occasional rain.

**5**. The reason that married students have high grades academically is that they have a definite goal in the future to come.

**6**. In the modern world of this day and age, economical operation has become an indispensable condition for business success.

**7**. Many steps toward equal opportunities were taken in the early days of our government's reign.

**8**. To be right at home in this modern age of today, one should choose a hobby like flying, which is right up to date with the times.

**9**. The majority of the time the literature of the nineteenth century was didactic in nature.

**10**. One important factor in the accident situation is the consumption of alcohol by the drinking driver.

**E**. Rewrite the following sentences to reduce padding. Try to convey the same idea, using *half as many words* as the original.

**1**. The act of effective teaching is an art that not many teachers are capable of doing.

**2**. Being a salesman, an individual has many responsibilities both to his employer as well as to his customers.

**3**. As a traveler who has made several trips to Europe of varying lengths of stay, I venture to say that I have reasonable background to discuss the merits of the various different types of transportation now available for travel to Europe.

**4**. The fact that the college forces one to pay for membership in a student organization seems to me a coercion of the student's funds.

# D 6   Directness

*A writer must know how to be blunt and direct.*

At times, a writer will be deliberately indirect for tactical reasons. More common is the kind of careless indirectness that for no good reason slows down the reader.

## D 6a   Euphemisms

*Much roundabout diction results from the desire to be elegant.* Refined or impressive names for unpleasant or prosaic things are known as **euphemisms**. The most familiar euphemisms are those for elementary facts of human existence.

| | |
|---|---|
| (birth) | *blessed event, new arrival* |
| (pregnancy) | *to be expecting* |
| (spinsterhood) | *bachelor girl, career woman* |
| (age) | *senior citizens, the elderly* |
| (death) | *pass on, expire, the deceased, mortal remains* |

Euphemisms are "beautiful words"—words more beautiful than what they stand for. Often they are required by politeness or tact. When referring to people you respect, you will prefer *stout* to *fat, intoxicated* to *drunk, indolent* to *lazy,* and *remains* to *corpse.* More often, however, euphemisms mislead or even deliberately deceive. Waitresses become "hostesses," plumbers "sanitary engineers," file clerks "research consultants," undertakers "funeral directors," door-to-door salesmen "customer-contact personnel," and fortune tellers "clairvoyant readers." In much public-relations prose and political propaganda, euphemisms cover up facts that the reader is entitled to know: *straitened financial circumstances* for "bankruptcy"; *planned withdrawal* for "disorganized retreat"; *resettlement* for "forcible expatriation."

Many readers are annoyed by such evasive tactics; they will be grateful when you call a spade a spade.

| Euphemism | Blunt |
|---|---|
| immoderate use of intoxicants | heavy drinking |
| lack of proper health habits | dirt |
| deteriorating residential section | slum |

NOTE: The use of euphemisms to avoid the repetition of more unpretentious words is called **elegant variation**. A writer describing the habits of the swordfish will rightly feel that repeating the name of the fish in every second sentence would be monotonous. However, his writing will sound strained if he starts using circumlocutions like "scaled creature," "aquatic marauder," "denizen of the deep," and "knight of the brine."

## D 6b Jargon

*Much inflated diction results from a writer's using two high-brow words where one lowbrow word would do.* **Jargon** reflects the desire to make the trivial seem important. It cultivates an impressive pseudo-scientific air by using indirect, impersonal constructions; by blowing up simple ideas through abstract or roundabout diction; and by seeking out technical-sounding Latin and Greek terms.

The jargon addict says "Reference was made" rather than "I mentioned"; "the hypothesis suggests itself" rather than "I think." He prefers *effectuate* to "bring about," *hypothesize* to "assume," *magnitude* to "size," *methodology* to "methods," *interrelationship* to "relation." He uses terms like *essential, primary,* and *individual* where no distinction between essential and nonessential, primary and secondary, or individual and society is implied or important. He discusses simple everyday happenings in terms of "factors," "phases," "aspects," "situations," "criteria," "data," "problems," "facets," "phenomena," "structures," "levels," and "strata."

| | |
|---|---|
| **Jargon:** | Procedures were instituted with a view toward the implementation of the conclusions reached. |
| **Plain English:** | We started to put our ideas into practice. |
| **Jargon:** | Careful consideration of relevant data is imperative before the procedure most conducive toward a realization of the desired outcomes can be determined. |
| **Plain English:** | Look before you leap. |

## D  6c    Flowery Diction

*Flowery and extravagant diction interferes with a writer's doing justice to his subject.* Flowery diction results from an attempt to give a poetic varnish to prose. Some writers cannot resist the temptation to call a policeman a "minion of the law," an Irishman a "native of the Emerald Isle," a colonist who served in the War of Independence a "gallant warrior defending our infant republic."

| | |
|---|---|
| **Flowery:** | The respite from study was devoted to a sojourn at the ancestral mansion. |
| **Plain English:** | I spent my vacation at the house of my grandparents. |
| **Flowery:** | The visitor proved a harbinger of glad tidings. |
| **Plain English:** | The visitor brought good news. |

In the more showy kinds of journalism, the flowery phrase is supplemented by **hyperbole**, exaggeration for dramatic effect. "Crises" are constantly "racing toward a climax," "tragedies" are "stunning" peaceful communities, "daring" new detergents are overjoying housewives by bleaching clothes to a "dazzling" white. Basketball teams "clobber," "bludgeon," and "exterminate" each other; a 250-pound fullback "gambols," "capers," or "romps" to a touchdown; a boxer "slaughters" his opponent. A hyperbolical style sounds breathless or juvenile in serious discussion.

# Exercises

**A.** Investigate the *current use of euphemisms* in one major area, such as education, medicine, or the funeral industry. Examine such euphemisms for intention, appropriateness, effect.

**B.** Translate the following specimens of jargon into *plain English.*

**1.** Innovations have to be judged as useful according to the possibility of their implementation.

**2.** To answer this question without clarification of my rationalizing would be senseless, since there are a great number of determinants that can be expressed pro and con.

**3.** Being in a profession marks a tangible asset usable as a means of support throughout life, including advancing years.

**4.** The individual's mental attitude is the factor that seems to make time spent in one geographical location more enjoyable than time spent in another.

**5.** Finding genuine leadership is a deciding factor in the possibility of the existence of good government.

**6.** As far as the status of women is concerned, I feel the strong tendency toward domestication in our society will never change, only modify. The physical aspect plays an important part, it being the role of a woman to reproduce the offspring.

**7.** If an observation of the streets in various cities were to be made, it would reveal a considerable number of situations where traffic is delayed because of congested conditions.

**8.** Aid along the lines of scholastic achievement and integration into the social group is accorded the younger members of a fraternity by their older brothers.

**9.** The student commencing matriculation in the institution of his choice should not be subjugated to general education requirements above and beyond the prerequisites stipulated in his major field.

**10.** The existence or nonexistence of sufficient socio-economic incentives can be presumed to be a major factor in determining the availability of instructional personnel requisite to the successful functioning of the nation's educational establishment.

**C**. Point out specific features that make the following passage jargon. Rewrite the passage in a *less pompous, more natural* style.

> We think of our audio-visual program as a method or medium, not as an end in itself. For example, a curriculum committee at its inception does not necessarily include a visual-aids representative. However, following the formulation of general philosophy and basic content, visual aids become an active and integral part of curriculum organization. The materials available then serve in many ways to orient and implement the program. The individual teacher is responsible for enriching the individual learning situation through the preplanned utilization of visual materials that vitalize interest. The principal must provide for physical and monetary aspects. But perhaps the greatest contributing factor to the success of the program is provision for continuous growth. Our concentration of effort is on individual evaluations of materials immediately following their use. This is further implemented by periodic evaluations by groups, on the vertical and horizontal grade-level basis.

**D**. What makes the language of the following *student-written paragraphs* pretentious? Rewrite one of the paragraphs in a more direct and natural style.

> **1.** For some people the cartoons shown at the theaters are the high spot of the program. The majority of these people is the children. The slapstick comedy affords loads of laughs to the younger folks. However, the cartoons have more than a little effect on the older people too. Sometimes this effect is negative, and sometimes it is positive. The main criticism against the cartoons is that they are so completely abstract and ridiculous. For those people who enjoy the cartoons, the abstractness is the backbone of their favoritism.

> **2.** The representation of the sub-teenagers at the scene of the accident was better than that of the teenagers. The sub-teeners, mostly girls, had a different attitude than did their elderly teenaged friends. One aspect of their different attitude centered on the concern for the people in the collision. The girls attempted to give any assistance that they could while the teenagers didn't even offer. The sub-teens' interest also revolved about the details of the incident although none of them kept quiet long enough to find out. Sprinkled among the outer edge of teenagers and the core of sub-teens stood the parents.

Those garbed in aprons illustrated the time as being the dinner hour; those in short-sleeved shirts and pants characterized the "gardening in the summertime."

**E.** Investigate the use of *jargon* in government publications or in professional publications in a major field of study. Use detailed examples, explaining what they show about the nature of jargon.

**F.** Study the language used by your favorite *sports writer, fashion analyst, or society editor.* Write a brief report, providing samples of characteristic diction.


# D 7    Expressive Language

*A writer who has something fresh to say should say it in fresh and expressive language.*

Careful word choice can make the difference between colorless language and language that is fresh, graphic, and concrete.


## D 7a    Specific Words

*A good writer uses specific, informative words.* Instead of a colorless general word like *building*, he will use a more expressive word like *barn, mansion, warehouse, bungalow, tenement, shack, workshop*, or *cabin. Tenement* carries more information than *building*. It also comes closer to concrete experience, making it possible for the reader to visualize an actual structure. When diction remains unnecessarily general, the reader is too far removed from what he can see, hear, and feel.

**General:**  All the animals of the farm joined in singing "Beasts of England."

**Specific:**  The whole farm *burst* out into "Beasts of England" in tremendous unison. The cows *lowed* it, the dogs *whined* it, the sheep *bleated* it, the horses *whinnied* it, the ducks *quacked* it.   (George Orwell)

A good writer is a patient observer of language and as a result has at his fingertips the right word for specific objects, shapes, sounds, textures, motions:

sand crabs *wriggling* and *scuttling* . . . heavy little creatures, shaped like *scarabs,* with grey-*mottled* shells and orange underparts . . . (John Steinbeck)

a big, squarish *frame house* that had once been white, decorated with *cupolas* and *spires* and *scrolled* balconies in the heavily lightsome style of the seventies . . .   (William Faulkner)

## D  7b   Figurative Words

*Figurative expressions make writing graphic and colorful by exploiting similarities between different things.* A compressed but explicit comparison, introduced by *as* or *like,* is called a **simile**. An implied comparison that uses one thing as the equivalent of another is called a **metaphor**. Literally, *monkey* refers to a small, long-tailed animal. Metaphorically, it may mean a person who, like a monkey, is agile, mischievous, imitative, or playful.

Figurative language makes writing come to life. It provides one way of translating the abstract into the *concrete:*

There is always one moment in childhood *when the door opens* and lets the future in.   (Graham Greene)

Presenting us with images that we can visualize, figurative language brings into play not only our reason but also our *emotions:*

No book has ever revealed more starkly the senselessness of the disasters of war, nor shown up *with sharper X-ray vision, under the torn flesh of war,* the hidden, all-corrupting sickness of the vindictive world of peace-behind-the-lines.   (Kenneth Rexroth)

Observe the following cautions in your own use of figurative language:

(1) *Figurative expressions should be apt.* The implied analogy must fit:

**Apt:** Putting the hubcap back on the rim is *like putting an undersized lid on an oversized jar.*
(As one side of the hubcap is pounded into place, the opposite side pops out.)

**Inept:** Lacking the ignition of advertising, our economic engine would run at a slower pace.
(An engine without ignition would not run at a slower pace; it would just be dead.)

**Inept:** The reader's interest, *like so many feathers,* must be handled with extreme care. *Too rapid a wind of facts* will disperse his interest quite readily.
(Facts seem too solid to be compared to a wind; facts might *crush* the reader but would hardly *blow away* his interest.)

(2) *Figurative expressions should be consistent.* When several figurative expressions appear closely together, they should blend into a harmonious whole rather than clash because of contradictory association. Avoid the **mixed metaphor**:

**Consistent:** Fame cannot spread wide or endure long that is not *rooted* in nature, and *manured* by art. (Samuel Johnson)

**Mixed:** America's colleges are the *key* to national survival, and the future of the country lies in their *hands.*
(The second part of the statement is illogical, because keys do not have hands.)

**Mixed:** Enriched programs give the good student a chance to *dig* deeper into the large *sea* of knowledge.
(Most people do their digging on solid ground rather than at sea.)

(3) *Figurative expressions should not call excessive attention to themselves.* Avoid metaphors that are strained enough to become distracting:

**Extravagant:** When the average overmothered college student is removed from parental control, the severance of the umbilical cord causes him to bleed to death, psychologically speaking.

## D 7c    Fresh Words

*Phrase ideas freshly in your own words; avoid familiar ready-made phrases.* Many phrases that may once have been striking have become trite through overuse. Such tired phrases are called **clichés**. They seduce the writer, because they spring to mind ready to use and thus help a paper write itself:

Trite:    He was always *wrapped up* in his own thoughts and feelings.
Fresh:    Only the *cocoon* of his own thoughts and feelings existed for him.

Trite:    The dean let us have it, *straight from the shoulder.*
Fresh:    The dean spoke to us directly and urgently, *like a scout just returned from the enemy camp.*

Everyday language is full of ready-made phrases that invite unthinking repetition. To the cliché expert, ignorance is always "abysmal," fortitude "intestinal," and necessity "dire." Daylight is always "broad," silence "ominous," and old age "ripe." People make a "clean break" and engage in "honest toil" till the "bitter end." They make things "crystal clear"; they wait "with bated breath"; they work "by the sweat of their brow." Last but not least, sadder and wiser and a little the worse for wear, they retire to the sidelines to let a new generation make its appearance upon the busy stage of life.

Here are some of the clichés that at times spill over into student writing:

believe it or not              the finer things
better late than never         first and foremost
beyond the shadow of a doubt   free and easy
bolt out of the blue           get in there and fight
burn the midnight oil          good time was had by all
couldn't care less             green with envy
crying shame                   in one fell swoop
dire straits                   in the last analysis
easier said than done          it goes without saying
the facts of life              it stands to reason
few and far between            last but not least
fine and dandy                 the last straw

let's face it
malice aforethought
nature's glory
off the beaten track
pride and joy
proud owner
rear its ugly head
rude awakening
a shot in the arm
sink or swim
a snare and a delusion

sneaking suspicion
something tells me
straight and narrow
strike while the iron is hot
tender mercies
to all intents and purposes
truer words were never
    spoken
truth is stranger than
    fiction
up in arms

## Exercises

**A**. From your current reading, select five short sentences in which a writer uses words *more specific* than you might have expected. Here are two examples:

> The voyage of the best ship is a *zigzag* line of a hundred *tacks*. (Ralph Waldo Emerson)

> The sunlight *pressed* through the windows, *thieved* its way in, *flashed* its light over the furniture and the photographs. (Katherine Mansfield)

**B**. Evaluate the use of figurative language in the following passages. Are the figurative expressions apt, consistent, unforced? Point out mixed or extravagant metaphors.

> **1**. Unnecessary precision is pedantic and fuzzy, like honing a razor to cut butter.   (Monroe C. Beardsley)

> **2**. Each professor has four faces. The first face is that of the scholar; it was started with Socrates, sharpened by science, and honed on experience.

> **3**. The man who merely "plays back" what he has heard or read without any understanding of it is not truly educated.

> **4**. Today our industrial giant, streamlined in accordance with the needs of the atomic age, stands on the threshold of a horizon of unlimited prosperity.

> **5**. Powered by the germ cell of the Ruhr, the truncated Reich had surpassed the economic peak of 1936, Hitler's best year. (William Manchester)

**6**. Selling an international language is like selling telephones. No one will buy either unless he thinks a lot of other people will do the same.

**7**. Scientific progress is a stream that owes its strength to many tributaries.

**8**. By taking the initiative in the current propaganda battle, the State Department has scored a bull's-eye of great magnitude.

**9**. This is one of those watershed moments in history, when the pendulum swing of public needs and public policies happens to coincide with a historical breaking point.   (Richard Nixon)

**10**. Africa is on the brink of television, and in one fantastic giant step the Dark Continent will be hurtled from the tomtom to the television screen.

**11**. The Congressman insults his constituents' intelligence by dragging a red herring into the arena and by wrapping himself in the mantle of his war record to shield himself from honest criticism.

**12**. In this poem, the poet seems to be coming out of a dream world and stepping into the face of reality.

**13**. No sooner does a teen-ager's car go off the road than he hits the front page of the newspaper.

**14**. A career is like a garden in that it, too, requires much plotting and planning, much preliminary spadework, the right seeds sown in the right soil, and a long period of careful cultivation.

**15**. Moral progress is at a low ebb and has reached the acme of stagnation. We have many outstanding religious and moral leaders, but their words of gold are falling on arid soil rather than on fertile ground.

**C**. Rewrite the following sentences to *eliminate clichés*. Try to make your phrasing fresh enough to revive the reader's attention.

**1**. They will have to get his signature by hook or by crook.

**2**. After one more defeat, he will have to throw in the sponge.

**3**. The reporter swallowed their story hook, line, and sinker.

**4**. The typical organization man knows which side his bread is buttered on.

**5**. Party platforms never get down to brass tacks.

**6**. In trying to revitalize our neighborhoods, we too often throw out the baby with the bath water.

**7**. When we are asked to change administrations in the midst of a serious international crisis, we should remember that it is unwise to change horses in midstream.

**8**. The opposing candidate is a Johnny-come-lately who entered the campaign only at the urging of his influential backers.

**D**. Compile a list of ten clichés widely used in news reporting, campaign oratory, or advertising. What explains their popularity?

# 3

# SENTENCE STYLE

An effective writer knows his tools. His most basic but also his most versatile tool is the sentence. Just as an effective writer must learn to exploit the rich resources of the English vocabulary, so he must learn to employ to advantage the rich structural resources of the English sentence. Notice how the basic idea in the following sentence may be stated in a variety of ways:

> The old man recited the verses with many a splendid gesture.
> With many a splendid gesture, the old man recited the verses.
> The verses were recited by an old man gesturing splendidly.
> A man—old, gesturing splendidly—was reciting verses.
> There was an old man reciting verses, gesturing splendidly.
> The man who recited the verses with many a splendid gesture was old.

When you work on sentence style, you focus on what makes sentences apt, varied, vigorous—a pleasure to read.

## S 1    Sentence Building

*A well-built sentence clearly signals important relationships.*

Many simple sentences are built on the "Who does what?" model. When such a sentence moves with few or no modifiers from subject to verb and from there to one or more complements, we are likely to encounter few problems of clarity or proper perspective.

> *My friend waited* outside the restaurant.
> *The relatives* of the deceased *crowded the room.*
> *The heavens declare the glory* of God.

Our problem is to maintain the same clarity and directness when we build sentences designed to carry more, and more complicated, information.

## S 1a   Effective Predication

*Give directness and vigor to a weak sentence by rewriting it on the "Who does what?" model.* Often a sentence gains in directness if the subject and the predicate carry a crucial part of the meaning. Try to make the subject name the key agent. Then make the predicate state the key point:

**Weak:**      *One crucial factor* in the current revolution in our social structure *is the relationship* between the white policeman and the black community.
(Subject and predicate carry little of the meaning; they are semantic blanks.)

**Stronger:**   *The white policeman* standing on a Harlem street corner *finds himself at the very center* of the revolution now occurring in the world.—James Baldwin, *Nobody Knows My Name*
(Sentence structure now makes the "crucial factor" also *grammatically* crucial—by making *policeman* the subject of the sentence.)

Check abstract nouns (ending in *-ment, -ion, -ism,* and the like) that serve as the subject of a sentence. Often these refer to actions, events, and activities that could be more vigorously expressed by a verb, with the agent clearly identified and serving as the subject.

**Weak:**      Violent *arguments* frequently *took place.*
**Revised:**   *We* often *argued* violently.

| Weak: | *A certain element* of confusion *was present.* |
| Revised: | *The speaker confused us.* |

| Weak: | *A criticism* which is prevalent against modern poetry *is* that *its appeal is* only to the super-sophisticated. |
| Revised: | *Many critics charge* that *modern poetry appeals* only to the super-sophisticated. |

| Weak: | *The solution* to the problem *was the result* of a careful examination of available records. |
| Revised: | *We solved the problem* by carefully examining available records. |

NOTE: You can often make the subject and predicate of a main clause carry your main point by eliminating tag statements like "The simple fact is that . . ." and "The question now confronting us is whether . . ."

| Weak: | *The question* now confronting us *is* whether we should yield to intimidation, and thus encourage other groups to resort to the same tactics. |
| Revised: | *Should we yield* to intimidation, and thus encourage other groups to resort to the same tactics? |

## S  1b    Effective Coordination

*Coordination is most appropriate when two ideas are about equally important.* In sentences like the following, both clauses are about equally relevant to the general trend of the report, narrative, or argument:

> We tried to locate the files, *but* we were unsuccessful.
>
> We shall have to build several new classrooms, *for* we expect a large increase in the school-age population.
>
> Our press is essentially provincial in this country, *and* except for a few syndicated columnists the reputation of our newspapermen is mainly local.

If you doubt the appropriateness of a coordinating connective like *and* or *but*, test the sentence by inserting a parenthetical "equally important":

**Effective:**     Under one of the plans, a reservist spends only six
months on active duty, *but* [equally important] he remains in the Ready Reserve for seven and one-half years.

*Excessive coordination* often results from the overuse of
*and*. Avoid *and* when it suggests a failure to examine the connection between ideas. The following sentence merely rambles
on from one point to the next, without connectives that would
prepare the reader for what is coming:

**Rambling:**     A member of the Reserve has to participate in weekly
drills, *and* it may be called up in emergencies, which
came as an unpleasant surprise to me, *and* you would do
better to stay away from it.

## S 1c   Effective Subordination

*Subordination is most appropriate when details, reasons, or
qualifications accompany a main point.* Subordinating connectives
(*when, while, since, because, if, though*) and relative pronouns
(*who, which,* and *that*) can make the material they subordinate
seem of secondary importance. They often seem particularly
apt when the main clause states a major point, with the dependent clauses establishing relations in place, time, or logic:

The edge of the cape was wet with blood *where* it had swept along
the bull's back *as* he went by.—Ernest Hemingway, "The Unde-
feated"

Remember the following points:

(1) Effective subordination *clarifies relationships in a sentence.* Merely placed next to each other, the following two
statements may seem disjointed: "Kroger organized a counterfeiting ring. He had studied printing in Germany." When
one is subordinated to the other, the connection between
them becomes more obvious:

**Effective:**     Kroger, *who had studied printing in Germany*, organized a
counterfeiting ring.

Coordinated by *but*, the following two statements leave the relationship between fishing and strong wind vague: "We spent the days fishing, but sometimes there was a strong wind." The subordinating connective *unless* leaves no doubt about the relationship:

**Effective:**    We spent the days fishing *unless there was a strong wind.*

(2) Unskillful subordination *blurs emphasis.* "*I was ten* when we moved to Alaska" focuses the reader's attention on you and your age. "When I was ten, *we moved to Alaska*" focuses the reader's attention on Alaska. **Upside-down subordination** results when the wrong item seems to stand out. When tucked away in a subordinate part of a sentence, important information may catch the reader unaware and, as a result, have an ironic effect. *Avoid upside-down subordination when no irony is intended:*

**Upside-Down:**    The salary was considered good by local standards, *though* it was not enough to feed and clothe my family.

**Improved:**    *Though* considered good by local standards, my salary was not enough to feed and clothe my family.

**Upside-Down:**    He had a completely accident-free record up to the last day of his employment, *when* he stepped on a power line and almost lost his life.

**Improved:**    On the last day of his employment, *after* ten years without a single accident, he stepped on a power line and almost lost his life.

Dependent clauses are harder to focus on, to remember, and to quote than independent ones. Your reader may lose the trend of your argument if too many essential points appear in unobtrusive dependent clauses.

## S 1d    Effective Modifiers

*Part of the secret of effective prose is skillful use of modifying words and phrases where an inexperienced writer might use separate clauses.* Observe the tightening of relationships and the gain in continuity in the following pairs:

**Routine:** She had shiny eyes, an upturned nose, and a lively mouth, and her face never seemed to be at rest.

**Effective:** Her face, *with its ever-shining eyes, its upturned nose, and mobile mouth,* was never in repose.—John Mason Brown, "Blithe Spirit," *Saturday Review*

**Routine:** We caught two bass. We hauled them in briskly, as though they were mackerel. After we pulled them over the side of the boat, we stunned them with a blow on the back of the head.

**Effective:** We caught two bass, *hauling them in briskly* as though they were mackerel, *pulling them over the side of the boat* in a businesslike manner without any landing net, and *stunning them with a blow on the back of the head.*—E. B. White, *One Man's Meat*

The following sentences, from a bull-fighting story by Ernest Hemingway, illustrate the variety in sentence rhythm made possible through the effective use of one or more modifiers *at different positions* in the sentence:

• breaking up subject and verb:

The horse, *lifted and gored,* crashed over with the bull driving into him.
Manuel, *lying on the ground,* kicked at the bull's muzzle with his slippered feet.
Manuel, *facing the bull, having turned with him each charge,* offered the cape with his two hands.

• at the end of the sentence:

Manuel walked towards him, *watching his feet.*
The bull was hooking wildly, *jumping like a trout, all four feet off the ground.*

• at the beginning of the sentence:

Now, *facing the bull,* he was conscious of many things at the same time.

*Heads up, swinging with the music, their right arms swinging free,* they stepped out.
*Arrogant, swinging,* they looked straight ahead as they marched.

• more than one position:

The bull, *in full gallop,* pivoted and charged the cape, *his head down, his tail rising.*

## Exercises

**A**. Rewrite the following sentences for *more effective predication.*

**1**. A conscientious teacher's satisfaction is incomplete unless he reaches a full realization of his goals.

**2**. As the result of unruly demonstrations, repeated interruptions of the committee's deliberations took place.

**3**. The conclusion is inevitable that considerable impairment of our country's military strength has come about.

**4**. A plan for safe driving is of no use if the cooperation of the individual driver is not present.

**5**. The accumulation of pressures to conform is so great that the student is in constant awareness of their presence.

**6**. The contribution of the alumni to the growth of the college will be in proportion to their information about its educational needs.

**B**. Write three pairs of related clauses. Then combine each pair in different ways, illustrating different possibilities of *coordination, subordination, or modification.*

EXAMPLE

The spring rains were heavy. The weeds grew at a furious rate.
The spring rains were heavy, *and* the weeds grew at a furious rate.
The weeds grew at a furious rate, *for* the spring rains were heavy.

*Because* the spring rains were heavy, the weeds grew at a furious rate.

*The spring rains being heavy*, the weeds grew at a furious rate.

The weeds, *with the spring rains heavy*, grew at a furious rate.

**C**. Rewrite the following passages, making effective use of *subordination or modifiers*.

   **1**. The monkey family is large. It includes monkeys, baboons, lemurs, and apes. The animals in the monkey family are closely related to man. They are imitative. They can be trained to perform simple tasks. However, their intelligence is low.

   **2**. My father came from a wealthy family, and my mother came from a very poor home, and it was strange that she held the purse strings in the family.

   **3**. Many high school teachers follow a textbook word for word, and they go over each page until everyone understands it. In college, many teachers just tell the student to read the textbook, and then they start giving lectures on the material covered in the text, but they don't follow it word for word.

**D**. In the first three sentences, point out effective subordination. In the next three sentences, point out effective use of modifiers. Your instructor may ask you to use one or more sentences in each group as *model sentences*. For each such sentence, write a sentence of your own on a different topic but preserving as far as possible the grammatical structure of the original.

   **1**. In Roman comedy the heroine, who is usually a slave or courtesan, turns out to be the daughter of somebody respectable, so that the hero can marry her without loss of face. (Northrop Frye)

   **2**. She stopped for a moment beside one of the prickly dark shrubs with which the city had beautified the Home, and then proceeded slowly toward the building, which was of whitewashed brick and reflected the winter sunlight like a block of ice. (Eudora Welty)

   **3**. The fame of each discovery rightly attaches to the mind that made the formula which contains all the details, and not to the manufacturers who now make their gain by it; although the mob uniformly cheers the publisher, and not the inventor. (Emerson)

**4**. Curiosity, like all other desires, produces pain as well as pleasure.  (Samuel Johnson)

**5**. All electric appliances, far from being labor-saving devices, are new forms of work, decentralized and made available to everybody.  (Marshall McLuhan)

**6**. The young moon recurved, and shining low in the west, was like a slender shaving thrown up from a bar of gold, and the Arabian Sea, smooth and cool to the eye like a sheet of ice, extended its perfect level to the perfect circle of a dark horizon.  (Joseph Conrad)

# S 2   Sentence Variety

*Keep your sentences from becoming plodding and monotonous.*

An effective writer uses sentences of different length and structure for variety and emphasis.

## S 2a   Sentence Length

*Use short sentences for emphatic, memorable statement; use long sentences for detailed explanation and support.* A short, incisive sentence is often appropriate for summing up a key idea or for giving pointed advice. The following sentences are quotable, emphatic, to the point:

> Economy is the art of making the most of life.  (G. B. Shaw)
> As long as possible live free and uncommitted. (Thoreau)
> Perversity is the muse of modern literature.  (Susan Sontag)

A complex, elaborate sentence is often appropriate for detailed explanation or argument. The following sentences from Thoreau's "Civil Disobedience" are carefully worked out, with all ifs and buts fully stated:

> There will never be a really free and enlightened State until the State comes to recognize the individual as a higher and independent power, from which all its own power and authority are derived, and treats him accordingly.

It is not a man's duty, as a matter of course, to devote himself to the eradication of any, even the most enormous wrong; he may still properly have other concerns to engage him; but it is his duty, at least, to wash his hands of it, and, if he gives it no thought longer, not to give it practically his support.

In order to use short and long sentences to advantage, remember the following points:

(1) Excessive use of *short, isolated sentences* can make your writing sound immature. The more you develop your capacity for sustained thinking, the more you will get away from sentences like the following:

**Choppy:**      Many teachers can give students information. Very few can inspire students to learn. Information is of little use to the student. Soon he will leave college. Then he will forget what he has memorized. He must be inspired to learn on his own.

**Improved:**      Many teachers can give students information, but few can inspire them to learn. When a student leaves college, the information he has memorized will be of little use and will soon be forgotten. What he needs most is the ability to learn on his own.

(2) Your writing will gain in clarity and emphasis if you occasionally make your reader stop short at a *concise, memorable statement of an important point.* Notice the emphatic short sentences in the following passages:

With the great growth in leisure-time activities, millions of Americans are turning to water sports: fishing, swimming, water skiing, and skin diving. *Clean water exhilarates and relaxes.*—Vance Packard, "America the Beautiful—and Its Desecraters," *Atlantic*

Bennett was always facing the wonder of the actualities of living. It was wonderful to him that we live as we do, that time will pass and change us, that we will die and perhaps die painfully, that life is what it is. *He never decorates or embroiders. He is wholly materialistic. Common sense is the salt of his plate.* We are never swept away, but we are curiously won over, and we, too, are filled with wonder at the slow unspinning of life.—John Van Druten, "My Debt to Arnold Bennett," *Saturday Review*

(3) A short sentence can be especially effective if it sets off an important conclusion or a *key observation at the end of a passage composed of longer sentences:*

They have a constitutional right, of course, to tell us what we must do to be saved; as they have always done. Twenty years ago they were telling us the direct opposite of what they tell us now; but they were just as sure then as now that they had the sole and sufficient key to salvation, and that those who did not accept it were forever damned. *One becomes bored.*—Elmer Davis, "History in Doublethink," *Saturday Review*

## S 2b   Varied Word Order

*Variations from normal word order can keep sentences from being tiresomely alike.* Though most of your sentences will follow the subject-verb sequence, there will usually be enough variety in the remaining sentence elements to prevent tiresome repetition. Monotony is most likely to result when a number of sentences start with the same subject, especially a pronoun like *I* or *he:*

**Monotonous:**   A good example of a topic drawn from personal experience is a bus accident I once had. I wrote a paper about this experience of mine. I remembered the events which took place during the accident. I could describe them well. After all, I had experienced them. It was a shocking experience. I will never forget it. The facts stand out in my memory because it was so shocking.

(1) One way to break up a monotonous sequence is to *make a modifier that usually occurs later in the sentence precede the subject.* The **introductory modifier** can introduce variety into a group of plodding sentences:

**Varied:**   He reversed the direction of the canoe. *After a few seconds* he stopped paddling. *Slowly* he made the canoe drift to the bank. *When within a yard of the shore*, he grabbed one of the overhanging branches.

**Varied:**    The Trans World Terminal stems from the work of contemporary architects like Corbusier of France and Nervi
of Italy, masters of the curve in concrete. *Like a true eagle,*
this building is all curves and muscle, no right angles. *Built
of reinforced concrete,* the whole structure swoops and turns
and rises.—Ken Macrorie, "Arriving and Departing," *The
Reporter*

(2) A less frequent variation from normal word order
is to *make a verb precede its subject.* The subject-verb sequence
is usually reversed only in questions, where all or part of
the verb characteristically precedes the subject: "*Are* you
ready?" "*Will* he *be* back?" "Why *did* your wife *leave* the car?"
Writers aiming at poetic or dramatic effects occasionally
use **inversion** even in ordinary declarative sentences:

Slowly *climbs* the summer moon.
Everywhere *was* silence.

## S 2c   Emphatic Word Order

*Variations from normal word order can direct attention to
the word or phrase occurring in an unusual position.*

(1) To gain emphasis, a writer may *shift a complement to
a more emphatic initial position.* The **introductory complement**
is normal in exclamations beginning with *what* or *how*: "*What
stories* that man told!" "*What a liar* you are!" "*How true* that
is!" In other sentences, the introductory complement is
especially effective when it takes up something mentioned
earlier:

**Effective:**    The committee has asked me to resign. *That* I will never
do.

**Effective:**    Mr. Schlumpf fried two small pieces of fish. *One of these*
he fed to his cat. *The other* he ate himself.

**Effective:**    We really should not resent being called paupers. *Paupers*
we are, and *paupers* we shall remain.

NOTE: Like other attention-getting devices, the introductory complement sometimes attracts attention to the

speaker rather than to what he is saying. Sometimes the construction smacks of old-fashioned oratory:

> *More patient wife* a husband never had.
> *Gone* are the days of my youth.
> *Such deeds of glory* we shall see no more.

(2) Often a sentence becomes clearer after you *shift the predicate of the main clause toward the end* and work some of the modifiers into the sentence earlier. Such treatment may strengthen a sentence especially if a **final modifier** is a belated qualification or concession, unexpectedly weakening the main point:

**Weak:**    We shall never dismiss a teacher because of the political beliefs of his associates without careful investigation. (*Without careful investigation* is a lame reversal of what starts out as a strong statement in support of teachers with controversial associations.)

**Improved:**    We shall never, *without careful investigation,* dismiss a teacher because of the political beliefs of his associates.

**Weak:**    Richard Wagner became one of the most successful composers of all time in spite of the jeers of his contemporaries. (This version may make your readers remember the jeers rather than the man's success.)

**Improved:**    Richard Wagner, *though jeered at by his contemporaries,* became one of the most successful composers of all time.

## S 2d    Loose and Periodic

*Experiment with shifts from the more common loose sentence to the more tightly structured periodic sentence.* A loose sentence finishes one major statement relatively *early* but then leads on to further points or further detail. It is an expandable or cumulative sentence that looks as if it might have been built in stages, or as if it grew by addition. Can you see how the following sentences finish one major point and then "move on"?

**Loose:**  *Comedy usually moves toward a happy ending,* and the normal response of the audience to a happy ending is "this should be," which sounds like a moral judgment.—Northrop Frye, *Anatomy of Criticism*

**Loose:**  *The whistle of the locomotive penetrates my woods summer and winter,* sounding like the scream of a hawk sailing over some farmer's yard, informing me that many restless city merchants are arriving within the circle of the town, or adventurous country traders from the other side.—Thoreau, *Walden*

In a periodic sentence, an essential part of the main statement is *held in suspense* until the end, so that the sentence ends when the main statement ends. Everything else is worked into the sentence along the way, contributing its share to the main effect. As a result, the periodic sentence has an air of finality, of emphatic assertion. It makes the main idea stay with us.

**Periodic:**  *Even Tom Jones,* though far more fully realized, *is still deliberately associated,* as his commonplace name indicates, *with the conventional and the typical.*—Northrop Frye, *Anatomy of Criticism*

**Periodic:**  *Prayer* that craves a particular commodity, anything less than all good, *is vicious.*—Emerson, *Essays, First Series*

## Exercises

**A.** Study the variations in sentence style in the following passages. Describe the functions performed or the effects produced by sentences of different *length.* Which passages make use of variations in *word order?*

**1.** Why conform to a group? Why throw away your birthright for a Greek pin or a peace button, for security and nonentity? This goes especially for the typical college student, who merely wants to do what "everyone else is doing." What everyone else is doing isn't best. It's merely common. One of the synonyms of "common" is "vulgar."

**2**. The dictionary can neither snicker nor fulminate. It records. It will offend many, no doubt, to find the expression *wise up*, meaning to inform or to become informed, listed in the Third International with no restricting label. To my aging ears it still sounds like slang. But the evidence—quotations from the *Kiplinger Washington Letter* and the *Wall Street Journal*—convinces me that it is I who am out of step, lagging behind.   (Bergen Evans)

**3**. The production of a work of art is not the result of a miracle. It requires preparation. The soil, be it ever so rich, must be fed. By taking thought, by deliberate effort, the artist must enlarge, deepen and diversify his personality. Then the soil must lie fallow. Like the bride of Christ, the artist waits for the illumination that shall bring forth a new spiritual life. He goes about his ordinary avocations with patience; the subconscious does its mysterious business; and then, suddenly springing, you might think from nowhere, the idea is produced.   (W. Somerset Maugham)

**B**. Which of the following sentences would you classify as loose, which as periodic?

**1**. Louise is the most lonely girl I have known, a beautiful little porcelain figurine placed into a world where porcelain figurines have gone out of style.

**2**. A thirty-hour ride in a troop train (model 1890) from Los Angeles had changed the dapper young man who had received personal greetings from the President of the United States into a sodden, wrinkled, tired, and bewildered draftee.

**3**. His friend Philinte, who is ready to lie quite cheerfully in order to enable other people to preserve their self-respect, is the more genuinely sincere of the two.   (Northrop Frye)

**4**. Far am I from denying in theory, full as far is my heart from withholding in practice (if I were of power to give or withhold) the *real* rights of man.   (Edmund Burke)

**5**. Liberals should not be ashamed to make positive claims about American society and politics, not only because they are true, but also because today's youth is being told so many other and contradictory things.

**C**. Select three sentences from your recent themes. For each, write down first the original version. Then add two or more revised versions, using *variations in word order* to make the sentence more emphatic or less routine.

EXAMPLE

We have always settled any disagreement over policy amiably by full and frank discussion.

By full and frank discussion, we have always settled any disagreement over policy amiably.

Any disagreement over policy we have always settled amiably by full and frank discussion.

# S 3   Awkward Construction

*Avoid constructions that make for an indirect, awkward, wooden style.*

Effective sentences may be long and complicated, as long as the words and structural relationships convey meaning clearly and directly. On the other hand, the grammatical equipment even in short sentences may become so heavy that it interferes with effective communication.

## S 3a   Deadwood

*Often a sentence proceeds more smoothly after it has been pruned of deadwood.* Avoid unnecessary *there ares* and *who weres:*

**Awkward:**    *There are* many farmers in the area *who* are planning to attend the meeting *which is* scheduled for next Friday.

**Improved:**    Many farmers in the area plan to attend the meeting scheduled for next Friday.

Other sentences can be cleared of deadwood by effective use of pronouns:

**Awkward:**    A child of pre-school age often shows a desire to read, but *the child's* parents often ignore this *desire.*

**Improved:**    Often a child of pre-school age shows a desire to read— *which his* parents ignore.

Some connectives, prepositions, and pronouns are unnecessary or unnecessarily heavy:

**Awkward:**   I wrote little, *because of the fact that* my childhood had been *an* uneventful *one.*

**Improved:**   I wrote little, because my childhood had been uneventful.

## S 3b   Awkward Passive

*Unnecessary use of the passive makes sentences heavy or roundabout.* An active sentence is modeled on the "agent-action-target" relationship: "The woodsman *felled* the tree." A passive sentence reverses this perspective and looks at the action from the point of view of the original object: "The tree *was felled* by the woodsman." Students often overuse the passive under the mistaken impression that it will make their sentences more formal, more scholarly. Practice translating such pseudo-formal passives back into the active voice:

**Pseudo-Formal:**   Although Bradley Hall *is* regularly *populated* by students, close study of the building as a structure *is* seldom *undertaken.*

**Direct:**   The students *passing* through Bradley Hall seldom *pause to study* its structure.

**Pseudo-Formal:**   My experiences at writing *were* greatly *increased* due to two large essays due each week.

**Direct:**   I *wrote* more than ever, *having to turn in* two long essays each week.

Unnecessary use of the passive can make it hard for the reader to visualize actions or events. Since the agent or performer is often *omitted* from a passive sentence, the reader may find it hard to determine the person responsible for an action or idea:

**Evasive:**   A plan for popular election of Supreme Court justices *is* now *being advanced.*
(By whom? The passive spreads a protective cloak of anonymity around the authors of the proposal.)

**Evasive:**      The racial problem is clearly one that *could and should have been solved* decades ago.
(By whom?)

NOTE: Not all passives are bad. The passive is appropriate when the *recipient or target of an action seems more important than the performer:*

*The unpretentious monarchs* of Scandinavia and the Low Countries are respectfully accepted by their sober subjects.—Kingsley Martin, "Strange Interlude," *Atlantic*

When no special emphasis is intended, the passive is most appropriate when the *originator or the performer of an action is unimportant, irrelevant,* or *hard to identify:*

Some of John's brain cells *were damaged* when he was a small child.
In World War II, millions of people *were driven* from their homes.

(On *shifts* to the passive, see G 12c.)

## S 3c    Impersonal Constructions

*Impersonal constructions are annoying when they obscure the identity of the forces at work.* Guard against the unnecessary use of such constructions:

(1) The **impersonal *one*** is often a tiresome substitute for fuller identification of the persons concerned, especially if their identity is indirectly revealed by modifiers:

**Tiresome:**    *When teaching, one* should be patient.
**Improved:**    *Teachers* should be patient.

**Tiresome:**    *As a father, one* should not spoil his children.
**Improved:**    *Fathers* should not spoil their children.

**Tiresome:**    *If one is a citizen of a democracy, he* should exercise his voting rights.
**Improved:**    *A citizen of a democracy* should vote.

(2) In *it-is* and ***there-is* sentences**, the first two words are mere structural props, which can make the sentences sound lame and indecisive. Sometimes the subject of a sentence receives needed emphasis if it is introduced by *it is* or *there is* and has its predicate changed into a modifying clause:

**Emphatic:**    It is *his competence* that we question—not his honesty.

More often, however, the rearrangement of sentence elements made necessary by *it is* or *there is* causes awkwardness:

**Awkward:**    In 1958, *there was* a strike participated in by five thousand union members.
**Improved:**    In 1958, five thousand union members went on strike.

## S 3d    Excessive Subordination

*Excessive subordination causes various types of overburdened sentences.*

(1) One common type *dovetails several dependent clauses into each other.* The resulting *that-if, if-because, which-when* **constructions** need not be awkward, but they almost always are when used by inexperienced writers:

**Awkward:**    I think *that if* there were less emphasis on conformity in high school, college students would be better prepared for independent thinking.

**Improved:**    In my opinion, college students would be better prepared for independent thinking *if* there were less emphasis on conformity in high school.

**Awkward:**    I am against football scholarships *because if* football players are given preferential treatment, who will want to participate in other college sports?

**Improved:**    I am against football scholarships. *If* football players are given preferential treatment, who will want to participate in other college sports?

(2) Another type of excessive subordination results in **"house-that-Jack-built" sentences**. Several dependent clauses

of the same type follow each other, making the sentence trail off into *a confusing succession of modifiers:*

**Awkward:**     When I was in Mexico City, I visited Jean, *who* was living with a Mexican girl *who* posed for the local artists, *who* are usually too poor to pay their rent, let alone the model's fee.

**Improved:**     When I was in Mexico City, I visited Jean. She was living with a Mexican girl *who* posed for the local artists but seldom received any money for her work. Most Mexican artists are too poor to pay their rent, let alone the model's fee.

Sometimes too many dependent clauses of the same type *delay* the main clause:

**Awkward:**     *When* a child is constantly watched *when* he is born and *while* he is a baby, the reason is that his mother wants to see whether he is developing as her books say he should.

**Improved:**     Some mothers constantly watch young children to see whether they are developing as the books say they should.

(3) Unskillful subordination sometimes causes sentences with a teeter-totter effect. Such **seesaw sentences** start with a dependent clause, proceed to the main clause, and then add a *second dependent clause that in a confusing way qualifies the meaning of the first:*

**Confusing:**     *Because many teen-agers marry hastily,* their marriages end in divorce, *because they are too immature to face adult responsibilities.*

**Clearer:**     Many teen-agers are too immature to face adult responsibilities. They marry hastily, and often their marriages end in divorce.

## S 3e    Awkward Modifiers

*Awkwardness results when heavy modifiers break up the pattern of a clause.* Lengthy appositives, verbal phrases, or dependent clauses sometimes separate elements that belong together:

**Awkward:**    The pilot told his friends that he had flown Clinton Morris, *a resident of New York City sought by the government for income tax evasion,* out of the United States.

**Awkward:**    The club treasurer, *being* the son of a father constantly *stressing* the importance of *maintaining* a proper sense of the value of money, refused to pay our expenses.

**Awkward:**    In 1943, Independence Hall, *which had been the first building built on the campus and which had housed the administration of the college for many decades,* was torn down.

# Exercise

Which of the following sentences seem clear and well built? Which seem awkward, overburdened, or confusing? If your instructor desires, revise the weak sentences.

**1.** Saturday mornings used to be my best time for studying, because I knew nothing was due the next morning (which was Sunday), until I started working.

**2.** From across the dinner-littered dining table, my father blinks myopically and asserts that current conflicts are no different from any other conflicts and that my dissent is no different from what his dissent used to be.

**3.** The magazine that is chosen by the reader is one that contains articles that the reader enjoys.

**4.** There are many ways in which a student who is interested in meeting a foreign student may come to know one.

**5.** A child's first impressions of people and places shape the course of his future life, frequently.

**6.** Knowing the right answers is sometimes less important than asking the right questions.

**7.** As we left the city, we approached a range of hills which seemed like giant waves which were about to break.

**8.** Having brothers and sisters to argue with and to adjust to was a useful experience because it helped me understand other people, because I don't always meet people sharing all my opinions.

**9**. John Milton was the first English writer who clearly and convincingly stated the idea that incompatibility is grounds for divorce, if I am not mistaken.

**10**. If someone is exercising his slightly off-key singing voice and a friend mockingly plugs his ears and winces in agony, the singer might well take the gesture as a personal insult if he didn't have a sense of humor.

**11**. As we were waiting for the doctor to see us, a boy with brown hair down to the small of his back played a flute, tears streaming down his face.

**12**. Various ways of living are being tested today and experimented with by youth whose dominant characteristic is the desire for flexibility.

# S 4   Repetition

*Make effective use of repetition and parallelism.*

Unintentional, haphazard repetition can make a passage sound clumsy. Deliberate repetition, on the other hand, can emphasize important points and give continuity to a sentence or a paragraph.

## S 4a   Awkward Repetition

*Unintentional repetition of sounds, syllables, words, or phrases violates the requirements of* **euphony**. A passage should sound pleasing, or at least inoffensive, when read aloud. Carelessly repeated sounds grate on the reader's ears.

**Awkward:**   Commercials seldom make for entertain*ing* and relax-*ing* listen*ing*.
**Improved:**   Commercials seldom entertain and relax the listener.

**Awkward:**   Close examin*ation* of the results of the investig*ation* led to a reorganiz*ation* of the department.
**Improved:**   Close study of the results of the inquiry led to a reorganization of the department.

**Awkward:** We listened to an account *of* the customs *of* the inhabitants *of* the village.

**Improved:** We listened to an account of the villagers' customs.

Unintentional repetition is especially annoying when the similarity in sound covers up a *shift in meaning or relationship:*

> My father lost his savings during the depression because he had *banked* on [better: "relied on"] the well-established reputation of our hometown *bank.*

## S 4b Emphatic Repetition

*Intentional repetition makes for clarity and continuity.* A writer may repeat important words and phrases for emphasis:

**Emphatic:** When I returned to State, *I studied* as I have never studied since. *I studied* before classes. *I studied* after classes. *I studied* till English, history, and zoology merged into one blurry mass of incoherent erudition.

**Emphatic:** In my mother's world, *no one ever* shrugged his shoulders; *no one* was *ever* bored and lazy; *no one* was *ever* cynical; *no one ever* laughed.—Alfred Kazin, "The Bitter 30's," *Atlantic*

Notice the cumulative effect of intentional repetition in the following passage from Stephen Crane's "The Open Boat":

> In the meantime, the oiler *rowed*, and then the correspondent *rowed*, and then the oiler *rowed*. Grey-faced and bowed forward, they mechanically, turn by turn, plied the leaden oars.

## S 4c Parallel Structure

*Effective use of parallel structure channels the reader's attention.* Parallel structure pulls together related ideas through the repetition of characteristic grammatical patterns. The following passages make effective use of parallelism:

My lack *of excitement,*
       *of curiosity,*
       *of surprise,*
       *of* any sort of pronounced *interest,*
           began to arouse his distrust.   (Joseph Conrad)

The air *must be* pure
    *if we are to* breathe;
the soil *must be* arable
    *if we are to* eat;
the water *must be* clean
    *if we are to* drink.

*Our* houses *are* built *with* foreign taste;
*our* shelves *are* garnished *with* foreign ornaments;
    *our* opinions,
    *our* tastes,
    *our* faculties,
       *lean* and
       *follow*
          *the* Past and
          *the* Distant.   (Emerson)

In prose of exposition and argument, parallel structure is used for some of the following purposes:

(1) Parallel structure helps to *line up related ideas in a sentence;* it *draws together related ideas in a paragraph:*

When the world wars came, the people of the liberal democracies could not be aroused to the exertions and the sacrifices of the struggle until they *had been frightened by* the opening disasters, *had been incited to* passionate hatred, and *had become intoxicated with* unlimited hope.

The people wanted to be told that when this particular enemy had been forced to unconditional surrender, they would re-enter the golden age. *This* unique *war would end* all wars. *This* last *war would make* the world safe for democracy. *This crusade would make* the whole world a democracy.—Walter Lippmann, *The Public Philosophy*

(2) Often, parallel structure helps to *line up dissimilar ideas for comparison or contrast:*

His remarks provoked much comment, *self-righteous from his enemies, apologetic from his friends.*

Whereas *it is desirable that* the old *should treat with respect* the wishes of the young, *it is not desirable that* the young *should treat with respect* the wishes of the old.

The European democracies *chose to rely on* unarmed appeasement, and the American democracy *chose to rely on* unarmed isolation.

(3) Parallel structure enables a writer to *make a series of parallel sentences build up to a* **climax**. Notice how the author of the following passage starts with fairly innocuous generalities and leads up to a specific point dear to his heart:

The future *is not for* little men with little minds. It *is not for* men without vision who fear progress. It *is not for* timid men who early were frightened by the story of Frankenstein. And it *is not for* those arch reactionaries who seek to shatter big enterprise and to force American industry back into the puny production patterns of its nineteenth-century infancy.

(On *faulty* parallelism, see G 11.)

## S 4d   Rhythm and Balance

*Frequent use of parallel constructions makes for regularity and balance, especially when the parallel elements are of approximately equal length.* Parallelism produces rhythmical patterns that are more distinctly felt than the variable rhythms of ordinary speech. A writer with an ear for rhythm makes use of the *variations* in sentence structure that prevent regularity from becoming predictable. In the following sentence the *which*-clause separating the subject and verb of the main clause makes for variety, while the prepositional phrases (*with remarkable vistas . . . , with weeping birches . . .*) make for balance:

Seattle, *which sits like Rome on seven hills,* was endowed by nature *with remarkable vistas* of water and mountains, *with weeping birches and monkey trees and dogwoods* big as maples.—Russell Lynes, "Seattle Will Never Be the Same," *Harper's*

Notice the role of variety and balance in the following passage:

India *is a poetic nation, yet it demands* new electrical plants. It *is a mystical nation, yet it wants* new roads. It *is* traditionally *a peaceful nation, yet it could,* if misled, *inflame* Asia.—James A. Michener, "Portraits for the Future," *Saturday Review*

There is just enough variation to keep the repetition of the pattern from becoming monotonous: "poetic—mystical—traditionally peaceful"; "demands—wants—could, if misled, inflame."

NOTE: Like other stylistic devices, patterns that make for euphony and balance are most effective when the reader responds to them without becoming consciously aware of them. Today, workaday expository prose avoids elaborate parallelism and obtrusive rhythm.

## Exercises

**A**. Examine the uses of *repetition and parallelism* in the following sentences. Your instructor may ask you to use one or more of these as model sentences. For each model sentence, write one of your own that as far as possible preserves the structure of the original.

**1**. Warren believed in applauding politely to reward effort, generously to reward competence, and frenetically to reward genius.

**2**. War, assuming that one does not love it for its own sake, or does not use it as a background for some isolated moral, or does not, worst of all, believe in its shabby rationale, can only produce one of two reactions: a tear, or a scream.

**3**. The businessman who writes a letter, the professor who fashions a lecture, the student who prepares a theme, needs style and covets style as much as the man who writes an editorial for the *Times.* (Charles W. Ferguson)

**4**. We are in such haste to be doing, to be writing, to be gathering gear, to make our voice audible a moment in the derisive silence of eternity, that we forget that one thing, of which these are but the parts—namely to live. (Robert Louis Stevenson)

**5**. The capital defect in the culture of These States is the lack of a civilized aristocracy, secure in its position, animated by an intelligent curiosity, skeptical of all facile generalizations, superior to the sentimentality of the mob, and delighting in the battle of ideas for its own sake.   (H. L. Mencken)

**6**. It requires enormous intelligence, innate or acquired by cultivation, to discharge the full responsibilities of managing a household; doing its endlessly repetitive work without deadening the mind; bringing up children, restraining, encouraging and helping them; being a companion and helpmeet to one's husband, helpfully and intelligently interested in his work; and being, at the same time, able to take on his duties and responsibilities if she must, as thousands of women have had to.   (Dorothy Thompson)

**B**. Examine the features that make for *rhythm and balance* in the following passages. Point out any other features that make for effective sentence style. Examine such features as sentence length, variety, emphasis. Point out any special or unusual effects.

**1**. We go to our libraries in order to read and take advantage of the experiences of others. I think we all realize that not every written word in a library is entirely true. Many different authors have here written what they think, what they have experienced, what they believe is true, and sometimes what they wish were true. Some are wrong, a few are right, and many are neither entirely wrong nor entirely right.

**2**. This is not a Utopian tract. Some of those who complain about the quality of our national life seem to be dreaming of a world in which everyone without exception has talent, taste, judgment and an unswerving allegiance to excellence. Such dreams are pleasant but unprofitable. The problem is to achieve some measure of excellence *in this society*, with all its beloved and exasperating clutter, with all its exciting and debilitating confusion of standards, with all the stubborn problems that won't be solved and the equally stubborn ones that might be.—John W. Gardner, *Excellence*

**3**. We do not need to fear ideas, but the censorship of ideas. We do not need to fear criticism, but the silencing of criticism. We do not need to fear excitement or agitation in the academic community, but timidity and apathy. We do not need to fear resistance to political leaders, but unquestioning acquiescence in whatever policies those leaders adopt.—Henry Steele Commager, "The Problem of Dissent," *Saturday Review*

# 4

# THE PARAGRAPH

In some kinds of writing, paragraph division is arbitrary, in others conventional. In many newspapers, a paragraph break occurs after every long sentence and after every group of two or three short ones. In much informal writing, the writer starts a paragraph as nonchalantly as a speaker pauses momentarily in cultivated conversation. In dialogue, a paragraph break conventionally signals each change from one speaker to another.

In an expository essay, some paragraphs are primarily helps to continuity: programmatic paragraphs stating the author's intention, transitional paragraphs helping the reader see the connection between ideas, summarizing paragraphs recapitulating important points. Some are primarily helps to effectiveness: introductory paragraphs catching the reader's attention, one-sentence paragraphs setting off a statement for emphasis. However, the meat of an essay is likely to be contained in a different kind of unit: the expository paragraph that presents and develops an important idea or an important step in an argument.

## 0 1 Structural Devices

*In serious expository prose, the paragraph is a logical, rather than a typographical, unit.*

**149**

In studying paragraphs written by professional writers, and in strengthening paragraphs in your own papers, look for clues to their logical coherence. Look for devices that reveal structure and guide the reader.

## 0  1a    Topic Sentences

*Use topic sentences to improve clarity and continuity of discussion.* A **topic sentence** states the central idea of a paragraph. Typical topic sentences might look like this:

> Many animals are capable of emitting meaningful sounds.
> Most of us are less tolerant than we think.
> The African students I know are suspicious of the motives behind "foreign aid."

Well-chosen topic sentences help you structure your writing in several important ways:

(1) A good topic sentence *pulls together* a mass of closely related material. Notice how much detail has been brought together in the following paragraph. Notice how effectively the topic sentence sums up the generalization to which all the details point:

> *Latin American culture has been and is a dynamic element in the development of our own.* It has, for example, furnished more than 2000 place names to the United States postal directory. Its languages have influenced American English, as such simple examples as "rodeo" and "vamoose" indicate. Its customs are part of our "Westerns" on television. Its housing, its music, its dances, its scenery, its ruins and its romance have been imitated and admired in the United States. One third of the continental area of this republic was for a long period, as modern history goes, under the governance of Spanish viceroys or of Mexico. The largest single Christian church in the United States is identical with the dominant church in Latin America.—Howard Mumford Jones, "Goals for Americans," *Saturday Evening Post*

(2) A good topic sentence *gives clear direction* to a paragraph. It provides a clear test of what fits in and what is ir-

relevant. The topic sentence in each of the following examples steers the paragraph in a different direction:

> *The dormitory reminds me of a third-class hotel.* Each room has the
> same set of unimaginative furnishings: the same pale red chest of
> drawers, the same light brown desks. . . .

> *The dormitory reminds me of a big office building.* People who half
> know each other pass in the hall with impersonal friendliness. . . .

> *The dormitory reminds me of a prison.* The study room is enclosed
> by windows with lines on them, giving the student a penned-in
> feeling. . . .

(3) A good topic sentence *moves the presentation or the
argument ahead* one essential step. Then the rest of the paragraph fills in, illustrates, and supports the point made. Then
the next topic sentence again takes a step forward. Part of an
article on the influence of television on political campaigns
might proceed like this:

> *Television continues to change the look of political conventions.*
> Speeches are fewer and shorter. Sweaty orators, bellowing and wav-
> ing their arms for an hour or more, have yielded almost completely
> to TelePrompTer readers, younger and brisker fellows, some of
> them very slick and many of them no fun. Both parties have short-
> ened sign-waving, chanting demonstrations. . . .
>
> While many of the changes may be for the best, *there is something
> synthetic about this new kind of convention.* There is a lack of spontane-
> ity, a sense of stuffy self-consciousness. There is something unreal
> about seeing a well-known newscaster starting across the floor to
> interview a delegate and getting stopped for an autograph. . . .
>
> Nevertheless, *television coverage of conventions manages to get across
> to us a great deal about the way our political system works.* We are still a
> nation of disparate parts. The conventions are the occasions that
> bring various coalitions together every four years to pull and haul
> at one another; to test old power centers and form new ones; to
> compromise and, yes, to raise a little hell together in a carnival
> atmosphere. . . .

NOTE: The topic sentence is usually most effective early
in the paragraph. But sometimes a writer will make the para-

graph *lead up* to its topic sentence (see O 3b). Sometimes, the topic sentence appears at the end of an introductory or transitional paragraph rather than in the paragraph that develops it.

## O  1b    Transitional Phrases

*Transitional phrases help the reader see a paragraph as a well-ordered whole.* A well-written paragraph does not need elaborate directional signals. When used unobtrusively, however, **transitional phrases** help the reader proceed smoothly from sentence to sentence. Notice their use in the following paragraphs: ˉ

Many animals are capable of emitting meaningful sounds. Hens, *for instance,* warn their chicks of impending danger. *Similarly,* dogs growl at strangers to express distrust or hostility. Most of man's pets, *in fact,* have a "vocabulary" of differentiated sounds to express hunger, pain, or satisfaction.

Most of us are less tolerant than we think. *It is true that* we tend to be tolerant of things sufficiently remote, such as Buddhism or impressionist painting. *But* we lose our tempers quickly when confronted with minor irritations. My friends, *at any rate,* will rage at drivers who block their way, at acquaintances who are late for appointments, or at manufacturers of mechanisms that break down.

All the frontier industrial countries except Russia received massive waves of emigrants from Europe. They *therefore* had a more rapid population growth than their industrializing predecessors had experienced. As frontier countries with great room for expansion, *however,* they were also characterized by considerable internal migration and continuing new opportunities. *As a result* their birth rates remained comparatively high. In the decade from 1950 to 1960, with continued immigration, these countries grew in population at an average rate of 2.13 per cent a year, compared with 1.76 per cent for the rest of the world.—Kingsley Davis, "Population," *Scientific American*

Notice how unobtrusive and yet how effective the transitions are in the following excerpt:

What must be *even more surprising* is the thinness of coverage right here at home in the center of our national news, Washington. Washington has a very large press corps. The roster of the National Press Club is substantial, *and* the State Department auditorium is easily filled by a glamour press conference. *The trouble* is that most of the Washington press corps runs as a herd, concentrating on the "big" story of the day to the neglect of much else. The news services have large staffs, *and* a few papers priding themselves on their national news maintain bureaus ranging from a half-dozen full-time correspondents to three times that number. *But* most of the so-called bureaus in Washington are one-man affairs. Except for an hour of gossip at the Press Club or at one of the other informal meeting places, and for what a lonesome man picks up from his home Congressional delegation, and the steady stream of inspired handouts, the average Washington reporter never gets beneath the surface of the day's one obvious story.—Philip M. Wagner, "What Makes a Really Good Newspaper," *Harper's*

## 0 1c    Recurrent Terms

*A unified paragraph is often marked by the repetition or paraphrase of important words and phrases.* Such **recurrent terms** reflect continuity of thought and subject matter. Similar in effect is the recurrence of "pointers" like *he, it, they, this, these,* and *those.* Notice in the following excerpt how the idea of change recurs in each successive sentence:

It is an ominous fact that in the long chain of evolution the latest link, man, has suddenly acquired alchemic powers to *alter* whatever he touches. No other species before has been able to *change* more than a tiny fraction of his habitat. Now there is but a tiny fraction that he has *left unchanged.* A bulldozer *undoes* in an hour the work of a million years.—Paul Brooks, "Canyonlands," *Atlantic*

The following paragraph on the relation of the "ends" and "means" in politics keeps playing off these two terms, and their synonyms or related terms, against each other:

The *technical* man isolates one particular field or activity, in order to concentrate upon the *procedure* within it. In order for his work to proceed, he must assume the worth of the *end* to which his work is addressed; in order to get on to his own question, "*How?*," he must assume that the *end* he is serving has an assured place in a hierarchy of *values* that he does not himself examine. As a cobbler cannot continually be asking himself whether shoes as such are a *good*, so an economist cannot continually ask himself whether "productivity" or "satisfaction" or—now apparently—"economic growth" is a *good*; he must take that for granted and get on with his job. Where the *end* is simple and noncontroversial, such a *technical approach* raises no problems. But in social policy the *ends* to be served admit of no such description: it is of the essence of politics that their meanings shift, that *values* conflict, and that men differ about them. The *ends* of politics, moreover, are not neatly separable from the "*means*" the *technical man* thinks he deals with exclusively; usually he bootlegs in some assumptions about *ends* in his work on the *means.* One might argue that political leadership, which must interpret the situation and fit together these several and conflicting *ends,* is preeminently the activity that cannot properly be reduced to sheer *technique.*—William Lee Miller, "Some Academic Questions About a New Yale Man," *The Reporter*

NOTE: In the sample paragraphs reprinted in the rest of this chapter, words and phrases that make for unity or continuity are italicized.

## Exercises

**A**. Examine the structure of each of the following paragraphs. Is there a topic sentence? Is all the material in the paragraph relevant to the idea stated in the topic sentence? Does the author use transitional phrases? Does he make use of recurrent terms or their synonyms?

1. All the evidence indicates that the population upsurge in the underdeveloped countries is not helping them to advance economically. On the contrary, it may well be interfering with their economic growth. A surplus of labor on the farms holds back the mechanization of agriculture. A rapid rise in the number of people to be maintained uses up income that might otherwise be utilized for long-term investment in education, equipment and other capital needs. To put it in concrete terms, it is difficult to give a child the basic education he needs to become an engineer when he is one of eight children of an

illiterate farmer who must support the family with the produce of two acres of ground.—Kingsley Davis, "Population," *Scientific American*

**2**. Primarily, the brain is an organ of survival. It was built by nature to search for food, shelter, and the like, to gain advantage—before addressing itself to the pursuit of truth. Hence most human brains are unable to distinguish between truth and advantage, and accept as truth that which is only advantage. We use our brain mainly for finding ways to reach what we want. Simultaneously, we produce the thoughts and arguments which justify our feelings and dealings. I suspect that if I were in the business of selling shelters, my brain would tend to dwell rather steadily on the probability of nuclear war. If I were in politics, I might find my brain devoting itself less to the next generation than to the next election.—Albert Szent-Gyorgyi, "The Persistence of the Caveman," *Saturday Review*

**3**. The prestige of science was colossal. The man in the street and the woman in the kitchen, confronted on every hand with new machines and devices which they owed to the laboratory, were ready to believe that science could accomplish almost anything; and they were being deluged with scientific information and theory. The newspapers were giving columns of space to inform (or misinform) them of the latest discoveries: a new dictum from Albert Einstein was now front-page stuff even though practically nobody could understand it. Outlines of knowledge poured from the presses to tell people about the planetesimal hypothesis and the constitution of the atom, to describe for them in unwarranted detail the daily life of the cave-man, and to acquaint them with electrons, endocrines, hormones, vitamins, reflexes, and psychoses.—Frederick Lewis Allen, *Only Yesterday*

**4**. Detective stories tend to glorify crime. Murderers, gangsters, and crooks of all kinds are described as tough, cunning, and courageous individuals who know how to take care of themselves and who know how to get what they want. In James M. Cain's *The Postman Always Rings Twice*, for instance, the villain is a much more impressive character than his victim. He is casual, brave, smart, and successful with women. It is true that he finally gets caught. But he is punished for a crime that he did not commit, so that his conviction is hardly a triumph of justice. Besides, looking back over the exciting life of the criminal, the reader might conclude that it was worth the risk.

**B**. From a current magazine article, select a *model paragraph* that has a clear topic sentence and makes effective use of transitional phrases or other structural devices. Be prepared to defend your choice.

**C**. From a recent theme, select a substantial paragraph that *could be improved* by use of a clear topic sentence and other structural devices. Hand in both the "Before" and the "After" version.

# O 2    Organizing the Paragraph

*Make your paragraphs follow a clear pattern of organization.*

The first requirement for a successful paragraph is that it should be packed with relevant details. But their relevance will show only if they are arranged in a pattern clear enough for the reader to follow.

## O 2a    Space and Time

*In description, narrative, or technical writing, a well-organized paragraph often follows the most plausible order in space or time.* Typically, such a paragraph corresponds to one major unit in the material treated: It takes up one limited aspect of a scene, one episode in a larger chain of events, one step in a process. The reader has to know where he is at the beginning, and where and how he is expected to move from there.

Study the way the two following paragraphs move in space or time:

(1) *Spatial order:*

The jockey *came to the doorway of the dining room, then after a moment stepped to one side* and stood motionless, with *his back to the wall. The room* was crowded, as this was the third day of the season and all the hotels in the town were full. *In the dining room* bouquets of

August roses scattered their petals on the white table linen and from the *adjoining bar* came a warm, drunken wash of voices. The jockey *waited with his back to the wall* and *scrutinized the room* with pinched, crêpy eyes. He *examined the room until at last* his eyes reached a table in *a corner diagonally across from him,* at which three men were sitting. *As he watched,* the jockey raised his chin and tilted his head back to one side, his dwarfed body grew rigid, and his hands stiffened so that the fingers curled inward like gray claws. Tense *against the wall of the dining room, he watched* and waited in this way.—Carson McCullers, "The Jockey"

(2) *Chronological order:*

The *greeting ceremony* when one bird of the pair, after having been away at the feeding grounds, rejoins its mate *is also beautiful. Some little time before* the human watcher notes the other's approach, the waiting bird rises on its branch, arches and spreads its wings, lifts its aigrettes into a fan and its head-plumes into a crown, bristles up the feathers of its neck, and emits again and again a hoarse cry. The other approaches, settles in the branches near by, puts itself into a similar position, and advances toward its mate; and *after a short excited space* they settle down close together. *This type of greeting* is repeated *every day until* the young leave the nest; for after the eggs are laid both sexes brood, and there is a nest-relief four times in every twenty-four hours. *Each time* the same attitudes, the same cries, the same excitement; only now at the end of it all, one steps off the nest, the other on. One might suppose that this closed the performance. But no: the bird that has been relieved is still apparently animated by stores of unexpended emotion; it searches about for a twig, breaks it off or picks it up, and returns with it in beak to present to the other. *During the presentation* the *greeting ceremony* is again gone through; *after each relief* the *whole business of presentation and greeting* may be repeated two, or four, or up even to ten or eleven times before the free bird flies away.—Julian Huxley, *Essays of a Biologist*

## O 2b   Explanation and Illustration

*In many expository paragraphs, developing a key idea is a matter of explanation and illustration.* A topic sentence is often intentionally terse and emphatic. It may be developed by material that amplifies it, spells out its implications, clarifies a key term (**definition**). It may be developed by two or three representative examples or by one example that is exceptionally detailed (**illustration**).

Notice how the following sample paragraphs vary the basic pattern of *statement—explanation—illustration:*

key idea

detailed restatement

first example

second example

third example

The deep sea has its *stars,* and perhaps here and there an eerie and transient equivalent of *moonlight,* for the mysterious *phenomenon of luminescence* is displayed by perhaps half of all the fishes that live in dimly lit or darkened waters, and by many of the lower forms as well. Many fishes carry *luminous torches* that can be turned on or off at will, presumably helping them find or pursue their prey. Others have *rows of lights* over their bodies, in patterns that vary from species to species and may be a sort of recognition mark or badge by which the bearer can be known as friend or enemy. The deep-sea squid ejects a spurt of fluid that becomes a *luminous cloud,* the counterpart of the 'ink' of his shallow-water relative.—Rachel Carson, *The Sea Around Us*

key question

key idea

first set of examples

second set of examples

restatement of key idea

Where do the terms of businesese come from? Most, *of course,* are hand-me-downs from former generations of businessmen, *but* many are the fruit of cross-fertilization with other jargons. A businessman who castigates government bureaucrats, *for example,* is at the same time apt to be activating, expediting, implementing, effectuating, optimizing, minimizing, and maximizing—and at all levels and echelons within the framework of broad policy areas. *Similarly,* though he is amused by the longhairs and the social scientists, he is beginning to speak knowingly of projective techniques, social dynamics, depth interviewing, *and* sometime soon, if he keeps up at this rate, he will probably appropriate that hallmark of the sound sociological paper, "insightful." Businesese, *in fact,* has very nearly become the great common meeting ground of the jargons.—William H. Whyte, "The Language of Business," *Fortune*

introductory anecdote

When Paul Garrett arrived in Detroit twenty-five years ago to begin General Motors' public relations program, the first question fired at him was:

"How do you make a billion dollars look small?" Garrett said damned if he knew, and furthermore damned if he thought that was his job. Public relations, he argued, was not an "act," but a continuing effort on the part of management to win the confidence of the people with whom it came into contact. *Hence* you will find General Motors engaged in a host of activities in which altruism and self-interest come together in a creamy blend. Plant City and Field Relations, *for example*, stimulates local GM participation in the community affairs of the sixty-eight cities where it has factories, thereby helping both the community and itself. Educational Relations works with the schools, providing them with such useful education material as films on safe driving, and providing itself with a flow of applicants for jobs. The Speakers Bureau is glad to send a company-sponsored lecturer to your club or association to edify it with an inspirational talk—or to educate it with a "sound" economic one. Institutional Advertising tells the story of GM's role in supporting some twenty thousand suppliers, and leaves you with the pleasant impression that what's good for General Motors is good for small business, too. The billion dollars may not look any smaller as a *result of these efforts. But* it looks much, much nicer.—Robert L. Heilbroner, "Public Relations—The Invisible Sell," *Harper's*

Not the least remarkable thing about Huck's feeling for people is that his tenderness goes along with the *assumption that his fellow men are likely to be dangerous and wicked.* He travels incognito, never telling the truth about himself and never twice telling the same lie, for he *trusts no one* and the lie comforts him even when it is not necessary. He *instinctively knows* that the best way to keep a party of men away from Jim on the raft is to beg them to come aboard to help his family stricken with smallpox. And if he had not already had the *knowledge of human weakness and stupidity and cowardice,* he would soon have acquired it, for all his encounters forcibly teach it to him—the insensate feud of the Grainger-

*Margin annotations:*

key idea

first example

second example

third example

fourth example

restatement of key idea, alluding to initial anecdote

key idea

first example

second example

further support for key idea

fords and Shepherdsons, the invasion of the raft by the Duke and the King, the murder of Boggs, the lynching party, and the speech of Colonel Sherburn. Yet his *profound and bitter knowledge of human depravity* never prevents him from being a friend to man.—Lionel Trilling, *The Liberal Imagination*

*restatement of key idea*

Perhaps the most wearing thing about television is that most of the time it talks in a language so bare, so elementary, and so lacking in overtones that it can only be called baby talk. *Certainly* the commercials are baby talk, complete with coo and wheedle; and some of them even press the toddlers into service to do the selling for them. *I am thinking of* the little girls who wash their dolls' clothes in Ivory and of the one little girl who, holding up a roll of paper, says "Hudson tissues tear so stwaight!" —Marya Mannes, "Channels," *The Reporter*

*key idea*

*narrowed to limited area*

*specific examples*

NOTE: Observe in these paragraphs the satisfying and self-evident **relevance** of explanations and examples to the central idea. Not only is the illustrative material ample, but its appropriateness is immediately clear.

## O 2c  Logical Patterns

*Many expository paragraphs weigh several closely related points or work out a conclusion in a series of closely related steps.* Such a paragraph may follow a number of different logical patterns:

(1) *Comparison and contrast:*

Just as Alger's view of money as something to be made and kept no longer generally operates, [neither] does his view of how it should be given away. There is a great deal of "charity" in Alger, but *it is always man-to-man, even palm-to-palm.* It is a gesture in the tradition of the New Testament, a retail transaction between two individuals, spiritual in essence, monetary in form. The adjective that comes first to mind when we think of it is "Christian." *The adjective that comes first to mind when we think of*

*key idea (linked to preceding step in discussion)*

*first subtopic (situation in Alger's books)*

<table>
<tr>
<td>second subtopic<br>(contrasting<br>situation today)</td>
<td>

*charity today is "organized."* Via drives, community chests, red feathers, we can give more away more quickly. At the same time the primitive-Christian heart of the process, man-to-man giving, is weakened. Warmheartedness is communized.—Clifton Fadiman, "Party of One," *Holiday*

</td>
</tr>
</table>

### (2) *Examination of causes and effects:*

<table>
<tr>
<td>key idea</td>
<td>

Europeans with time-honored experience in the technique of painlessly extracting cash from foreigners' pockets have correctly gauged that Americans like to travel abroad provided they don't

</td>
</tr>
<tr>
<td>cause<br>(with specific<br>examples)</td>
<td>

really have to leave home. *They've seen* the U.S. armed forces and U.S. oil companies spend millions to give their personnel the illusion of living in a European or African suburbia filled with shopping centers, post exchanges, movie houses, ice-cream parlors, juke boxes, and American-style parking

</td>
</tr>
<tr>
<td>effect<br>(with specific<br>examples)</td>
<td>

lots. *Smart promoters now give* the American abroad exactly what he wants. Hotel rooms are furnished to please him, meal hours drastically advanced to suit the American habit of eating dinner at 6 p.m., arrangements made to satisfy the Americans' affection for crowds, action, and noise.—Joseph Wechsberg, "The American Abroad," *Atlantic*

</td>
</tr>
</table>

### (3) *Drawing logical conclusions from evidence* (**inductive order**):

<table>
<tr>
<td>detailed report<br>of experiment</td>
<td>

Psychologists studying race prejudice have many times made an interesting experiment. They seat a few people in a row, show a picture to the first in line, and ask him to whisper a description of it in a few words to a second who will whisper the information to the third, and so on. The picture is of a policeman and a badly dressed, uncouth Negro. The policeman is holding a knife in his hand; the Negro is unarmed. Almost never is the description transmitted to more than two or three individuals in succession, before the knife has passed from the hand of the policeman and is now being held in a threatening manner, by the Negro! *In other words,*

</td>
</tr>
</table>

interpretation
of experiment

the picture is transformed until it fits the preexisting concept in the mind, which is that an open knife is far more likely to be held by a Negro than a policeman. *This sort of unconscious alteration* of what is perceived, to make it accord with what is already believed, is universal and is one of the most important of all the facts with which communication has to deal.—Bruce Bliven, *Preview for Tomorrow*

general
application
of findings

(4) *Drawing logical conclusions from accepted premises* (**deductive order**):

first
observation

In the history books of the future this age of ours may come to be known as the Age of Statistics. In the biological and physical as well as the sociological sciences, statistics have become, as they never were before, the most important tool of investigation. *But* as every philosophical scientist knows, the conclusions drawn by a science depend to a considerable extent upon the tools used. *And* it is in the nature of statistics not only that they deal with quantity but that they emphasize the significance of averages and medians. What usually exists or usually happens establishes The Law, and The Law is soon thought of as identical with The Truth. In all the arts, *nevertheless*, it is the exceptional and the unpredictable which really count. It is the excellent, not the average, which is really important. And there is, *therefore*, one aspect of the cultural condition of a civilization to which statistical study is curiously inappropriate.—Joseph Wood Krutch, *Is the Common Man Too Common?*

second
observation

third
observation
(specific
application
of point 2)

fourth
(contrasting)
observation

logical
conclusion

(5) *Choosing among alternatives:*

first
alternative
examined and
rejected

History shows that wars between cities, states, and geographic regions cease once the originally independent units have amalgamated under the leadership of a single government with the power of making and enforcing laws that are binding upon individuals. *One might reason on this basis that* if all of the industrialized and semi-industrialized regions of the world were to federate under a common government, the probability of another war would

be greatly decreased. It seems likely that this conclusion would be valid if the resultant federation
were as complete as was the federation formed by
the original thirteen colonies in America. *On the
other hand,* it is extremely unlikely that such a highly
centralized federation could come into existence at
the present time; nationalistic feelings of individual
men and groups of men, and conflicts of economic
interests, are too strong to permit rapid transition.
*Also,* those nations which have high per capita re-
serves of resources and high per capita production
would be most reluctant to delegate their sovereign-
ties to higher authority and to abandon the economic barriers that now exist.—Harrison Brown,
*The Challenge of Man's Future*

*(margin note:)* second alternative presented and supported

## 0  2d     Emphatic Order

*Order of presentation in a paragraph is determined in part by
the intended effect upon the reader.* As in the theme as a whole,
the most emphatic positions in the paragraph are at the beginning and at the end. A short, strongly worded topic sentence at the very beginning can throw out a challenge to the
reader. A key detail or key point withheld until the end can
create suspense; it can make the paragraph as a whole *build
up* to a climactic ending.

### (1) *Emphatic initial assertion:*

*There is little doubt that the draft limits my freedom.* Although I have
a student deferment, I must carry a full load to maintain it. Since I
am not obsessed with the desire to graduate within four years, and
because I must work part time during the school term, I would like
to take my time and do well in a few courses each semester. In this
way I might really learn something. Unfortunately, because of the
draft I cannot do this, and so I feel as if I am being rushed through
an academic processing plant where education in the form of units
is quickly tacked onto me. At the end of four years I will emerge as a
finished product with a degree certifying that my processing has
been complete. That is not what I want, and yet I am forced to submit to it by a selective service system which leaves military service
as my only alternative.

(2) *Climactic order:*

The morning sun was streaming through the crevices of the canvas when the man awoke. A warm glow pervaded the whole atmosphere of the marquee, and a single big blue fly buzzed musically round and round it. Besides the buzz of the fly there was not a sound. He looked about—at the benches—at the table supported by trestles—at his basket of tools—at the stove where the furmity had been boiled—at the empty basins—at some shed grains of wheat —at the corks which dotted the grassy floor. Among the odds and ends he discerned a little shining object, and picked it up. *It was his wife's ring.*—Thomas Hardy, *The Mayor of Casterbridge*

## Exercises

**A**. From your recent writing, select the paragraph that comes closest to following the pattern of *statement—explanation—illustration*. Revise or expand it as needed to make it a clearly and solidly developed example of the type.

**B**. Select a key sentence from your current writing or reading. Use it as a topic sentence in three different paragraphs. Follow a *different pattern of organization* each time, using different supporting material as far as possible. Concentrate on making each pattern emerge clearly from the paragraph.

**C**. Describe in detail the pattern of organization in each of the following paragraphs. How clearly does it emerge from the paragraph as a whole? How would you rate these paragraphs as examples of student writing?

1. Newspapers give a distorted view of life. They have a tendency to exaggerate the morbid: the killings, the sex crimes, the fires, and the accidents. Newspapers are prone to overemphasize the unusual, such as a mother giving birth to quintuplets, the development of a Christmas tree that grows its own decorative cones, the minting of two pennies which were only half engraved, gang fights, teen-age drinking, or university riots.

2. Although I never attended a class there, the abandoned main building that crowned the top of the hill was a favorite monument of mine. It was weathered by salt air, wind, and

fog; its surface was scarred by dozens of holes where engineers and inspectors had bored into the plaster for samples; many of the windows were broken or missing, and they stared out at the rest of the campus like the huge, vacant eye-sockets of a skull. In spite of these mutilations, the old building radiated an atmosphere of dignity and benevolence. Its massive stone steps extended outward from the barricaded door like the arms of the Lincoln monument, inviting students to gather there.

**3**. When I attended my first class meeting in World History, I was disappointed to learn that during the year we were not to study and discuss the reasons why an event occurred; we were apparently expected to spend most of our time memorizing dates and names. At least, I thought, when a test came up I would have to think back to remember what happened in 1492, for instance. But when the students sat down for the final examination, the question was not "What important event occurred in 1492, and how did it affect world history?" No! It was as follows: "In 1492, Columbus sailed to the New World—true or false?" or "What year did Columbus sail to the New World? (a) 1942; (b) 1812; (c) 1912; (d) 1492." What kind of thought is provoked by tests such as these?

**4**. My own pet feature of the magazine are the advertisements. Well I know that their sole purpose is to induce the reader, including me, to spend as many dollars as possible for the product pictured. Knowing this in no way detracts from my enjoyment of the color and pictorial values of what I see. Fully aware as I am of the appeals being made to my baser instincts (snobbishness and greed, to name just two) by the artful devices of the advertising fraternity, I still enjoy looking at the pictures. The allure of an ordinary metal cooking utensil pictured in a setting more fit for a precious gem can spur me, a representative reader, on to the kitchen with grim determination to substitute for my own quite adequate pots just *such* pots, with or without daisies. Utilized more sensibly, the power of such an imaginative appeal can bring about many small changes in the average home simply by giving a new slant on an old topic.

**5**. One obvious result of modern technology has been the increasing dependence of one workman upon another. We have "geared the machines and locked all together into interdependence." In Detroit's factories, thousands of workers are specialized; each performs a specific task. On the assembly line, an automobile is mass produced in a matter of hours. One worker installs wires, a second fastens lining in the interior, a third installs the windshield. Further down the line, groups of specialized personnel have assembled the dashboard and the seats. The finished body is lowered onto a chassis that has come down a similar line, operating on the same principle of each man doing a particular job. In a short time, the test driver drives the finished car through the factory gates. This is division of labor. This is specialization.

**D**. The more sophisticated a professional writer, the more likely he is to combine or adapt familiar patterns of organization in his own way. Can you still recognize the patterns of organization at work in the following paragraphs? Which is the most conventional in organization? Which the least?

1. Nobody has succeeded in explaining the connection between the private sources and the public functions of art. But art does have its public functions, though we often lose sight of them. In primitive agricultural societies, and even in Western Europe until the Renaissance, the functions were more clearly defined. It was the duty of the artist to celebrate the community in its present oneness, in its divine past, and in its glorious future. Thus he invented dances and rituals for the group, he retold the stories of its gods and heroes, he fashioned their images, and he persuaded the "people"—his own tribe that is, the only genuine persons—that they were reenacting the lives of the gods, who would some day return and reinstitute the golden age. Thus the artist played a recognized part in the daily life of the people.—Malcolm Cowley, "Artists, Conscience, and Censors," *Saturday Review*

2. Abstractions are really disguised metaphors (most thoroughly disguised when they derive from the classical languages), and metaphors can only keep their sensuous content when poetry insists on reminding us of it. Take a scientific term like *parthenogenesis*, put it in a poem, and the poem will not be able to resist digging out the "virgin" image (with the help of the Parthenon and the New Testament) and showing, with reference to the Old Testament, precisely what *genesis* means. Not that etymology is necessarily much help in giving us an anchor for an abstraction; it just happens to be the only

source available, with some words, for a concrete image, the sense of a real thing out there in the world of the senses. The vague term "lady" at least takes on an image when we refer it back to the Anglo-Saxon *hlaefdige*, which has something to do with making a loaf. Somebody's there supervising the bread-making, perhaps. Or, even if she's actually baking it herself, her hands are clean. Superiority, neatness, calm, authority—those will do for a beginning.—Anthony Burgess, "The Future of Anglo-American," *Harper's*

**3**. In many simple societies, the "institutionalized ways" of controlling marriage run to diverse schemes and devices. Often they include special living quarters designed to make it easy for marriageable girls to attract a husband: the Bontok people of the Philippines keep their girls in a special house, called the *olag*, where lovers call, sex play is free, and marriage is supposed to result. The Ekoi of Nigeria, who like their women fat, send them away to be specially fattened for marriage. Other peoples, such as the Yao of central Africa and the aborigines of the Canary Islands, send their daughters away to "convents" where old women teach them the special skills and mysteries that a young wife needs to know.—John Finley Scott, "Sororities and the Husband Game," *Trans-action*

**4**. Reading is a habit. Once you've got the habit you never lose it. But you must somehow be exposed to reading early enough in life to have it become a part of your daily routine, like washing your face or breathing. Many an unfortunate grade-school child in our highly seasoned, electronic, picture-conscious age has never been exposed to the reading habit and cannot, therefore, read without effort. Some modern children seldom if ever read for fun. Like muscles that are almost never used, their concentration and interest give way quickly. They long for the automatic, pictorial sensation of TV (which can be highly instructive and entertaining at times) rather than the tedium of moving the eyes from left to right, from left to right, from left to right on line after line after line of unillustrated print. There's a certain sadness in realizing that a whopping segment of the exploding new teen-age generation never *really* reads anything, unless forced to do so.—Richard L. Tobin, "Reading Is a Habit," *Saturday Review*

**5**. When films first broke on the world, let's say with the full-length, full-scale achievement of D. W. Griffith, *The Birth of a*

*Nation,* one of its most persuasive and hitherto unexperienced powers lay in the absolute reality of the moving image. The camera is a scientific instrument, not a paintbrush: its special virtues are accuracy and actuality. Thus, when Griffith organized a pan-shot which began with a mother and child huddled in terror on a mountain and then moved slowly to a raging battle on the plain beneath, we were left breathless by a juxtaposition in scale—from the individual to the group, from the passive to the active—that was, quite literally, taking place before our eyes. Our belief in the medium had begun with actual railroad trains roaring down actual tracks right at us, with actual ocean waves breaking somewhere near our feet. Griffith moved from simple documentation to high imagination, from fact to fiction, from present to past; and he took us with him because he used his camera as a faithful recorder of something that was really and truly going on: he did not abandon his camera's ability to state visual facts.—Walter Kerr, "What Good Is Television?" *Horizon*

# O 3    Paragraph Revision

*Check your paragraphs for lack of focus and lack of supporting detail.*

In revising the first draft of a paper, you will do well to look for common sources of weak paragraph development. Generally, both a sequence of one- or two-sentence paragraphs and a page without any paragraph breaks at all are signals of inadequate paragraphing.

## O 3a    Lack of Focus

*Focus weak paragraphs more clearly on a central point.* A paragraph may be weak because the writer has not gone beyond the first jotting down of possibly useful detail. He has not done the kind of sorting and focusing that changes a first inventory of material into structured prose.

Do the following to give clear focus to your paragraphs:

(1) *Give unity to a rambling paragraph by formulating a topic*

*sentence that holds its details together.* Look for a logical connection you previously missed or ignored.

**Poor:**   San Francisco is a city of beautiful parks and public buildings. Golden Gate Park, with its spacious lawns and graceful ponds, enjoys international fame. The city's Bohemian section has become the national headquarters for jazzage poetry and philosophy. Every tourist must visit Fisherman's Wharf and Coit Tower. The city is famed for its cultural events and conventions.

**Revised:**   *Tourists and convention managers are irresistibly attracted to San Francisco.* Miles of varied waterfront, spacious parks, and impressive public buildings contribute to the city's unique appearance and cosmopolitan atmosphere. Fisherman's Wharf, with its seafood smells and colorful shops, attracts sightseeing crowds. Coit Tower affords a spectacular view of bay and city. Golden Gate Park, with its spacious lawns and graceful ponds, enjoys international fame.

(2) *Give focus to a blurred paragraph by eliminating material that does not bear on the central point.* A paragraph in a paper describing a magazine might contain a comment on a striking cover, information about the price, and a brief summary of an interesting article. However, once the eye-catching qualities of the magazine are mentioned, describing and illustrating them adequately will take at least one full paragraph. Observations and comments not **relevant** to eye appeal will have to make room for more unified material.

(3) *Split up paragraphs that are merely a series of undeveloped observations.* The following paragraph consists of sentences that should each become the topic sentence of a separate paragraph. Each sentence could then be fully developed by supporting detail.

**Poor:**   The poems I liked best were those by A. E. Housman. *His poems were easy to comprehend without being overly simple.* With most other poems I need the assistance of an expert who can "translate" them for me. *The thoughts and attitudes expressed in Housman's poems represent the wisdom of an experienced, educated man. His poems are short and to the point,* a great help to enjoyment. *They are written in such a manner that the reader does not feel the author is preaching to him.*

## O 3b    Filling in Detail

*Strengthen skimpy paragraphs by supplying relevant detail.* The weakest kind of paragraph merely repeats, in slightly different words, an idea that is already sufficiently clear:

**Poor:**    My roommate is very considerate. I have always found him helpful and eager to be of service. He has really taught me something about the role of kindness in everyday living.

But even a paragraph that does develop its topic sentence may remain too thin. Notice how the following passage gains in authenticity through the filling in of detail from the author's experience:

**Thin:**    I like politicians. I have spent a lot of time in their company. Mostly, I have reported their doings, but on occasion I have assisted them. On the whole, they have proved better company than any other professional group I have had a chance to know well.

**Authentic:**    I like politicians. *Ever since I started work as a city-hall reporter in New Mexico some thirty years ago,* I have spent a lot of time in their company—*in smoke-filled rooms, jails, campaign trains, shabby courthouse offices, Senate cloakrooms, and the White House itself.* Mostly I've been reporting their doings, but on occasion I have served them *as speech writer, district leader, campaign choreboy, and civil servant.* On the whole, they have proved better company than any other professional group I've had a chance to know well—*including writers, soldiers, businessmen, doctors, and academics.*—John Fischer, "Please Don't Bite the Politicians," *Harper's*

To keep your paragraphs from remaining too skimpy, try the following:

(1) *Practice building up detail in a multiple-example paragraph.* Try to build up your examples until the reader is likely

to say: "Enough! You have made your point, and you have made it well." Here is a paragraph that makes exceptionally ample use of relevant examples:

> *A person's touch makes what the other senses take in more real to the memory.* A *wood carving* appeals to the touch with deep grooves and parts that are rough as well as parts that are smooth. The fingers can interpret the richness of *brocade* and the rough warmth of wool. An ancient *book* becomes even older when one feels the fragile pages. A *puppy* tugging wildly at a leash feels like energy. *Winter* is felt in the hastily prepared snowball and the pine boughs that are brittle in the sharp air. A child must feel a *hot stove* before it becomes a thing to avoid touching, and words become meaningful when he loses the skin from his tongue to the *cold metal pipe* he was warned about. The energy of the *sun* becomes more apparent when one focuses a magnifying glass on his fingers. A *baby chick* is something altogether new when one holds the cotton-like ball of feathers and feels its nervous heartbeat. An *oil painting* is only paint and canvas until one touches the swirls made by the artist's brush. A *rose* is only a flower until one holds it in his hands and pulls the petals from the intricate pattern. A human *voice* becomes more than sounds when one speaks with his fingers to his throat to feel the vibrations. The surface of a *rock* is only light and shadow until one feels its ridges and ripples. Touching helps one to see and hear more clearly.

(2) *Give priority to supporting detail by practicing the examples-first paragraph.* When you reverse the usual order from topic sentence to supporting detail, you force yourself to provide the relevant examples that in the end will add up to a well-earned generalization:

> The shops of the border town are filled with many souvenirs, "pintas," pottery, bullhorns, and "serapes," all made from cheap material and decorated in a gaudy manner which the tourist thinks is true Mexican folk art. Tourists are everywhere, haggling with the shopkeepers, eager to get something for nothing, carrying huge packages and boxes filled with the treasures bought at the many shops. Car horns blare at the people who are too entranced with the sights to watch where they are going. Raucous tunes pour from the nightclubs, open in broad daylight. Few children are seen in the town, but some boys swim in the Rio Grande and dive to retrieve the coins that tourists throw as they cross the bridge above. People

come for a cheap thrill, a quick divorce, cheap liquor. *A border town is the tourist's Mexico, a gaudy caricature of the real country.*

## Exercises

**A**. For each of the following paragraphs, formulate a topic sentence that would sum up the *central idea* implied in them. Compare your own topic sentences with those of your classmates.

> **1**. I am sure that the Romans, whose lives were lived under stately porticoes and amid the pomp of great temples, found in that background an ever present dignity which must have followed them even into the poverty and confusions of the crowded, many-storied *insulae*. The wide forums and the glittering *thermae* did not arise merely from the vanity of emperors and the corruption of the people. These were the songs in which the Roman soul made itself known above the cries of the circus and the clash of civil swords. The Gothic cathedrals were, in part at least, prayers of thanksgiving for a joy discovered in the revival of cities, and the *piazze* into which Venice poured her compressed splendor are jubilant with that new enfranchisement. These are not each an ornament added to a city but summations of a city's spirit to which houses and streets, walls, canals, and the domes of public buildings are the harmonious counterparts. Florence, Padua, Cordoba; the Paris of Richelieu, the Philadelphia of Franklin: each of these might have been the work of a single architect so consistent is the ordinance and expression of their streets and structures.—Joseph Hudnut, *Architecture and the Spirit of Man*

> **2**. During my month of vigil and research, I heard an able physiologist who has a radio program say, quite simply, "We do not use up all the food we take in." He wasn't allowed to get away with that piece of clarity, however. "Ah," cut in his announcer, for the benefit of those no longer able to understand simplicity, "the utilization factor!" I turned from this station to a droning psychologist, just in time to hear him say, "The female is sometimes the sexual aggressor." Here a familiar noun of mental illness and military invasion was clumsily at work beating in the skull of love with a verbal bung-starter. The sweetheart now often wears the fustian of the sick man and the Caesar. In the evening, I tuned in on one of the space-patrol programs that gleefully exude the

great big blockyisms. "Your astrogation bank will tell you!" cried the captain of a space ship to another interplanetary pilot, meaning his navigational instruments. In a fairy tale, an astrogation bank would be a "star panel," but the quality of fairy tale is nowhere to be found in these dime novels of the constellations.—James Thurber, "The Psychosemanticist Will See You Now, Mr. Thurber," *The New Yorker*

**3.** More books have been written about Napoleon than about any other human being. The fact is deeply and alarmingly significant. What must be the day-dreams of people for whom the world's most agile social climber and ablest bandit is the hero they most desire to hear about? Duces and Fuehrers will cease to plague the world only when the majority of its inhabitants regard such adventurers with the same disgust as they now bestow on swindlers and pimps. So long as men worship the Caesars and Napoleons, Caesars and Napoleons will duly rise and make them miserable. The proper attitude toward the "hero" is not Carlyle's, but Bacon's. "He doth like the ape," wrote Bacon of the ambitious tyrant, "he doth like the ape that, the higher he clymbes, the more he shewes his ars." The hero's qualities are brilliant; but so is the mandril's rump. When all concur in the great Lord Chancellor's judgment of Fuehrers, there will be no more Fuehrers to judge. Meanwhile we must content ourselves by putting merely legal and administrative obstacles in the way of the ambitious. They are a great deal better than nothing; but they can never be completely effective.—Aldous Huxley, *Ends and Means*

**B.** Write a one-paragraph theme describing a face, a dress, the façade of a building, an abstract painting, or a tree. Pack the paragraph with specific detail that all supports the *same dominant impression* or central point.

**C.** Formulate a limited generalization about youth, education, or campus life. Support it in a *multiple-example* paragraph that presents at least half a dozen clearly relevant examples.

**D.** Write an *examples-first* paragraph about a place; an actor or a public figure; a type of play, concert, or program. Make all your details help lead the reader up to the final point.

# 5

# THE WHOLE
# THEME

The finished theme is the result of a process. Ideally, the process of composition moves through five overlapping stages:

(1) The writer *explores his subject,* gathering and examining possibly relevant material.

(2) The writer *limits his subject* to what he can treat in the necessary detail.

(3) The writer *works out a pattern of organization* that fits his material.

(4) The writer *writes his first draft,* presenting his material to advantage.

(5) The writer *revises* his first draft for continuity, clarity, and effectiveness.

The more substantial a project, the greater usually the need for systematic planning. Such planning is not the result of following a pat formula or a set of simple rules. If a writer forces his material into the straitjacket of a tried-and-true scheme, he may keep himself from doing justice to his subject and from discussing it with conviction. On the other hand, there are general principles of organization that can help a writer find his bearings. There are conventional de-

vices for checking and strengthening the structure of a paper
or of a paragraph.


# 0  4  The Need for Focus

*A writer must concentrate on one point at a time.*

Many papers begin with a vague interest in a general subject area. The instructor assigning a topic does part of the
job of narrowing down the general area to something manageable. The writer has to do the rest.


## 0  4a  Limiting the Subject

*The shorter the paper, the greater the need for restricting the area
to be covered.* No one could write a paper on a vast subject like
"Education in America." A writer interested in American
education may restrict this field according to *kind:* academic,
physical, religious. He may restrict it according to *area:* a
state, a town, the nation's capital, Indian reservations in
Arizona. He may limit himself to a particular *level:* kinder-
garten, grade school, high school, college. He may limit his
discussion to a certain *type of student:* gifted, retarded, emo-
tionally disturbed. A manageable topic might look like this:

> Space-age science at Washington High
> "Released time" and the Winchester Public Schools: No time
> 　　for God
> Talking typewriters for the retarded
> Home economics for boys
> Stagnant schools and the migrant child
> How to succeed in a military academy


Each large subject can be split up into several medium-
sized subjects. Each of these in turn will yield many limited
subjects narrow enough to serve as topics for short papers:

| General Area: | City life |
|---|---|
| Intermediate: | The inner city |
| | Suburbia |
| | Urban sprawl |

| Topics: | One major cause of urban blight |
|---|---|
| | Redeveloped vs. grown neighborhoods |
| | An alternative to teen-age gangs |
| | A new trend in city architecture |
| | Keeping up with the Joneses |
| | The suburb and the sense of community |
| | Who pays for the schools? |
| | Why I don't like supermarkets |
| | The passing of the neighborhood store |
| | Kids with nothing to do |
| | My church is a country club |
| | Good fences make good neighbors |

## O 4b    Choosing a Key Question

*Often, you can bring a subject into focus by asking a key question that the paper as a whole is designed to answer.* Merely writing *about* a subject often results in a catalog of miscellaneous impressions. The freshman who writes "about" his first week on campus may ramble from one thing to another. To give direction to his paper, he should ask a question that helps him to sort out his impressions: "What kind of advice would I give to an incoming freshman? What makes a person a good roommate? What can be done to help students find adequate housing?"

The more *specific* the key question you choose, the more likely your paper is to have a clear focus:

General:    How do crime comics shape their readers' attitudes?

Focused:    Is it true that crime comics equate physical ugliness with moral depravity, thus encouraging the reader to judge by appearances?

Is it true that heroes tend to look white, Anglo-Saxon, and Protestant, while villains are made to look Latin, for instance, or Oriental?

Is it true that in the crime comics people are either all good or all bad?

Do crime comics reveal the political sympathies of their authors?

NOTE: A *pointed* question is more likely to produce a focused paper than a question that is open or merely exploratory. Avoid questions like "What are some of the causes of adolescent crime?" or "What are some of the things every freshman should know?" The "What-are-some" kind of question almost always leads to a paper in which many different things are *mentioned* but too few of them studied in detail. Substitute a "What-is-the-most" or "What-is-the-best" kind of question: "What is the most important thing a freshman should know?" "What is the most serious obstacle to communication between a teenager and his parents?" "What are three key features shared by successful television comedians?"

## O 4c Defining Your Purpose

*Often a confusing subject comes into focus when the writer limits the purpose he is trying to achieve.* It is one thing to *explain* to your reader how a machine functions. It is another thing to *persuade* him that the machine will serve his needs. It is one thing to *define* a term like "modern liberalism." It is another to *convert* the reader to the cause so defined. The main purpose of a writer may be:

* *to inform:* to pass on to the reader facts gathered by firsthand observation or compiled from other sources;

* *to explain:* to show the workings of a process or trace the causes of an event;

* *to define:* to give definite meaning to a confusing or difficult term;

* *to argue:* to show the logic behind a conclusion or decision;

* *to persuade:* to influence the reader's opinions, decisions, actions.

These purposes are not mutually exclusive. Explanation, definition, and argument, when well done, have a persuasive effect on the reader. Nevertheless, failure to settle for one major purpose can easily make a writer's efforts seem scattered and ineffectual.

## Exercises

**A.** Choose *two* of the following general areas. For each, write down *five topics limited enough* to be covered in a short paper.

> Recreation
> Religion
> Industry
> Minority groups
> Transportation

**B.** Assume you are preparing five pointed questions for an *interview* with one of the following: a college president, a police chief, a Negro minister, a conscientious objector, a diplomat from a country currently in the news. Formulate questions *significant* enough to be worth following up but *limited* enough to steer the interview away from vague generalities. The class as a whole may want to choose the two or three sets of questions most likely to produce significant, detailed responses.

**C.** Write two paragraphs covering roughly the same area but serving a *different purpose.* Choose one: (1) In one version *describe* a product factually; in the other, *persuade* a skeptical customer to buy it. (2) In one version *report* an incident objectively; in the other, use it to *entertain* the reader. (3) In one version *explain* a current political slogan or idea; in the other version *make fun* of it.

## 0 5    Patterns of Organization

*Present your material in a clear and consistent sequence.*

Adequate restriction of the subject area sets the outside limits of a theme. In its internal organization, the theme is likely to follow one, or a combination, of a number of common patterns.

## O 5a   Space and Time

*Much descriptive writing, technical exposition, and autobiographical narrative follows a sequence inherent in the writer's material.* Often such material fits naturally into a **spatial** or **chronological order**. An account of a vacation trip may trace a trail up into mountainous country. An article on radio transmitting may follow the voice of the soprano through microphone and transmitter to the receiving set and the listener's ear. An autobiographical paper may follow a "before-and-after" pattern: family life before and after the loss of a parent; a boy's attitude toward military service before and after induction.

To strengthen a paper of this kind, observe the following cautions:

(1) *Make the progression in space or in time clear and consistent.* The professional may attain special effects by flashbacks and by calculated shifts of perspective. The amateur, however, especially when writing a short paper, usually does well to follow a consistent pattern: from the foothills to the wind-swept peak, from childhood to adolescence.

(2) *Break up the whole sequence into major divisions or emphasize the most significant steps.* Suppose a paper follows the assembly line in an automobile factory: the basic parts of the body are welded together; the doors are hung; the body shells are dipped into a chemical solution; they are spray-painted; they are dried in ovens; electrical wiring is laid; door locks and other mechanisms are installed; glass is installed; interior lining is installed; and so on. To protect the reader against a monotonous "and-then" sequence, the writer will probably break up the body's progress into three major stages:

   I. Building the body shell
  II. Painting the body
 III. Outfitting the painted shell

## O 5b   Thesis and Support

*In a short paper, limit yourself to one major point that you can fully explain, illustrate, and support.* Supporting a thesis requires us to relate a mass of material to a single point. It thus teaches us to *limit* ourselves to one major point, and to drive it home. In the following excerpt, from Gordon Parks' *A Choice of Weapons*, the first sentence serves as a thesis; and each of the three paragraphs of the excerpt takes up one incident that bears out the point made by the thesis:

*thesis*         *When I was eleven, I became possessed of an exaggerated fear of death.* It started one quiet summer afternoon with

*first incident*   an explosion in the alley behind our house. I jumped from under a shade tree and tailed Poppa toward the scene. Black smoke billowed skyward, a large hole gaped in the wall of our barn. . . .

*second incident*   Then once, with two friends, I had swum along the bottom of the muddy Marmaton River, trying to locate the body of a Negro man. We had been promised fifty cents apiece by the same white policeman who had shot him while he was in the water trying to escape arrest. . . .

*third incident*   One night at the Empress Theater, I sat alone in the peanut gallery watching a motion picture, *The Phantom of the Opera*. When the curious heroine, against Lon Chaney's warning, snatched away his mask, and the skull of death filled the screen, I screamed out loud. . . .

The following instructions will help you write papers that successfully support a thesis:

(1) *Make sure your thesis is a clear statement of a limited point.* Whenever possible, state your thesis in a single **thesis sentence**:

**Topic:**     Urban Redevelopment

**Thesis:**    "Redeveloped" neighborhoods lack the varied life of the "grown" neighborhoods they replace.

**Topic:**     Life in Suburbia

**Thesis:**    Living in the suburbs does not prevent people from developing a sense of community.

The thesis should be a true statement, a true assertion. It cannot be a question, though an excellent way of *arriving at* a thesis is to sum up in one sentence the answer to a question like "What is missing in the typical redeveloped neighborhood?" The thesis should not merely map out the general territory but focus on a limited issue:

| Too Vague: | A modern suburb is a good place to live. |
| Focused More Clearly: | Modern suburbs have kept alive the American tradition of being a good neighbor. |

| Too Vague: | Today's children are spoiled. |
| Focused More Clearly: | Grade school teachers lack the means of disciplining their students. |

(2) *Make your thesis pull together your previous observations or impressions.* Writing about the heroine of an Ibsen play, you may wish to say that she was bored and frustrated, cruel and selfish, hungry for excitement but at the same time afraid of scandal. Formulating a thesis, you try to make these various points add up to a coherent overall view: "This woman was dissatisfied and resentful because she was unable to adjust her desires to the limitations of her environment." Your paper could then give several examples of her acting frustrated and cruel when the setting she lived in thwarted her desires. Or perhaps you formulate a thesis like this: "She expected too much of people and as a result was invariably disappointed." Your paper could then give several examples of her approaching people with high hopes and then acting bored, frustrated, or cruel when her expectations fail to come true.

(3) *Arrange your supporting material in an intelligible order.* Try to sort out your examples under three or four major headings, as in the following sample outlines (see also O 5c):

| Thesis: | My high school teachers insisted on strictly formal language. |
| Support: | I. Colloquial language was forbidden in *student themes.* |
| | II. *Books* with outspoken and slangy dialogue were put on the "don't-read" list. |

III. *Classroom discussion* had to be carried on in strictly formal phrases.

**Thesis:**    A part-time job supplements a student's education.

**Support:**    I. Part-time work can provide a valuable *practical education* (training for do-it-yourself projects; knowledge useful to future housewife, car owner).

II. It can provide field work related to the student's *major field of study* (hospital work for future nurses, tutoring for future teachers, playing in a commercial band for music student).

III. It can provide valuable *psychological training* (association with people from different backgrounds, taking orders from superiors).

## O 5c   Classification

*Sort out or break up your material so as to group together related points.* A writer may have to sort out miscellaneous material into several major categories (**classification**). He may have to break up a sprawling, formless subject into three or four plausible parts (**analysis**). He may merely arrange several major points of equal importance in the most convenient sequence (**enumeration**).

Here is a typical preliminary collection of material for a paper about a person:

SUBJECT:  Last semester's psychology teacher
    (1) had a loud, clear voice
    (2) told interesting stories about students helped by psychology
    (3) came to class late several times
    (4) explained difficult words
    (5) wasn't sarcastic toward students
    (6) wore colorful neckties
    (7) walked with a limp
    (8) had been an exchange teacher in France
    (9) outlined subject clearly
    (10) spaced assignments well
    (11) talked over test I did poorly on
    (12) served in the Army Signal Corps

What goes with what? Here are four possible categories:

I. *Teaching methods:* (2) relevant anecdotes, (4) explanation of terms, (9) clear outline, (10) spacing of assignments, and perhaps (1) effective speech habits

II. *Attitude toward students:* (5) absence of sarcasm, (11) assistance after class

III. *Personal traits:* (6) sporty clothes, (7) limp, (3) lack of punctuality

IV. *Background:* (8) teaching experience abroad, (12) service in Signal Corps

A student concerned about his success in school would probably conclude that categories I, II, and IV are most significant. A second look at III might suggest an effective strategy for the paper as a whole: an introduction describing an unpromising first impression, belied by the teacher's effectiveness. The outline of the finished paper might look like this:

I. Unpromising external characteristics

II. Effectiveness as a teacher
   A. Interesting background
   B. Effective presentation of subject
   C. Positive attitude toward students

III. Lesson learned
   ("Don't judge a teacher by his ties.")

Here are some other subjects with relevant material sorted out into major categories:

SUBJECT: Types of comic strips
   I. Righteous crime fighters (Dick Tracy, Robin Malone)
   II. Comic stereotypes (Dennis the Menace, Blondie, Bugs Bunny)
   III. Social satire (L'il Abner)
   IV. Amusing human foibles (Peanuts, Pogo)

SUBJECT: Types of high school teachers

I. The *authoritarian* personality (strict discipline, one-way teaching, heavy assignments, severe grading)

II. The *journeyman* teacher (reliance on the textbook, moderate assignments, "don't-rock-the-boat" attitude)

III. The students' *friend* (chummy attitude, many bull sessions, unusual projects, fraternizing outside of school)

Remember the following advice when setting up and presenting such major categories:

(1) *Let the subject of your paper help you determine appropriate categories.* Writing about campus social life, you might divide students into Greeks, Coop dwellers, and Independents. Writing about "cultural" subjects for vocational students, you might divide them into nursing majors, engineering majors, police majors, and so on.

(2) *Avoid a confusing mixture of criteria.* It does not make sense to divide students into graduates of local high schools, disadvantaged students, and Catholics. It *does* make sense to sort them out according to geographical origin (local, rest of the state, out of state, foreign), *or* according to belief (Catholics, Protestants, Jews, agnostics), *or* according to social and economic background.

(3) *Try not to vary thoroughness of treatment drastically from one category to the next.* Some papers seem unbalanced because the writer has tried to analyze the subject exhaustively instead of fully developing perhaps three major categories. A paper on teen-age marriage might proceed like this:

THESIS: Often teen-age marriages result from motives other than mature affection.

I. One possible motive is the desire for independence from parental control. (Several case histories are discussed.)

II. Another motive may be the sense of satisfaction derived from marrying a popular boy or a popular girl. (No details or examples are given.)

III. A person may marry "on the rebound," marrying one person to spite another. (A sketchy and inconclusive case history is provided.)

IV. A couple may mistake physical attraction for love. (Several cases are discussed; similar cases in fiction and drama are cited.)

V. A boy about to be drafted may marry a girl for fear of losing her. (A case in point is discussed at length.)

The paper is likely to be unconvincing, because the author is stretching himself too thin. In a long paper, he might successfully tackle I, IV, and V. In a short paper, he might do well to limit himself to either I or IV.

(4) *If the major divisions of the paper vary in importance, make your presentation follow a consistent pattern.* Many effective papers move from the less important to the more important. This order produces a **climactic effect** and leaves the most important point firmly embedded in the reader's memory. The paper on teen-age marriage, for instance, might start with motives related to external circumstances (I, V) and end with the problem that is probably the most important and the hardest to discuss (IV).

## O 5d    Comparison and Contrast

*Comparison and contrast requires us to establish meaningful connections between things normally considered separately.* To justify our preference for a lackluster incumbent over a more dynamic challenger, we may compare their records on a number of crucial points. To identify a style of architecture, we may note the features it shares with other styles and those features that set it apart.

The most common failing of the comparison-and-contrast paper is that the author has left the actual brainwork for his readers. He has collected the necessary material but has failed to *work out* the parallels or differences. Often such a paper breaks apart in the middle: a discussion of the Volkswagen followed by a separate discussion of the Ford; a discussion of the villain in a Shakespeare play, followed by a discussion of the villain in a play by Ibsen. To make possible fruitful comparison and contrast, the author must *line up* his material so that one thing throws light upon the other.

Here are the two basic ways of organizing systematic comparison and contrast:

(1) *The author discusses two things together—feature by feature, point by point.* A **point-by-point comparison** takes up one feature of, say, the Volkswagen, and then immediately asks: "Now what does this look like for the Ford?" A typical outline would look like this:

 I. Economy
    A. Initial cost (data for both cars)
    B. Cost of operation (data for both cars)
    C. Resale value (data for both cars)

 II. Comfort and convenience
    A. Space for passengers and luggage (data for both cars)
    B. Maneuverability (data for both cars)

III. Performance
    A. Acceleration and speed (data for both cars)
    B. Durability (data for both cars)

Here is the same scheme applied to a discussion of two Dutch painters. The author is trying to show that the two, though superficially very different, share important traits.

THESIS: There are basic resemblances between Rembrandt and Van Gogh.

 I. Both were interested in people, in what is called "character" or "expression" (this point applied first to Rembrandt and then to Van Gogh).

 II. Both were deeply religious—but not in a remote or abstract way (applied first to Rembrandt and then to Van Gogh).

III. Even formally, in their brushwork and use of color, the two men are akin (applied first to Rembrandt and then to Van Gogh).

(2) *The author discusses two things separately but takes up the same points in the same order.* Such a **parallel-order comparison** makes it possible to give a coherent picture of each of the two things being compared, while at the same time helping the reader see the connections between the two. In the following portrait of two types of baseball fans, notice that the same three points are taken up both times in the identical order: I. absorption in the game; II. attitude toward fellow fans; III. interest in the players.

| | |
|---|---|
| *thesis* | The true baseball fan is found in the bleachers, not in the grandstand. |
| point 1 | The man in the bleachers *forgets himself in the game.* When he gets excited . . . |
| point 2 | He is apt to *turn to a total stranger,* tap him on the shoulder, and say, "Ain't that boy Aaron the berries!" . . . |
| point 3 | Though his seat is farthest from the diamond and he cannot see the batters' faces, he *recognizes each one* of them as they come up. . . . |
| transition | The man in the grandstand looks at the game differently. . . . |
| point 1 | He never quite *gives himself up to the game.* He never cuts loose with a wild yell. . . . |
| point 2 | If he is sitting among people who are strangers to him, he *treats them like strangers.* . . . |
| point 3 | He has to refer to his scorecard to get the *names of the players.* . . . |

Here is the same scheme applied to a comparison and contrast of the villain in a Shakespeare and an Ibsen play:

| | |
|---|---|
| *thesis* | Shakespeare's Iago represents spectacular and triumphant evil, whereas the villain in Ibsen's *The Pillars of the Community* represents the unheroic evil brought about by ordinary men. |
| point 1 | Iago is a *deliberate* villain, freely admitting his evil intentions to his audience. . . . |
| point 2 | Iago is forever plotting *ingenious schemes,* producing dramatic results. . . . |
| point 3 | Iago goes about his villainies with tremendous *gusto,* finding ever new objects for his cynical sense of humor. . . . |
| transition | Ibsen's villain is much less spectacular, and is in fact revealed as the villain only after a close second look. . . . |

point 1    Ibsen's villain is constantly *rationalizing* his guilt. . . .
point 2    The evil he does is represented by *acts committed half-heartedly and furtively.* . . .
point 3    Ibsen's villain is a *brooding, unhappy man,* ineffectually revolving his problems in his own mind. . . .

## O 5e    Logical Argument

*Many papers dealing with issues and ideas follow the order of a logical argument.* Several patterns of such argument are especially worth noting:

(1) The logical coherence of the paper may derive from *cause-and-effect relationships.* The following outline might represent an essay by a teacher concerned about his students' lack of interest in poetry:

> I. *First step:* The author states his central concern, bringing out its interesting, startling, or paradoxical aspects:
>
> Children like poetry; they make up jingles and keep chanting them to each other; they listen avidly to poems about little pigs and clever cats. Most college freshmen, on the other hand, are either indifferent or hostile toward poetry, both traditional and modern.
>
> II. *Second step:* The author asks and answers the obvious question: Why?
>
> Poetry is often presented to students as something special and solemn; memorizing and reciting make many students regard it as drudgery; prose paraphrase necessarily emphasizes the most prosaic aspect of poetry.
>
> III. *Third step:* The author suggests remedies at least partly implied in the diagnosis:
>
> Teachers of poetry should emphasize oral reading; they should cater to their students' interest in song and story by including ballads and narrative poetry; they should encourage discussion and writing rather than make poetry the subject of objective tests.

(2) A second logical pattern leads to the desired conclusion through *qualification of* or *attack upon a familiar idea:*

I. *First step:* A familiar idea is confirmed:

It is true that many required courses do not help to prepare the student for his professional career (detailed illustrations).

II. *Second step:* A qualification or objection is stated:

But a responsible citizen must be able to recognize competence and quackery in fields other than his own (detailed illustrations).

III. *Third step:* A balanced conclusion is drawn:

Therefore, a student needs required courses that give him a basic understanding of some important disciplines outside his own field.

The same scheme is applicable to more general or more demanding subjects. When the resulting paper clearly plays two *opposed* ideas off against each other, it mirrors the **dialectic** process:

I. *Thesis:* It is true that modern industrial society makes for unprecedented interdependence among its citizens.

II. *Antithesis:* But such interdependence is an essential condition of mass production and mass consumption.

III. *Synthesis:* Interdependence is the price modern society pays for a high standard of living.

(3) A third logical pattern is modeled on the **inductive argument**, which *presents examples, case histories, or evidence and then draws a general conclusion.* Inductive order is especially effective when a writer has to overcome prejudice or distrust:

I. *First step:* Data are presented:

Carlotta Brink, heroine of *Vengeance Is Mine,*

A. is rude to her servants (examples)

B. insults tradesmen (examples)

C. attempts to put other people in the wrong (examples)

D. is unconcerned about her husband's business problems (examples)

E. scolds her children without provocation (examples)

II. *Second step:* The conclusion is drawn:
Carlotta is inconsiderate and unkind.

(4) In many papers an inductive paragraph becomes one link in a logical chain. Sustained logical reasoning makes unusual demands both on writer and reader. It is necessarily rare in popular or informal exposition and most common in scholarly controversy. Here is a rough outline of a **deductive argument**, which *draws conclusions from premises previously established* or *applies generalizations to specific instances:*

I. A college should develop in its students a sense for spiritual values (elaboration and support).

II. Architecture gives tangible expression to such values as dignity and permanence (elaboration and support).

III. The buildings facing the traditional Inner Quad of the college exhibit several of these qualities (elaboration and support).

IV. Of the modern classroom buildings on this campus, few suggest a sense of tradition, a sense of style, a feeling of dignity (elaboration and support).

V. Therefore, the buildings surrounding the Inner Quad should not be torn down to make room for additional "cell block" structures.

NOTE: The more substantial an essay or an article becomes, the less likely it is to fit into any one simple organizational scheme. A chapter in a book may follow a chronological order in its main outline, with different sections illustrating various kinds of analytic, inductive, and deductive order.

## Exercises

**A**. Identify the ten or twelve *essential steps* in a complicated process that is well known to you from first-hand observation or experience. Try to group the various steps into several major stages. Use the following outline form to report your findings.

I. _____ (first major stage)
        A. _____ (first step)
        B. _____ (second step)
        C. _____ (third step)
    II. _____ (second major stage)
        A. _____ (first step)
        [and so on]

**B**. Of the thesis sentences presented in the following brief passages, select the three that come closest to your own views. For each one, jot down briefly what *supporting material* you could supply from your own experience and reading to back up the point made.

> **1**. In today's high schools, *there is too much competition for grades.* The student constantly worries about tests and has little chance to think and explore on his own.

> **2**. *Students profit as much (or more) from a summer of work, travel, or reading as from additional coursework in summer sessions.* Though such experiences are less systematic than academic learning, they are educational in the sense that they broaden the student's perspective.

> **3**. *The public schools do not fully practice the constitutional principle of separation of church and state.* Students, whether of Christian, Jewish, or agnostic parents, participate in Christmas plays and Easter pageants, and sing religious songs.

> **4**. *Teen-age fads and fashions have increasing influence on the adult world.* Teen-age styles set the pace for much advertising and strongly influence adult fashions and even hair styles.

> **5**. *The population of the typical big city is declining in income and social status.* The unskilled and the less educated remain, while the middle class moves out to the suburbs to find living space and better schools for the children.

> **6**. *Fear of violence restricts the activities of many Americans.* People stay away from public parks; older people are afraid to venture out into the streets.

**C**. Consult recent issues of several of the following general-interest magazines: *Atlantic, Harper's, New Republic, National Review, Commentary, Commonweal.* Choose *three thesis sentences* that illustrate exceptionally well the kind of thesis that makes a definite assertion on a limited point.

**D**. State *three possible theses* that your experience or background equips you especially well to support. For each thesis, outline the paper you would write in support of it. Your instructor may ask you to write a thesis-and-support paper based on the most promising of your outlines.

**E**. The following "interest inventory" was adapted from a student paper. How would you *classify* the items in order to present them in a plausible sequence? Prepare a brief outline showing how you have sorted them out.

1. contact sports
2. coffee dates
3. religious retreats
4. taking a girl to the movies
5. work for worldwide disarmament
6. long hikes
7. beach barbecues
8. vacation trips
9. fellowship meetings
10. swimming
11. social work
12. student government

**F**. Sort out the suggestions in the following list into major categories. Arrange both your major categories and their subdivisions in the *most plausible or the most logical order.*

### Study Hints

1. Make study time as regular as possible.

2. Work out an understanding with friends and roommates concerning unnecessary interruptions.

3. Avoid dim or glaring light.

4. Get an understanding of the purposes and organization of a course from course outlines, introductory materials in a textbook, or chats with the instructor.

5. If you can, work at an uncluttered desk.

6. Ask yourself practice questions about what you study.

7. Make a point of not protracting lunch hours and coffee breaks indefinitely.

8. If you can, find a congenial corner in a library or study hall.

9. Start studying the first week of each term.

10. Take two or three *short* breaks during each two- or three-hour period of study.

11. In studying a textbook, try to relate what you read to the instructor's lectures or to class discussion.

12. If a subject does not seem immediately practical or interesting, treat it as a challenge to your resourcefulness, agility, and perseverance.

13. Break up the material to be studied into convenient chunks.

14. Reserve the cramming session before final examinations for review and for attention to special difficulties.

15. Summarize, review, and think about one major section before going on to another.

**G.** What is your favorite reading matter? Have you ever sorted it out into recurrent types? Choose one of the following: science fiction, detective novels, Western novels, historical novels, nineteenth-century British fiction, current American short stories, biographies, autobiographies, books on travel or exploration. Sort the books you have read in this major category out into a few major types. For each, write a short paragraph indicating the major features that examples of the type have in common.

**H.** Of the following topics, choose the one that seems most promising for fruitful comparison and contrast. Write *two* rough outlines—one for a point-by-point comparison, the other for a parallel-order comparison. Choose one: your high school campus and your present college campus, two successful television comedians with different styles, old-style and "adult" Western movies, a student hang-out and an expensive restaurant.

**I.** Write a rough outline for a comparison and contrast of *two major* *characters* from imaginative literature. Choose the central figures of two Shakespeare plays, two nineteenth-century British novels, or two modern American novels. Make it *either* a point-by-point or a parallel-order comparison, and be prepared to defend your choice.

**J**. Write an outline for a paper modeled on the dialectic method. Have you recently become strongly aware of two different or opposed views on a familiar problem or current issue? Use your outline to line up the *pros and cons* and to lead up to your own conclusion. Among possible topics are

> Antisemitism in Shakespeare's *Merchant of Venice*
> The commitment to nonviolence in political demonstrations
> Legal control of the ownership and sales of guns
> Stepped-up freeway construction in urban or scenic areas

**K**. Write an outline for an *inductively organized* paper on a subject of your choice.

**L**. Write an outline for a paper in which you derive a *specific, limited proposal* for the reform of high school or college education from basic assumptions about the nature or purposes of education. Try to make each major point in your outline a necessary step in your argument.

# O 6   Beginnings and Endings

*Learn how to enlist the reader's attention and how to leave him with a strong final impression.*

Many writers spend too much time wondering how to begin and how to conclude. Often, the best advice is to begin in the middle and to stop when he has finished what he has to say. Nevertheless, once a writer has worked out the body of his essay, he should think seriously about how to approach his readers and how to shape their final reaction to the paper as a whole.

## O 6a   Titles

*The ideal title attracts the reader without promising more than the author is going to deliver.* It is specific enough to stake out a limited area, honest enough to prevent later disappointment, and striking enough to compete with other claims on the reader's time. A good title often has a dramatic or humorous touch:

> At Last Lincoln Found a General
> The Crime of Punishment
> Second Things First
> On Becoming Human

Bad titles tend to be vague, colorless, sprawling, or deceptive. Here are some weak titles followed by a choice of possible improvements:

**Before:**  Business Success

**After:**  Selling Home Encyclopedias
Where the Customer Is King

**Before:**  Qualities of a Future Husband

**After:**  What Makes Eligible Men Eligible
Breadwinner or Prince Charming?

**Before:**  Juvenile Delinquency

**After:**  My Stay at Juvenile Hall
The Boy From a Good Family

**Before:**  Neutrality of Political Science Teachers

**After:**  Impartiality in the Classroom
Teachers, Too, Have Opinions

## O 6b  Introductions

*The ideal introduction attracts the reader but at the same time does important groundwork for the paper.* An effective introduction *sketches out the territory* to be covered, often by narrowing down a more general subject. It *sets the tone* for the rest of the essay. Here are some typical examples, each serving one or more of the purposes for which an effective introduction may be designed:

(1) The writer may attract the reader's attention by relating his subject to a *topical event or a current controversy:*

### Russian, Anyone?

On August 12 . . . the Soviet government announced the construction of Russia's first . . . Though Russian scientific journals had published detailed accounts of . . . , the lack of qualified translators had kept American scientists unaware of the Russians' rapid progress in this field. . . .

(2) The writer may make the reader take a *new look at a familiar situation:*

### The Life of Stress

A lot of sympathy is being wasted on executives for leading lives so full of stress and strain that it impairs their health. Actually, their subordinates suffer more from high blood pressure and artery disease. These surprising findings . . . —*Time*

(3) The introduction may limit the subject by *proceeding from a general situation to a specific instance:*

### The Wastelands Revisited

School people have to put up with a lot, not only from the kids, who must be bad enough, but also from the grown-ups, who probably are worse. Pummeled, pressured, and advised from every side, still bearing the wounds inflicted by super-patriots, super-religionists, super-taxpayers, and super-superintendents, the educators now have to deal with yet another attack from Arthur E. Bestor, Jr.—William Lee Miller, *The Reporter*

(4) An *initial quotation* may serve as the keynote for the rest of the paper:

### Who Is Hamlet?

"It is a commonplace that the character of Hamlet holds up the mirror to his critics."[1] Shakespeare's Hamlet has been aptly described as the sphinx of the Western world, with each critic giving his own subjective answer to the riddle it proposes. . . .

(5) *Striking facts or statistics* may dramatize the issue to be discussed:

### Monolingualism Is Obsolete

Last year, only one out of ten American high school graduates had studied a foreign language. In spite of the publicity recently given to the teaching of foreign languages in primary and secondary schools . . .

(6) A *striking contrast* may heighten the point to be made:

### American Children Are Spoiled

Not too many decades ago, young children were early taught the difference between what they were, and were not, allowed to do. Today, many American parents treat their children as if they could do no wrong. The most obvious manifestation of this change . . .

(7) An *initial definition* may clarify a key term:

### What Is Automation?

Economists do not agree among themselves on what "automation" means. Some writers use the term for any type of large-scale mechanization of industrial or administrative processes. Others, more plausibly, use it in referring to the mechanization of planning, supervision, and control.

(8) Biographical or personal comment may help establish the *writer's qualifications* for dealing with his subject:

### Victory and After

When I first came to Germany in November 1945, all the major cities seemed to be curiously alike. . . .

(9) A *provocative statement* may challenge a familiar belief or ideal:

### Freedom Is Impossible

Freedom in society is impossible. When the desires of two people do not agree, both cannot be satisfied. Who is going to be free to realize his desire—the man who wants to walk down the street shouting and singing, or his neighbor who seeks peace and quiet? The man who wants to build a new highway, or the one who wants to retain the unspoiled natural beauty of the land? . . .

(10) A *controversial question*, provocatively worded, may stir up an apathetic reader:

### Divided Loyalties

Should a man put loyalty to his country above loyalty to a friend? Does loyalty to the government come before loyalty to one's family? How we answer such a question depends on . . .

(11) By *anticipating damaging objections*, the writer may disarm would-be critics:

### The High Cost of Misfortune

Nowadays anyone who advocates public health insurance is called a socialist. Thanks to years of skillful and well-financed publicity . . .

(12) An *amusing anecdote* may at the same time convey an important idea:

### Medical Journalism—
### With and Without Upbeat

As a veteran writer of medical and psychological articles for the mass-circulation "slicks," I have a fellow feeling for the violinist who rebelled after having been with an orchestra for thirty years. One day, so the story goes, he sat with his hands folded during rehearsal, and when the conductor rapped on the podium with his baton and demanded furiously, "Why aren't you playing?" replied, with a melancholy sigh, "Because I don't like music." Sometimes I feel like sitting at my typewriter with my hands folded. I don't like popularization. It has gone too far. The little learning—with illustrations— which the magazines have been pouring into a thirsty public has become a dangerous thing. . . . —Edith M. Stern, *Saturday Review*

Some common ways of introducing a theme are usually *ineffective:*

(1) A *repetition,* often verbatim, *of the assignment.*

(2) A *colorless summarizing statement:* "There are many qualities that the average college graduate looks for in a job. Most of them probably consider the following most important. . . ."

(3) An *unsupported claim to interest:* "Migratory birds are a fascinating subject. Ever since I was a little child I have been interested in the migration of birds. Studying them has proved a wonderful hobby. . . ."

(4) An *unsubstantiated claim that the paper is going to deal with a burning issue:* "There has been much controversy over the question of whether public schools should give their students released time for religious instruction. This question has been debated many times. . . ."

(5) *Complaints:* "I find it hard to discuss prejudice in a paper of 500 words. Prejudice is a vast subject. . . ."

(6) *Apologies:* "I am really not very well qualified to write about the qualifications that good children's books should have. . . ."

(7) *Evasions:* "Everyone feels differently about the merits of required courses. I think everyone has a right to his own opinion. . . ."

(8) A *dictionary definition* that is not really followed up, applied, or argued with in the rest of the paper.

## 0  6c    Conclusions

*An effective conclusion ties together different parts of a paper and reinforces its central message.* It may simply be an emphatic restatement of an important idea, an explicit assertion of what the writer has been hinting at. At the end of a fairly long and involved paper the conclusion may offer a convenient summary of major points. Often an essay concludes with a detail symbolic of the prevailing mood, or with an anecdote reaffirming the central idea in a witty or memorable way.

Here are some examples of effective conclusions:

(1) A *memorable restatement* of the central idea:

. . . Underneath our shiny fronts of stone, our fascination with gadgets and our new toys that can blow the earth into a million stars, we are still outside the doorway through which the great answers wait. Not all the cameras in Christendom nor all the tricky lights will move us one step closer to a better understanding of ourselves, but only, as it always was, the truly written word, the profoundly felt gesture, the naked and direct contemplation of man which is the enduring glamour of the stage.—Arthur Miller, "The American Theater," *Holiday*

(2) A *final anecdote* that reinforces the central idea without explicit restatement:

. . . Only once did I ever hear of an official football speech which met with my entire approval. It was made by a Harvard captain. His team had lost to Yale but by a smaller score than was expected. It had been a fast and interesting game. At the dinner when the team broke training the captain said, "We lost to Yale but I think we had a satisfactory season. We have had fun out of football and it seems to me that ought to be the very best reason for playing the game."

A shocked silence followed his remarks. He was never invited to come to Cambridge to assist in the coaching of any future Harvard eleven. His heresy was profound. He had practically intimated that being defeated was less than tragic.—Heywood Broun, "A Study in Sportsmanship," *Harper's*

(3) An apposite *final quotation:*

. . . Should there be codes of ethics for honesty in government? Must public men declare themselves in writing to be honest men just as some professors have been required to swear solemnly that they do not really intend to overthrow the Government of the United States? Personally, I have no faith in such oaths. A gentleman who much influenced my early life once told me:

"Son, by God, when I invite a man to dinner I do not propose to count the silver—before or after he leaves the table!"—William S. White, "The American Genius for Hypocrisy," *Harper's*

(4) A sober estimate of the *significance of the conclusions* reached:

. . . Criticism by outsiders will not miraculously transform the quality of network programs. But as long as criticism finds its way into print, and as long as network presidents take their critics seriously enough to cajole or denounce them, the cause of informative and satisfying television is not lost.

(5) A *forecast or warning* based on facts developed in the paper:

. . . In education we have not yet acquired that kind of will. But we need to acquire it, and we have no time to lose. We must acquire it in this decade. For if, in the crucial years which are coming, our people remain as unprepared as they are for their responsibilities and their mission, they may not be equal to the challenge, and if they do not succeed, they may never have a second chance to try.— Walter Lippmann, "The Shortage in Education," *Atlantic*

(6) An essential *condition for future progress:*

. . . When public relations people become as a group more forthright, less designing, more strict in their standards, and more respectful of the public, then—and only then—will the discerning public accept them as real professionals.—Vance Packard, "Public Relations: Good or Bad," *Atlantic*

(7) A suggestion for *remedial action:*

. . . If the leading citizens in a community would make it a point to visit their state prison, talk with the warden, then return to their communities with a better understanding of actual down-to-earth prison problems, they would have taken one of the most important and most effective steps toward a solution of our crime problem.— Erle Stanley Gardner, "Parole and the Prisons—An Opportunity Wasted," *Atlantic*

(8) A *return from the specific to the general*, relating the findings of the paper to a general trend:

. . . Inge's family plays constitute a kind of aesthetic isolationism upon which the world of outside—the world of moral choice, decision, and social pressures—never impinges. Although he has endowed the commonplace with some depth, it is not enough to engage serious attention. William Inge is yet another example of Broadway's reluctance or inability to deal intelligently with the American world at large.—Robert Brustein, "The Men-Taming Women of William Inge," *Harper's*

Here are some examples of *ineffective* conclusions:

(1) The *platitude:* "This problem deserves the serious attention of every right-thinking American."

(2) The *silver lining:* "When things look their grimmest, a turn for the better is usually not far away."

(3) The *panacea:* "The restoration of proper discipline in the nation's schools will make juvenile delinquency a thing of the past."

(4) The *conclusion raising problems* that weaken or distract from the point of the paper: "Of course, a small car has obvious disadvantages for a family with numerous children or for the traveler in need of luggage space."

## Exercises

**A.** Study the following *book titles* and rank the three best titles in order of their effectiveness. Explain what makes them effective.

1. *George Washington, Man and Monument*
2. *Freedom in the Modern World*
3. *The City in History*
4. *The New Radicalism in America*
5. *The Free World Colossus*
6. *Number: The Language of Science*
7. *Lost Worlds of Africa*
8. *The Feminine Mystique*
9. *The Naked Ape*
10. *The Second Sex*

**B.** Look through recent issues of general-circulation *magazines* to find five articles whose titles you consider exceptionally effective. Defend your choices.

**C**. What would you do to improve the title of a theme you have recently written? Write down the original title and *three* alternative titles that seem equally or more effective. Make sure the new titles do justice to the content of the actual theme.

**D**. Describe the approach chosen in each of the following introductions. Comment on the effectiveness of both *introduction and title.* Do they make the reader want to go on reading? Do they seem to lead clearly and directly into a specific subject? What kind of paper would you expect in each case?

**1**.                    Hydroponics in the Home

Hydroponics is a subject about which many people have little or no knowledge, yet there is nothing really new or mysterious about it. It is merely a system by which plants are grown in water solutions containing the essential minerals for plant growth. The terms *water culture* and *water gardening* refer to this same system. . . .

**2**.                    The Latest Style

If you picked this paper up expecting a dissertation on frills, frocks, and new brassieres to dream in, you had best put it down again. I am concerned here with a new style in automotive power plants, the free-piston turbine engine. You may ride behind one sooner than you think. . . .

**3**.                    The New Illiteracy

We hear much about the reawakening interest in the humanities, the new appreciation of the generalness in the liberal arts, the growing dissatisfaction with overspecialization. Maybe so. But these signs are minute, I suggest, [compared with] those coming from the other direction. I offer the proposition that the trends that have been working against the humanities are likely to increase, not decrease, in the decade ahead. . . .—William H. Whyte, Jr., *Saturday Review*

**4**.                    Mary Had a Little Delinquent

In today's world, the worst kind of juvenile delinquent is not the one who has become a public blotch on the good name of society, or who has been blasted to fame in a newspaper headline. More frightening is a silent, sneaking kind of young rebel. Normal enough in looks, this person creeps through our culture until suddenly — POW — his disrespect for authority is revealed. The delinquent of this second variety with whom I am most intimately acquainted is — *me*! I am very good at being bad.

**5**.　　　　　　　Thoreau and Human Nature

Our histories of American literature are deficient in a number of categories. They seldom or never, for example, recognize the greatness of American biographical writing. . . . They do not know what to do with the powerful library of travel literature written by Americans. . . . But I think the greatest deficiency in these manuals is their failure to recognize the existence of that type of writer the French call the moralist.—Howard Mumford Jones, *Atlantic*

**6**.　　　　　College—From the Outside Looking In

Why waste four years going to college? In four years an ambitious high school graduate can become happily established with a company and have a sizable lead on the road to fame and fortune over his former schoolmates. This is how I felt when I left high school. Three years of pursuing fame and fortune altered my thinking radically. . .

**7**.　　　　　　The Educated Anti-Intellectuals

It is a curious fact that the American people spend more per capita on the schooling of their children than any other people on this globe and yet they persist in proclaiming their anti-intellectualism. Consider the epithets "brain trusters" and "eggheads." Look at the general disdain for the very word "intellectual" . . .

**8**.　　　　　　Brute Strength Is Not Enough

Football has often been called a game for men who are all muscle and have no brains. This charge may have been justified in the infant years of the game, when it consisted entirely of running plays and when the players used brute strength to crash through the opposing line. Today, a team may use as many as fifty different plays, involving complicated deception and a wide variety of passes. . . .

**9.**                    The Role of Government

The decision between a strong government which governs the people or a weak government is one of importance and one that needs careful thought and consideration. Throughout history, the proper role of government has been a subject of discussion. . . .

**10.**                    The Bent and Blunted Free Lance

In the chivalry of the thirteenth century, an important figure was the free lance, an independent knight who sold his fighting skill to the highest bidder and, so legend says, tilted his bold weapon in defense of the helpless against all sorts of dragons and outrages. So far in the twentieth century an important adjunct to communication has been the free-lance writer who has made a living, and a considerable social impact, with his pen. . . .—Hartzell Spence, *Saturday Review*

**E.** Examine the introduction or "lead" in three current articles from different general-interest magazines. Write a well-developed paragraph about each one. Describe the approach followed and evaluate its effectiveness.

**F.** Formulate a central idea for a short theme on a topic of your choice. Then write *three different possible introductions,* each time using a different approach.

**G.** Describe the function and estimate the probable effectiveness of the following conclusions:

**1.** (A paper describing the game of badminton)

. . . Badminton can be very exciting. If you are ever looking for a good time I suggest that you try this game. I know from experience that it can really be a lot of fun.

**2.** (A paper discussing a veteran's visit to his former high school)

. . . As I walked, alone, down the familiar and yet strangely different hall, I began to realize a truth that nostalgic people like myself find hard to learn: Distance gives glamor to the past.

**3.** (A paper defending women against the charge that they are poor drivers)

. . . that the woman driver, inexperienced and timid as she may be, is less of a highway menace than the arrogant, inconsiderate male. Of course, this is only one woman's opinion, and yours may be different from mine.

**4**. (A paper trying to demonstrate the futility of censoring comic books)

. . . the parents can do most to counteract the comic-book habit. If they read to their children from good books, if they teach their children to treat good books as treasured possessions, if they make it a habit to talk about good books in the home, the positive attraction of good literature may prove more effective than censorship possibly can.

**5**. (A paper discussing several examples of "tolerance")

. . . We thus conclude that by "tolerance" we mean allowing beliefs and actions of which we do not wholly approve. Since many of us approve wholeheartedly of only very few things, life without tolerance would be truly intolerable.

**6**. (A paper examining the proposition that "that government governs best that governs least")

. . . Government must effectively govern to be a true government, but it must govern with restraint and not to excess. The government that governs least is not necessarily the best one. I would rather say that the government that governs ablest, in the interest of most of its citizens, is the best government.

**7**. (A paper on race prejudice)

. . . What can the individual do to combat racial prejudice? This question is very hard to answer, because nobody can predict the future.

**8**. (A paper on the democratic process)

. . . The benefits society derives from the democratic process are often unspectacular, and slow in coming. Its weaknesses and disadvantages are often glaringly evident. By its very nature, democracy, in order to survive, must give its enemies the right to be heard and to pursue their goals. As Chesterton has said, "The world will never be safe for democracy—it is a dangerous trade."

**H**. Rewrite the conclusion to one of your recent themes. Write two new versions, each reinforcing in a different way the same central idea as the original.

## O 7    Continuity and Transition

*Learn how to take your reader along from point to point.*

In a competent piece of writing, sentence follows sentence, and paragraph follows paragraph, in a smooth, natural sequence. When such progression is lacking, the reader will soon start asking exasperated questions: Where are we going? How does this fit in? What are you leading up to?

### O 7a    Key Sentences

*Emphatic key sentences serve as guideposts to the reader.* Thus, a **topic sentence** becomes a guide to the intention of a paragraph (see O la). A **thesis sentence** gives direction to the paper as a whole. From paragraph to paragraph, and even within a paragraph, the most basic method of moving a paper along is to make a key statement that calls for an explanation, to make an assertion that calls for proof.

Study the following excerpted version of an article that is exceptionally deliberate and clear-cut in its organizational scheme. Can you see how the key sentences the author formulates in response to his four major questions help the reader follow him step by step?

*What are the students like?* They come from all sorts of backgrounds. . . .

Only one thing they are certain to have in common: they are roughly in the same age group. . . .

*Why do they come to college?* They come because it is assumed that they will come, because almost everyone they know does. . . .

A second and related reason why students come is to make good contacts. . . .

Many come simply to learn to make a living. . . .

To have fun is still another motive. . . .

There are students who actually come because they learn. . . .

*What happens to students in college?* It is the students' first meeting, most likely, with a national and perhaps international group of men and women of their own age. . . .

Furthermore, college is the students' first encounter with live intellectuals. . . .

Students are surprised, too, at their first meeting with really violent political opinion of all possible varieties. . . .

It is in college, too, that the sharp bitter sting of failure is first experienced to any appreciable extent. . . .

*What does the student learn?* On the simplest level he has acquired a considerable amount of information. . . .

He will also have learned to question. . . .—James K. Feibleman, "What Happens in College," *Saturday Review*

## O 7b    Transitions

*Apt transitional phrases help the reader move smoothly from one point to the next.* In a well-written paper, the reader can see how and why the writer moves from point to point. But the connection is seldom as obvious as the writer thinks. Transitional phrases are directional signals that help the reader move along without stumbling.

Here are common transitional phrases:

| | |
|---|---|
| addition | *too, also, furthermore, similarly, moreover* |
| illustration | *for example, for instance* |
| paraphrase or summary | *that is, in other words, in short, to conclude, to sum up* |
| logical conclusion | *so, therefore, thus, accordingly, consequently, as a result, hence* |
| contrast or objection | *but, however, nevertheless, on the other hand, conversely, on the contrary* |
| concession | *granted that . . . , no doubt, to be sure, it is true that . . .* |
| reiteration | *indeed, in fact* |

The following advice should help you make effective use of transitional phrases:

(1) *Avoid transitions that merely add without showing why.* Shun expressions like "Another interesting point is . . ." or

"We might also take a look at . . ." These make it sound as though the writer asked himself: "What else?" They make the reader feel that what follows is at best optional and at worst mere padding.

(2) *Use enumeration sparingly, for emphasis.* Lining major points up in a numerical sequence makes for a formal, systematic presentation. In the following discussion of language, the key points gain force from marching across the page in a 1-2-3 order:

> There are *five simple facts* about language in general which we must grasp before we can understand a specific language or pass judgment on a particular usage. . . .
> *In the first place,* language is basically speech. . . .
> *In the second place,* language is personal. . . .
> *The third fact* about language is that it changes. . . .
> *The fourth great fact* about language . . . is that its users are, in one way or another, isolated. . . .
> *The fifth great fact* about language is that it is a historical growth of a specific kind. . . .—Donald J. Lloyd, "Snobs, Slobs, and the English Language," *The American Scholar*

Though effective when used for special emphasis, such enumeration easily becomes too rigid and unimaginative. When used in a perfunctory manner, it makes for heavy, plodding reading. The next example, though also presenting several major points in order, uses less obtrusive transitional expressions:

| | |
|---|---|
| *thesis*<br><br>first point | An arrangement of shapes is satisfying, or otherwise, to the human eye, because of certain elementary natural laws. *The most essential of these* is the law of balance. . . . |
| second point | A picture *also* demands harmony. . . . |
| summarizing definition | *In speaking* of the harmony, or unity, of a picture, *we mean* that . . . |
| further development of point 2 | The colors, *too,* must be related harmonious⌐ |
| summary of points 1, 2; third point | *Thus* we have balance and harmony as ne⸍ in a picture. We must *also* have variety and subt⸍ |

definition
summarizing
points 1–3

The design of a picture, which includes *these quali-ties of* balance, harmony, and variety, is its basis and essential skeleton. . . .—K. W. Maurer, "On the Appreciation of Paintings," *Queen's Quarterly*

(3) *Fill in the logical connections that help the reader follow an argument.* Take special care to take your reader along when an argument moves systematically through a number of essential steps:

| | |
|---|---|
| introduces main point | It is plain that . . . |
| begins to enumerate reasons | Here are some reasons for . . . |
| elaborates on one of several points | The second of these . . . |
| summarizes what precedes | In short, . . . |
| raises a possible objection | Yet . . . |
| concedes a point | It is true that . . . |
| returns to original trend of thought | Nevertheless, . . . |
| draws balanced conclusion | At the very least, . . . |

NOTE: Overuse of transitional expressions like *however, therefore,* and *all things considered* can make a paper awkward and mechanical. But when used sparingly, and when varied to avoid monotony, they help to keep both writer and reader from leaving the tracks.

## O 7c   Synonyms and Recurrent Terms

*In much well-focused discussion, key terms and their synonyms echo from one paragraph to the next.* In a paper on academic freedom, terms and phrases like "freedom," "liberty," "independent thought," "free inquiry," "responsible choice," "absence of interference," and "self-government" show that the writer is never straying far from the central issue. Look for the network of synonyms and near-synonyms that helps keep together much well-written prose:

Throughout his public career, Taft was lampooned as an *anachronism*, a man *out of touch with modern needs* and aspirations. . . . Reading over his speeches and debates, one detects an *antiquarian* flavor. . . . the lawyerly precision and the candor are decidedly *old-fashioned*. . . .

In the following excerpt, notice how the repetition of key terms like *work, toil,* or *labor* helps lead the reader through a passage consisting of several substantial paragraphs:

What elements of the national character are attributable to this long-time agrarian environment? First and foremost is *the habit of work.* For the colonial farmer ceaseless striving constituted the price of survival. . . .

The *tradition of toil* so begun found new sustenance as settlers opened up the boundless stretches of the interior. "In the free States," wrote Harriet Martineau in 1837, "*labour* is more really and heartily honoured. . . ."

One source of Northern antagonism to the system of human bondage was the fear that it was jeopardizing this basic tenet of the American creed. "Wherever *labor* is mainly performed by slaves," Daniel Webster told the United States Senate, "it is regarded as . . ."

Probably no legacy from our farmer forebears has entered more deeply into the national psychology. If an American has no *purposeful work* on hand . . .

This *worship of work* has made it difficult for Americans to learn how to play. As Poor Richard saw it, "Leisure is . . ."

The first mitigations of the daily grind took the form of hunting, fishing, barn-raisings and logrollings—*activities that* had no social stigma because they *contributed to the basic needs of living.* . . .

The importance attached to *useful work* had the further effect of helping to make "this new man" indifferent to aesthetic considerations. . . .—Arthur M. Schlesinger, *Paths to the Present*

## Exercises

**A**. In each of the following pairs of sentences, a *transitional word or phrase* has been left out. Fill in a transition that will help the reader move smoothly from the first sentence to the second.

**1**. There are many special schools which should be considered by the young person who is not going on to college. The boy who wishes to be an X-ray technician and the girl who wishes to be a practical nurse, _____, will find many schools at which they may receive training.

**2**. Apprenticeship systems are still operating in every industry and offer wide opportunities for the ambitious youngster. He must be warned, _____, that in some of the older crafts entry is jealously guarded.

**3**. The home environment is the largest single factor determining the grade school youngster's "scholastic aptitude." _____, how well he learns in school depends on what he has learned at home.

**4**. Rennie was lazy, self-indulgent, spoiled. _____, he did remarkably well in his favorite subjects.

**5**. The basic promise that American society has always held out to its citizens is equality of opportunity. The typical substandard big-city school, _____, is profoundly un-American.

**6**. Negro athletes are not as pampered as some white sports fans seem to think. _____ the outstanding Negro athlete enjoys many privileges, but when a black and a white man are equally well qualified, coaches are likely to give preference to the latter.

**7**. The European system of education very early separates youngsters permanently on the basis of ability. The American system, _____, is designed to make possible numerous second chances.

**8**. In many Latin-American countries, more young men study to be lawyers than are needed in their country. _____ _____, in many underdeveloped countries more young men study to be engineers than a pre-industrial society could support.

**9**. A highly specialized skill limits a person's job opportunities. It _____ makes the specialist a potential victim of technological unemployment.

**10**. Our leaders are fond of the phrase "the free world." In actual fact, _____, societies that foster political freedom are the exception rather than the rule.

**B.** Point out the *logical connections* that give continuity to the following excerpted student paper about the work of an American painter.

> . . . The "window series" captivated me for it implied glimpses into the privacy of humanity; each soul was shielded, barely, by a fragile lace curtain, or a shade, or perhaps a shadow . . . Exquisite and delicate, the details of the curtain, for instance, were so tangible that I was tempted to push it aside; but then, I'd have been intruding.

In contrast, the civil rights drawings almost scream for involvement—they beg to be studied, and to study them means to lose one's complacency. . . .

Perhaps his interest in the civil rights struggle helped the artist to identify with Lincoln. Certainly he created a striking interpretation in his Lincoln portrait. . . .

If it could be said that Lincoln symbolizes the simplicity of the Midwest, then the artist's prairie landscapes glorify it. There is a sense of infinity in the vast expanse of heavens over rain-soaked fields and rolling prairies. . . .

**C.** In a page of expository prose selected by your instructor, point out all key sentences, transitional phrases, and words or devices making for continuity.

# O  8    Outlines and Summaries

*Practice in outlining and in summarizing helps a writer achieve a firm grasp of organization.*

## O  8a    Working Outlines

*Construct a working outline by jotting down major points in a tentative order.* To be useful as a help in *writing* a paper, an outline should be informal and flexible. Such a working outline resembles an architect's preliminary sketches rather than the finished blueprint. Here is a first tentative outline for a short paper on anti-intellectualism in the high schools:

emphasis in high school on
    athletics
    social activities

little recognition for intellectual achievement
    honor roll
    debating society
    drama society ("intellectual"?)

attitude now changing?
    stress on college entrance

Use such an informal outline as a *tool* in working out a plausibly organized paper. As you look at your tentative points, ask: Would this order make sense to the reader? Suppose you want to discuss an important common element in books that have enjoyed a tremendous vogue with adolescents. You might first jot down titles as they come to mind:

> *Catcher in the Rye*
> Goethe's *Young Werther*
> *Catch-22*
> *The Prophet*
> *The Stranger*
> *Lord of the Flies*

To arrange these titles in a plausible order, you might decide to start with the *classic* example: Goethe's *Werther,* the book that "invented adolescence." You could then discuss outstanding *recent* examples, taking them up roughly in the order in which they became popular. Finally, you could discuss in detail a *personal* example—a book that meant a great deal to you. Your working outline might look like this:

> classic example: Goethe's *Werther*
>
> recent examples
> > *Catcher in the Rye*
> > *The Stranger*
> > *Lord of the Flies*
> > *Catch-22*
>
> my own favorite
> > poems of Dylan Thomas

## O 8b    Final Outlines

*The final outline, intended as a guide to the reader, usually follows one of several conventional forms.*

(1) The **topic outline** is most useful for quick reference. It presents, in logical order, the topics and subtopics (and often the sub-subtopics) that a paper covers. Like other out-

lines, it is often preceded by a thesis sentence summarizing the central idea of the paper:

### Sororities and the Single Girl

THESIS: The social activities of a sorority are designed to help girls conclude desirable middle-class marriages.

   I. Keeping girls away from undesirable men
   A. Dating arrangements with fraternities
   B. Busy social calendar discouraging independent dating
   II. Husband-hunting opportunities
   III. Emphasis on formal courtship rather than casual dating
   A. "Pinnings" as formal ceremonies
   B. The role of pinnings and engagements in sorority "news"

(2) In a **sentence outline**, the writer sums up, in one complete sentence each, what he has to say on each topic and subtopic. The sentence outline thus forces him to think through his material thoroughly and systematically:

### Main Street Isn't Pennsylvania Avenue

THESIS: A successful business career alone does not qualify an executive for government work.

   I. Prominent businessmen have often occupied high positions in the federal government.
   II. Businessmen often have qualifications that government officials tend to lack.
   A. They are in close contact with the wishes and opinions of the general public.
   B. They have thorough training in organizational problems.
   1. They are trained in administrative efficiency.
   2. They are cost-conscious.
   III. But business executives often lack preparation for other aspects of government work.

A. They tend to lack the tact and experience necessary for dealing with people from foreign cultures.

   1. They may alienate foreign diplomats.

   2. They tend to ignore public opinion abroad.

B. They tend to lack the legal training required in interpreting and administering laws.

C. They have had little experience with the delays inherent in democratic processes.

IV. The personal qualifications of the individual executive are more important than his business background.

To eliminate common weaknesses, check your finished outlines against the following list of suggestions:

(1) *Be consistent* in the use of symbols, indention, and spacing.

(2) *Avoid using "Introduction," "Conclusion,"* etc., as substitutes for individual headings.

(3) *Avoid single subdivisions.* If there is a subdivision *A,* there should be a subdivision *B.* If there is a section numbered *1,* there should be a section numbered *2.* If a section covers only one major point or one major step, leave it undivided.

(4) *Avoid a long sequence of parallel elements,* such as *I-X, A-F,* or *1-8.* Unless the subject matter justifies mere undifferentiated enumeration, try to split the sequence into two or three major groups.

(5) *Use parallel grammatical structure* for headings of the same rank in order to emphasize their logical relation. For instance, if *A 1* reads "To revive the student's interest," *A 2* and *A 3* should also be worded as infinitives: "To promote the student's participation"; "To develop the student's independent judgment."

(6) *Make sure the thesis is a complete statement*—not a question, not a phrase without a predicate, not a dependent clause.

(7) In a topic outline, *make each topic specific and informative.* In a sentence outline, make each subdivision a complete sentence. *Make each sentence sum up an idea* rather than merely indicate a topic.

NOTE: The divisions of an outline do not always correspond exactly to the paragraph divisions in the paper—though in a well-organized paper the two often coincide. Several minor subdivisions may be treated in the same paragraph; one subdivision, developed by detailed examples, may spread through several paragraphs; short transitional paragraphs may intervene between subdivisions.

## O 8c   Summaries

*Related to skill in outlining is skill in the writing of summaries—* of your own work or, more commonly, of the work of others.[1] To summarize a piece of writing, you need to grasp its organization. You can then state essential points and qualifications in the most concise possible form, omitting illustrations, lengthy explanations, and incidental comment. A summary can preserve the gist of an article or a paper for efficient study, for future reference, or for the use of a busy reader.

In writing a summary, you will have to observe several essential requirements.

(1) *Make sure you grasp the main trend of thought.* Isolate key sentences; formulate the major point implied in a paragraph; distinguish between incidental comments and important steps in an argument.

(2) *Reduce explanation and illustration to the essential minimum.* Omit passages that are mere paraphrase. Preserve only the most important details, examples, statistics. Reduce or omit elaboration by metaphor, comparison, anecdote.

(3) *Use the most economical wording possible.* Use the simpler of two alternative terms, the shorter of two synonyms. If you can, substitute a single word for a phrase, a phrase for a clause.

Study the differences between the full text and the summary in the following pairs:

[1] See Chapter 8 for detailed discussion of how to summarize and paraphrase quoted material.

ORIGINAL: The invention of the process of printing from movable type, which occurred in Germany about the middle of the fifteenth century, was destined to exercise a far-reaching influence on all the vernacular languages of Europe. Introduced into England about 1476 by William Caxton, who had learned the art on the continent, printing made such rapid progress that a scant century later it was observed that manuscript books were seldom to be met with and almost never used. Some idea of the rapidity with which the new process swept forward may be had from the fact that in Europe the number of books printed before the year 1500 reaches the surprising figure of 35,000. The majority of these, it is true, were in Latin, whereas it is in the modern languages that the effect of the printing press was chiefly to be felt. But in England over 20,000 titles in English had appeared by 1640, ranging all the way from mere pamphlets to massive folios. The result was to bring books, which had formerly been the expensive luxury of the few, within the reach of all. More important, however, was the fact, so obvious today, that it was possible to reproduce a book in a thousand copies or a hundred thousand, every one exactly like the other. A powerful force thus existed for promoting a standard uniform language, and the means were now available for spreading that language throughout the territory in which it was understood.—Albert C. Baugh, *A History of the English Language*

SUMMARY: Printing from movable type, invented in Germany about 1450 and brought to England about 1476, had a far-reaching influence on all European languages. Within a hundred years, manuscript books had become rare. Though at first most printed books were in Latin, over 20,000 titles in English had appeared by 1640. Books were now within the reach of everyone and could exert a powerful standardizing influence upon language.

ORIGINAL: The tendency to erect "systems"—which are then marketed as a whole—affects particularly the less mature sciences of medicine and psychology. In these subjects we have had a succession of intellectual edifices originally made available only in their entirety. It is as if one cannot rent a room or even a suite in a new building, but must lease the whole or not enter. Starting with a substantial contribution to medicine the authors of such systems expand their theories to include ambitious explanations of matters far beyond the original validated observations. And after the first pioneer, later and usually lesser contributors to the system add further accretions of mingled fact and theory. Consequently systems of this kind—like homeopathy, phrenology, psychoanalysis, and conditioned reflexology (the last dominant for years in Russia)—eventually contain almost inextricable mixtures of sense and nonsense. They capture fervid adherents, and it may take a generation or several for those who preserve some objectivity to succeed in salvaging the best in them while discarding the dross.—Dr. Ian Stevenson, "Scientists with Half-Closed Minds," *Harper's*

SUMMARY: Medicine and psychology have produced a number of intellectual systems that one is asked to accept as a whole or not at all. The ambitious authors and adherents of such systems go beyond original valid findings to produce a mixture of truth and error that attracts enthusiastic supporters. Objective observers may not succeed in separating the valuable from the worthless till much later.

NOTE: Unless the original version is already severely condensed, a summary of about one third or one fourth the original length can usually preserve the essential points. However, the shorter the summary, the greater the danger of oversimplification or outright misrepresentation. You will have to be careful to preserve essential conditions and distinctions: *if-* and *unless*-clauses; differences between *is, will,* and *might;* qualifiers like *only, almost,* and *on the whole.* You will have to preserve the relative emphasis of the original, giving more prominence to a point treated at great length than to one mentioned in passing.

## Exercises

**A**. Sort out the following material and arrange it in a topic outline:

Education Without Representation

THESIS: Students would profit greatly from being given greater influence on curricula and teaching methods than they now have.

    1. Training for citizenship through active participation
    2. Present lack of student influence
    3. Sense of belonging through participation
    4. Attitudes toward elective as compared with required courses
    5. Success of experimental programs

6. Attitude of night school and business college students toward freely chosen subjects

7. Training for adult responsibilities in business and family through participation

8. Improved motivation through active participation

**B**. Sort out the following material and arrange it in a sentence outline:

### The Value of Group Discussion

THESIS: Training in the techniques of group discussion is an indispensable part of the student's general education.

1. Discussion teaches us to look for evidence that will withstand criticism.

2. Discussion teaches us to control emotional reactions.

3. The primary goal of a discussion is to solve immediate problems.

4. Successful discussion requires ability to focus on the subject at hand.

5. In modern American society, more and more decisions are reached as the result of group discussion.

6. Successful discussion requires willingness to consider the viewpoints of others.

7. Discussion teaches us to estimate the reliability of evidence submitted by others.

8. Comparison of different views enables us to distinguish valid from invalid arguments.

9. The give-and-take of discussion is a humane alternative to one-sided propaganda and the use of force.

10. Discussion teaches us to get along with others.

11. Discussion teaches us to respect people whose knowledge or ability is superior to ours.

12. A successful discussion has educational value.

13. Discussion teaches us to be patient with people whom we assume to be wrong.

14. Discussion teaches us to evaluate evidence.

15. Successful discussion requires careful investigation of the relevant facts.

16. Discussion teaches us how to think.

17. Disagreement forces us to reexamine our views.

**C.** Select a current magazine article whose organization you find exceptionally clear or effective. Prepare both a topic and a sentence outline. Your instructor may wish to suggest a maximum number of words for each outline.

**D**. Select a passage of about 250 words from a history or science textbook. Prepare a summary running to about a third of the original length. Provide a copy of the original.

## Review Exercise: Sample Themes

Study the following *student themes.* How successful has the author been in gathering relevant material? Is the subject adequately restricted? How effective are title, introduction, and conclusion? What features make for continuity? Rate these papers from most to least successful, and be prepared to defend your choices.

1.                    Ceramics—My Hobby

Have you ever picked up a piece of free-form earthenware and thought how very satisfying and enjoyable it must have been for the person who worked it up from mere earth and water? By "free form," I mean the potter's own creative idea modeled in clay. Such free-form modeling is rather an involved process—many times, it is true, heart-breaking, but nevertheless an enjoyable and thoroughly gratifying experience.

It is possible to dig one's own clay from the earth. By moistening it with water and adding certain chemicals, one can make the clay mass more elastic, more workable, and stronger. Then follows the mixing of a glaze which, according to a specialized formula, will have an affinity to the original clay body. This in itself can become a long and tedious procedure. So, unless one has a pioneering spirit, it is better to find a standard clay body and glazes which have already been processed according to the manufacturer's own formula.

Cutting, shaping and molding the clay mass into the desired form with one's own hands is one of the biggest thrills imaginable. It is surprising what can be done with moist clay! A creative spirit can really go "wild" and still come up with something both beautiful and practical—say a flower vase or planter in the exaggerated form of some sea shell.

When the piece is thoroughly dry, it is known as "greenware" and is very fragile, but it becomes hardened through firing in a kiln. The firing is done slowly. The heat goes up to about 2000°F. It is measured by a cone-shaped pin set in a clay base and made to melt at the desired temperature. This is known as the pyrometric cone. The entire firing period takes about eight hours. Then the kiln is cooled slowly. It should not be opened or disturbed during the cooling time, which may take twelve hours or more. The greenware is now referred to as "bisque."

Bisque may be painted in a variety of colors, called underglaze, and then dipped in a transparent glaze. It may be sprayed or brushed with or dipped in any of the colored glazes. A second firing to bring out the glaze effect is now necessary. Usually, this firing is slow too, with the temperature not as intense as before—about 1800°F. However, the pyrometric cone must be watched more closely than in the bisque firing, especially with certain glaze formulas.

Glazes are extremely difficult to control, and many unexpected effects are obtained—probably caused by moisture in the air, uneven firing elements, firing time, dirt particles, or some chemical reaction. Many unique and unusual effects can be obtained through experimentation with underglazes, overglazes, colored clay bodies, sifted sands, crushed colored glass and even salt! I remember my first experiment. I used sifted sand which I found in my backyard. I dusted the sand over the glaze coating and, after firing, found there were bright red and black raised granules throughout the glaze.

One can look at this hobby from a practical point of view. Gifts alone, especially at Christmas time, make it worth while. But it is the ideas and experiments that make it a truly fascinating and worthwhile hobby.

**2.**                          My Friend, My Enemy

Mimi is practically my best friend. On the outside, she is a loud-talking, big-mouthed, obnoxious girl. At a party, her only aim seems to be fun, with no feelings about anyone else. During the course of a conversation, she tells all she knows about her friends and their personal lives, never leaving out a detail or personal remark. Though Mimi is my best friend, her utter disregard for other people's feelings also makes her my worst enemy.

After seeing Mimi once, you won't forget her. She has a wild mop of short blond hair, which is combed once a day. Her big blue eyes are continually covered by a pair of heavy, coke-bottle lens glasses. She weighs well over her quota, a fact she explains by saying "there's more of me to love" and "I was thin once, but I wasn't as jolly." Her clothes are in the casual range of tennis shoes, big sweaters, and skirts.

What's ticking inside her head? Most noticeable is a bad, bad temper. She has the idea that no man is good enough to be his brother's keeper. This is her basic philosophy: If she decides to swear or dress sloppily, it's her business and nobody else's. Her temper makes her rage at people who make noise while she sleeps and at such things as a dirty bathroom basin. Usually her rage is a short atomic blast, but it never has a fallout of grudges. After waking, Mimi speaks to no one for at least two hours. She simply glares at any bystander.

A greater sense of humor never was found in one human being. In high school she called herself "Sherman" because she was as big as a tank. Everyone loved and hated her at the same time. Some people claimed that she sold beer and wine from her hall locker and made stencils of the teachers' signatures. When she was sent to the dean, she presented her ideas on how to improve the school honor code.

The parties Mimi goes to are never boring. She cuts everyone to pieces, including—and especially—me. At one time, she told everyone that I mixed my make-up in a huge vat and spread it on with a spatula. She is always talking to my friends and warning them about my numerous shortcomings.

Mimi lives across the hall in our boarding house. There she can sit for hours with a piece of clay or even a cigarette box and create small things for her enjoyment. Her jolly laugh is heard around the house when small things amuse her.

Few people understand what provokes Mimi, and they resent her carefree attitude. When I see her sitting like a fat little baby on the floor reading the college daily or a letter from home, enjoying every word like a piece of candy, I would like to hug her. However, as she slowly reveals my life to all present, I would like to kill her.

To many people, Mimi is just another coed. But to me she is a villain, the Medusa, Eleanor Roosevelt, Jerry Lewis, and Jack the Ripper, with a heart as big as a statue, all rolled into one fat, fun-loving, childlike package.

**3.**                     Thou Shalt Not Lie

Although most people believe it is wrong to lie, it is doubtful that anyone can go through his entire life without ever telling a lie. But are all lies equally wrong? Or are some lies actually justified? To answer this we must examine the four basic types of lies. Each type is told for a different reason.

The first, and probably the most common type of lie, is the lie of exaggeration. This is the type of lie we tell to make an incident sound more interesting. Or we may lie about our achievements to make ourselves seem more intelligent or clever. We justify this type of lie by convincing ourselves it cannot harm anyone. But there is one disadvantage to this type of lie. If we are found out, we are left feeling like a fool and wondering why we bothered to lie about something so unimportant.

The second type of lie is the one told to avoid hurting someone. This type of lie is often considered necessary. When someone asks, "Do you like my new dress?" we prefer to answer yes because we know that is what she wants to hear. But even this type of lie is not always wise. For example, if a patient asks his doctor if he has terminal cancer, he wants and expects an honest answer in most cases.

The third type of lie is the exact opposite of the second. It is the deliberately malicious lie told for the express purpose of hurting someone. Few mature adults tell this kind of lie, but it is fairly common among children. They may shout "I hate you" at another child one day but be back playing with him the next day.

The last type of lie is the one we tell to cover up something we should or should not have done in the first place. Rather than admit we made a mistake, we lie about it. This is the type of lie that gets us into the most trouble. No one has a good enough memory to tell this type of lie. One lie leads to another. Then before we know it, we have forgotten what we said to whom, and we are afraid to open our mouth for fear we will put our foot in it. Then we realize what is meant by the phrase, "Oh, what a tangled web we weave when first we practice to deceive."

**4.**                    No More Favors, Please

Many times in a conversation I have heard it said that "a boss's son has it made." I doubt whether a person who makes this statement has ever worked for his father. At any rate, during the four years that I worked for my father's water softener firm, I was not treated nearly as well as were the other employees.

With them my father was generous and tolerant. They received $2.50 an hour or $100.00 for their standard forty-hour week. And if Jerry or Fred helped to sell a new water softener to one of our customers, he was awarded a $20.00 commission. Whenever Jerry asked for a little time off to go fishing, my father promptly granted his request. And once Fred got two days off to take a trip to Chicago, and Dad didn't even dock his pay. If Jack and Kenny botched an installation job, my father would reprove them in a kindly tone and explain how they could have avoided the mistake. Once Kenny failed to tighten a packing nut on a valve, and the water leaked all over the customer's floor. Father sent over a man to clean up the mess and just told Kenny to be more careful next time. On another occasion Jack and Kenny dropped a softener down a customer's stairs, ruining the softener and damaging several steps. When they reported the incident to him with worried and anxious looks, Father calmed their fears and told them his insurance would cover the loss. If one of his men became involved in a dispute with a customer over a repair bill, it was his employee, and not the customer, who was always right.

But where I was concerned, my father was a close-fisted and harsh employer. My weekly paycheck was an unvarying fifty dollars, whether I worked forty hours or fifty-five, and the occasional salary raises the other employees enjoyed were never extended to me. I rarely received a commission on the sales I made; my father would either say that he couldn't afford to pay me any extra just then, or else that I wasn't really entitled to the money. If I wanted to take part in some school activity or go on a beach party with some friends, my father would not only refuse to give me time off, but he would often find extra jobs that would force me to work overtime. My mistakes called forth only anger from my father, never understanding. If anything went wrong with one of the company trucks while I was driving, he always assumed I had been driving like my "hot rod friends." If a customer complained about my service or her bill, my father bawled me out for giving him and his business a bad name. Once when I forgot to reduce the water pressure in the backwash machine and caused about twenty dollars worth of mineral to be washed down the drain, he spent half an afternoon sarcastically analyzing my mistake and showing me, in minute detail, how my carelessness had "cut into the profits for the year." Insurance never covered *my* accidents; their cost was deducted from my salary, "to teach me to be more careful."

I don't know whether my father was so harsh with me because he didn't want to appear to be favoring me; but I do know that his constant criticism convinced me that the role of boss's son is a role I don't want to play for a lifetime.

# Theme Topics

## Process

**1.** Assume that your reader is a high school graduate with little detailed knowledge of science or engineering. Describe the *process* underlying one of the following: the operation of a television set, jet engine, or computer; the life cycle of a butterfly or frog; the manufacture of paper, sugar, or other product that goes through numerous stages in the production process.

**2**. Write *instructions* that will help your readers perform a difficult task well. Choose one requiring a skill that you have acquired but that is not generally shared. Preferably the task to be performed should require loving care: the preparation of an unusual and difficult dish; the grafting of a bush or tree; the grooming of a horse.

**3**. Write a *job description* that would help a newcomer do a fairly complicated kind of work. Make it a step-by-step account that would take the novice through a typical hour (morning, evening) on the job.

**4**. For a foreign student with a good command of English but little experience with *American sports*, prepare a step-by-step account of a typical quarter in football or a typical inning in baseball. Make sure your reader will have a clear and graphic picture of how the game proceeds. Make sure to cover features that you have long taken for granted but that are essential to the outsider's understanding of the game.

## Thesis and Support

**5**. Write a paper in which you support as fully as you can *one limited assertion* in one of the following areas: learning how to drive, learning a foreign language, P.E. in American schools, women teachers and high school boys, student journalism, the school band or orchestra.

**6**. Of the following statements, select the one you most whole-heartedly *endorse or reject*. Make your affirmation or denial of it the thesis of your paper, and support it as fully as you can.

    **a**. High school administrators are too authoritarian in their exercise of discipline.

    **b**. Students seldom receive meaningful vocational guidance.

    **c**. Girls today receive little encouragement to become truly feminine.

    **d**. Popular songs repeat the same sentiments over and over.

   **e**. American society is intolerant of unconventional dress or appearance.

   **f**. The typical American male takes sports too seriously.

## Classification

**7**. Write a paper in which you divide *a group of people* into three or four major categories. For instance, you might classify children as leaders, followers, and loners; or teachers as authoritarian, chummy, and withdrawn. Make sure to establish categories that reflect your own experience and that you can fill in with graphic detail.

**8**. Have you found that one of the following labels covers an exceptionally diverse assortment of *different things*? Classify them, setting up several major categories and describing them as fully as you can. Choose one of the following: jobs, hobbies, comics, popular songs, television game shows, poems. Do not rely on conventional categories; set up divisions that reflect your own experience.

**9**. Have you ever watched closely the people present at a demonstration, riot, protest march, "confrontation with authority," or similar occasion? Can you *classify* them, setting up three or four major categories? For instance, is it possible to distinguish between "demonstrators" and mere "spectators"?

## Comparison and Contrast

**10**. Compare and contrast two fairly complicated pieces of *equipment or machinery* designed for basically the same job. For instance, compare and contrast an ordinary car motor with a diesel or jet engine. Or compare and contrast two related forms of *music or dance*: the polka and the waltz, dixieland and progressive jazz, gospel and blues.

**11**. Compare and contrast one of the following: current men's fashions and women's fashions, girls' talk and boys' talk, men's and women's ways of dealing with children. Limit your subject so as to make possible a unified, well-focused paper.

**12**. Compare and contrast *two styles of talk* used by the same person on different occasions: shop talk and sports talk, customer talk and "insider's" talk, talking with friends and talking with strangers, or the like. Base your paper on your *own* use of language or that of people to whom you listen frequently.

## Logical Argument

**13**. Write a paper in which you examine the pros and cons in order to lead the reader to a balanced conclusion. Choose a topic for which you can identify *two strong opposing views*. For instance, should the primary goal of higher education be the creation of an intellectual élite equipped to understand and deal with the complex issues of our time? Or should higher education aim at providing the best possible education for everyone?

**14**. We are often told that a whole generation of boys took as a model the Horatio Alger hero, who made his way to fame and fortune through self-reliance, honesty, and hard work. Do young people today find any such *culture hero* in what they read or watch? Can you identify a recurrent type that might serve as a model or ideal for large numbers of young people? Use the *inductive approach* in presenting your findings.

**15**. Argue as fully as you can your position on one of the following issues. Try to make your reader see as fully as you can the steps by which your argument proceeds.

> **a**. Should a newspaper represent the opinions of its journalists, its publishers, its advertisers, or its public?
>
> **b**. Should a college make it a policy to bar undesirable or controversial speakers?
>
> **c**. Should college professors be allowed to bring their own political views into the classroom?
>
> **d**. Is there ever any justification for censorship of the arts?

# 6

# MECHANICS AND SPELLING

## M 1 Manuscript Mechanics

*Submit neat and competently prepared copy.*

Whenever you hand in a theme or a report, the outward appearance of your manuscript is the first thing to strike your reader. A good first impression is likely to put him in a receptive mood. A bad first impression is likely to linger even after he discovers compensating virtues in the text.

### M 1a Penmanship and Typing

*All copy, whether handwritten or typed, should be neat and legible.* To produce legible handwritten copy, use composition paper of standard size, preferably ruled in *wide lines,* and a reliable pen. You may find that you don't write fast enough, especially when you are asked to write in class. Don't try to develop speed by substituting a smudge for letters like *a, e,* or *i;* by running together combinations like *mm* or *mn;* or by substituting a vague scrawl for endings like *-ing* and *-tion.* Instead, practice speed writing while at the same time forcing yourself to make every *a* and *e* as distinct as your grade school penmanship book required. Dot all your *i*'s and cross all your *t*'s. Distinguish clearly between capitals and lower-case letters.

Prune your writing of flourishes; avoid excessive slanting or excessive crowding. Unconventional handwriting is much more likely to annoy than it is to impress the reader.

To prepare typewritten copy, use unlined paper of standard size. Onionskin paper or semitransparent sheets are for carbon copies; use solid, *nontransparent* paper of good quality for the copy you turn in. Change your typewriter ribbon at reasonable intervals.

*Double-space* all material except block quotations and footnotes. Leave two spaces after a period or other end punctuation; use two hyphens—with no space on either side—to make a dash. Proofread all typewritten copy carefully for typographical errors and for errors in transcription.

## M 1b   Corrections

*Last-minute corrections are permissible on the final copy, provided they are few in number, look neat, and conform to standard practice.* (On papers written outside class, all major revisions are of course made on the rough draft.)

(1) Draw a line through words and phrases that you want to omit; *do not use parentheses or square brackets for this purpose.*

(2) To correct a word, draw a line through it and insert the corrected word in the space immediately above; avoid crossing out or inserting individual letters.

(3) To add a missing word, insert a caret ( ∧ ) and write the word immediately above.

## M 1c   Titles of Themes

*Titles of themes follow the general rules for the capitalization of words in titles of publications* (see SP 7b). Do *not* underline or put in quotation marks the title that you assign to one of your own themes. Use a question mark or an exclamation mark after it where appropriate, but do *not* use a period even if your title is a complete sentence:

Chivalry Is Dead
Is Chivalry Dead?
Chivalry Is Dead!

## M 1d  Spacing and Syllabication

*Observe conventional spacing and syllabication.* Whether your papers are handwritten or typed, leave adequate margins. An inch and a half on the left and at the top, and an inch on the right and at the bottom are about standard. Indent the first lines of paragraphs, about an inch in longhand or five spaces in typed copy. To make a last-minute change in the paragraphing of a paper, insert the symbol ¶ to indicate an additional paragraph break. Insert "*no* ¶" in the margin to indicate that an existing paragraph break should be ignored.

On the whole, a somewhat uneven right margin is preferable to the practice of dividing words at the end of every second or third line. Dictionaries generally use centered dots to indicate where a word may conventionally be divided (*com·pli·ment*). A few generally observed practices are worth remembering:

(1) The setting off of single letters saves little or no space and tends to confuse the reader. Do not divide words like *about*, *alone*, and *enough* or like *many* and *via*. Similarly, do not set off the ending -*ed* in words like *complained* or *renewed*.

(2) Hyphenated words become confusing when divided at any other point than at the original hyphen. Do not break up the *American* in "un-American" or the *sister* in "sister-in-law."

(3) Do not divide the last word on a page.

## M 1e  Italics

**Italics** (or slanted type) are indicated in the handwritten or typed manuscript by underlining.

(1) *Italics identify technical terms and words borrowed from foreign languages.* (See P 8e.)

(2) *Italics serve to emphasize or call special attention to part of a sentence:*

The judge told me to apologize *in person* to everyone who had sat down in the freshly painted pews.
The company is not liable for accidents caused by the negligence of employees or *by mechanical defects.*

Like other means of procuring emphasis, such italics lose their value if overused.

(3) *Italics set off the title of a publication from the text in which it is cited.* Italicize titles of periodicals and of works published as separate units. Use **quotation marks** to set off titles of articles, chapters, or poems that are merely a part of a complete publication:

> Kipling's "Recessional" can be found in *A Treasury of Verse.*
> "We Shall Overcome" has the ring of a gospel hymn rather than that of a *New Republic* editorial.

# M  2    Abbreviations and Numbers

*Avoid the overuse of abbreviations in ordinary expository prose.*

Abbreviations save time and space. Here as in other matters, however, formal written English discourages excessive short cuts.

## M  2a    Acceptable Abbreviations

*Some abbreviations are generally appropriate in expository writing:*

(1) Before or after names, the titles *Mr., Mrs., Dr., St. (Saint);* the abbreviations *Jr.* and *Sr.;* degrees like *M.D.* and *Ph.D.* (Mr. John J. Smith, Jr.; Dr. Alfred Joyce or Alfred Joyce, M.D.). Use *Prof.* only before the *full* name: Prof. James F. Jones.

(2) Before or after numerals, the abbreviations *No.,* A.D. and B.C., A.M. and P.M., and the symbol $ (in 1066 A.D.; at 5:30 A.M.; $275).

(3) Initials standing for the names of agencies, organizations, business firms, technical processes, chemical compounds, and the like, when the full name is awkward or unfamiliar: *AFL-CIO, FBI, PTA, TVA, UNESCO, DDT, FM radio.*

(4) Some common Latin abbreviations: *e.g.* (for example),

*etc.* (and so on), *i.e.* (that is), *viz.* (namely). However, the modern tendency is to prefer the corresponding English expressions.

## M 2b    Restricted Abbreviations

*Some abbreviations are appropriate in addresses, newspaper reports, technical reports, and other special contexts.* Most of these have to be written in full in ordinary expository prose:

(1) With a few exceptions, names of countries, states, streets, and the like, are spelled out in ordinary writing: *United States; Schenectady, New York; Union Street.* (Exceptions: *USSR; Washington, D.C.*)

(2) The ampersand ("&") and abbreviations like *Inc.* and *Bros.* occur in ordinary writing only in references to organizations that employ those abbreviations in their official titles: *Smith & Company, Inc.* Spell out % and ¢.

(3) In ordinary expository prose, *lb.* (pound), *oz.* (ounce), *ft.* (foot), and *in.* (inch) are usually spelled out. Some units of measurement are more unwieldy and are abbreviated, provided they are used with figures: *45 mph, 1500 rpm.*

NOTE: Check your dictionary whenever you are not sure of the use of capitals and periods with an abbreviation. Some dictionaries include common abbreviations in the main listing; others list them in a special appendix.

## M 2c    Numbers

*In ordinary expository prose, the use of figures is to some extent restricted.* They are generally appropriate in references to the day of the month (*May 13*), the year (*1917*), street numbers (*1014 Union Avenue*), and page numbers (*Chapter 7, page 18*). For other uses of numbers, the following conventions are widely observed:

(1) Numbers from one to ten, and *round numbers* requiring no more than two words, are usually spelled out: *three dollars a seat, five hundred years later, ten thousand copies.*

(2) Figures are used for *exact sums, technical measurements,*

*decimals, and percentages,* as well as for references to time using A.M. or P.M.: *$7.22; 500,673 inhabitants; 57 per cent; 2:30 P.M.*

(3) Figures are avoided at the beginning of a sentence: "Fifteen out of 28 replied . . ." or "When questioned, 15 out of 28 replied . . ." Except in special situations like this one, changes from figures to words (and vice versa) in a series of numbers are generally avoided.

(4) When spelled out, *compound numbers* from 21 to 99 are hyphenated: *twenty-five, one hundred and forty-six.*

## Exercise

Rewrite the following passage, using abbreviations and numerals in accordance with standard practice:

> Mister Geo. Brown had resided at Eighteen N. Washington St. since Feb. nineteen-hundred and forty-four. Though he weighed only one hundred and twenty-six lbs. and measured little more than 5 ft., he was an ardent devotee of the rugged life. He did his exercises every a. m. and refused to send for the Dr. when he had a cold. 3 yrs. after he moved here from Chicago, Ill., the Boy Scouts of America made him an honorary member, & he soon became known in scout circles for the many $ he contributed to the Boy Scout movement. One Sat. afternoon B. forgot to spell out the amount on a check for one-hundred and twenty-five dollars intended for a bldg. drive and payable to the B. S. of A. The treasurer, Bernard Simpson of Arlington, Va., wrote in 2 additional figures, spelled out the changed amount, and left the U. S. after withdrawing B.'s life savings of twelve-thousand five-hundred and fifty dollars from the local bank. "Ah," said Geo. when he found 2$ and 36 cts. left in his account, "if I had only spelled out the No.'s and abbrev.!"

## SP 1 Spelling Habits

*Correct spelling is the result of good spelling habits, estab-lished by study and drill over the years.*

The average high school graduate spells correctly most of the words he uses. According to recent studies, most of the trouble that college students have with spelling is caused by perhaps fewer than 250 words out of the 5,000 or 10,000 they are likely to use. The most common troublemakers are everyday words like *believe* or *definite*. The spelling of such a word may look right not because you have seen it in this particular word but because you have seen it in another word that is confusingly similar. Thus, you may spell the main syllable in *believe* like the main syllable in *receive*. You may spell the ending in *definite* like the ending in *ultimate*. To spell such a word correctly, you have to memorize it letter by letter, while at the same time seeing each letter as a part of the whole.

Merely looking up misspelled words has little long-range effect. The following procedure has a good chance of producing favorable results:

(1) *Find out which words you tend to misspell.* Make a list of all spelling errors pointed out to you in your themes, quizzes, and exams. Work your way through a list of common spelling demons (such as the one printed under SP 4). Copy out those that you have found troublesome in your own writing.

(2) *Put in twenty minutes three times a week over a fairly long period of time.* Unless you work on your spelling regularly, you will make little progress. You cannot unlearn in two or three hours the spelling habits that you developed over many years.

(3) *Work out a definite routine and stick to it.* At each sitting, take up a group of perhaps ten or twenty spelling words. If you are a "visualizer," place your spelling words before you in clear, legible handwriting. Try putting them on a set of small note cards that you can carry around with you. Run your eyes over each word until you can see both the individual letters and the whole word at the same time. Circle the letters that cause the most trouble. If you learn primarily by ear, read each word aloud. Then spell each letter individually: *Receive*—R-E-C-E-I-V-E. If you learn best when you can bring your nerves and muscles into play, try writing each word in large letters. Trace it over several times. Combine or alternate the three methods in the manner that seems to yield the best results.

(4) *Make use of memory devices like the following:*

MAC got ACquainted.

ALL RIGHT means ALL is RIGHT.

There's an INNING in begINNING.

Don't beLIEve LIEs.

There's a CRITIC in CRITICism.

There's IRON in the envIRONment.

Men who GOVERN are a GOVERNment.

PERhaps he will give a PERfect PERformance.

There's a COG in reCOGnition.

There's a VILLA in VILLAin.

(5) *Copy difficult new terms and names that you encounter in your reading for various courses.* Study and memorize them. If you are a science major, master words like *enzyme, anesthesia, protein,* or *arteriosclerosis.* If you are taking a literature course, focus on the exact spelling of names like *Oedipus, Xanthippe,* or *Omar Khayyam.*

# SP 2    Spelling Problems

*Learn to identify and master recurrent spelling problems.*

Some words can be conveniently grouped together because they share common characteristics. Others are best studied together because they need to be carefully distinguished from each other.

## SP 2a    Spelling and Pronunciation

*Some words become spelling problems because the gap between spelling and pronunciation is unusually wide.*

(1) Some words are difficult to spell because of *silent*

*consonants.* Be sure to insert the silent consonants in "condem*n*," "de*b*t," "dou*b*t," "forei*g*n," "mor*t*gage," and "sovereig*n*."

(2) Frequent causes of confusion are *vowels occurring in unstressed positions. A, e,* and *i* become indistinguishable in the endings *-ate* and *-ite, -able* and *-ible, -ance* and *-ence, -ant* and *-ent.* You can sometimes learn to choose the right ending by associating the word with a closely related one: *definite* (fin*i*sh, defin*i*tion); *separate* (separ*a*tion); *ultimate* (ultim*a*tum); *indispensable* (dispens*a*ry). For many other words no such crutches are available. Watch out for the following:

> accept*able,* accept*ance,* advis*able,* attend*ance,* attend*ant,* brilli*ant,* perform*ance*

> consist*ent,* excell*ence,* excell*ent,* exist*ence,* experi*ence,* independ*ent,* persist*ent,* tend*ency*

> irresist*ible,* plaus*ible,* poss*ible,* suscept*ible*

(3) Some words are hard to spell because of *sounds not pronounced* in much nonstandard or informal speech:

> accident*a*lly, can*d*idate, Feb*r*uary, gover*n*ment, lib*r*ary, prob-*ab*ly, quan*t*ity

(4) In unstressed positions, words like *have, can,* or *will* tend to appear in shortened forms. Do not substitute *of* for *have* in combinations like *could have been, might have been, should have seen.*

## SP 2b    Variant Forms

*Some words are confusing because they appear in a variety of forms.* Especially confusing are different spellings in variant forms of the *same root word:* "ti*ll*" but "unti*l*," "fo*u*r" and "fo*u*rteen" but "fo*r*ty," "fo*r*ward" but "fo*r*emost," "ni*ne*" and "ni*ne*ty" but "ni*n*th."

(1) Watch out for spelling differences in pairs of words representing different parts of speech:

absor*b*–absor*p*tion, advi*s*e (v.)–advi*c*e (n.), conscien*ce*–conscien*t*ious, court*eous*–court*esy*, curi*ous*–curi*o*sity, dissen*t*–dissen*s*ion, gener*ous*–gener*o*sity, geni*us*–ingeni*ous*, proc*eed*–proc*e*dure, pron*ou*nce–pron*u*nciation, ren*ou*nce–ren*u*nciation

(2) Sometimes a confusing change in spelling accompanies a *change in the grammatical form* of the same word. For instance, you "ch*oo*se" and "l*ea*d" in the present, but you "ch*o*se" and "l*e*d" in the past. Some plural forms cause spelling difficulties: one *man* but several *men*, one *woman* but several *women*. Remember these especially:

| Singular: | hero | Negro | potato | tomato | wife |
| --- | --- | --- | --- | --- | --- |
| Plural: | hero*es* | Negro*es* | potato*es* | tomato*es* | wi*ves* |
| Singular: | freshman | postman | life | veto | calf |
| Plural: | freshm*en* | postm*en* | li*ves* | veto*es* | cal*ves* |

(3) Be sure to add the *-ed* for *past tense* or *past participle* in words like the following:

He us*ed* to come.
She was suppos*ed* to write.
They were prejudic*ed* (bias*ed*).

NOTE: Your dictionary lists the correct spelling of plural forms that are difficult or unusual. Sometimes it lists two acceptable forms: *buffalos* or *buffaloes*, *scarfs* or *scarves*.

## SP 2c   Confusing Words

*Some words need attention because they sound similar but differ in spelling or in meaning.* Here is partial list of these:

| Accept: | to *acc*ept a bribe; to find something *acc*eptable; to make an *acc*eptance speech |
| --- | --- |
| Except: | everyone *ex*cept Judy; to make an *ex*ception; to *ex*cept (exempt, exclude) present company |

| | |
|---|---|
| **Adopt:** | to ado*p*t a proposal (in its present form); the ado*p*tion racket |
| **Adapt:** | to ada*p*t it to our needs (to make it more suitable); an ada*p*table worker; an ada*p*tation from a novel |
| **Capital:** | unused capit*a*l; modern capit*a*lism; the capit*a*l of France; capit*a*l letters |
| **Capitol:** | the cupola of the Capit*o*l; remodeling the façade of the Capit*o*l |
| **Censor:** | to cens*o*r a reporter's dispatch; to object to cens*o*rship |
| **Censure:** | to cens*u*re (blame, condemn) someone for his behavior; a vote of censure |
| **Cite:** | *c*ited for bravery; to *c*ite many different authorities; a *c*itation for reckless driving |
| **Site:** | the *s*ite of the new high school (where it is *s*ituated or located) |
| **Consul:** | the American c*o*nsul in Berlin; the French c*o*nsulate in New York |
| **Council:** | the members of the city coun*c*il; Coun*c*ilor Brown |
| **Counsel:** | the coun*s*eling staff of the college; camp coun*s*elors |
| **Desert:** | he lost his way in the de*s*ert; he de*s*erted his family; he got his just de*s*erts |
| **Dessert:** | the dinner did not include a de*ss*ert |
| **Effect:** | to *e*ffect (produce, bring about) a change; immediate *e*ffects; an *e*ffective speech |
| **Affect:** | it *a*ffected (had an influence on) his grade; he spoke with an *a*ffected (artificial) British accent |
| **Loose:** | lo*o*se and fast; lo*o*sen your grip |
| **Lose:** | win or l*o*se; a bad l*o*ser |
| **Personal:** | a perso*n*al appeal; speak to him perso*n*ally |
| **Personnel:** | a perso*nn*el bureau; hire additional perso*nn*el |
| **Presents:** | visitors bearing presen*t*s |
| **Presence:** | your presen*c*e is requested; presen*c*e of mind |
| **Principal:** | his princip*al* (main) argument; the princip*al* of the school |
| **Principle:** | princip*les* (rules, standards) of conduct; the princip*les* of economics |
| **Quiet:** | be qui*e*t; a qui*e*t neighborhood |
| **Quite:** | qu*ite* so; not qu*ite* |

| | |
|---|---|
| **Right:** | *right* and wrong; *right* and left; all *right* |
| **Rite:** | savage *rites* (ceremonies); the *rites* of spring |
| **-wright:** | a play*wright;* a wheel*wright* (a man who wrought, or made, wheels and carriages) |
| **Than:** | bigger th*a*n life; more trouble th*a*n it is worth |
| **Then:** | now and th*e*n; until th*e*n |
| **There:** | here and th*ere*; th*ere* you are; no one was th*ere* |
| **Their:** | they lost th*eir* appetite; mental ills and th*eir* cure |
| **To:** | go *to* bed; cut *to* pieces; easy *to* do; hard *to* deny |
| **Too:** | *too* good to be true; bring your children, *too* |
| **Two:** | *two* and *two* makes four |
| **Whether:** | *whe*ther good or bad |
| **Weather:** | bad *wea*ther; to *wea*ther the storm |

# Exercises

**A**. In available dictionaries, check the status of simplified spellings like trave*l*ed, thr*u*, an*e*sthetic, th*o*, catal*o*g, or any others you have encountered.

**B**. Insert the missing letter in each of the following words: accept____nce, attend____nce, brilli____nt, consist____ncy, defin____te, excell____nt, exist____nce, experi____nce, independ____nt, indispens____ble, occurr____nce, irresist____ble, perform____nce, persist____nt, separ____te, tend____ncy.

**C**. Look up the plural of *cargo, Eskimo, hoof, mosquito, motto, piano, solo, soprano, wharf, zero.*

**D**. Select the appropriate word in each of the numbered pairs:

**1**. After Jean-Pierre *(1)accepted/(2)excepted* our invitation to spend a month in the nation's *(3)capital/(4)Capitol,* he applied to the American *(5)consul/(6)counsel* for a visa.   **2**. The *(7)presence/(8)presents* of federal troops prevented further *(9)incidence/(10)incidents.*   **3**. The city's émployees presented the members of the city *(11)council/(12)counsel* with a declaration of *(13)rights/(14)rites* and *(15)principals/(16)principles.*   **4**. My moral *(17)principals/(18)principles* do not permit a *(19)personal/(20)personnel* appearance at a play depicting *(21)loose/(22)lose* behavior.   **5**. Though he can *(23)cite/(24)site* no precedent, the city *(25)council/(26)counsel* advises us to *(27)adapt/(28)adopt* a motion providing for the *(29)censoring/(30)censuring* of foreign films. **6**. After our *(31)censor/(32)censure* of conditions at the plant, the owner *(33)affected/(34)effected* changes *(35) affecting/(36)effecting* most of his *(37)personal/(38)personnel*. **7**. The teachers wanted to wait on the steps rather *(39)than/(40)then* enter the *(41)capital/(42)Capitol*, for all *(43)accept/(44)except* the *(45)principal/(46)principle* had already been *(47)their/(48)there*.

**E**. Explain the difference in meaning between the words in each of the following pairs: *aid–aide, causal–casual, complimentary–complementary, costume–custom, emigrant–immigrant, eminent–imminent, isle–aisle, key–quay, meet–mete, rational–rationale, stationary–stationery, straight–strait*.

# SP 3    Spelling Rules

*Spelling rules provide a key to a group of words that you would otherwise have to study individually.*

The purpose of spelling rules is *not* to make English spelling appear more regular than it is but to help you memorize words that follow a common pattern.

## SP 3a    *i* Before e

*Identical sounds are often spelled differently in different words.* For instance, *ie* and *ei* often stand for the same sound. If you sort out the words in question, you get the following:

achieve, believe, chief, grief, niece, piece (of pie), relieve
ceiling, conceited, conceive, perceive, receive, receipt

In the second group of words, the *ei* is regularly preceded by *c*. In other words, it is *i* before *e* except after *c*. About half a dozen words do not fit into this pattern:

either, leisure, neither, seize, weird
financier, species

## SP 3b Doubled Consonant

*In many words a single final consonant is doubled before an ending* (or **suffix**) *that begins with a vowel: -ed, -er, -est, -ing.* Doubling occurs under the following conditions:

(1) The vowel preceding the final consonant *must be a single vowel.* It cannot be a "long" or double vowel (**diphthong**) indicated in writing by combinations like *oa, ea, ee,* and *ou* or by a silent final *e* (k*ite,* h*ope,* h*ate*). Note the differences in pronunciation and in spelling in the following pairs:

| | |
|---|---|
| bar–barred | bare–bared |
| bat–batted | boat–boating |
| hop–hopping | hope–hoping |
| plan–planned | plane–planed |
| red–redder | read–reading |
| scrap–scrapped | scrape–scraped |
| slip–slipped | sleep–sleeping |
| stop–stopped | stoop–stooped |

(2) In words of more than one syllable, the last syllable before the suffix *must be the one stressed in pronunciation.* Sometimes a shift in stress will be reflected in the spelling of different forms of the same word. Compare the following groups:

| | |
|---|---|
| ad**mit**, ad**mit**ted, ad**mit**tance | **ed**it, **ed**ited, **ed**iting |
| for**get**, for**get**ting, for**get**table | **ben**efit, **ben**efited |
| be**gin**, be**gin**ning, be**gin**ner | **hard**en, **hard**ened |
| over**lap**, over**lapp**ing | de**vel**op, de**vel**oping |
| re**gret**, re**gret**ted, re**gret**table | pro**hib**it, pro**hib**ited, pro**hib**itive |
| pre**fer**, pre**ferr**ed, pre**ferr**ing | **pref**erence, **pref**erable |
| re**fer**, re**ferr**ed, re**ferr**ing | **ref**erence |

NOTE: There is doubling after the single vowel *i* in *equip–equipped* (the *u* does not combine with *i* but is part of the consonant *qu*); there is no doubling of the final *x* in *mix–mixed* (*x* is really a double consonant: *ks*).

## SP 3c   *y* as a Vowel

*Y* is sometimes used *as a consonant* (*y*ear, *y*outh), some-times *as a vowel* (m*y*, dr*y*; hurr*y*, stud*y*). As a single final vowel, it changes to *ie* before *s*, to *i* before all other endings except *-ing*.

family–families, fly–flies, study–studies, try–tries, quantity–quantities

beauty–beautiful, bury–burial, busy–business, copy–copied, dry–drier, lively–livelihood, noisy–noisily

burying, copying, studying, trying, worrying

When it follows another vowel, *y* is usually preserved: *delays, joys, played, valleys.* A few common exceptions are *day–daily, gay–gaily, lay–laid, pay–paid, say–said.*

## SP 3d   Final e

*In some words a silent final vowel is omitted before an ending starting with a vowel.*

(1) A silent *e* at the end of a word is dropped before an ending that begins with a vowel; it is preserved before an ending that begins with a consonant:

| | | |
|---|---|---|
| bore | boring | boredom |
| hate | hating | hateful |
| like | liking, likable | likely |
| love | loving, lovable | lovely |

The following words do *not* fit into this pattern: *argue–argument, due–duly, dye–dyeing* (as against *die–dying*), *mile–mileage, true–truly, whole–wholly.*

(2) A final *e* may signal the difference in pronunciation between the final consonants in *rag* and *rage* or in *aspic* and *notice.* Such a final *e* is preserved not only before a consonant but also before *a* or *o:*

advantage–advantageous, change–changeable, courage–courageous, outrage–outrageous

notice–noticeable, peace–peaceable

# Exercises

**A**. Insert *ei* or *ie:* ach__vement, bel__ver, dec__tful, f__ld, inconc__vable, misch__f, perc__ve, rec__ving, rel__f, s__ze, w__rd, y__ld.

**B**. Select the appropriate word in each of the numbered pairs: *(1)bared/(2)barred* from office; his *(3)bating/(4)batting* average; *(5)caned/(6)canned* meat; *(7)biding/(8)bidding* their time; *(9)hoping/(10)hopping* for the best; *(11)pined/(12)pinned* to the mat; a *(13)well-planed/(14)well-planned* outing; *(15)robed/(16)robbed* in white; a boy *(17)spiting/(18)spitting* his parents; *(19)taped/(20)tapped* him on the shoulder.

**C**. Combine the following words with the suggested endings: accompany__ed, advantage__ous, argue__ing, benefit__ed, carry__s, come__ing, confide__ing, differ__ing, excite__able, friendly__ness, lively__hood, occur__ing, prefer__ed, remit__ance, sad__er, satisfy__ed, shine__ing, sole__ly, study__ing, tragedy__s, try__s, use__ing, valley__s, whole__ly, write__ing.

## SP 4 Words Often Misspelled

*Studies of the words most frequently misspelled in student writing have resulted in substantial agreement on words most likely to cause spelling difficulties.*

In addition to words listed in SP 1–3, the following list will repay careful study:

| | | | |
|---|---|---|---|
| absence | accomplish | acquaintance | admit |
| abundance | accumulate | acquire | adolescence |
| accessible | accurately | acquitted | advantageous |
| accidentally | accuses | across | advertisement |
| acclaim | accustom | actuality | afraid |
| accommodate | achievement | address | against |
| accompanied | acknowledgment | adequate | aggravate |

aggressive
alleviate
allotted
allowed
all right
already
altar
altogether
always
amateur
among
amount
analysis
analyze
annual
anticipate
anxiety
apologize
apology
apparatus
apparent
appearance
applies
applying
appreciate
approach
appropriate
approximately
area
argue
arguing
argument
arising
arrangement
article
artistically
ascend
assent
athlete
athletic
attendance
audience
authority
balance

basically
basis
beauty
becoming
before
beginning
belief
believe
beneficial
benefited
boundaries
breath
brilliant
Britain
buses
business
calendar
candidate
career
careless
carrying
category
ceiling
cemetery
challenge
changeable
character
characteristic
chief
choose
chose
clothes
coarse
column
comfortable
comfortably
coming
commission
committed
committee
companies
competition
competitive
completely

comprehension
conceivable
conceive
concentrate
condemn
confident
confidential
conscience
conscientious
conscious
considerably
consistent
continually
continuous
control
controlled
convenience
convenient
coolly
courageous
course
courteous
criticism
criticize
cruelty
curiosity
curriculum
dealt
deceit
deceive
decision
definite
definitely
definition
dependent
describe
description
desirability
desirable
despair
desperate
destruction
devastate
develop

development
device
difference
different
difficult
dilemma
dining
disappear
disappearance
disappoint
disastrous
discipline
disease
disgusted
dissatisfaction
dissatisfied
doesn't
dominant
due
during
ecstasy
efficiency
efficient
eighth
eliminate
embarrass
embarrassment
eminent
emphasize
endeavor
enforce
enough
entertain
environment
equipped
erroneous
especially
etc.
exaggerate
excellent
exceptionally
exercise
exhaust
exhilarate

| | | | |
|---|---|---|---|
| existence | indefinite | ninety | privilege |
| experience | independent | noticeable | probably |
| explanation | indispensable | obstacle | procedure |
| extraordinary | inevitable | occasion | proceed |
| extremely | influence | occasionally | professor |
| familiar | ingenious | occurred | prominent |
| families | intellectual | occurrence | propaganda |
| fascinate | intelligence | omit | prophecy |
| finally | interest | operate | psychology |
| financial | interpret | opinion | pursue |
| financier | interrupt | opponent | quantity |
| foreign | involve | opportunity | really |
| forward | irrelevant | optimism | recommend |
| friend | irresistible | original | regard |
| fulfill | itself | paid | relief |
| fundamentally | jealous | parallel | relieve |
| further | knowledge | paralysis | religion |
| gaiety | laboratory | paralyze | repetition |
| generally | laid | particularly | representative |
| genius | leisure | passed | resource |
| government | likelihood | past | response |
| governor | literature | peace | rhythm |
| grammar | livelihood | peculiar | ridiculous |
| guaranteed | loneliness | perceive | roommate |
| guidance | losing | perform | safety |
| happily | magnificence | performance | satisfactorily |
| happiness | maintain | permanent | schedule |
| height | maintenance | persistent | seize |
| heroes | manageable | persuade | sense |
| heroine | manufacturer | pertain | separate |
| hindrance | marriage | phase | sergeant |
| hopeful | mathematics | phenomenon | shining |
| huge | meant | philosophy | significance |
| humorous | medieval | physical | similar |
| hundred | merely | piece | sincerely |
| hurriedly | mileage | pleasant | sophomore |
| hypocrisy | miniature | possess | speech |
| hypocrite | minute | possession | sponsor |
| ignorant | mischievous | possible | strength |
| imaginary | muscle | practical | stretch |
| imagination | mysterious | precede | strictly |
| immediately | naïve | prejudice | studying |
| immensely | necessarily | prepare | subtle |
| incidentally | necessary | prevalent | succeed |

| successful | therefore | tries | various |
| summarize | thorough | undoubtedly | vengeance |
| surprise | together | unnecessary | villain |
| temperament | tragedy | useful | weird |
| tendency | transferred | using | writing |

## SP  5    The Apostrophe

*The **apostrophe** has no exact equivalent in speech and is therefore easily omitted or misplaced.*

### SP  5a    Contractions

*Use the apostrophe in contractions to indicate that one or more letters have been omitted (I'll go now; I'm too tired; we're almost ready).* It appears most frequently in contractions using a shortened form of *not: haven't, can't, wouldn't, won't, isn't.* Take care not to misspell *doesn't,* which is a shortened form of "*does* not."

A few contractions are easily confused with words of different spelling and different meaning. *It's,* meaning "it is," differs from *its,* meaning "of it" or "belonging to it." *Who's,* meaning "who is," differs from *whose,* which means "of whom" or "of which." *They're* means "they are" and differs from both *there* and *their:*

> *It's* time to give the cat *its* milk.
> *Who's* to say *whose* fault it is?
> If *their* lights are turned off, *they're* not *there.*

NOTE: Contractions are characteristic of informal conversation. Avoid them in formal reports, research papers, and letters of application. Some readers approve of contractions only in distinctly informal writing.

### SP  5b    Possessives

*Use the apostrophe for the possessive of nouns.* A person closely associated with something named by another noun often appears in the **possessive**, usually produced by adding an apostrophe plus -*s* to the plain form of a noun: *my sister's purse, Mr. Smith's garage, the student's notebook.* Often the possessive indicates where something belongs, or who owns an article. It also, however, indicates many other relationships: *the boy's friends, the firemen's ball, a man's world, the child's innocence, the children's capers, the general's dismissal.* Possessives occur in many familiar expressions: *an hour's drive, the day's news, a moment's notice, a dollar's worth, tonight's paper.*

Note the following variations:

(1) Sometimes the plain form of a noun already ends in -*s*. The possessive then adds an apostrophe *only*. This applies especially to plural forms. Compare the following pairs:

the Turk's wives (one Turk)     the Turks' wives (several Turks)

a week's pay     two weeks' pay

Names of individuals do not always follow this rule. The writer *may* add a second -*s*, depending on whether he would expect an extra syllable in pronunciation: *Mr. Jones' car– Mr. Jones's car; Dolores' hair–Dolores's hair; Charles Dickens' first novel–Charles Dickens's first novel.*

(2) The apostrophe is *not* used in the *possessive forms of personal pronouns.* No apostrophe appears in *his, hers, its, ours, yours,* or *theirs.* It does appear, however, in the possessive forms of such indefinite pronouns as *one* (one's friends), *everyone* (to everyone's surprise), *someone* (at someone's suggestion; also, at someone else's house).

## SP 5c    Plurals of Letters and Symbols

*The apostrophe is often used to separate the plural -s from the name of a letter or a symbol or from a word named as a word* (two large 7's; if's and but's):

Those great big beautiful A's so avidly sought, those little miserly C's so often found, were meant for another time and another student

body.—Oscar Handlin, "Are the Colleges Killing Education?"
*Atlantic*

## Exercise

Check for appropriate use of the apostrophe in choosing between
the spellings in each of the following pairs.

**1.** When the mother and the father respect each *(1)other's/(2)
others'* opinions, children learn to live harmoniously by following their *(3)elders/(4)elders'* example.    **2.** Since the *(5)chair-
mans/(6)chairman's* resignation, all the *(7)members/(8)member's*
have been speculating about *(9)whose/(10)who's* going to succeed him.    **3.** *(11)Mrs. Beattys/(12)Mrs. Beatty's* husband still
sends her *(13)flowers/(14)flower's* on *(15)Valentines/(16)Valen-
tine's* Day.    **4.** We were all overjoyed when my *(17)sister's/
(18)sisters'* baby took *(19)its/(20)it's* first faltering steps.    **5.** A
*(21)student's/(22)students'* lack of interest is not always the *(23)
teachers/(24)teacher's* fault.    **6.** *(25)Its/(26)It's* the *(27)parents/
(28)parents'* responsibility to provide for their *(29)children's/
(30)childrens'* religious education.    **7.** *(31)Lets/(32)Let's* borrow
*(33)someones/(34)someone's* car and go for an *(35)hour's/(36)
hours'* drive.    **8.** *(37)Charles/(38)Charles's* father murmured
audibly that the assembled *(39)relatives/(40)relative's* had con-
sumed at least ten *(41)dollars/(42)dollars'* worth of food.

## SP 6    The Hyphen

*Use of the **hyphen** is the least uniform and the least stable
feature of English spelling.*

In doubtful cases, the most recent edition of a reputable
dictionary is the best guide.

### SP 6a    Compound Words

*Treatment varies for words habitually used together as a single
expression.* Some compound words are clearly distinguished
from ordinary combinations by differences in both writing
and pronunciation: *black bird* (black BIRD) but *blackbird*
(BLACKbird), *dark room* (dark ROOM) but *darkroom* (DARK-
room). Such unmistakable compounds are *bellboy, bridesmaid,*

*headache, highway, newsstand, summertime,* and *stepmother.* In many similar compounds, however, the parts are conventionally kept separate: *bus boy, commander in chief, goose flesh, high school, labor union, second cousin.* Still other compound words conventionally require a hyphen: *able-bodied, bull's-eye, cave-in, great-grandfather, merry-go-round, mother-in-law.*

NOTE: Be sure to spell *today, tomorrow, nevertheless,* and *nowadays* as single words. Be sure *not* to spell as single words *all right, a lot* (a lot of time), *be able,* and *no one.*

## SP  6b    Prefixes

*Many hyphenated compounds consist of a prefix and the word it precedes.*

(1) *All-, ex-* (in the sense of "former"), *quasi-, self-,* and sometimes *co-* require a hyphen: *all-knowing, ex-husband, quasi-judicial, self-contained, co-author.*

(2) All prefixes require a hyphen before words beginning with a capital letter: *all-American, anti-American, pro-American, un-American.*

(3) Often a hyphen prevents the meeting of two identical vowels: *anti-intellectual, semi-independent.*

NOTE: Sometimes a hyphen distinguishes an unfamiliar use of a prefix from a familiar one: *recover–re-cover* (make a new cover), *recreation–re-creation* (creating again or anew).

## SP  6c    Group Modifiers

*Several words may temporarily combine as a modifier preceding a noun.* They are then usually joined by hyphens: *a flying-saucer hat, a middle-of-the-road policy, a question-and-answer period, a step-by-step account, a devil-may-care attitude.* No hyphens are used when the same combinations serve some other function in a sentence: *tend toward the middle of the road; explain a process step by step.*

NOTE: No hyphen is used when a modifier preceding a noun is in turn modified by an adverb ending in *-ly: a fast-*

*rising executive, a well-balanced account;* but *a rapidly growing city, a carefully documented study.*

# Exercise

Insert hyphens or combine elements where appropriate.

> **1**. The prospective son in law listened self consciously to Mother's praise of the bride to be.　**2**. Those who denounced the parking privileges for out of town students were obviously not from out of town.　**3**. Both pro British and anti British Arabs were united in their contempt for ex king Farouk.　**4**. The anti intellectual local news paper had called our candidate an absent minded ex professor and a tool of the labor unions; never the less he was elected.　**5**. Now a days few self respecting candidates conduct old fashioned campaigns taking them into out of the way places.　**6**. Mr. Andrews and his co author have written a well documented account of the un democratic procedures followed by quasi judicial agencies.

# SP 7　Capitals

*Although practice varies on minor points, certain conventions of capitalization are widely observed.*

## SP 7a　Proper Names

　　*Proper names are always capitalized.* Capitalize the names of persons, places, regions, historical periods, ships, days of the week, months (but not seasons), organizations, religions: *James, Brazil, the Middle Ages, S.S. Independence, Sunday, February, Buddhism.* Capitalize words derived from proper names: *English grammar, French pastry, German beer, Parisian fashions, Christian charity, Marxist ideas.*

　　Note the following difficulties:

　　(1) In some words the proper name involved has been lost sight of, and a lower-case letter is used: *guinea pig, india rubber, pasteurized milk.*

(2) The same word may serve as a general term but also as a proper name for one person, institution, or place:

| | |
|---|---|
| democratic (many institutions) | Democratic (name of the party) |
| orthodox (many attitudes) | Orthodox (name of the church) |
| history (general subject) | History 31 (specific course) |
| west (general direction) | Middle West (specific area) |
| my mother (common relationship) | Mother (name of the person) |

(3) The general term for a title, a family relationship, an institution, or a geographical feature is capitalized when it combines with a proper name: *Major Brown, Aunt Augusta, Sergeant Barnacle, Campbell High School, Indiana University, Tennessee Valley Authority, Medora Heights, Lake Erie.* Some titles refer to only one person and can take the place of the person's name: *the Pope, the Queen* (of England), *the President* (of the United States).

## SP 7b    Titles of Publications

*A capital letter marks the first and all major words in the title of a book, other publication, or work of art.* The only words not counting as major are articles (*a, an,* and *the*), prepositions (*at, in, on, of, from, with*), and connectives (*and, but, if, when*). Prepositions and connectives are usually capitalized when they have five or more letters. Observe these conventions in writing the titles of a theme:

Life in a Dormitory
Get Rich Through Hypnosis
New Facts About the Common Cold
How to Become Extinct

The same conventions apply to titles of publications cited in a sentence:

Several generations of Americans read *Sink or Swim, Phil the Fiddler, Mark the Match Boy,* and *From Canal Boy to President,* records of achievement which rewarded personal goodness with happiness and goods.—Saul Bellow, "The Writer as Moralist," *Atlantic*

## Exercise

Revise the following passage to make it conform to the conventions governing the use of capitals.

Boris was a young american pianist. His father came from a calvinistic new england family. His mother, who had been born in the caucasus, spoke french, german, and russian, as well as english and her native armenian. She had studied classical music in european cities like paris and vienna. Before he was ten, boris could play everything from viennese waltzes to presbyterian hymns. In high school he read books like *the life of beethoven, all about wagner,* and *brahms through the eyes of a friend.* At east bloomingdale city college, he took a course in music appreciation as well as a course entitled "the great composers." After he graduated, he spent the summer in california and the winter giving concerts in the middle west.

Fame came to boris in march one year when, armed with his bible, he set off for a contest in a country dominated by marxist ideology but susceptible to capitalist music. Even orthodox socialists cheered wildly when boris was awarded the first prize. Back home, the united states senate promptly commended boris's achievement as a national triumph and a vindication of democratic principles. Only one democratic and two republican senators abstained. The national broadcasting company paid the back rent on boris's piano after he performed in a sunday morning concert given by the new york philharmonic orchestra and broadcast from carnegie hall. In june, *lifemanship* magazine had an article on boris in its section entitled "speaking of pianists." The article said: "So catholic is the appeal of music that it reconciles, for a time, yankees and southerners, protestants and catholics, russians and americans."

## PUNCTUATION MARKS

### Reference Chart

**COMMA**

| | |
|---|---|
| before coordinating connectives and, but, for, nor | P 3c |
| with nonrestrictive adverbial clauses | P 4b |
| after introductory adverbial clauses | P 4c |
| with nonrestrictive modifiers (other than adverbial clauses) | P 5b–c |
| after introductory modifiers (other than adverbial clauses) | P 5c |
| with adverbial connectives | P 3b |
| with *especially, namely, for example*, etc. | P 2b |
| with *after all, of course,* and other sentence modifiers | P 5c |
| between items in a series | P 6a |
| in a series of parallel clauses | P 3d |
| between coordinate adjectives | P 6b |
| with dates and addresses, etc. | P 6c |
| with direct address and other parenthetic elements | P 7c |
| between repeated or contrasted elements | P 6d |
| with quotations | P 8a–b, d |

**SEMICOLON**

| | |
|---|---|
| between closely related sentences | P 3a |
| before adverbial connectives | P 3b |
| before coordinating connectives between clauses containing commas | P 3c |
| in a series with items containing commas | P 6a |

**COLON**

| | |
|---|---|
| to introduce a list or explanation | P 2b |
| to introduce a formal quotation | P 8a |
| between closely related sentences | P 3a |

**PERIOD**

| | |
|---|---|
| at end of sentence | P 1c, P 2 |
| ellipsis | P 8c |
| with abbreviations | M 2 |

**DASH**

| | |
|---|---|
| break in thought | P 2a, P 7a |
| before summary at end of sentence | P 7a |

**QUOTATION MARKS**

| | |
|---|---|
| with quotations | P 8a–d |
| quotation within quotation | P 8a |
| with terminal marks | P 8b |
| with slang or technical terms | P 8e |
| to set off titles | M 1e |

| | |
|---|---|
| **EXCLAMATION MARK** | P 1a |
| **QUESTION MARK** | P 1b |
| **PARENTHESES** | P 7b |

254

# 7

# PUNCTUATION

When we speak, we do more than put the right words together in the right order. We pause at the right times, raise our voices for emphasis. To the structures and forms we study in the grammar of the written sentence, speech adds **intonation**: differences in timing, pitch, and stress that make our words mean what we want them to mean. Such differences are further supplemented by facial expressions and gestures: the knowing wink that indicates irony, the raised forefinger that signals emphasis. When writing, we use punctuation marks for similar purposes.

The English system of punctuation has relatively few ways of indicating differences in emotion or attitude. In speech, "George is an honor student" can express many different shades of meaning. When we try to reproduce these differences in writing, we are soon reduced to devices frowned upon by conservative readers:

George is an honor student!
George is an honor student?
George is an honor student (!).
George is an honor (?) student.
George is an "honor" student.

*English punctuation is best equipped to signal differences in structure.* Punctuation marks may separate groups of words from each other. They may establish different kinds of connection between them. For instance, punctuation may show two closely related groups of words to be a general statement followed by detailed explanation:

> The room was full of noisy men: ranchers, merchants, and lawyers.

It may show them to be an important statement followed by incidental additional information:

> Richard inherited his uncle's estate, which had been in the family since 1632.

## P 1    End Punctuation

*Use end punctuation to put a stop to an utterance that is grammatically complete.*

Utterances terminated by end punctuation may have to become part of a coherent narrative or argument before their full *meaning* becomes clear. They do not need anything before them or after them to be complete as far as *grammatical structure* is concerned.

### P 1a    Exclamations

*Use the exclamation mark to give an utterance unusual emphasis.* Such utterances range from a groan, curse, or shout to an order or a command. The **exclamation mark** can signal excitement, insistence, surprise, indignation, or fear:

> Ouch!
> Hurrah!
> Silence! Get up! Close the book!
> He loves me!
> And this man wants to be President!

NOTE: Avoid using the exclamation mark as an easy way of making trivial things seem important. Avoid using more than one exclamation mark at a time.

## P 1b   Questions

*Use the question mark whenever an utterance is worded as a request for information.* Whenever you raise your voice inquiringly at the end of something you say, you should terminate the written equivalent with a **question mark** (*He sent you a check?*). Not all questions, however, are marked by intonation:

Who are you?
What did he want?

Do not forget to use question marks at the end of questions that are long or involved:

How is the student who enters college as a freshman supposed to find his way through the maze of instructions and regulations printed in small print in the college catalog?

(1) Use question marks even after *rhetorical questions.* Rhetorical questions do not really ask for an answer but already indicate what the correct answer is supposed to be by the way they are worded:

Are you implying that our candidate is a liar?
Am I, life-long servant of this great republic, going to betray the trust placed in me by my constituents?

(2) You are free to omit the question mark after *requests phrased as questions* for the sake of politeness.

Will you please notify your clients of our decision?
Will you please notify your clients of our decision.

## P 1c   Statements

*Use the period at the end of a simple statement.* In formal writing, the units separated by **periods** are grammatically self-contained; they are complete sentences. Guard against using a period to set off a unit that is not a complete sentence but merely a **sentence fragment** (see P 2). Guard against omitting the period between two complete sentences, thus producing a **fused sentence** (see P 3e).

| | |
|---|---|
| **Complete:** | He is gone. *He left for Alaska.* |
| **Fragment:** | He left yesterday. *For Alaska* |
| **Fused:** | You won't find him *he left for Alaska.* |

## P 2    Eliminating Fragments

*Identify and eliminate from your writing all objectionable sentence fragments.*

The type of sentence fragment most common in student writing results when an afterthought is added to the main statement. After making a statement (*I left home*), a writer may add an explanation that is not a second complete sentence (*To go to college*). He may make a statement (*These are my relatives*) and add a comment (*A fine group of people*). Each of these afterthoughts is a sentence fragment when separated from the main statement by a period.

Grammatically, such fragments are of several common types:

| | |
|---|---|
| appositives | A great man. My history teacher. Carts loaded with fruit |
| adjectives, adverbs | Beautiful in the morning sun. Carelessly as usual. |
| prepositional phrases | For the last time. With great trepidation. On behalf of the management. |
| verbals, verbal phrases | Leaving the car behind. Other things being equal. |
| dependent clauses | Because I did not study. Though nobody replied. Which came far too late. (See P 4a.) |

Many such fragments can be joined to the main statement either without any punctuation at all (*I left home to go to college*) or by a comma (*These are my relatives, a fine group of people*). Whenever a fragment is pointed out to you, try first to connect it with the main idea in such a way that the sentence flows smoothly, without interruption:

**Fragment:**  Be sure to be there. *At seven o'clock.*
**Revised:**  Be sure to be there *at seven o'clock.*

**Fragment:**  He bought a used car. *In spite of my warnings.*
**Revised:**  He bought a used car *in spite of my warnings.*

If the fragment cannot become part of either the preceding or the following statement, you may have to develop the material it contains into a complete sentence:

**Fragment:**  He appealed to a higher court. *Being a futile effort.*
**Revised:**  He appealed to a higher court. *The effort was futile.*

## P 2a  Breaks in Thought

*At times, material added to the main statement is kept clearly separate as an afterthought.* To indicate the break in thought, use a **dash** instead of a period:

These are my relatives—*a motley crew.*
He would close his eyes and talk into the dictaphone—*a strange way to write an English theme.*

Use dashes sparingly, since they can suggest the casual rambling of conversation or the jerky movement of an improvised speech. They are most effective when used only occasionally, to emphasize a break for ironic or dramatic effect. (See also P 7a.)

## P 2b  Explanation and Enumeration

*To establish a definite connection between an explanatory afterthought and the preceding statement, use a colon or a common transitional expression.*

(1) The **colon** serves to introduce a *list or description* of something that has already been mentioned in a more general way:

> We have two excellent players this year: *Phil and Tom.*
> She served an old-fashioned breakfast: *fishballs, brown bread, and baked beans.*
> Your friend lacks an essential quality: *tact.*

NOTE: The colon, like the period, ordinarily has a complete statement *in front of it.* Do *not* use the colon to separate verb and complement ("The chest contained: . . ."; "The two best players were: . . .").

(2) Explanations or examples added to a complete statement are often introduced by expressions like *especially, such as, namely,* or *for example.* When they introduce material that is not a complete sentence, these expressions are usually preceded by a **comma**:

> He took several courses in the humanities, *such as French Literature and Elementary Logic.*
> Plato and Aristotle wrote in the same language, *namely Greek.*

In formal usage, another comma often keeps *namely, for example, for instance,* and *that is* separate from the explanations or examples they introduce:

> Professor Miller objected to my system of punctuating, for example, my use of dashes.

Do not use another comma if the introductory expression is *especially* or *such as.*

## P 2c    Permissible Nonsentences

*Permissible fragments are common in speech and are used in writing for special effects.* Experienced writers use permissible fragments, better called **nonsentences**, for special purposes. The following examples illustrate the most common of these:

(1) *Common transitional expressions:*

*So much for* past developments. *Now for* a look at our present problems.

(2) *Answers to questions,* suggesting the give-and-take of conversation:

What did we gain? *Nothing.*

(3) *Descriptive passages,* especially when designed to give a static, pictorial effect:

We stood in the hot dry night air at one in the morning, waiting for a train at an Arizona station. *Nothing but the purple arc of sky and at the end of the platform the silhouette of a cottonwood tree lapped by a hot breeze. The stars big as sunflowers.*—Alistair Cooke, *One Man's America*

(4) In narrative, *passages suggesting random, disconnected thought:*

*Fifty dollars to Dorothy's piano teacher. His sister. Another plain girl.* She might as well learn how to play the piano.—Irwin Shaw, "Main Currents of American Thought"

There he is: the brother. *Image of him. Haunting face.*—James Joyce, *Ulysses*

(5) Transcripts of *conversation or dialogue:*

In one part of the picture you see five young men in white coats conferring around a microscope. The voice on the sound track rings out boldly, *"No geniuses here. Just a bunch of good Americans working together."*—William H. Whyte, Jr., "The New Illiteracy," *Saturday Review*

(6) Afterthoughts deliberately delayed for *ironic effect:*

Man is the only animal that blushes. *Or needs to.*   (Mark Twain)

Most teachers discourage their students from experimenting with such incomplete sentences until they have learned to use complete sentences effectively and confidently.

# Exercises

**A.** In which of the following passages is the second unit a *sentence fragment*? In which is the second unit a complete sentence?

1. The ocean has always beckoned to man. Daring him to risk all to sail the seas.

2. What I mean by good music is not popular music but the more classical type. It is music that can be evaluated and criticized by experts.

3. The dictionary usually gives the etymology of a word. Its origin and later history.

4. We made our way to the train station in a blizzard. Only to find the ticket window closed.

5. My uncle gave me not only advice but also money. Without his help I could never have started college.

6. Writers in recent decades have done battle against the forces of censorship. Not just for their own benefit but for the benefit of all.

7. The population explosion has brought with it many major problems. One urgent problem is the education of the growing mass of children.

8. In "The Real Thing," a painter employs as his models a couple with true upper-class manners. Mr. Monarch being the picture of a true gentleman, and Mrs. Monarch that of a lady.

9. Bradley Hall is a large building. Not immense in height, but of considerable length and width.

10. The typical eighteen-year-old is really still a fledgling in the family nest. Untried in many of the everyday happenings of life.

**B.** Check the following passages for *conventional use of end punctuation*. Label each passage *S* (satisfactory), *F* (unsatisfactory because containing a fragment), or *U* (unsatisfactory for some other reason).

1. Fred was collecting pictures of architectural marvels, such as Gothic cathedrals and Aztec pyramids.    2. The next sum-

mer I tried a new sales technique. With good results. **3**. You will not be able to reach them. They left no address. **4**. I remember the festive spirit of the Christmas season in my home town. The many colorful lights along the city streets. **5**. When will parents realize that their children's education is not someone else's responsibility but their own. **6**. He left school after two years. To take over his father's business. **7**. The airline refused to transport his pet: a tame puma. **8**. Rapidly growing housing tracts have created many problems. The most serious one being inadequate school facilities. **9**. Why should I spend my time making excuses for an incorrigible liar. **10**. He remembered his first glimpse of the United States. The Manhattan skyline. **11**. Many of my friends were studying a foreign language, especially Spanish or French. **12**. The club invited a well-known guest lecturer. An anthropologist from Cornell. **13**. The osprey dives into the water to seize its prey. Plunging down from heights of up to one hundred feet. **14**. Please stop at the post office. We need some stamps. **15**. The gallery was showing the work of several French painters, especially Degas and Monet.

**C**. From your current writing and reading, select ten sample sentences that illustrate the various conventions of punctuation discussed in the preceding section.

# P 3   Joining Independent Clauses

*Use a semicolon to join independent clauses unless they are linked by a coordinating connective.*

    The semicolon is the most typical punctuation between two statements that are still grammatically self-contained but that are closely enough related in meaning to combine in a single larger sentence. The semicolon then functions as a "semi-period," signaling a less definite break than the period but appearing in positions where a period would also be possible.

## P 3a   Closely Related Sentences

   *A semicolon or colon may replace the period between two complete sentences.*

(1) The **semicolon** joins *complete sentences that are closely related.* Often two statements go together as related pieces of information, develop the same mood or point of view, line up related ideas for contrast. When a semicolon replaces the period between two such statements, the first word of the second statement is *not* capitalized.

> Sunshine was everywhere; orchards were in bloom.
>
> Some librarians circulate books; others hoard them.
>
> The Queen is not allowed to wear a crown; nothing less than a halo will suffice.—Kingsley Martin, "Strange Interlude," *Atlantic*

(2) In informal writing, a **colon** often replaces the semicolon when the second statement gives the reader information or explanation that helps him understand the first one. Formal usage prefers the semicolon unless the *first statement clearly introduces the second.*

> One thing was certain: he would never race again.

## P 3b   Adverbial Connectives

*Adverbial connectives overlap with other groups of connectives in meaning but differ from them in typically requiring a semicolon.* **Adverbial connectives** are *therefore, consequently, hence, accordingly, moreover, furthermore, besides, however, nevertheless, indeed,* and *in fact.* Since they show that two statements are closely related, these statements often are separated by a **semicolon** rather than by a period. A period, nevertheless, would still be possible and acceptable.

> Business was improving; *therefore,* we changed our plans.
> Business was improving. *Therefore,* we changed our plans.
>
> The hall was nearly empty; *nevertheless,* the curtain rose on time.
> The hall was nearly empty. *Nevertheless,* the curtain rose on time.

Notice the following points:
(1) The adverbial connective need not be placed at the

point where the first statement ends and the second begins. The *semicolon appears at the point where the two statements join,* regardless of the position of the connective:

Attendance is compulsory; *therefore*, the students have no choice.
Attendance is compulsory; the students, *therefore*, have no choice.
Attendance is compulsory; the students have no choice, *therefore*.

The possibility of a shift in position is a test that you can employ to identify members of this group. They share their freedom of movement with adverbs (and are therefore called "*adverbial* connectives" or "connective *adverbs*").

(2) Adverbial connectives are often *set off from the rest of the second statement* by **commas**, as in the examples already given. You then have to make sure that there is a punctuation mark both before and after the connective:

The food, *however*, was impossible.

NOTE: Whether you should set off an adverbial connective depends partly on the level of formality of your writing. Informal and journalistic writing tend toward **open punctuation**, using fewer commas than formal writing does. Accordingly, the authors of popular books and magazine articles tend not to separate adverbial connectives from the rest of a clause.

## P 3c　Coordinating Connectives

*Coordinating connectives typically require a comma. And, but, for, or, nor, so,* and *yet* establish a close relation between two clauses without making the one more important than the other. They are typically preceded by a **comma**:

The bell finally rang, *and* George rushed out of the room.
She saw me, *but* she did not recognize me.
We went inside, *for* it had started to rain.
You had better apologize, *or* she will not speak to you again.

Notice the reversal of subject and verb after *nor*:

We cannot through the courts force parents to be kind, *nor can we force* men to be wise by the pressure of committees.—Dan Lacy, "Obscenity and Censorship," *The Christian Century*

Do not use the comma with these connectives when they merely join two words or two phrases (came in *and* sat down, tired *but* happy, for cash *or* on credit) rather than two independent clauses.

Notice the following variations:

(1) *And, but,* and *or* are often used without a comma *when the clauses they join are short:*

The wind was blowing *and* the water was cold.

*Yet* and *so* are often used with a **semicolon**:

The critics praised Oliver's work; *yet* no one bought his paintings.

(2) Any coordinating connective may be used with a semicolon, especially if the connective joins *clauses that already contain commas* or that are unusually long:

Previously the river has always been accompanied by mountains near or far; *but* they lay generally parallel to its course. Now in the Big Bend the river encounters mountains in a new and extraordinary way; *for* they lie, chain after chain of them, directly across its way.—Paul Horgan, "Pages from a Rio Grande Notebook," *New York Times Book Review*

(3) Unlike adverbial connectives, coordinating connectives *are not set off from the rest of the clause* they introduce; there is no comma after *and, but,* or *yet* unless it is required by some other convention of punctuation. Like adverbial connectives, however, coordinating connectives leave the clauses they join self-sufficient or independent grammatically. Thus, the clauses they connect may still be kept separate from each other by a **period**:

I called your office twice. *But* nobody answered. *So* I left without you.

## P 3d    Comma Splice

*Do not use a comma alone to join two independent clauses.* Next to the sentence fragment, the most noticeable departure from conventional punctuation is the **comma splice**, which runs on from one independent clause to the next with only a comma to keep them apart:

**Comma Splice:**     The doctor looked worn, he had stayed up all night.

**Revised:**     The doctor looked worn; he had stayed up all night.

One way of avoiding the comma splice is to insert a co-ordinating connective ("The doctor looked worn, *for* he had stayed up all night"). Note, however, that a sentence *remains* a comma splice even if there is an adverbial connective (which requires a semicolon instead of the comma):

**Comma Splice:**     French Canadians insist on preserving their language, therefore federal employees are being taught French.

**Revised:**     French Canadians insist on preserving their language; therefore, federal employees are being taught French.

Note the following exceptions to the traditional rule against the comma splice:

(1) Commas may appear between the independent clauses in a sentence composed of *three or more parallel clauses.* Note that the clauses in the following examples are closely related in meaning and similar in structure:

Be brief, be blunt, be gone.

Students in India demonstrate against the use of English, Vietnamese reformers protest against the use of French, young Israelis have no use for the languages once spoken by their parents.

(2) Some of the best modern writers use the comma between *two* clauses when the logical connection or similarity

in structure is especially close. For instance, there may be a close *cause-and-effect* relationship, or a *carefully balanced contrast:*

> The fire was dead, the ship was gone.—William Golding, *Lord of the Flies*

> The grass is rich and matted, you cannot see the soil.—Alan Paton, *Cry, the Beloved Country*

> Rage cannot be hidden, it can only be dissembled.—James Baldwin, *Notes of a Native Son*

Conservative teachers and editors consider this practice careless or, at best, informal. *Avoid it* in formal writing.

### P 3e Fused Sentence

*Never merely juxtapose two independent clauses without any punctuation. And, but,* and *or* sometimes appear between very *short* independent clauses without any punctuation (see P 3c). A **fused sentence** results when two such clauses are simply run together with any other type of connective, or with no connective at all:

**Fused:** I am not sick or anything I just like to sit in a chair and think.

**Revised:** I am not sick; I just like to sit in a chair and think.

**Fused:** Today's young people do not readily affiliate with political factions instead they align themselves with causes.

**Revised:** Today's young people do not readily affiliate with political factions; instead, they align themselves with causes.

## Exercises

**A**. Check the following sentences for punctuation between independent clauses. Label each sentence *C* (conventional), *CS* (comma splice), or *FS* (fused sentence).

**1**. He ultimately followed Scully across the corridor, but he had the step of one hung in chains.

**2**. The most precious right of a free man is to choose for himself therefore no one should have the right to ban or censor books.

**3**. Today's demonstrators are not sensation seekers, they are using the only available means to call attention to their views.

**4**. He now seemed all eagerness, and his eyes glowed.

**5**. My father never answered my questions, he always countered with questions of his own.

**6**. Hitches for horses were in front; however, they had not been used for half a century.

**7**. The typical juvenile delinquent drives without a license it doesn't matter to him.

**8**. The two major types of characters in *Animal Farm* are the human oppressors and the rebellious animals.

**9**. He would promise to reform then a few days later he had forgotten everything.

**10**. John Montgomery was tall for his age; in fact, he measured almost six feet at the age of thirteen.

**11**. In today's society a person is no longer a human being, he is a social security number.

**12**. She was not merely sophisticated; she was sophistication itself.

**13**. I must give my friend credit at least he has his pride.

**14**. Most of the people there were old-timers, there was seldom a young face in church.

**15**. To raise esteem we must benefit others; to procure love we must please them.

**B**. Check the following passages for conventional use of punctuation marks in joining clauses. Label each passage *S* (satisfactory), *CS* (unsatisfactory because of a comma splice), *U* (unsatisfactory for some other reason).

**1**. I asked my father for a car instead he gave me a bicycle.
**2**. I know the city very well; I used to live there, in fact.   **3**. In Europe family ties are close, the whole family does things together.   **4**. There is a growing audience for ballet, and the theater flourishes in half a dozen centers outside New York.
**5**. All the polls favored our candidate; the election, however, told a different story.   **6**. Previews consist of short selections from the movie being advertised, usually these are the most exciting or the most daring parts.   **7**. Children are like tape recorders; they repeat everything they hear.   **8**. We had planned to look for driftwood on the beach, but the rain kept us indoors.   **9**. The horses must have been frightened by the crowd, for they started rearing and tugging nervously at their bridles.   **10**. High costs make orchestra deficits perennial, yet almost everywhere performances are sold out.   **11**. I hurriedly went downstairs for breakfast was ready.   **12**. His landlady did not know his whereabouts, nor could she name his companions.   **13**. A teacher cannot do everything for his students they must meet him half way.   **14**. Classes are large, therefore few students have a chance to participate in discussion.   **15**. Our school annual was to give many students a chance to participate; the captain of the football team, consequently, became our sports editor.

## P 4   Adverbial Clauses

*Distinguish between adverbial clauses set off by commas and those requiring no punctuation.*

Adverbial connectives and coordinating connectives leave the clauses which they join independent. A third type of connective subordinates the second clause to the main clause of the sentence.

### P 4a   Subordinating Connectives

*Distinguish subordinating connectives from other types of connectives.* They normally introduce adverbial clauses, which tell us something about the circumstances of an action or event described in the main part of the sentence. *When, when-*

*ever, while, before, after, since, until, as long as,* and *where* introduce information about time and place. *Because, if, provided,*
and *unless* introduce reasons or conditions.

(1) A *subordinating connective can turn a group of words into
a sentence fragment* even though the group has both a subject
and a predicate. An *if* or a *because* changes a self-sufficient,
independent clause into a **dependent clause**, which normally
cannot stand by itself. "If I were a boy" does not become a
complete sentence until you answer the question "If you were
a boy, then what?" Beware of dependent clauses added to a
main statement as an afterthought:

**Fragment:**    He failed the test. *Because he did not study.*
**Revised:**    He failed the test *because he did not study.*

(2) *Subordinating connectives introduce material that may
precede rather than follow the main clause.* To identify a subordinating connective, try to reverse the order of the two
statements which it joins:

Vote for me *if you trust me.*
*If you trust me,* vote for me.

I drove more slowly *after I noticed the police car.*
*After I noticed the police car,* I drove more slowly.

## P 4b    Restrictive and Nonrestrictive Adverbial Clauses

*Do not separate restrictive adverbial clauses from the rest of
the sentence; set off nonrestrictive ones by a comma.*

(1) Adverbial clauses usually *restrict or qualify in a significant way the meaning of the clause to which they are joined.* Suppose a father tells his son, "I'll raise your allowance *after I
strike oil.*" Without the proviso about striking oil, the sentence
would sound like an immediate promise of more money. With
the proviso, it means that the son will get more money only
by a very remote chance. When they *follow* the main clause,
such **restrictive** clauses are not set off by punctuation:

I consulted my notes *before I spoke.*
Do not sign anything *until you hear from me.*
We cannot keep you on the team *unless you improve.*

Occasionally, the *time, place, or condition for an action or event is already indicated in the main clause.* In that case, the dependent clause may merely *elaborate* on the information already given. Such dependent clauses are called **nonrestrictive** and are separated from the main clause by a **comma**:

Bats were well developed *as far back as the Eocene, when man's ancestors were still in the trees.*
He was born *in California, where one can pick oranges during the Christmas holidays.*

(2) *Though, although,* and *whereas* usually introduce nonrestrictive material and as a result require a **comma**. Rather than adding essential qualification, these words establish a *contrast between the statements they connect*:

I like the work, *though the salary is low.*
Her friend wore a sports shirt and slacks, *whereas the other men wore tuxedos.*

Combinations like *whether or not* and *no matter how* indicate that the main statement is true *regardless* of possibilities mentioned in the dependent clause:

We are canceling the lease, *whether you like it or not.*
She will never forgive you, *no matter what you do.*

(3) Some subordinating connectives introduce *either restrictive or nonrestrictive material, depending on the meaning of the sentence.* Notice the comma that signals the difference between the members of each of the following pairs:

Why are you going to town? I am going to town *because I want to do some shopping.*
(The reason for your trip is the essential part of the sentence.)

What are you going to do? *I am going to town,* because I want to do some shopping.
(The reason for your trip is added, nonrestrictive explanation.)

I am telling you this *so that* there will be no misunderstanding.
(*So that* reveals purpose or intention.)

The cafeteria was small, *so that* it was always overcrowded.
(*So that* introduces an unintended result.)

NOTE: Some connectives belong to different groups of connectives depending on their meaning in the sentence. *However* is normally an adverbial connective and requires a semicolon. It sometimes takes the place of the subordinating connective *no matter how* and requires a comma:

I cannot please him; *however, I am trying hard.*
I cannot please him, *however hard I try.*

*Though,* normally a subordinating connective, is often used in informal English as an adverbial connective placed in the middle or at the end of a clause:

I felt entitled to more freedom; *my parents, though, didn't agree with me.*

## P 4c   Introductory Adverbial Clauses

*Set off an adverbial clause that precedes rather than follows the main clause.* After an introductory adverbial clause, a **comma** normally indicates where the main clause starts:

*If you want to do well,* you will have to work hard.
*Whenever there is a heavy rain,* the area is threatened by floods and slides.

Some writers consider this comma unnecessary, provided the sentence would be clear without punctuation:

*As the cowboy drew his fur cap down over his ears* his hands trembled.—Stephen Crane, "The Blue Hotel"

NOTE: Subordinating connectives are not the only way of relating a dependent clause to another clause. Two other types of dependent clauses are treated under P 5. (See P 5a for noun clauses, P 5b for adjective clauses.)

## Exercises

**A**. Explain the use of punctuation marks in the following passage. Which adverbial clauses are *restrictive*? Which are *nonrestrictive*?

> English and French were widely used in Africa until most African nations became independent. Now these countries are trying to assert their linguistic independence, although their people often speak several mutually incomprehensible native tongues. After the Belgians left the Congo, names like Leopoldville and Stanleyville disappeared. Swahili could become an official language in much of East Africa if linguistic minorities were willing to accept it. Similar developments accompanied the passing of colonialism in the Far East, where Batavia turned into Jakarta many years ago. A Malaysian city recently changed its name from Jesselton to Kinabalu, because Jesselton had been named for a British empire-builder.

**B**. Check the following passages for conventional use of punctuation marks with subordinating connectives. Label each passage *S* (satisfactory), *F* (unsatisfactory because of a sentence fragment), or *U* (unsatisfactory for some other reason).

> **1**. Though his paintings were truly remarkable, few of them found buyers among museums or private collectors.  **2**. Cleaning pots and pans looks easy on television. Whereas at home it takes a lot of hard work.  **3**. Unless a man has an unusual fondness for teaching grade school children are best taught by women.  **4**. Most of the animals were extremely shy, so that photographing them required much patience.  **5**. After the camera had followed the hero to his destination in the West, it switched back to the freshly plowed fields of Iowa.  **6**. The city is desperately short of hospital space because, most people don't appreciate the need for adequate facilities.  **7**. Myrna has been afraid of heights since she was a small child.  **8**. Mountain climbing does not appeal to me; however exciting it may be to others.  **9**. Because many educated people in India know English, foreign visitors seldom

learn Hindu. **10**. If we didn't know the teacher usually supplied the answers in class. **11**. In Mexico architecture seemed to flourish, whereas at home it had seemed a lost art. **12**. The city relinquished one hundred acres of city-owned land so that the local baseball team could build a new stadium there. **13**. Ralph was suspended last year. After he put war paint on the bronze Indian decorating the principal's lawn. **14**. Our house is a shambles, whenever my uncle's family pays us a visit. **15**. Ask me when you need advice; ask your father when you need money.

**C**. From your current writing and reading, select ten sample sentences that illustrate the various conventions of punctuation discussed in P 3–4.

# P 5  Punctuating Modifiers

*Distinguish between modifiers set off by commas and those requiring no punctuation.*

Often nouns and verbs are accompanied by further material that develops, embroiders, or modifies the meaning they convey. Such material is punctuated in accordance with its function and importance in the sentence.

## P 5a  Unnecessary Commas

*Unless extraneous material intervenes, do not use punctuation between basic elements of a sentence.* Do not put a comma between a subject and its verb, between verb and complement, or between the basic elements and various phrases added to the sentence to describe circumstances, reasons, or conditions:

| Andrew | studies | his textbooks | in bed. |
| Gaston | had been | a mess sergeant | during the war. |
| Jones | left | his wife | to shoot elephants. |

The rule against punctuation breaking up the basic sentence pattern applies even when the place of the subject or complement is taken by a *clause within a clause*. Such clauses, which appear in positions frequently occupied by nouns, are called **noun clauses**. They become *part* of another clause and should not be confused with clauses which are *joined* to another clause:

| | |
|---|---|
| **Noun (subject):** | *The writer* knew your name. |
| **Noun Clause:** | *Whoever wrote it* knew your name. |

| | |
|---|---|
| **Noun (object):** | John announced *his plans.* |
| **Noun Clause:** | John announced *that he would retire.* |

| | |
|---|---|
| **Noun (description):** | Your net gain is *a small sum.* |
| **Noun Clause:** | Your net gain is *what little remains after taxes.* |

Be careful not to put a comma before or after a noun clause, especially one introduced by *that*:

We knew *that he is unreliable.*
*That he failed to answer your letter* is a bad sign.

## P  5b    Restrictive and Nonrestrictive Modifiers

*Do not separate restrictive modifiers from what they modify; set off nonrestrictive modifiers by commas.* This convention applies especially to modifiers inserted after a noun (or noun equivalent) to clarify or develop its meaning. Such modifiers become an essential part of the main statement if *used for identification.* In that case, they are **restrictive**; they restrict or narrow down a general term like *student* to help the reader single out one particular student, or type of student. Restrictive modifiers are *not* set off:

(*Which* student studied the book?)
The student *wearing the red hunting cap* studied the book.

(*Which* man took the money?)
The man *dressed in the pink shirt* took it.

(*What kind* of course appeals to you?)
Courses *which require hard work* appeal to me.

Often information accompanying a noun is not necessary for identification. It merely gives your reader *further information* about something on which he has already focused; it is **nonrestrictive**. Nonrestrictive material is set off from the rest of the sentence by a **comma**, or by a comma both before and after it if it occurs in the middle of the sentence:

> The student studied his book.
> (*What else* about him?)
>> The student, *a freshman,* studied his book.
>> The student, *looking weary,* studied his book.
>> The student, *who had little time,* studied his book.

> I talked to my lawyer.
> (*What else* about him?)
>> I talked to my lawyer, *a well-known Boston attorney.*
>> I talked to my lawyer, *who is a very impatient man.*

The commas used to set off nonrestrictive modifiers often make the difference between a cautious and a sweeping statement. "Americans *who do not speak French* need not apply" narrows the scope of the statement to *certain* Americans, those that do not speak French. "Americans, *who do not speak French,* need not apply" is aimed at *all* Americans and at the same time makes a sweeping claim about their linguistic abilities. The commas used to signal the difference in meaning correspond to a break signaled in speech by a characteristic change in the tone of voice. You can train your ear to catch the distinction by going over the sample sentences already given and reading them out loud.

Note the following points:

(1) **Dashes** occasionally set off a nonrestrictive *modifier that contains internal punctuation* and that would not be clearly marked without them:

> His lawyer—*a gruff, stubborn, impatient man*—stalked out of the hall.

(2) A *proper name* is usually adequate identification; a

modifier following the name usually becomes nonrestrictive and is set off by commas. Several such modifiers may succeed each other:

> Mr. Smith, *my history teacher,* dismissed his class early.
>
> In 1942, he joined the Actors' Theater, *a repertory company with strong political views.*
>
> David Daiches, *English-born but Scottish-educated, formerly a professor at Chicago and Cornell, now at the University of Sussex,* chaired the meeting with the skill and courage of a lion-tamer.—Ralph W. Condee, "Bedlam at Edinburgh," *The Reporter*

But occasionally a *restrictive* modifier is needed to help the reader distinguish between several people of the same name:

> I find it hard to distinguish between Holmes *the author* and Holmes *the Supreme Court justice.*

NOTE: When your reader already knows whom you have in mind, even a proper name may be additional, nonrestrictive information:

> His oldest sister, *Martha,* has always helped him when he was in trouble.

(3) **Adjective clauses** modify a noun (or noun equivalent) and usually begin with *who, which,* or *that.* Clauses beginning with *when, where,* and *why* are also adjective clauses if they are used to modify a noun. Adjective clauses, like other modifiers, may be *either restrictive or nonrestrictive:*

**Restrictive:**    According to my sister Irene, all boys *who carry briefcases* are "brains."

**Nonrestrictive:**    Grade school teachers, *who have become more militant over the years,* are no longer satisfied with genteel poverty.

But note that two types of adjective clauses are *always* restrictive: those beginning with *that,* and those from which the pronoun or connective has been omitted:

The book *that you sent me* was exciting reading.
Most of the things [*that*] *I like to eat* are fattening.
She wrote a long passionate letter to the man [*whom*] *she loves.*

## P 5c Sentence Modifiers

*Many sentence modifiers are set off by commas.* Modifiers may modify sentence elements other than nouns. They may also modify the sentence as a whole rather than any part of it.[1]

(1) *Verbals and verbal phrases modifying a verb* may be either restrictive or nonrestrictive. Notice the **comma** indicating the difference:

| | |
|---|---|
| **Restrictive:** | He always came into the office *carrying a shirt box full of letters under his arm.* |
| **Nonrestrictive:** | Deadline newspaper writing is rapid because it cheats, *depending heavily on clichés and stock phrases.* |

Always set off *verbal phrases modifying the sentence as a whole:*

*To tell you the truth,* I don't even recall his name.

*The business outlook being rosy,* he invested his savings in highly speculative stocks.

Our new manager has done rather well, *considering his lack of experience.*

(2) If a *sentence is introduced by a long or substantial modifying phrase,* a **comma** usually indicates where the main sentence starts:

*After an unusually solemn Sunday dinner,* Father called me into his study.

*Like all newspapermen of good faith,* Mencken had long fumed at the low estate of the journalistic rank and file.—Philip M. Wagner, "Mencken Remembered," *The American Scholar*

Set off *introductory verbals and verbal phrases* even when they are short:

[1] Adverbial clauses, which can be classified as sentence modifiers, are treated under P 4.

*Smiling,* she dropped the match into the gas tank
*To start the motor,* turn the ignition key.

The comma after an introductory modifier can be an important clue to the meaning of a sentence. Omitting the comma may cause serious misreading. Compare the following two sentences:

*When hunting,* lions stay away from wooded areas.
*When hunting lions,* stay away from wooded areas.

(3) Expressions like *after all, of course, unfortunately, on the whole, as a rule,* and *certainly* often do not modify the subject or the predicate of a sentence but establish a connection between one sentence and another. Depending on the amount of emphasis you would give such a modifier when reading, you can make it stand out from the rest of the sentence by a **comma**:

*After all,* we are in business primarily for profit.
*On the other hand,* the records may never be found.
You will submit the usual reports, *of course.*

Sentence modifiers that are set off require *two* commas if they do not come first or last in the sentence:

We do not, *as a rule,* solicit applications.
A great many things, *to be sure,* could be said for him.

# Exercises

**A.** Explain the use (or lack) of punctuation in the following sentences. Point out *restrictive and nonrestrictive* modifiers.

**1.** A person who leases a car still has to pay for repairs and maintenance.

**2.** During Joe's practice rides, the few children who do remain outside huddle behind the nearest tree or bush.

**3**. Thoreau was well aware that no one can alert his neighbors who is not wide awake himself. (E. B. White)

**4**. On the main island of Britain, the Welsh, whose own Gaelic tongue is radically different from English, are now mostly bilingual.

**5**. Those who guide our worries on large issues regularly ask us to ponder man's losing competition with the machine. (John Kenneth Galbraith)

**6**. Few people in the West study Mandarin, the traditional literary and official language of China.

**7**. The Latin of the Roman Empire, once established as a world language, continued in that role through the Middle Ages.

**8**. I am not the only one who has worked fifty hours a week and every instant ached to be elsewhere.

**9**. During sessions of the United Nations, the Soviet representatives have almost always used Russian in their addresses, letting the chips fall where they may.

**10**. Americans, who had long been isolationists in matters of language as well as politics, became acutely language-conscious during World War II.

**B**. Check the following passages for conventional punctuation of modifiers. Label each passage *S* (satisfactory), *F* (unsatisfactory because of a sentence fragment), or *U* (unsatisfactory for some other reason).

**1**. With only a cautious enthusiasm, newspapers are giving a little extra Sunday space to culture. **2**. Despite the opposition of a crooked sheriff, the hero, a handsome screen cowboy on a $5,000 horse, succeeded in straightening things out. **3**. The proctor—a waspish, restless man—kept his eye on the whispering students. **4**. Everyone, who is physically able, should have some exercise each day. **5**. The kind of history that we were taught dealt mainly with the pageantry of princes and with the intrigues of empire. **6**. Queen Victoria, brought from retirement by the skill of Disraeli, became the adored symbol of domestic virtue and imperial greatness. **7**. Having swallowed enough water to last me all summer, I decided to leave water skiing to those who had an aptitude for it. **8**. My father who taught both in high school and in college gave me many helpful pointers on how to budget my time.    **9.** Major medical news—the discovery of a new surgical technique, the development of a cure for heart disease—is sometimes buried on the back pages.    **10.** Work after school can cut severely into study time, forcing the student to study late at night. **11.** All kinds of opinion-makers—people who would never dream of insulting a Negro, Jew, Catholic, or Paiute Indian— delight in slipping their daily needle of sarcasm into the politician.    **12.** Usually a selfish person is a spoiled person. One who must have his way or else.    **13.** A good example of our neglect of public health problems, is the lack of hospital space for the mentally ill.    **14.** With print orders now running fourteen million monthly, the *Reader's Digest* faces no serious competition in its field.    **15.** Pontius Pilate, Procurator of Palestine, the highest judge and top administrator of the country, had few of the marks of greatness.

**C.** From your current writing and reading, select ten sample sentences that illustrate the various conventions of punctuation discussed in P 5.

# P 6    Coordination

*Use the comma (and some other marks) as appropriate when several elements of the same kind appear together.*

## P 6a    Series

*Use commas to separate three or more items of the same kind appearing in a series.* The most common pattern separates the elements from each other by **commas**, with the last comma followed by a connective tying the whole group together:

*Phil, Jim,* and *Harry* came to see me.

After dinner, we *talked, laughed,* and *sang.*

*The new students enter* after a rigid selective process, *they present* few disciplinary problems, and *they arrive* after good and uniform preparation.—Oscar Handlin, "Are the Colleges Killing Education?" *Atlantic*

This basic *A, B, and C* pattern can be expanded to accommodate any number of elements:

The boys had spread out around them the homely tools of mischief—*the long wires, nails, hammers, pliers, string, flashlights, paraffin* saved from the tops of their mothers' jelly jars, *knives* for cutting a clothesline or carving out insults to the grown-up world, and *tin cans* filled with rocks for making a farewell noise after the damage was done.—Lois Phillips Hudson, "The Buggy on the Roof," *Atlantic*

Notice the following variations:

(1) Occasionally, you will want to arrange in a series *groups of words that already contain commas.* To prevent misreading, use **semicolons** instead of additional commas to indicate the major breaks:

Three persons were mentioned in her will: *John, her brother; Martin, her nephew;* and *Helen, her faithful nurse.*

(2) The *last comma* in a series is often left out, even in formal writing. (Most teachers, however, insist on its use.)

Then amid the silence, he *took* off his hat, *laid* it on the table and *stood* up.—James Joyce, "Ivy Day in the Committee Room"

(3) For variety or special effect, a writer may use *commas only,* leaving out the connective:

The idea was to pool all the needs of all those who had in one way or another been bested by their environment—*the crippled, the sick, the hungry, the ragged.*—John Lear, "The Business of Giving," *Saturday Review*

## P 6b   Coordinate Adjectives

*Separate coordinate adjectives by a comma corresponding to a characteristic break in speech.* Two adjectives describing different qualities of the same noun may be coordinated by a **comma** rather than by *and.* They are then called coordinate adjectives:

|  |  |
|---|---|
| a *black* and *shaggy* dog | a *black, shaggy* dog |
| a *starved* and *exhausted* stranger | a *starved, exhausted* stranger |
| a *grand* and *awe-inspiring* sunset | a *grand, awe-inspiring* sunset |

Not every sequence of adjectives falls into this pattern. Often an adjective combines with a noun to indicate a type of person or object (a *public* servant, a *short* story, a *black* market). An adjective preceding such a combination modifies the combination *as a whole* and should not be separated from it by a comma. Use the comma only if you could use *and* instead.

a *secretive* public servant (not "secretive *and* public")
a *long* short story (not "long *and* short")
a *lively* black market (not "lively *and* black")

NOTE: One method of distinguishing between the two kinds of adjective is to read the sentence out loud. This method will help when the difference in meaning is not obvious (a *tired, weary old man* but *an old, tired, weary man; chattering, giggling little girls* but *tiny, anemic, undernourished children*).

## P 6c  Dates and Addresses

*Use commas with dates, addresses, page references, and similar information consisting of three or four parts.* The different items are kept separate from each other by a **comma**; the last item is followed by a comma unless it is at the same time the last word of the sentence:

The date was *Tuesday, December 16, 1952.*
Please send my mail to *483 Tulane Street, Jackson, Oklahoma,* starting the first of the month.
The quotation is from *Chapter V, page 43, line 7,* of the second volume.

Commas are also used to keep separate the different parts of *measurements* employing more than one unit of measurement. Here the last item is usually *not* separated from the rest of the sentence:

> The boy is now *five feet, seven inches* tall.
> *Nine pounds, three ounces* is an unusual weight for this kind of fish.

## P 6d　Repetition and Contrast

*Use commas between expressions that are identical or give two different versions of the same meaning.* Use the **comma** after a word or phrase to be repeated or to be followed by a definition or explanatory paraphrase:

> *Produce, produce!* This is a law among artists, or rather it is their inner compulsion.—Malcolm Cowley, "Artists, Conscience, and Censors," *Saturday Review*
>
> I am asking *whether you recall his exact language, whether you remember exactly what he said.*

Commas also separate words or groups of words that establish a *contrast:*

> *His wife, not his brother,* needs the money more.
> *The days were warm, the nights cool.*

# Exercises

**A**. Explain the use of punctuation in the following passages, paying special attention to coordinate or closely related elements.

> **1**. The floor of the room was gritty with cigarette butts, superfluous correspondence, crushed coffee cartons, and honest gray dirt.
>
> **2**. Shortly after seven o'clock, a taxi disgorges a bearded, bearlike man, who shambles slowly toward the brownstone.

**3**. Ralph ran stumbling along the rocks, saved himself on the edge of the pink cliff, and screamed at the ship.    (William Golding)

**4**. After a while the bagelman arrives with a large box full of breakfast: coffee, steaming hot; a triple order of bacon; two fried eggs; and bagels, split and buttered.

**5**. In the simplified, censored biographies I read as a child, courteous, considerate heroes displayed magnanimity in victory and dignity in defeat.

**6**. Great writers can be temporarily put off by illness, by disappointment, or by some difficulty inherent in the process of composition, one of those snags, those pitfalls that lie in wait on every page.

**7**. One corner of the room is fitted with three worn turntables, a huge electric clock, and a cantilevered microphone that hangs over a console of switches, buttons, and dials.

**8**. Lee was known as a strategist, not as a tactician.

**B**. Check the following passages for conventional punctuation of coordinate or closely related elements. Label each passage *S* (satisfactory) or *U* (unsatisfactory).

**1**. Congress has the right to approve presidential appointments, to override presidential vetoes, and to impeach the President.    **2**. The old, the infirm and the widowed, are the most frequent victims of the confidence man's schemes. **3**. While living there, I knew I was sharing a room with a friend, not just a roommate.    **4**. To my weary, apprehensive parents, November 12, 1951, was a momentous day.    **5**. More people than ever are painting pictures going to museums and listening to classical music.    **6**. The new hospital was faced partly with aluminum sun-breakers, partly with ceramic tile.    **7**. The alderman complained that the Henry E. Lee Memorial Library was a gigantic, white elephant.    **8**. Our editorial and executive offices are located in the Newsweek Building, Broadway and 42nd Street, New York 36, New York.    **9**. The ores of the Comstock Lode not the natural beauty of the sierras had brought my family to Nevada.    **10**. The miles upon miles of small houses are new, spick-and-span, and highly sanitary, but they are also indistinguishable from those in Kankakee, Illinois; Lincoln, Nebraska; or Oakland, California.

**C.** From your current writing and reading, select ten sample sentences that illustrate the various conventions of punctuation discussed in P 6.

## P 7   Parenthetic Elements

*Use dashes, parentheses, or commas to set off parenthetic elements.*

To some extent, conventions of punctuation follow the rhythms of speech. This is true of conventional ways of setting off parenthetic elements, which *interrupt* a sentence without becoming grammatically a part of it.

### P 7a   Dashes

*Use the dash—sparingly—to signal a sharp break in a sentence.* A speaker may stop in the middle of a sentence to supply some preliminary detail or additional clarification. In writing, such material is set off from the rest of a sentence by **dashes**. Dashes tend to emphasize or dramatize the material they set off. (See also P 2a.)

Use dashes sparingly for the following situations:

(1) A *complete sentence is inserted into another sentence*, without a connective or relative pronoun to join them:

Lady Macbeth—*has this been noted?*—takes very little stock in the witches.—Mary McCarthy, "General Macbeth," *Harper's*

(2) A *list enumerating details or examples* interrupts rather than follows a clause:

Women tolerate qualities in a lover—*moodiness, selfishness, unreliability, brutality*—that they would never countenance in a husband.—Susan Sontag, *Against Interpretation*

(3) After a list, a sentence starts anew with a summarizing *all, these,* or *those:*

*The visual essay, the rhythmic album, the invitation to drop in on a casual conversation*—these are the idiosyncratic traits by which television, as television, has come to be recognized.—Walter Kerr, "What Good Is Television?" *Horizon*

(4) A word or phrase is made to stand out for emphasis or for a *climactic effect:*

After twenty-three years, he was leaving Newston jail—*a free man.*

## P 7b    Parentheses

*Use parentheses to enclose inserted material that supplies relatively unimportant data (or mere asides).* **Parentheses** play down the importance of what they enclose; they are most appropriate for things mentioned in passing:

Fatal accidents (*we had three of them last year in a town of 5,000 people*) can often be traced to excessive speed.

Kazan directed the rest of his considerable steam into studying English (*he graduated with honors*), waiting on tables, and joining as many extracurricular campus clubs as he could.—Thomas B. Morgan, "Elia Kazan's Great Expectations," *Harper's*

Parentheses are commonly used to enclose dates, addresses, page references, chemical formulas, and similar information if it might be of interest to some readers but is not an essential part of the text. Here are some typical examples: (*p. 34*) (*first published in 1910*) (*now called Market Street*).

NOTE: When inserted into another sentence, a sentence in parentheses, like a sentence set off by dashes, usually begins with a lower-case letter and has no end punctuation. When a sentence in parentheses begins *after* end punctuation, end punctuation is required inside the final parenthesis:

Select your purchases with care. (*No refunds are permitted.*)

## P 7c   Commas for Parenthetic Elements

*Use commas for parenthetic elements that blend into a sentence with only a slight break.* Take note especially of the following possibilities:

(1) Use commas when you interrupt a statement to *address the reader* or to *comment* on the source, validity, or plausibility of what you are saying:

Marriage, *dear boy,* is a serious business.
Politicians, *you will agree,* were never popular in this part of the country.
Our candidate, *it seems,* is not very well known.

(2) Commas set off the *introductory greetings and exclamations,* as well as the introductory *yes* and *no,* which frequently precede a statement in conversation and in informal writing:

*Why,* I don't even know that man.
*Yes,* you can now buy Pinko napkins in different colors.
*Well,* you can't have everything.

(3) Commas set off the *"echo questions"* often added to a statement to elicit agreement or confirmation:

You are my friend, *aren't you?*
So he says he is sick, *does he?*

(4) Slight breaks similar to those caused by parenthetic elements are sometimes caused by *sentence elements that have changed their usual position in the sentence:*

Laws, *to be cheerfully obeyed,* must be both just and practicable.
Philip, *for no apparent reason at all,* got up and left the room.
Marriage, *unless it is to be a failure,* must be completely voluntary.

(5) Commas may take the place of dashes to set off a word for emphasis. They suggest a *thoughtful pause* rather than a dramatic break:

We should act, *and suffer,* in accordance with our principles.
People cannot, *or will not,* put down the facts.

# Exercises

**A.** Explain punctuation in the following passages, paying special attention to *parenthetic elements.*

1. Fashions (especially adolescent fashions) do not as a rule outlast their generation.

2. The good grey people of Washington—the civil servants—are not renowned for the courage of their convictions.    (David Sanford)

3. Many people would agree, offhand, that every creature lives its life and then dies. This might, indeed, be called a truism. But, like some other truisms, it is not true. The lowest forms of life, such as the amoebae, normally (that is, barring accidents) do not die.    (Susanne K. Langer)

4. The underdeveloped countries have about 69 per cent of the earth's adults—and 80 per cent of the world's children. (Kingsley Davis)

5. Your true artist, let us note, always does finish. Sometimes he rages, like Wagner. Sometimes he finishes in serenity, and writes at the bottom of his music paper, like Palestrina and Bach, the words *Soli Dei Gloria.* But he finishes.    (Catherine Drinker Bowen)

6. Nowhere in the world has the old cliché of European romanticism—the assassin mind versus the spontaneous heart—had such a long career as in America.    (Susan Sontag)

**B.** Check the following passages for conventional punctuation of parenthetic elements. Label each passage *S* (satisfactory) or *U* (unsatisfactory).

1. Photography, you will agree, is not yet generally accepted as an art form.    2. For years, English Methodists have debated the merits of reunion with the Anglican Church (2,922,000 members).    3. Many fine programs though presented mainly for entertainment, supplement what the child learns in school. 4. Painter Du Bois—his work is represented in Manhattan's Metropolitan Museum of Art—resisted the modern trend toward abstraction.    5. The lone rider, the barroom fight, and the gingham-clad heroine—these are the indispensable ingredients of the third-rate cowboy movie.    6. At one time

President Wilson was a university president wasn't he?  **7**. A dozen last-inning victories (six of them since July 4) have given hometown fans something to cheer about.  **8**. He reports that political independents—his term is the mugwumps—have ejected the old-line party hacks from the city government.  **9**. Why if I were you Alice I would see a lawyer first thing tomorrow morning.  **10**. Peter Minuit I am sure you remember bought Manhattan Island from the Indians for a handful of trinkets.  **11**. The government, many businessmen feel, should insure foreign investments against expropriation.  **12**. A trip abroad, to be truly enjoyable, should be carefully planned.

**C**. From your current writing and reading, select ten sample sentences that illustrate the various conventions of punctuation discussed in P 7.

# P 8   Quotation

*Know how to punctuate different kinds of quoted material.*

Often, you will need to indicate that you are reproducing information or ideas derived from a specific source, that you are quoting something first said or observed by someone else.

## P 8a   Direct Quotation

*In repeating someone's exact words, distinguish them clearly from your own text.* Such direct quotations are enclosed in **quotation marks**. They are usually separated by a **comma** from the credit tag (the statement identifying the source):

She said, "Leave me alone."
"I don't care," he said.

Often the *credit tag interrupts the quotation* instead of introducing or concluding it. You then need **commas** both before and after the credit tag if it splits one complete sentence:

"All men," Aristotle wrote, "naturally desire knowledge."

You need a comma before and a **period** after the credit tag if it comes between two complete sentences:

> "All men are curious," Aristotle wrote. "They naturally desire knowledge."

The following variations are important:

(1) No comma is required with extremely *short quotations* or with *quotations worked into the pattern of a sentence* that is not a mere credit tag:

> Your saying "I am sorry" was not enough to soothe his wounded pride.
>
> The clatter of dishes and tableware, mingled with lusty shouts of "Seconds here!" and "Please pass the butter!", will resound across the county.—John Crawford, "A Plea for Physical Fatness," *Atlantic*

No comma is required when the credit tag follows a question or an exclamation:

> "Is everybody all right?" he shouted at the top of his voice.

(2) *Long or formal quotations* are often introduced by a **colon** instead of a comma. Whether you use a comma or a colon, capitalize the first word of the quotation if it was capitalized in the original source (or if it would have been capitalized if written down):

> Saarinen's definition of architecture's purposes describes his work: "To shelter and enhance man's life on earth and to fulfill his belief in the nobility of his existence."

(3) *Long quotations* (more than ten typed lines) should be set off from the rest of a paper *not* by quotation marks but by indention and single-spacing. The same applies to quotations consisting of more than a full line of poetry. (See Chapter 8 and the sample paper that follows it for examples of such **block quotations**.)

(4) Indicate when the person you are quoting is quoting someone else. In a quotation marked by the conventional set of double quotation marks, **single quotation marks** signal a *quotation within a quotation:*

> He said, "Our Congressman's constant cry of 'Cut that budget!' deceives no one."

> In the words of Chester Bowles, "In our national efforts to prove that we are 'realists' who do not 'go off half-cocked,' we have developed an appalling gap between the moral beliefs to which we subscribe and our day-to-day performance."

## P 8b    Terminal Marks in Quotations

*Observe conventional sequence when quotation marks coincide with other marks of punctuation.*

(1) Commas conventionally precede the final quotation mark, whereas semicolons and colons conventionally follow it:

> As he said, "Don't worry about me," the ship pulled away from the quay.
> You said, "I don't need your sympathy"; therefore, I didn't offer any.

(2) End punctuation usually precedes the final quotation marks, as in all the examples given so far. Sometimes, however, you will have to use a question mark or an exclamation mark after the quotation has formally ended. This means that the quotation itself is not a question or an exclamation. Rather, you are asking a question or exclaiming about the quotation.

> Who said, "We are strangers here; the world is from of old"?
> Don't ever tell a girl, "There'll never be another woman like my mother"!

NOTE: *A terminal mark is not duplicated at the end of a quotation,* even when logic might seem to require its repetition.

For instance, use only one question mark even when you are asking a question about a question:

> Were you the student who asked, "Could we hold the class on the lawn?"

## P 8c    Insertions and Omissions

*In direct quotation, any changes you make in the original text should be clearly indicated to your reader.*

(1) If for any reason you insert *explanations or comments of your own*, set them off from the quoted material by **square brackets**:

> As Dr. Habenichts observes, "Again and again, they [the Indians] saw themselves deprived of lands of whose possession they had been assured with solemn oaths."
>
> The note read: "Left Camp B Wednesday, April 3 [actually April 4]. Are trying to reach Camp C before we run out of supplies."

A comment sometimes inserted in a quotation is *sic*, the Latin word for "thus," which indicates that a passage that seems questionable or contains errors was transcribed exactly the way it occurred in the original source.

> The police records contained this short entry: "The accomplices of the suspect is [*sic*] unknown."

(2) When you *omit unnecessary or irrelevant material* from a quotation, indicate the omission by three spaced periods (called an **ellipsis**). If the omission occurs after a period in the original text, retain the sentence period and then insert the ellipsis.

> The report concluded on an optimistic note: "All three of the patients . . . are making remarkable progress toward recovery."
>
> "To be a bird is to be alive more intensely than any other living creature, man included. . . . They live in a world that is always

present, mostly full of joy." So wrote N. J. Berrill, Professor of Zoology at McGill University.—Joseph Wood Krutch, "If You Don't Mind My Saying So," *The American Scholar*

To indicate extensive omissions (a line or more of poetry, a paragraph or more of prose), you may use a single typed line of spaced periods.

NOTE: An ellipsis can *distort* a quotation by omitting important qualifications. A testimonial reading "This might have been a good book if it had been more carefully planned" should not be shortened to read ". . . a good book."

## P 8d  Indirect Quotation

*In indirect quotations, reproduce someone else's ideas or thoughts but translate them into your own words.* Indirectly quoted statements often take the form of noun clauses introduced by *that*; indirectly quoted questions take the form of noun clauses introduced by words like *whether, why, how,* and *which.* Such clauses are *not* separated from the statement indicating the source by a comma or colon. They are *not* enclosed in quotation marks:

Aristotle stated *that all men naturally desire knowledge.*
General Grant replied *that he doubted the wisdom of such a move.*
The artist asked me *which of the drawings I liked best.*

Note two exceptions:

(1) The following passage shows ways of *working the source statement into the indirect quotation as parenthetic material,* requiring **commas**:

*As Gandhi remarked,* the first consequence of nonviolent action is to harden the heart of those who are being assaulted by charity. But, *he continued,* all the while they are being driven to a frenzy of rage, they are haunted by the terrible knowledge of how wrong they are.—Michael Harrington, "Whence Comes Their Passion," *The Reporter*

(2) Even in an indirect quotation, you may reproduce some words or phrases exactly as they were used by the person you quote. To indicate that you are *preserving part of the original wording*, enclose such directly quoted words and phrases—but not any other part of the quotation—in **quotation marks**:

> The author felt that students could not be "tricked or coerced into thinking."
> The government radio referred to the accused men as "bandits" and "murderers" and promised that justice would be upheld "regardless of the cost."

## P 8e   Words Set Off from Context

*Use quotation marks to indicate words and phrases that are not part of the vocabulary you would normally employ.* Use them for expressions that are not your own, even though you may not be quoting them from any specific source.

(1) **Quotation marks** may identify words that you employ for *local color or comical effect.* They enable you to show irony by holding an expression, as it were, at arm's length:

> At the school I attended, a girl who did not go on "dates" or take an interest in "fellows" was not accepted as a normal human being.
> It would seem that every modern child's pleasure must have its "constructive aspects."—Lois Phillips Hudson, "The Buggy on the Roof," *Atlantic*

Avoid using such quotation marks by way of apology for undesirable or inappropriate expressions.

(2) Quotation marks may call attention to familiar words used in *unfamiliar* ways:

> *Partisan Review* thrived on its mutual interests in radicalism in politics and experimentalism in literature, each helping to "generalize" the other's concerns.—Theodore Solotaroff, "Radicals and Writing," *The New Republic*

(3) Either quotation marks or italicized print (under-lining in a typed manuscript) identifies *technical terms* presumably new to the reader or *words discussed as words*, as in a discussion of grammar or meaning:

> She wore a "Mother Hubbard," a loose, full gown long since out of fashion.
> In logic, the term *inference* refers to a conclusion or deduction arrived at by reasoning.
> The word *mob* was attacked as slang by some eighteenth-century writers.

(4) **Italics** rather than quotation marks identify *words that have been borrowed from foreign languages* and have not become part of the general vocabulary of English:

> Logrolling and back scratching are his exercises; *Quid pro quo* and *Cui bono?* are his mottoes.—William Lee Miller, "Confessions of a Conferencegoer," *The Reporter*

Many legal and scientific terms borrowed from Latin belong in this category:

> A writ of *certiorari* is issued by a superior court to obtain judicial records from an inferior court or quasi-judicial agency.
> The sperm whale, *Physeter macrocephalus,* is valuable for its oil and spermaceti.

## Exercises

**A**. Explain the use of punctuation in the following passages. Pay special attention to *quoted material.*

> **1**. Young Southerners often admire the somewhat anarchic qualities Latin Americans refer to as *machismo.*

> **2**. The *Michigan Daily* called him "a planner, an innovator, a persuader, a sympathizer . . . who is willing to align himself on the side of the students interested in getting an education here."

**3**. "I weep for you," the walrus said; "I deeply sympathize."

**4**. Shepley, Bulfinch, Richardson & Abbott were retained to design a "championship amphitheater."

**5**. In the *Random House Dictionary*, the reader can find such concoctions as *Franglais* and *Guesstimate.*

**6**. "The *Random House Dictionary*," I learn from a press release, "demanded seven years of editorial research and about $3,000,000 to produce."

**7**. Punctuation was unknown to the ancients. Latin teachers used to give their students a sentence that can mean: "My mother, O pig, is wicked." It can also mean: "Priestess, my sow is ugly"; or, "Come on, goddess, a boar is eating the apples."

**8**. How many students will understand what Marlowe meant by "the topless towers of Ilium"?

**B**. Check the following passages for conventional punctuation of quotations. Label each passage *S* (satisfactory) or *U* (unsatisfactory).

**1**. "Everything has already been said," wrote André Gide, "but since nobody ever listens we always have to start all over again."

**2**. "I am Grace Anders," she said, "do you mind if I come in?"

**3**. "Terrible!" the director shouted. "Let's take that passage again, starting from 'O, that this too too solid flesh would melt . . .' "

**4**. Newspaper veterans turned the phrases "culture beat" and "culture editor" over in their mouths with the gusto of a man biting into an unripe olive.

**5**. The lady from Buffalo kept asking the guide "what he meant by primitive?"

**6**. Wild applause and shouts of "Encore!" greeted us when the curtain parted.

**7**. Instead of congratulating me, John said, "Beauty contests—what a farce!"

**8**. According to one irate bystander, the murderer deserved no more sympathy than a "rabid dog."

**9**. "I'm all right," said my uncle, "just watch what you are doing the next time."

**10**. The speaker charged "that the television audience resembled the ancient Romans, who liked to see gladiators do battle to the death."

**11**. The speaker quoted Jefferson as saying that "our new circumstances" require "new words, new phrases, and the transfer of old words to new objects."

**12**. The constant war cry of my high school English teachers was give an example!

**C.** From your current writing and reading, select ten sample sentences that illustrate the various conventions of punctuation discussed in the preceding section.

**D.** (**Review of punctuation**) Explain the use of punctuation marks in each of the following passages. Point out sentences that you would have punctuated differently and explain why. Explain effects achieved by unconventional punctuation.

**1**. In recent years it has been possible to make motionpicture films of events on the surface of the sun, and by speeding them up several hundred times to project on the screen the life story of cataclysmic solar events which may occupy hours of time and quadrillions of cubic miles of space. Some of these films are awe-inspiring: they show immense fountains of flame spurting to heights of a hundred thousand miles from the sun's edge; bridges of fire, which could span a dozen earths, forming and crumbling; exact replicas of A-bomb bursts—but a thousand times as large—shooting up into space.—Arthur C. Clarke, "The Secret of the Sun," *Holiday*

**2**. Many of the greatest classics were written, assuredly, without children in mind, and were taken over by children who cheerfully disregarded what they could not understand and cherished what they could. Thus Defoe, old and cantankerous, did not mean to write for children, but they adopted Robinson Crusoe and own him still; soon Crusoe spread all over the globe; he was celebrated in every language; he suffered one metamorphosis after another, most famously in "Swiss Family Robinson," but in dozens of others as well. After two hundred years he is read avidly by children in Montana and Tasmania and Norway, and very little by their parents. Nor did the harsh and embittered Jonathan Swift mean to write for the young, but he could not help himself either, it seems. The children took over Gulliver and went with him on his travels, they made him into a fairy-story character.—Henry Steele Commager, "When Majors Wrote for Minors," *Saturday Review*

**3**. Men are brought to these conferences, regularly, in a sort of balanced ticket: one Jew, one Catholic, one Protestant; one labor leader to every businessman; one Republican to every Democrat; very carefully, a Negro and a woman; an economist with the Economist's View, a psychoanalyst with the Psychoanalytical View, a philosopher with the Standpoint of Philosophy. In my earliest conferencegoing days I myself was a College Student, attending as representative decoration conferences composed mainly of older people. Invariably there would come a golden moment when—since I then had sense enough to keep my mouth shut and would not have spoken— the chairman would pounce: "But let us hear from the Student Mind"; or "And how does this sound to Young People?"— William Lee Miller, "Confessions of a Conferencegoer," *The Reporter*

# 8

# THE RESEARCH PAPER

An effective writer has learned to assemble, interpret, and correlate material from a variety of sources. He has learned to build on the work of previous investigators. He knows how to present his findings in such a way that they will be accepted as the result of detailed and comprehensive exploration, conducted by a competent and responsible observer.

## Choosing a Subject

*Select a subject limited in scope and suitable for objective investigation.*

As a student writing a research paper, you need to produce definite results in a limited time. Your first task, therefore, is to select a subject that you can profitably treat within the time and with the materials at your disposal. Obviously, you will avoid subjects for which you are completely unprepared. For instance, recent developments in the natural sciences or in medicine may call for a knowledge of mathematics, physics, or chemistry that many college freshmen do not have. If you can, start from a foothold of previously acquired knowledge. If you grew up in the South, you might be prepared to investigate the influence of a Confederate leader like Jefferson Davis. If your home state is known for its Indian reservations, you might investigate the cultural traditions of an Indian tribe.

Select a subject that will allow you to observe a number of basic requirements for a successful paper:

(1) *The paper should center on one limited aspect of a general subject.* Avoid subjects that would lead you to compile miscellaneous information. Many research papers are unsuccessful because they cover too much ground. Restrict your general subject area until you arrive at something that you can explore in detail. "The early history of American universities" is a general subject area; "the training of Puritan divines at Harvard" is a specific subject.

(2) *The paper should show that the author has made detailed use of several different sources.* Avoid subjects that would tempt you to summarize preassembled information from one main source. Whatever points you make should require careful sifting and comparing of evidence from different, and possibly conflicting, sources.

(3) *The conclusions elaborated in the paper should stay close to the evidence actually presented.* When you write a research paper, the stance you adopt toward your audience is: "Here is the evidence. This is where I found it. You are welcome to verify these sources and to check these facts." Avoid subjects whose discussion would require you to appeal frequently not to objective evidence but to personal preference or partisan allegiance.

Here are some general areas for research:

**1**. The past history and future prospects of English spelling: reasons for its irregularity; causes that led to standardization; attempts at spelling reform.

**2**. The history of dictionary making: the principles and practices of lexicographers like Samuel Johnson or Noah Webster; the history of the *Oxford English Dictionary;* problems of lexicography.

**3**. Bilingualism: problems encountered by French Canadians, Mexican-Americans, or Flemish-speaking Belgians; assimilation versus the preservation of a separate linguistic and cultural tradition; the schooling provided for children who speak a different language at home.

**4**. Foreign-language teaching in the public schools: arguments for and against the study of Latin; current trends toward increased study of foreign languages; public school offerings in Russian and other languages not often taught.

**5**. The early history of outstanding universities or colleges: the philosophical, religious, or political motives of their founder; the purposes, vocational or otherwise, for which the institutions were originally intended; the educational principles of their founder or their original faculties.

**6**. The education or the reading of a prominent early American: books that influenced Washington, Jefferson, Franklin, or Madison; the influence of the classics or of contemporary trends of thought.

**7**. The public reception of a controversial author: Henrik Ibsen, D. H. Lawrence, James Joyce, Henry Miller, Jean Genet; changing standards of taste and public morals.

**8**. The history or the extent of the censorship of imaginative literature: standards applied by critics, courts of law, civic groups; legal means and indirect pressures at the disposal of would-be censors.

**9**. The self-image of the young Negro in white society as reflected in several books by Negro authors: Richard Wright, James Baldwin, Ralph Ellison.

**10**. Religious trends: the growth of Catholicism; the spread and influence of evangelistic movements; the prospects for closer association of the various Protestant denominations; tendencies within American Judaism; interest in religious subjects among college students.

## Using the Library

*Learn to use the resources of your college library.*

In an adequate college library, every imaginable subject is covered by books, articles, and reports that are often the result of painstaking and comprehensive study.

## General Reference Works

*Learn to use the reference tools available to every investigator regardless of his specific subject.*

**Encyclopedias.**  An encyclopedia is a good place to start—but not to finish—your investigation. Typically, the encyclopedia provides a convenient summary of what is generally known, or easily accessible to the layman, on your subject. The purpose of your investigation is to go *beyond* the encyclopedia—to take a closer first-hand look.

The *Encyclopaedia Britannica,* now an American publication, is considered by many the most authoritative of the general encyclopedias. It provides extended articles on general subjects, with exceptionally full bibliographies at the ends of articles. It is brought up to date each year by the *Britannica Book of the Year.* Although you would normally consult the most up-to-date version, you will occasionally find references to scholarly articles in earlier editions.

The *Encyclopedia Americana* is sometimes recommended for science and biography. General subjects are broken up into short articles, arranged alphabetically. The annual supplement is the *Americana Annual.*

*Collier's Encyclopedia* is another multivolume general encyclopedia, aiming somewhat more directly at a popular audience.

The one-volume *Columbia Encyclopedia* provides a bird's-eye view. It serves well for a quick check of people and places.

**Bibliographies.**  At the end of many encyclopedia entries you will find a short bibliography, a list of important books and other sources of information. The encyclopedia may suggest only very general books, but these in turn will often contain more detailed bibliographical listings or direct you to book-length bibliographies. Any general survey of a subject is likely to provide information about more detailed studies. College textbooks often provide a short bibliography at the end of each chapter.

Take up first those books that a bibliography labels "standard," "indispensable," or "the best introduction" to your subject. If the bibliographies you have consulted merely *list* books, take up those that are most frequently mentioned. Study their tables of contents, prefaces, introductory or concluding chapters. Find out what each book is trying to do and whether all or parts of it would be useful for your project.

The *Book Review Digest* contains short selections from book reviews written shortly after publication of the book reviewed. These can give you an idea of the intention and importance of books on subjects of general interest.

**Periodical Indexes**.   When writing on a current problem, you may have to rely primarily on articles in both general and technical magazines. Since the card catalog of your library lists magazines but not individual magazine articles, you will have to locate the latter in the **periodical indexes**. These are published in monthly or semimonthly installments and then combined in huge volumes, each listing articles for a period of one or more years.

The *Readers' Guide to Periodical Literature* indexes magazines written for the general reader. If you are writing on American policy in the Far East, the *Readers' Guide* will direct you to speeches by government officials reprinted in full in *Vital Speeches of the Day* or *U.S. News & World Report.* It will direct you to discussions of American foreign policy in such magazines as *Newsweek* and *New Republic.*

The *Social Sciences and Humanities Index* (formerly *International Index*) lists articles in more scholarly magazines. If you are writing on the status of the American Negro, this index will direct you to articles in sociological and psychological journals.

*Poole's Index to Periodical Literature* lists articles published between 1802 and 1906. It can help you find contemporary reviews of Noah Webster's dictionary or the novels of James Fenimore Cooper.

NOTE: Whatever index or bibliography you use, read

its introductory pages and study its list of abbreviations. *Study the list of the periodicals indexed*—it may not include a magazine that you have seen mentioned elsewhere and that you know to be important. Look at sample entries to study the listing of individual articles (usually by subject) and the system of cross references.

## Specialized Reference Works

*Learn to use the reference tools of a special area of study.* Every major area, such as education, history, or art, has its own specialized reference guides: yearbooks, specialized encyclopedias, dictionaries of names and technical terms, general bibliographies.

To find specialized reference works relevant to your research project, turn to Constance M. Winchell's *Guide to Reference Books,* including the supplements bringing it up to date. It lists the standard sources of information for all major fields of study.

**Biography.**   One type of library project that is often assigned in writing classes is the biographical paper. In addition to the biographical entries in the major encyclopedias, most libraries have ample material for this kind of project.

*Who's Who in America,* a biographical dictionary of notable living men and women, provides a brief summary of dates and details on important contemporaries.

The *Dictionary of American Biography* (*DAB*) contains a more detailed account of the lives of important persons. The British counterparts of these two volumes are *Who's Who* and the *Dictionary of National Biography* (*DNB*).

The *Biography Index* is a guide to biographical material in books *and* magazines. By consulting both recent and earlier volumes, you can compile a comprehensive bibliography of material on the married life of George Washington or on the evangelistic campaigns of Billy Graham.

**Literature**. Courses that stress reading and discussion of imaginative literature may include a library project on a subject from literary history—an author's schooling or early reading, recurrent themes in the books of a well-known novelist, the contemporary reputation of a nineteenth-century American poet.

The fifteen-volume *Cambridge History of English Literature* and the *Cambridge Bibliography of English Literature* provide comprehensive information about English authors and literary movements.

The Spiller-Thorp-Johnson-Canby *Literary History of the United States,* with its supplementary bibliographies, lists as its contributors an impressive and representative roster of contemporary American literary scholars.

*Harper's Dictionary of Classical Literature and Antiquities* is a comprehensive scholarly guide to Greek and Roman history and civilization. (Robert Graves' *The Greek Myths* and Edith Hamilton's *Mythology,* both available as paperbacks, provide an introduction to famous names and stories.)

**Current Events**. A number of special reference guides are useful for papers on a political subject or on current events.

*Facts on File* (published since 1941) is a weekly digest of world news, with an annual index. It gives a summary of news reports and comments with excerpts from important documents and speeches. It can serve as a convenient review of day-to-day happenings in politics, foreign affairs, entertainment, sports, science, and education.

The *New York Times Index* (published since 1913) is a guide to news stories published in the *New York Times.* By looking up an event or a controversy in either index, you can ascertain the approximate dates for relevant articles in newspapers and magazines.

The annual index to the *Monthly Catalog of the United States Government Publications* lists reports and documents published by all branches of the federal government.

## Choosing Your Sources

*Learn to evaluate the library resources available to you.* Learn to choose authoritative sources and to evaluate conflicting evidence. Consider such points as the following:

(1) Is the author an *authority on his subject* or merely a casual observer? If you can, find out whether a book was written by an economist whose specialty is Russian agriculture or by a columnist who spent four weeks surveying Russian agriculture from the windows of a train.

(2) Does the author have an *established reputation in his field?* Keep an eye open for comments on the background and the scholarly competence of authors you are reading, or on the reputation of institutions and organizations with which they are connected.

(3) Does the publisher of the book or magazine represent a *tradition of scholarly and serious work?* Does he have a reputation to maintain? Know whether your material comes from a university press or from a popular book club, from a technical journal or from a mass-circulation magazine.

(4) Regardless of the reputation of the author and the publisher, *is the present work a thorough and carefully documented study* or a sketchy, improvised survey of the topic? Is it short on opinion and long on evidence, or vice versa? Does it weigh the findings of other authorities, or ignore them?

(5) Does the author settle important questions by *referring to primary sources*—that is, legal documents, letters, diaries, eyewitness reports, transcripts of speeches and interviews, reports on experiments, statistical surveys? Or does he rely exclusively on *secondary sources*—other authors' accounts and interpretations of primary materials?

(6) Is the author's treatment *balanced or one-sided?* An early phase in the history of the American labor movement is likely to be treated one way in the success story of a famous industrialist, another way in the biography of a pioneering labor leader. An objective historian will weigh both pro-business and pro-labor views.

(7) Is the work *recent enough to have profited from current scholarship?* If it was originally published ten or twenty years ago, is the current version a revised edition? Consider the possibility that an author's views may have been invalidated by new findings and changing theories in a rapidly expanding field of study.

## Exercises

**A**. Select one of the three major encyclopedias discussed in this section and one other encyclopedia not mentioned here. Compare their treatment of *one* of the following subjects: atonality, cybernetics, Gestalt psychology, impressionism, quantum theory, semantics, stream-of-consciousness technique, surrealism, transcendentalism, transformational grammar.

**B**. Study the general scheme of the *Book Review Digest* and check it for reviews of books you have read. Describe its treatment of one or two of the books.

**C**. Study the general scheme and sample entries of *one* of the following reference works: *American Universities and Colleges, Art Index, Business Periodicals Index, Cambridge Modern History, Catholic Encyclopedia, Concise Dictionary of American History, Dictionary of World Literature, Education Index, Grove's Dictionary of Music and Musicians, Oxford Companion to American Literature, Standard Jewish Encyclopedia, Van Nostrand's Scientific Encyclopedia.* Report your findings, commenting on the scope, usefulness, and possible limitations of the work.

**D**. Select *one* of the following books and study its preface, table of contents, bibliography (if any), and introductory or concluding sections. Study its treatment of one or two limited topics. Then write a brief report on the intention, scope, level of difficulty, and special features of the book: (1) Ruth Benedict, *Patterns of Culture;* (2) James B. Conant, *On Understanding Science;* (3) Myron Lieberman, *The Future of Public Education;* (4) Erwin Panofsky, *Meaning in the Visual Arts;* (5) Otto Jespersen, *Growth and Structure of the English Language;* (6) David Riesman, *The Lonely Crowd;* (7) Marshall McLuhan, *Understanding Media;* (8) René Wellek and Austin Warren, *Theory of Literature.*

**E**. Study the general scheme of Constance M. Winchell's *Guide to Reference Books* and report on its treatment of a field that is of special interest to you, such as journalism, medicine, business, folklore, or religion.

**F**. Consult the *Readers' Guide* and find recent articles on *one* of the following: Benjamin Franklin, Alexander Hamilton, Andrew Jackson, Thomas Jefferson, Thomas Paine, George Washington. Compare the intention, tone, and level of difficulty of articles taken from three different periodicals.

**G**. Consult the *International Index (Social Science and Humanities Index)* to find a scholarly article on *one* of the following: (1) the hypothetical parent language of all Indo-European languages, (2) the historical background of Homer's epics, (3) the Roman occupation of ancient Britain, (4) the earliest extant versions of the Old Testament, (5) the origins of medieval drama, (6) Freud's view of imaginative literature. Examine the author's use and identification of the source materials on which he has drawn.

**H**. Consulting more than one index, locate at least five reviews or critical discussions of one of the following: an essay by James Baldwin, a play by Peter Weiss or Richard Hochhuth, a novel by Günter Grass, the poems of Theodore Roethke. Report on your success in locating relevant material.

# Using Bibliographical Information

*Learn to make competent use of bibliographical information.*

When you make extensive use of printed sources, you will realize the usefulness of systems of classification that help you to locate books. You will have to be able to interpret information about books that describes their origin, authorship, publication, content, and the like.

## Library Catalogs

*Learn to make efficient use of the card catalog.* Your research projects will ordinarily be geared to the resources of your college library. Its central card catalog is a complete alphabetical index of the materials available to you.

A card for a general-interest book brought out by a commercial publisher will look something like this:

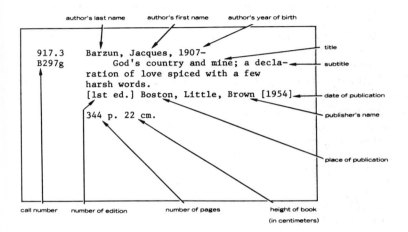

Such cards give you several kinds of information:

(1) After the *full name of the author,* you will find the *date of his birth* and, if applicable, his death.

(2) After the title of the book, you will find *the number or description of the edition.* If the catalog lists both the original edition and another one marked "2nd ed." or "Rev. ed.," you will generally choose the one that is most nearly up to date.

(3) The *name and location of the publisher* can be a clue to the nature of a book. For instance, a book published by a university press is more likely to be a scholarly and specialized study than a book published by a commercial publisher. The *date of publication* is especially important for books on scientific, technological, or medical subjects, since new scientific discoveries can rapidly invalidate old theories.

(4) The *number of pages*, with the number of introductory pages given as a lower-case Roman numeral, can indicate whether the book is a short pamphlet or a full-scale treatment of the subject. If the book contains *illustrations* or a *bibliography*, the card will carry a notation to that effect.

In most card catalogs, the same book is listed several times: by *author* (under the author's last name), by *title* (under the first word of the title, not counting *The*, *A*, or *An*), and by *subject*. Often, a card lists the several major *subject headings* under which the book can be found. For instance, a catalog card for a sociological study of a town in the Middle West may carry the following notation concerning various headings under which the study is listed:

1. U.S.—Social conditions. 2. Cities and Towns—U.S. 3. Cost and standard of living—U.S. 4. U.S.—Religion. 5. Social surveys. 6. Community life.

**Subject cards** can direct you to many books that are relevant to your topic. Look for subject headings under which books on your topic might be listed. Books on progressive education might appear under *Education—Aims and Objectives*, under *Education—Experimental Methods*, or under *Educational Psychology*. Books on the Civil War might appear under *U.S.— History—Civil War*, under *U.S.—History—Military*, under *Slavery in the United States*, or under *Abolitionists*.

*Once you decide that you should consult a book, copy its call number*. The **call number** is the group of letters and numbers usually found in the upper left-hand corner of the card. It directs you, or the librarian, to the shelf where the book is located. Your library may use either of two numbering systems: the Library of Congress system or the Dewey decimal system. The **Library of Congress system** divides books into categories identified by letters of the alphabet. It then uses additional letters and numerals to subdivide each main category. For instance, the call number of a book on religion would start with a capital *B*; the call number of a book on education starts with a capital *L*. The **Dewey decimal system** uses numerals to identify the main categories. For instance, 400–499 covers books on language; 800–899 covers books on literature. The 800 range is then further subdivided into American literature (810–819), English literature (820–829), and so on. Additional numerals and letters distinguish among individual authors and among individual works by the same author.

Along with the call number, you may find a notation directing you to a special section of the library. The book you are looking for may be located in a *reference room*, where encyclopedias, dictionaries, and other reference works are kept. It may be located in a *special reading room* where books for a particular field of study are on reserve.

NOTE: Although the card catalog lists magazines and newspapers, most libraries have a separate, compact catalog for periodicals. It lists, in alphabetical order, all periodicals to which the library subscribes. For each periodical it indicates the location of recent issues (often on the shelves of a separate periodical room) as well as of back issues (usually in bound volumes in the book stacks of the library).

## Bibliography Cards

*Make your own card catalog of all materials that seem promising or worthy of investigation.* Include a separate note card for each book, pamphlet, or magazine article you intend to use. Your instructor may suggest a minimum number of sources he wants you to consult.

On each bibliography card, include the library call number or the place in the library where the publication is to be found. (This information is for your own personal use; do *not* reproduce it in your finished paper.) Other entries on your cards will serve as the basis for references to a source in your final manuscript. Check all entries carefully against the title page of the book or the heading of the magazine article in order to correct discrepancies. Be especially careful to get the *exact spelling* of unfamiliar names.

Often, a bibliography card for a book need list no more than the following information:

509        Conant, James Bryant
C743o      *On Understanding Science: An Historical Approach*
           New Haven: Yale University Press, 1947

Usually, the first item you record is the *full name of the author.* Put the last name first to facilitate alphabetizing. If a work has been collected or arranged by a person other than the author (or the authors), you may start with that person's name, followed by "ed." for "editor." Ordinarily, however, the name of an editor or of a translator (followed by "trans.") appears on a separate line below the title. If an article in an encyclopedia is identified only by the author's initials, you may be able to find his full name by checking the initials against a list of contributors.

Start a new line for the *full title of the publication,* including a subtitle, if any. Underline the title of a book, pamphlet, or other work published as a separate entity. (Underlining in a typed manuscript corresponds to italics in print.) Put the title of an article or short poem in quotation marks and underline the title of the magazine, collection, or encyclopedia in which it appears.

Use a separate line for the *facts of publication.* For a book or pamphlet these may include a number of different items:

(1) The *number or description of the edition* (unless a book has not been re-edited since publication).

(2) The *number of volumes* (if a work consists of several, and all are relevant to your investigation).

(3) The *place of publication* (usually the location of the main office of the publishing house, or of the first branch office listed if several are given).

(4) The *name of the publisher.*

(5) The *date of publication* (not always given on the title page, though it can usually be inferred from the copyright date, found on the reverse side of the title page).

(6) The *number of the specific volume used* (if only one of several volumes is relevant to your investigation).

A bibliography card for an article is likely to contain something like the following:

| Periodical | Whyte, Lancelot Law |
| Room | "Can We Grow Geniuses in Science?" |
| | *Harper's Magazine,* CCXIV (June 1957), 46–50 |

For a magazine or newspaper article, the facts of publication ordinarily do *not* include the name of the publisher and the place of publication, though the latter is sometimes needed to identify a small-town journal. The pages of most professional or technical magazines are numbered consecutively through the several issues comprising one volume, usually the issues published during one year. For an article in such a magazine, record the *number of the volume* (preferably in Roman numerals), the *date of the issue,* and the *page numbers of the article.* For articles in other magazines and in newspapers, record the date of the issue and the page numbers. If the pages in separate sections of a newspaper are not numbered consecutively, identify the section where the article is to be found.

## Annotation

*You will greatly increase the usefulness of your bibliography cards by annotation.* Write down brief reminders concerning characteristic features of your sources. You might note, for instance, that an article on atomic energy is extremely technical; perhaps it requires more knowledge of physics than you command. Another article on the same subject may be a popularized treatment and give none of the specific data you need. Or you may want to note that a book has a glossary of technical terms, or an annotated bibliography, or a convenient summary of historical facts.

```
Humanities     Neville, Mark A.
Room           "Who Killed Poetry?"
               The English Journal, XLVII (March 1958)
                                            133-138
     Examines, with examples, conventional methods
of teaching poetry in high schools.  Concludes
that teachers of poetry should stress appreciation
and enjoyment rather than the study of versifica-
tion.
```

# Exercises

**A**. Study the arrangement of cards in the central card catalog of your college library in order to answer the following questions: (1) What are the major subdivisions for subject cards under the heading "Education"?    (2) Where would you find a book by an author named John McMillan (under *Mc, Mac, Mi?*), George St. John (under *St., Sa, Jo?*), Antoine de Saint-Exupéry (under *De, Sa, St.?*)? (3) Do subject cards for books on the Civil War precede or follow cards for books on the War of Independence? Is the arrangement alphabetical or chronological?    (4) Are books about George Washington listed before or after books about the State of Washington, or about Washington, D.C.?    (5) Check under *John Keats*: What is the relative order of the author's individual works, his collected works, and books about the author?

**B**. Transcribe and explain the information that the card catalog of your college library provides concerning *one* of the following books: Leonard Bloomfield, *Language;* H. W. Fowler, *A Dictionary of Modern English Usage;* Otto Jespersen, *Modern English Grammar;* H. L. Mencken, *The American Language;* Stuart Robertson, *The Development of Modern English.*

# The Technique of Note-Taking

*Learn how to take efficient and usable notes.*

While you are investigating source materials, your reading will be exploratory. You may read an article in an encyclopedia or a chapter in a textbook. You may glance through introductory material and selected chapters in a number of promising books. Even at this stage you may be jotting down tentative questions and observations. It will be some time, however, before you have a clear idea of the scope and point of your paper. Only then will you be ready to start taking notes in a systematic manner.

## Gathering Material

*Select material for its relevance to the tentative generalizations that you formulate as you go along.* Suppose you are writing a research paper on trends toward increased teaching of foreign languages in the public schools. You are consulting a number of books published in the fifties and sixties and devoted to the improvement of American public education. By glancing over the table of contents and consulting the index of each book, you locate a number of discussions bearing on your subject. The following passages seem particularly relevant:

The school board should be ready to offer a third and fourth year of a foreign language, no matter how few students enroll. . . . I have met no teachers of foreign language who felt that anything approaching mastery could be obtained by the study of a foreign language for only two years in high school, nor have the students felt that two years of study had given them any real working knowledge of the language. Four years of study, on the other hand, will yield dividends for those capable of handling foreign languages. This is the recommendation of the foreign language panel of the NEA Conference on the Identification and Education of the Academically Talented held in Washington in February, 1958.

Almost without exception, I found a deplorable state of affairs in regard to foreign languages. . . .—James B. Conant, *The American High School Today*, p. 69.

. . . In the third field of importance today—foreign languages—the situation is even more serious. One consequence is that we have a diplomatic service where only 50 per cent now have command of a foreign language and where—still worse—a mere 30 per cent of the incoming recruits speak any foreign language; clear evidence of the deterioration of foreign-language teaching in the last generation. . . .

Progressive education must be blamed in large part for our neglect of foreign-language teaching. . . . We are the only major country which neglects the early years when a child can learn foreign languages most easily—from 10 onward.—H. G. Rickover, *Education and Freedom*, p. 109 and App., p. 65.

The American attitude toward the study of foreign languages has changed remarkably in the last decade. Twenty years ago, the future for these subjects seemed bleak indeed. Greek was gone, Latin was going, and enrollments in French and German were steadily declining. . . . In the early fifties, the Modern Language Association of America received from the Rockefeller Foundation a substantial grant for the purpose of setting up a Foreign Language Program. . . . It collected and disseminated information of all sorts and tried with some success to persuade the nation that a revival of foreign languages was in the national interest. The movement called FLES—Foreign Languages in the Elementary Schools—was greatly encouraged by this project.

The shudder that the launching of the Russian satellite sent through the world accelerated the swing back to foreign languages, as to other solid subjects. . . . The most dramatic response was the National Defense Education Act of 1958, which provided funds for the improvement and expansion of instruction in science, mathematics, and modern foreign languages.—Albert R. Kitzhaber e.a., *Education for College*, pp. 113–116.[1]

From these and related passages, a number of tentative areas of agreement emerge. The first is the relatively low

[1] Albert R. Kitzhaber, Robert M. Gorrell, and Paul Roberts, *Education for College: Improving the High School Curriculum.* Copyright © 1961 The Ronald Press Company.

state of foreign-language teaching in the past. The second is a growing concern in the last one or two decades with the improvement of foreign-language instruction. In further reading, you will look for material that will support or clarify these tentative points. At the same time, these passages suggest avenues for further exploration. You will try to find some of the "information of all sorts" disseminated by the Modern Language Association, some of it likely to be found in its official quarterly, *PMLA*. You will try to find out more about the role of the National Education Association (NEA), again perhaps turning first to an official publication like the *NEA Journal*. You will try to locate authoritative accounts of the original National Defense Education Act, both its original intent and its impact on the schools.

## Recording Material

While recording information and ideas, you will have to employ a combination of techniques:

(1) *Learn to extricate important points from long passages, to summarize or condense lengthy quotations.* A formal abridgment, sometimes called a **précis**, preserves all essential points while curtailing or omitting altogether explanations, examples, and incidental comments. It uses the most economical kind of wording, substituting one word for a lengthy phrase wherever possible. (See O 8.)

When you condense material for reproduction in the finished paper, you are likely to be more selective than in preparing a formal précis. You will pick out only those points of a report or of an argument that are directly relevant to your investigation. For instance, you may be investigating Woodrow Wilson's unsuccessful defense of the Treaty of Versailles and the League of Nations in 1919. After reading several pages of a historical study that reviews relevant political facts, you may decide to summarize them for use in an introductory paragraph. Your note might look like this:

---

American Politics 1918-1920

    Election of Republican Congress in 1918.
Bitter opposition to President's role in peace
conference from such men as ex-President
Roosevelt and Senator Lodge.  Unprecedented
Republican majority in congressional elections
of 1920.  Final rejection of treaty and of
League of Nations by U.S. Senate in March
1920.


Commager, History, pp. 411-413

---

(2) *Learn to translate information and ideas into your own
words.* Many of the notes you will take for a research project
will record information fairly specifically and fully. A flexible
method of recording such material is the **paraphrase**:

---

Wilson's Campaign in Support of League

    Speech at Pueblo, Colorado, shows that Wilson
is very much aware of the activities of men creating
what he considers erroneous impressions concerning
the League of Nations.  Speech is designed to dispel
mistaken impressions created in the public's mind.

    The proposed peace treaty is based not on the
desire for territorial acquisition but on the
principle that people should freely choose their own
governments.  The League of Nations is needed to
mobilize the united moral force of the great nations
of the world in support of the principles of non-
agression and of self-determination for all nations.

Heffner, Documents, p. 235

---

(3) *Use well-chosen quotations to pinpoint key ideas or to clinch*

*an argument.* The following note reproduces verbatim an author's position on a debatable point:

```
Dangers of Conformity

     "The idea that men are created free and
equal is both true and misleading:  men are
created different; they lose their social
freedom and their individual autonomy in
seeking to become like each other."


Riesman, Lonely Crowd, p. 349
```

Use **direct quotation** sparingly or not at all in reproducing information, in outlining an author's argument, and in covering minor or noncontroversial points. Frequent use of undigested direct quotations tempts the reader to skip the quoted material and to look in the accompanying text for your main point.

NOTE: Make sure that your notes differentiate clearly between paraphrase or indirect quotation on the one hand and direct quotation on the other. In other words, *use quotation marks to identify all material quoted verbatim.*

## Note Cards

*Separate note cards enable you to sort out and reshuffle information.* Most composition instructors require that their students take notes for a research project on 3x5 or 4x6 cards. Observing the following suggestions will help you make efficient use of your cards:

(1) Each card should record either *one single item of information or material so closely related that there is no chance of your having to separate it* in order to use it in different parts of your

paper. However, generalizations should be accompanied by the specific detail that you will need to illustrate or support them in a paragraph. Include selected examples, statistical figures, definitions of difficult terms.

(2) The *material on each card should be full and clear enough* to make sense to you even after the context in which it originally appeared is no longer fresh in your mind. Excessive use of condensation and of abbreviations may make notes worthless later.

(3) The *material on each card should be representative* of the source from which it was taken. Be careful not to copy, as bare assertion, statements that are modified or qualified by the context in which they originally appeared.

(4) Each card should clearly *identify the source of the material recorded.* Use a shortened form of the author's name and the title of the work. (Some instructors recommend using a code number that you have assigned to the work in your preliminary bibliography.) *Include the exact page reference.*

(5) If you have arrived at tentative subdivisions for your paper, the *heading to which the material on the card relates* should appear at the top of the card. Use headings that will divide your material into sizable but convenient units. Having too many cards per heading will make your notes unwieldy. Having too few cards per heading will make your notes confusing.

## Exercise

Select an article (or chapter from a book) for its possible relevance to a future research project. Prepare a dozen note cards, grouped around two or three related headings and illustrating the various techniques of note-taking.

## Writing and Revising the First Draft

*Learn to organize and adapt material from your note cards for use in your finished text.*

By taking notes on separate cards, you can sort your notes into tentative categories while you are still studying your sources. When you have done most of the necessary reading, you should review your note cards to consider the main divisions they suggest.

## Organizing the Research Paper

*Group together cards that contain related material.* Make sure your finished paper will not strike the reader as a collection of loosely connected bits of information. Often a group of cards will record details pointing to a common generalization, evidence backing up the same major point. Often a group of cards will record related causes combining to produce a common result. Two related groups of cards may contain parallel sets of data for detailed comparison.

As your paper begins to assume definite shape in your mind, remember the following advice:

(1) *Work toward a unifying thesis.* Ask yourself: "What is this paper as a whole going to tell the reader?" Suppose you are writing a paper on the present state of gambling in the United States. Keep your paper from becoming a repository of miscellaneous facts about gambling laws, famous gamblers, different games of chance, and tourist life in Las Vegas. To unify your paper, you might concentrate on the legal aspects of gambling. You could then review in some detail the laws of Nevada as exceptions to anti-gambling laws in other states, the legal status of horse and dog races, the question of lotteries and games conducted for charitable purposes. Everything you say in the paper could support one single major point: "Gambling laws in the United States are paradoxical and unpredictable."

(2) *Plan to state your thesis early in your paper.* Do not merely start by indicating the *direction* of your inquiry. Instead, early state the *conclusion* you have reached. No one can quarrel with a program like the following, but no one will get excited about it either:

Volumes have been written about the character of Hamlet. Careful study is required to separate the mere fanciful theories from those that deserve our attention. . . .

Commit yourself to an assertion that can be argued, challenged—and remembered:

The great majority of Shakespeare's critics agree that the ghost's appearance, urging Hamlet on to revenge, imposes a task on a man unfitted by nature to accomplish such an undertaking.

(3) *Work out a logical overall scheme.* When writing about critical interpretations of Hamlet's character, do not simply give a survey following straight chronological order. Instead, try to identify three or four major schools of thought. Group together critics interested in the *lone* Hamlet, listening to him most intently in his monologues and solitary musings. Group together critics interested in the *social* Hamlet and absorbed by his playacting and verbal fencing. Group together critics interested in the *child* Hamlet, listening, in psychoanalyst's fashion, for hints of his early psychological history.

(4) *After arranging your cards in a tentative sequence, write a preliminary outline that reflects their order.* Formulate a tentative thesis sentence summarizing the conclusion that your paper seems to suggest. Your outline and your thesis sentence will enable you to decide which of your note cards contain *irrelevant* material and should be set aside. They will also help you to decide in which areas your notes need to be supplemented by further reading. A definitive outline preceding the final paper usually shows whether the paper has a unifying purpose, whether the major subdivisions of the paper contribute to that purpose, and whether unrelated odds and ends have been eliminated. (For forms of outlines, see O 8.)

Once you have a preliminary outline, you can start writing a first rough draft of your paper. Keep your eyes on your overall plan and decide to be temporarily satisfied with less than perfection in details. Where necessary, modify your plan or reorganize your note cards as you proceed. If you notice unanswered questions or missing evidence, note the inadequacies in the margin and follow them up later.

## Adapting Quoted Material

In writing a research paper, you will be working into the text an often considerable amount of quoted material. The following examples illustrate some legitimate, and some illegitimate, ways of incorporating material from a source into the text of a paper:

(1) *Extensive quotation—to be used sparingly:*

```
such a view.  In an article in Fortune that has been fre-
quently reprinted, Adlai Stevenson stated his belief that
American postwar prosperity was due to the cooperation of
business and government:

            It is a curious thing that the two institutional
        forces in the democratic capitalistic society that
        contributed most directly to this emergence of the
        powerful consumer during this quarter-century seemed
        to snarl at each other every step of their common way.
        The bounding prosperity of postwar America has been
        due in large measure to processes in which government
        and business have in effect played complementary and
        cooperative roles.  The New Deal legislation of the
        Thirties helped to provide a "built-in" consumer
        demand that business could then work to satisfy, and
        the increase of 70 per cent in the scale of the
        American economy between 1939 and 1944 was achieved
        by the closest cooperation between government and
        industry in America's war effort.
```

---

```
    ⁷Adlai E. Stevenson, "My Faith in Democratic
Capitalism," Fortune, October 1955, p. 126.
```

In this example, a lengthy excerpt from a source is used to buttress an important point. The excerpt is indented and set off from the text as a **block quotation**—*no quotation marks, single-spaced lines.* The sentence introducing the excerpt gives credit to author and publication; the footnote numeral at the end directs the reader to the footnote providing the name of the article and an exact page reference. *The introductory sentence also summarizes the main point or the significance of the quotation.* A reader easily becomes bored and discouraged if he cannot make out why he is given numerous lengthy quotations.

(2) *Plagiarized version—illegitimate, unacknowledged paraphrase:*

```
has had lasting effects.  But it is surprising that the

two forces in our society that contributed most to the

emergence of the powerful consumer seemed to snarl at each

other every step of the way.  The prosperity of postwar

America has been due to the fact that government and

business have played complementary and cooperative roles.

The New Deal legislation of the Thirties provided a built-in

consumer demand for business to satisfy.  The increase of

70 per cent in the American economy was achieved by the

cooperation between government and industry in America's

war effort.
```

Much **plagiarism** takes this form: a slightly abridged version of the original source. Even if the source were identified, this way of adapting the material would be unsatisfactory. It preserves far too much of the original author's way of putting things—without using direct quotation. Sentence structure corresponds closely to that of the original. Much of the characteristic phrasing is preserved ("emergence of the powerful consumer," "seemed to snarl," "complementary and cooperative roles"). The only changes are the omission or shortening of incidental phrases. As in much hasty adaptation, qualifications that made the original cautious have been lost ("due to" for "due *in large measure* to"; "provided" for "*helped* to provide").

(3) *Legitimate paraphrase—attributed to the original author:*

Like other observers, Mr. Stevenson points out the irony in the apparent hostility of the two major institutions that made the American consumer a powerful force in the nation's economy. He attributes the rapidly growing prosperity of postwar America at least partly to the cooperation, intentional or unintentional, of government and business. Thus, legislation enacted under the Roosevelt administration helped to increase consumer purchasing power. Similarly, the extraordinary growth of the American economy between 1939 and 1944 was the result of government and industry working together in building up the country's military strength.[7]

This **paraphrase**, documented by a footnote, preserves the essential meaning of the original. At the same time, by translating the passage into his own words, the adapter shows that he has understood it. He shows how he interprets phrases that are in any way unusual or metaphorical. For instance, he takes the phrase "a curious thing" to express irony. For the graphic "seemed to snarl" he substitutes its literal equivalent, "apparent hostility." Instead of using percentage points, the adapter describes the growth of the economy as "extraordinary." Though general, this term does

justice to the intention of the original. Although some of the
sentences are roughly parallel to the original in grammatical
construction, others—for instance, the first and second
ones—are completely reorganized. This kind of close paraphrase is useful when detailed interpretation and evaluation
of a source is desirable.

(4) *Part paraphrase, part direct quotation—worked closely
into the text:*

    Like economists and sociologists before him, Mr.

Stevenson emphasizes that government and business in this

country have in effect worked together in assuring postwar

prosperity--even though they "seemed to snarl at each other

every step of their common way."  As he implies but does

not directly state, business has never openly acknowledged

that "New Deal legislation . . . helped to provide a

'built-in' consumer demand that business could then work

to satisfy."  He attributes an "increase of 70 per cent in

the scale of the American economy between 1939 and 1944"

to "the closest cooperation" between government and

industry.[7]


This technique is the most flexible and most generally
useful one for adapting source material to the adapter's own
use. He condenses, restates, and interprets the material he
has selected, at the same time using brief direct quotations
for important points and characteristic phrases. Competent
use of this technique can effectively break up the deadly

"So-and-So says such-and-such" pattern found in many library papers.

(5) *Legitimate summary:*

Mr. Stevenson feels that postwar prosperity in this country was to a large extent the result of cooperation between government and business. Specifically he refers to the role of New Deal legislation in restoring consumer demand and to the joint participation of government and industry in the war effort.[7]

This **summary** gets at the gist of the passage. At the same time it lists briefly arguments or details supporting the main point in the original.

## Integrating Quoted Material

*Work material from different note cards smoothly into a coherent paragraph of your own.* To keep your text moving smoothly in spite of the bulk of quoted material, remember the following points:

(1) *Link quoted and paraphrased material clearly to its source.* There is considerable difference between "Capitalism is a moribund system" and "According to Marx, capitalism is a moribund system." If you are citing several authors, make sure that the references like "he," "this author," or "the writer" point clearly to the person you have in mind. Show clearly where a paraphrase stops and your own comment starts:

*Lewis Theobald, an eighteenth-century critic,* sees Hamlet as the heroic prince. *Theobald* is engrossed with the neoclassical principle of decorum as he criticizes Hamlet's coarseness and obscenity toward Ophelia. *The modern reader* is not likely to think of this part of Hamlet's behavior in the same terms. . . .

(2) *Review carefully the conventions governing the punctuation of quoted material.* Pay special attention to the distinction between direct and indirect quotation, to differences in handling long and short passages, and to ways of indicating omissions and insertions. (See chart.)

(3) When a quotation becomes part of one of your own sentences, *fit it into the grammatical pattern of your sentence, without changing the original wording* of the material enclosed in quotation marks:

| | |
|---|---|
| **Unsatisfactory:** | Pope Pius described a just war in this way: "If it has been forced upon one by an evident and extremely grave injustice that in no way can be avoided." |
| **Satisfactory:** | Pope Pius stated that a war is just "if it has been forced upon one by an evident and extremely grave injustice that in no way can be avoided." |
| **Unsatisfactory:** | The writer suggests that Whittaker Chambers, "Having experienced at first hand the evils of communism, he now sees himself clad in shining armor, engaged in deadly combat with that evil." |
| **Satisfactory:** | The writer says of Whittaker Chambers that "having experienced at first hand the evils of communism, he now sees himself clad in shining armor, engaged in deadly combat with that evil." |

(4) *Make sure quotations are logically complete.* Suppose you quote Albert Schweitzer as saying, "I therefore stand and work in the world, as one who aims at making men less shallow and morally better by making them think." To keep the quotation from being logically incomplete, you will have to let your reader know what the "therefore" stands for. If you don't want to include the reasons to which it refers, you will have to shorten or paraphrase the quotation in such a way as to omit it.

## HOW TO PUNCTUATE QUOTATIONS
### A Brief Guide (see also P 8)

*Word or phrase directly quoted,* becoming part of a larger sentence (quotation marks, but *no* comma or colon):

> A. E. Housman is generally known as "a writer of elegiac pessimism in strikingly simple form." [1]

*Indirect quotation* or paraphrase (no quotation marks, no comma or colon):

> These dissertations on death and its aftereffects are merely Housman's stoical explanation of actuality. He once observed that the love of truth with most people is the faintest of passions. [14]

*A sentence or more,* directly quoted (quotation marks, introduced by comma or colon):

> George Santayana, American poet and philosopher, commented on the use of melancholy in many of Housman's poems: "I read *A Shropshire Lad,* always with tears. There is not much else than tears in them, but they are perfect of their kind." [4]

*Long prose passage,* set off as block quotation (indented, single-spaced — *no* quotation marks):

> During Housman's teaching career at Princeton, his work was very influential on those close to him. According to one of his students,
>
>> Instinctively we felt he knew all about us, that some would die young, some fail in love, some end in jail. His wisdom was a bitter brew, but it did not inspire bitterness or despair, and his poems with a marvelous economy told us the strengthening truth that we were very ordinary fellows whose only portion was the estate of man. Those of us who learned this young owe him much. [6]

*Words or phrases from poetry,* becoming part of a larger sentence (quotation marks; diagonal line to show start of a new line in original poem):

> The poet and his guide journey "like the cloudy shadows / Across the country blown . . ." (p. 55), and the entire expedition is a very pleasant one with no hardships or miseries.

*Complete lines of verse,* set off as block quotation (indented, single-spaced, centered on the page):

> Housman does not deny his use of despondency but rather seems to think it essential to the universality of his work:
>
>> They say my verse is sad: no wonder;
>>   Its narrow measure spans
>> Tears of eternity, and sorrow,
>>   Not mine but man's. [3]

## Revision

*Careful revision of the first draft is an essential step, and your timetable should make adequate allowance for it.* A first draft usually makes jerky reading. The writer is likely to have concentrated on arranging his material in the most logical or the most convenient order, without always explaining to his readers how he got from one paragraph to the other. He is likely to have concentrated on getting the main body of the paper into shape, providing no more than a routine introduction and allowing the paper to run out without a definite conclusion.

In revising your first draft, you will make changes ranging from the substitution of a semicolon for a comma to the rearrangement of major sections of your paper. However, regardless of the specific improvements needed, your revision should concern itself with several basic requirements for a successful paper:

(1) Check for *adequacy of detail.* See to it that individual points are clearly stated and well illustrated or documented. Make sure that the evidence you present in support of your generalizations is adequate to prevent questions such as "Is this really so?" "Is this merely a superficial impression?" or "Do the experts agree on this point?"

(2) Check for *clarity of explanation.* Many papers suffer from too much quotation, too much paraphrase, too much summary, and not enough explanation and comparison. Examine key terms to see whether they need to be more explicitly defined. Explain terms like *Hellenistic, psychosomatic,* or *lingua franca.*

(3) Check for *adequate paragraph structure.* Avoid sequences of short paragraphs that give bits of information or quotation from different sources. Instead, work material from different note cards into a coherent paragraph that coordinates, compares, contrasts. Choppy paragraphing makes continuous reading difficult, if not impossible.

(4) Check for *clear attribution.* If you are comparing dif-

ferent sources, keep your reader from getting hopelessly confused about who says what. Constant repetition of phrases like "according to Dewey" or "as his biographer observes" can make a paper seem heavy-handed. However, awkward but exact identification is preferable to elegant but misleading continuity of discussion.

(5) Check for *coherence.* Make your reader see the relationship between different parts of your paper. Anticipate and answer the questions of a reader mired in a mass of details: "How did this get in here?" "Why do I have to study this particular set of statistics?" Make sure there is a clear **transition**, implied or explicitly stated, from paragraph to paragraph. Inserting a *therefore,* a *nevertheless,* or a *for instance* in a few strategic places can help transform a rambling discussion into a tightly knit argument. Check the organization of the paper against your tentative outline and adjust your outline to reflect any changes you made while writing the first draft and while revising it.

(6) Check for *clarity of overall intention.* Make sure that the main points you are trying to bring out are not merely implied but clearly and fully stated. State them preferably at the beginning of the paper following your introduction or, if more appropriate, toward the end of the paper in the form of a summary. Don't take it for granted that your reader will automatically arrive at the same conclusions that you did if you merely present "the facts."

## Exercises

**A.** Select a passage of paragraph length from an article or book relevant to a future research project. Illustrate various legitimate ways of quoting, excerpting, or summarizing it in the text of a research paper.

**B.** In the following passage from *Eminent Victorians,* Lytton Strachey documents the period of spiritual unrest that Cardinal Manning experienced before his conversion to Catholicism. Study the way Strachey has worked *short, revealing* quotations from Cardinal

Manning's diary into a coherent paragraph. Your instructor may ask you to write a similar paragraph, using quotations from the autobiography, diary, or memoirs of one of the great Victorians—Cardinal Newman, Charles Darwin, General Gordon, or another major figure of your choice.

> He decided to mortify himself, to read St. Thomas Aquinas, and to make his "night prayers forty instead of thirty minutes." He determined during Lent "to use no pleasant bread (except on Sundays and feasts) such as cake and sweetmeat"; but he added the proviso "I do not include plain biscuits." Opposite this entry appears the word *"kept."* And yet his backslidings were many. Looking back over a single week, he was obliged to register "petulance twice" and "complacent visions." He heard his curate being commended for bringing so many souls to God during Lent, and he "could not bear it"; but the remorse was terrible: "I abhorred myself on the spot, and looked upward for help." He made out list upon list of the Almighty's special mercies towards him, and they included his creation, his regeneration, and (No. 5)
>
> > the preservation of my life six times to my knowledge—
> > (1) In illness at the age of nine.
> > (2) In the water.
> > (3) By a runaway horse at Oxford.
> > (4) By the same.
> > (5) By falling nearly through the ceiling of a church.
> > (6) Again by a fall of a horse. And I know not how often in shooting, riding, etc.
>
> At last he became convalescent; but the spiritual experiences of those agitated weeks left an indelible mark upon his mind, and prepared the way for the great change which was to follow.

**C**. After finishing the first draft of a research paper, write a *one-page abstract* that spells out the thesis and summarizes the argument. (Your instructor may ask you to submit a *preliminary* summary of findings at an earlier stage of your investigation.)

## Preparing Footnotes and Bibliographies

Documentation enables your readers to identify, trace, and check your sources. Its purpose should not be to impress your readers but to provide exact and comprehensive information in condensed form.

## Footnotes

*In your own paper, the main purpose of footnotes will be to document your sources.* Use footnotes to indicate the origin of facts, opinions, and illustrative material. Use them not only when you quote an author directly, but also when you merely paraphrase or summarize what he said.[2] A footnote is *not* necessary when the author has merely repeated something that is widely known or believed.

**No Footnote:** George Washington was elected to the Virginia assembly in 1758. (This is "common knowledge," the kind of fact likely to be recorded in public documents and found in many history books.)

**Footnote:** Samuel Eliot Morison describes Washington as "an eager and bold experimenter" in new agricultural methods.[17] (This is a judgment the historian made on the basis of first-hand investigation. The text already mentions his name; the footnote, not reprinted here, will give the exact source.)

Current practice favors consecutive numbering of all footnotes for a paper, article, or chapter of a book. In other words, footnotes are not indicated by asterisks or similar symbols. Nor do the footnote numbers start anew on each individual page. The **footnote number** is placed outside whatever punctuation goes with the item to which it refers. The footnote itself is indented like a paragraph and is intro-

[2] Not all footnotes serve exclusively for documentation. **Explanatory footnotes**, of which this note is an illustration, may define technical terms unfamiliar only to some of the readers. They may provide information not necessary to the main trend of the argument. They may contain reservations that would confuse ordinary readers but are needed to satisfy critical ones. Use such material sparingly. Many readers check all footnotes to make sure they miss nothing of importance. Do not make them interrupt their reading for the sake of something trivial or irrelevant.

duced by a raised numeral; the numeral is *not* followed by a period or other punctuation. The footnote begins with a capital letter and ends with appropriate terminal punctuation, most commonly a period.

In printed publications, the footnotes for each page appear in small print at the bottom of each page. In typed manuscripts, footnotes are usually single-spaced and placed in one of three possible positions:

(1) Footnotes may be placed *between two unbroken lines immediately below the line of typed material* to which they belong. This system, when permitted by the instructor, helps the inexperienced researcher to make the right footnote go with the right portion of the text.[3]

---

[3] Even when a different system of placing footnotes is required in the final paper, students may find the system of which this footnote is an illustration the most convenient one to follow in the first draft. It prevents errors when footnotes have to be renumbered because of changes in the manuscript.

---

(2) Footnotes may be placed *at the bottom of the page,* separated from the text by an unbroken line or by triple spacing. This system is convenient for the reader, who is used to a similar arrangement in printed material, but it is hard on the amateur typist. It requires him to type his footnotes on a separate sheet of paper so that he can estimate the amount of space needed for each and leave exactly enough space at the bottom of each page for the footnotes that go with it.

(3) Footnotes may appear *on a separate sheet at the end of the paper.* This system is usually required when a manuscript is submitted for publication.

### First References

*Fully identify a source the first time you refer to it.* The most common type of footnote gives full information about a source the first time it is mentioned or drawn on in the text.

The following sample footnotes illustrate the standard form for such a first reference, as well as the most important variations. *Pay special attention to the way punctuation marks are used in these sample footnotes.* Use commas, colons, parentheses, and quotation marks exactly as here illustrated unless you are otherwise instructed by the teacher or editor who is to pass judgment on your work.

(1) *Standard reference to a book.* Give the author's full name, putting the first name *first.* After a comma, add the title of the book—*underlined* in typescript (italicized in print). Give the facts of publication in parentheses. Many teachers and editors require only *place and date* of publication (separated by a comma). But adding the publisher's name can help the reader identify different editions or paperback reprints of standard authors. After a comma, add the page reference ("p." for single page; "pp." for several pages: pp. 163–165).

[2] Albert H. Marckwardt, *American English* (New York, 1958), p. 17.

[4] Irving H. Anderson and Walter F. Dearborn, *The Psychology of Teaching Reading* (New York, 1952), pp. 70–72.

[7] Henry James, *The Portrait of a Lady* (New York: Random House, 1951), p. 140.

(2) *Newspaper or magazine article.* Enclose the title of the article in quotation marks; underline the title of the newspaper or magazine: "How to Deep-Freeze Bait," *The Fisherman's Monthly.* Give the date of issue, separated from what precedes and follows by commas. If a magazine provides a volume number, give it as a Roman numeral, enclose the date in parentheses, and give the page reference *without* using "p." or "pp.": XV (September 1969), 47.

[3] "U.S. Asked to Aid Youth Exchanges," *New York Times,* June 15, 1968, p. 8, col. 1.

[6] Jeanne Contini, "The Illiterate Poets of Somalia," *The Reporter,* March 14, 1963, p. 36.

[9] Constance M. Drake, "An Approach to Blake," *College English*, XXIX (April 1968), 545.

NOTE: Linguists often follow an alternative style used in the sciences: The volume number appears as an Arabic numeral, separated from the page number by a period: *College English*, 29.545 (April 1968).

(3) *Partial footnote.* If the text of your paper has given the author's full name, do not repeat it but start your footnote with the title. If you have given both the full name and the full title, start your footnote with the facts of publication (without parentheses):

[2] *American English* (New York, 1958), p. 17.

[2] New York, 1958, p. 17.

(4) *Work with subtitle.* Separate the subtitle from the title by a colon unless the original has other punctuation. Underline the subtitle of a book; enclose both the title and the subtitle of an article in the same set of quotation marks.

[11] Marshall McLuhan, *Understanding Media: The Extensions of Man* (New York, 1964), p. 20.

[2] John J. Gross, "The Writer in America: A Search for Community," *Queen's Quarterly,* LXIII (Autumn 1956), 387.

(5) *Edited or translated work.* Insert the editor's or translator's name after the title, separating it from the title by a comma. Use the abbreviation "ed." or "trans." The editor's name may come *first* if the author is unknown, if the editor has collected the work of different authors, or if the editor has brought together an author's work from different sources.

[2] H. L. Mencken, *The Vintage Mencken*, ed. Alistair Cooke (New York, 1956), p. 49.

[8] André Siegfried, *America at Mid-Century*, trans. Margaret Ledésert (New York, 1955), p. 227.

[5] Kenneth Sisam, ed. *Fourteenth Century Verse and Prose* (London, 1948), p. 14.

(6) *Revised editions.* If a work has been brought up to date since its original publication, indicate the number of the edition you are using. Place it before the facts of publication, separating it from what precedes it by a comma.

[2] Albert C. Baugh, *A History of the English Language*, 2nd ed. (New York, 1957), pp. 7–8.

[9] M. B. Forman, ed. *The Letters of John Keats*, 3rd ed. (London, 1948), pp. 67–68.

(7) *Work published in several volumes.* Specify the number of the volume you are citing. Use a capital Roman numeral, insert it after the facts of publication, and separate it from what precedes and follows it by commas. Remember that after a volume number "p." and "pp." are omitted.

[3] Vernon Louis Parrington, *Main Currents in American Thought: An Interpretation of American Literature from the Beginnings to 1920* (New York, 1930), III, 355.

(8) *Article in a collection.* Identify fully both the article and the anthology of which it has become a part.

[13] Eliseo Vivas, "Kafka's Distorted Mask," in *Kafka: A Collection of Critical Essays,* ed. Ronald Gray (Englewood Cliffs, N.J., 1962), pp. 137–138.

(9) *Encyclopedia entry.* Page numbers and facts of publication are unnecessary for *short* entries appearing in alphabetical order in well-known encyclopedias or dictionaries. Date or number of the edition used, however, is usually included because of the frequent revisions of major encyclopedias.

[2] M. J. Politis, "Greek Music," *Encyclopedia Americana*, 1956.

[4] "Drama," *Encyclopaedia Britannica*, 1958, VII, 596

(10) *Bible or literary classic.* References to the Bible usually identify only book, chapter, and verse. The name of a book of the Bible is *not* underlined or put in quotation marks. References to a Shakespeare play available in many different editions may specify act, scene, and line; references to an epic poem book, canto, and stanza.

> [4] Judges 13:5.   or   [4] Judges xiii.5.
>
> [3] *Hamlet* II.ii.311–322.

Note, however, that you will have to specify the edition used if textual variations are important, as with a new translation of the Bible. No identification is necessary for well-known or proverbial lines: "To be or not to be"; "The quality of mercy is not strained"; "They also serve who only stand and wait."

(11) *Quotations at second hand.* Make it clear that you are not quoting from the original or complete text.

> [5] William Archer, letter of October 18, 1883, to his brother Charles; quoted in Henrik Ibsen, *Ghosts,* ed. Kai Jurgensen and Robert Schenkkan (New York, 1965), p. 135.

(12) *Pamphlets and unpublished material.* Indicate the nature and source of materials other than books and magazines: mimeographed pamphlet, unpublished doctoral dissertation, and the like. Start with the title if no author or editor is identified. Use quotation marks to enclose unpublished titles.

> [6] Walter G. Friedrich, ed. "A Modern Grammar Chrestomathy" (Valparaiso, Indiana, mimeo., 1961), p. 12.
>
> [7] U. Fuller Schmaltz, "The *Weltschmerz* of Charles Addams," (Ph.D. dissertation, Columbia, 1959), p. 7.
>
> [8] *Grape Harvesting,* California Department of Viticulture Leaflet (Sacramento, 1969), pp. 8–9.

## Subsequent References

*Keep subsequent references short but clear.* There is no need to repeat the full name and title, or the facts of publication. Here are the most common possibilities:

(1) *Shortened reference.* Once you have fully identified a book, use the author's last name to identify it in subsequent footnotes. Separate the name from the page reference by a comma.

> ¹¹ Baugh, p. 9.

When you are using *several works by the same author,* use the author's last name and a shortened form of the title:

> ¹¹ Baugh, *History,* p. 9.

(2) *One footnote for several quotations.* Avoid long strings of footnotes giving different page references to the same work. If several quotations from the same work follow one another in the same paragraph of your paper, incorporate the page references in a single footnote. Use this method only when *no* quotations from another source intervene.

> ¹³ Harrison, pp. 8–9, 12, 17.

(3) *Page references in the text.* If all or most of your references are to a single work, you may put page references in parentheses in the body of your text: (p. 37). Identify the source in your first footnote and explain your procedure.

> ¹ Jerome S. Bruner, *On Knowing: Essays for the Left Hand* (New York: Atheneum, 1965), p. 3. All page references in the text of this paper are to this source.

(4) *Latin abbreviations.* An alternative system for shortened reference is frequently found in earlier scholarship but

no longer in frequent use. Instead of repeating, in a shortened form, the author's name or the title, the writer may use *ibid.*, an abbreviation of Latin *ibidem*, "in the same place." When used by itself, without a page reference, it means "in the last publication cited, on the same page." When used with a page reference, it means "in the last publication cited, on the page indicated." Like other Latin abbreviations used in footnotes, *ibid.* is no longer commonly italicized. It can refer only to *the last source cited.*

[1] G. B. Harrison, *Introducing Shakespeare* (New York, 1947), p. 28.

[2] Ibid., p. 37.

If a reference to a *different* work has intervened, the author's name is followed by *op. cit.*, short for *opere citato,* "in the work already cited." (This abbreviation cannot be used when *several works* by the same author have already been cited.)

[1] G. B. Harrison, *Introducing Shakespeare* (New York, 1947), p. 28.

[2] B. Ifor Evans, *A Short History of English Drama* (Hammondsworth, Middlesex, 1948), pp. 51–69.

[3] Harrison, op. cit., p. 37.

## Abbreviations

*Footnotes in scholarly books and articles employ a number of abbreviations and technical terms in addition to those you will regularly use in your own work.* The meaning of many of these will be clear from their context or position; for example, *anon.* for "anonymous," *ch.* and *chs.* for "chapter" and "chapters," *col.* and *cols.* for "column" and "columns," *l.* and *ll.* for "line" and "lines," *n.* and *nn.* for "note" and "notes." Others are not self-explanatory:

| | |
|---|---|
| © | copyright (© 1961 by John W. Gardner) |
| c. or ca. | Latin *circa*, "approximately"; used for approximate dates and figures (*c.* 1952) |
| cf. | Latin *confer*, "compare"; often used loosely instead of *see* in the sense of "consult for further relevant material" (Cf. Ecclesiastes xii.12) |
| et al. | Latin *et alii*, "and others"; used in references to books by several authors (G. B. Harrison et al.) |
| f., ff. | "and the following page," "and the following pages" (See pp. 16f.) |
| loc. cit. | Latin *loco citato*, "in the place cited"; used without page reference (Baugh, loc. cit.) |
| MS, MSS | manuscript, manuscripts |
| n.d. | "no date," date of publication unknown |
| passim | Latin for "throughout," "in various places in the work under discussion" (See pp. 54–56 et passim) |
| q.v. | Latin *quod vide*, "which you should consult" |

## Final Bibliography

*The final bibliography, based on your bibliography cards, includes all the information required to identify a source when first cited.* Its main purpose is to describe in one single alphabetical list all sources you have used. You may include sources that you have found helpful or enlightening but have not had occasion to quote from in your paper. However, do *not* list every book or article whose title you have come across during your investigation.

Entries in the bibliography differ from footnotes both in the arrangement and in the punctuation of the material presented:

(1) The *last name of the author* (or of the first author listed when a book has several authors) is placed first—since the bibliography is an *alphabetical* listing. The full name of the author is separated from what follows by a period.

(2) The *facts of publication* for a book usually include the publisher's name. They are *not* enclosed in parentheses and are separated from what precedes and what follows by periods.

(3) Entries for books do not include page references; entries for parts of books or items in magazines give the *inclusive page numbers* for the whole selection.

In a typed manuscript, single-space each individual item but leave a double space between items. Indent two spaces for the second and for subsequent lines of each item. If you list *several publications by the same author*, substitute a line composed of six consecutive hyphens for his name in second and subsequent entries. If *no name of author or editor is known to you*, list the publication alphabetically by the first letter of the title, not counting "The," "A," or "An."

The following might be the final bibliography for a paper investigating theatrical conventions and stage techniques in the time of Shakespeare. Study the different kinds of entries it includes. (See also the bibliography at the end of the sample research paper.)

BIBLIOGRAPHY

Adams, John Cranford.  The Globe Playhouse:  Its Design and
    Equipment.  Cambridge, Mass.:  Harvard University Press,
    1942.

Bailey, Margery.  "Shakespeare in Action," College English,
    XV (March 1954), 307-315.

Brooke, C. F. Tucker.  "The Renaissance," in A Literary
    History of England, ed. Albert C. Baugh.  New York:
    Appleton-Century-Crofts, Inc., 1948.

Chambers, E. K.  The Elizabethan Stage.  4 vols. Oxford:
    The Clarendon Press, 1923.

Davies, W. Robertson.  Shakespeare's Boy Actors.  London:
    J. M. Dent & Sons, Ltd., 1939.

Frye, Northrop, "The Argument of Comedy," in Shakespeare:
Modern Essays in Criticism, ed. Leonard F. Dean, 2nd ed.
New York: Oxford University Press, 1967.

Granville-Barker, Harley, and G. B. Harrison, eds.
A Companion to Shakespeare Studies. New York: The
Macmillan Company, 1934.

Greg, W. W., ed. Henslowe's Diary. 2 vols. London:
A. H. Gullen, 1904-1908.

Harbage, Alfred. Shakespeare's Audience. New York:
Columbia University Press, 1941.

------, Theatre for Shakespeare. Toronto: University
of Toronto Press, 1955.

"A New Shakespearean Festival," The Oakland Herald,
August 12, 1958, p. 7, col. 2.

North, Sir Thomas, trans. Shakespeare's Plutarch: The Lives
of Julius Caesar, Brutus, Marcus Antonius, and Coriolanus,
ed. T. J. B. Spencer. Baltimore: Penguin Books, 1964.

Rosenberg, Marvin. "Elizabethan Actors: Men or Marionettes?"
PMLA, LXIX (September 1954), 915-927.

Shaw G. B. Shaw on Shakespeare, ed. Edwin Wilson. New York:
E. P. Dutton & Co., 1961.

Spargo, J. W. "The Knocking on the Gate in Macbeth, An
Essay in Interpretation," in John Quincy Adams Memorial
Studies, ed. J. G. McManaway et al. Washington, D.C.:
Folger Shakespeare Library, 1948.

Sprague, A. C. Shakespeare and the Actors: The Stage
Business in His Plays (1660-1905). Cambridge, Mass.:
Harvard University Press, 1948.

## Exercises

**A.** Interpret the information provided in the following footnotes:

[3] Robert E. Spiller et al., *Literary History of the United States*,
rev. ed. (New York, 1953), p. 1343.

[1] James Brown, "Eight Types of Puns," *PMLA*, LXXI (March 1956), 20.

[9] Euripides, *The Trojan Women*, trans. Richmond Lattimore, in *Greek Plays in Modern Translation*, ed. Dudley Fitts (New York, 1947), p. 161.

[2] "America—the Beautiful?" *Life*, June 3, 1957, p. 34.

[8] Kenneth Muir, ed. *Collected Poems of Sir Thomas Wyatt* (Cambridge, Mass., 1950), p. xx.

[7] I Corinthians iii.18–20.

[6] Joannes Caius, *Of English Dogs*, trans. Abraham Fleming (1576), in *An English Garner*, ed. Edward Arber (London, 1877–83), III, 225–268.

[12] Cf. *The Complete Works of William Hazlitt*, ed. P. P. Howe (London, 1932), XI, 88ff.

**B**. Study the style of documentation followed in a scholarly journal in your major field of interest. Determine to what extent its style coincides with that outlined in the preceding discussion and in what respects it differs from it.

# Review Exercise: Sample Research Paper

Study the following sample research paper, adapted from a student-written paper. Pay special attention to the way the author has adapted and worked into the text a variety of quoted material. Compare the different kinds of footnotes used. Contrast the way sources are identified in the footnotes and in the final bibliography. How successful has the author been in meeting the standards outlined in the preceding chapter?

THE FUROR OVER IBSEN

by

John Balfour

English 2, Section 5

March 22, 1969

OUTLINE

Thesis:   Ibsen's plays were denounced as immoral and at the same time celebrated as advancing a new morality.

Introduction:   The divisive effect of Ibsen's plays

      I.   Ibsen's plays and his time

         A.   The morality of his plays

         B.   The moral views of his contemporaries

     II.   The attack on Ibsen

         A.   Scott's denunciation

         B.   Archer's collection of criticism

    III.   Shaw's defense of Ibsen's plays

    IV.   Ibsen's portrait of his critics

         A.   The moralist in his plays

         B.   Ibsen's letters

Conclusion:   Ibsen as father of the modern drama

THE FUROR OVER IBSEN

What did Henrik Ibsen do?  According to Granville-
Barker, he "split the English theater in two."[1]  Indeed,
"as everyone knows, the introduction of Ibsen into England
was not a peaceful one.  In its wake came one of those great
outbursts of critical frenzy and inflamed controversy which
at regular intervals enliven literary history."[2]  In England,
as in the rest of Europe, the public was split into two
factions:  those who placed Ibsen on the blacklist as
"immoral"; and those who saw in him the champion of a new
morality.

Ibsen's plays aroused both indignation and enthusiasm
because he fought against maintaining appearances at the
expense of happiness, or what he termed hypocrisy.  Una
Ellis-Fermor, a translator and lifelong student of Ibsen,
said that he "took upon himself the task of exposing the
makeshift morality of his contemporaries in private and
public life":

---

[1]Harley Granville-Barker, "When Ibsen Split the English
Stage in Two," The Literary Digest, IIIC (April 28, 1928),
24.
[2]"A Retrospective Eye on Ibsen," Theatre Arts Monthly,
XII (March 1928), 199.

-2-

> In The Pillars of the Community he examines
> the lie in public life, the tragic struggle
> of Karsten Bernick to hide his sin and pre-
> serve his reputation at the expense of another
> man's good name. . . . In A Doll's House and
> Ghosts the subject is the lie in domestic life;
> the first shows the destruction of a marriage
> by an unreal and insincere relationship between
> husband and wife, and the second the destruction
> of the lives and souls of the characters by the
> oppressive tyranny of convention.[3]

In Ghosts, a dutiful and unloving wife keeps up an elaborate

façade of respectability for a profligate husband.  She

finds herself defeated when her cherished son returns home

suffering incurably from the syphilis he has inherited from

his father.  According to Bernard Shaw, the play was "an

uncompromising and outspoken attack on marriage as a useless

sacrifice," the story of a woman who had wasted her life in

manufacturing a "monstrous fabric of lies and false appear-

ances."[4]

Against the tyranny of middle-class standards, Ibsen

pitted his own concept of individual integrity.  He felt,

according to Georg Brandes, that "the individuality of the

human being is to be preserved for its own sake, not for

---

[3]Henrik Ibsen, Three Plays, trans. Una Ellis-Fermor
(Hammondsworth, Middlesex, 1950), pp. 9-11.
    [4]The Quintessence of Ibsenism, 3rd ed. (New York, 1957),
pp. 86, 88.

-3-

the sake of higher powers; and since beyond all else the
individual should remain free and whole, all concessions
made to the world represent to Ibsen the foul fiend, the
evil principle."[5] One of the main ideas fused into Ibsen's
plays, according to an article in the Encyclopaedia
Britannica, is "the supreme importance of individual character, of personality: in the development and enrichment
of the individual he saw the only hope for a really cul-
tured and enlightened society."[6]

A Doll's House was particularly loaded with the "first
duty to oneself" theme. Nora, in the last act, wakes to the
fact that she is not worthy to be a good mother and wife
because she has been merely a submissive servant and foil
first for her father and then for her husband; she has been
so protected and guided by them that she has no individual
conception of life and its complexities. Nora realized that
she did not know enough about the world and her place in it
to be really "a reasonable human being," and she felt a
duty to become one.[7] Her life all at once seemed so

---

[5]Creative Spirits of the Nineteenth Century, trans.
Rasmus B. Anderson (New York, 1923), p. 373.
[6]"Ibsen, Henrik Johan," Encyclopaedia Britannica, 1958,
XII, 38.
[7]Henrik Ibsen, Four Great Plays by Ibsen (New York,
1959), p. 65.

-4-

artificial and meaningless to her that she felt like a doll living in a doll's house, Nora left her husband and children to try to gain an understanding of real life, and when she "banged the door of A Doll's House, the echo of that violence was heard across the continent."[8]

Ibsen wrote these plays at a time when people felt a general ferment, a "spirit of the age" or "movement of the century" that had introduced everywhere a tendency toward change. Spokesmen for the modern age referred to the "new phase into which humanity is passing" and expressed the conviction that "society must undergo a transformation or perish."[9] But the voices resisting the clamor for "innovations" were equally strong. Their watchword was devotion to duty--toward God, country, one's family and husband. Self-denial for the sake of greater forces was the commendable action. The churches taught it was sinful to assert one's own wishes and desires. The people, especially the dominated wife with whom Isben frequently deals, were exhorted to live for the good of everyone but themselves.

---

[8]"Drama," Encyclopaedia Britannica, 1958, VII, 600.
[9]William Barry in The Nineteenth-Century (1889); quoted in Michael Goodwin, ed. Nineteenth-Century Opinion: An Anthology (1877-1901) (Hammondsworth, Middlesex, 1951), pp. 124, 122.

-5-

Spokesmen for the emancipation of women were told in the public press that "men are men and women, women"; that "sex is a fact--no Act of Parliament can eliminate it"; that "where two ride on a horse, one must needs ride behind."[10]  They were told that in women's hands "rests the keeping of a pure tone in society, of a high standard in morality, of a lofty devotion to duty in political life." If she were to enter openly into political conflict, she would "debase her sex" and "lower the ideal of womanhood amongst men."[11]

The old-fashioned moralists were shocked by the "Ibsenist" view that self-fulfillment is more important than the sanctity of marriage, one's duty to others, and even business success.  According to Arthur Bingham Walkley, drama critic for the London _Times_, "Ibsen became a bogey to many worthy people who had never read or seen a single one of his plays."  To these people, "Ibsenism was supposed vaguely to connote 'Woman's Rights,' Free Love, a new and fearful kind of wildfowl called 'Norwegian Socialism,' and

---

[10]Quoted in _Nineteenth-Century Opinion_, pp. 103, 109.
[11]_Opinion_, pp. 103-104.

-6-

generally, every manifestation of discontent with the
existing order of things."[12]  Clement Scott, a prominent
drama critic, led such formidable opposition against Ibsen's
dramas, especially A Doll's House and Ghosts, that they were
actually banned for a time from English stages.  "Ibsen
fails," Scott says, "because he is, I suppose, an atheist,
and has not realized what the great backbone of religion
means to the English race."  Scott continues, "He fails
because his plays are nasty, dirty, impure, clever if you
like, but foul to the last degree; and healthy-minded
English people don't like to stand and sniff over an ash-
pit."[13]

Many of the people causing the uproar against Ibsen
used similar exaggerated and irrational language.  William
Archer, the first English translator of Ibsen, collected some
of the attacks appearing in the English press when Ghosts
was first produced.  The play was called "disgusting,"
"loathsome," "gross," and "revoltingly suggestive and blas-
phemous."  It was compared to "a dirty act done publicly"

---

[12]"Ibsen in England," The Living Age, XII (September
21, 1901), 790.
[13]Quoted in "Inside Views of Ibsen in the Nineties,"
The Literary Digest, IIIC (May 12, 1928), 24.

-7-

and was called "a piece to bring the stage into disrepute
and dishonour with every right-thinking man and woman."[14]

Those who defended Ibsen--Shaw, Archer, Walkley--
blamed his unpleasant reception in England on both his
revolutionary themes and his new dramatic technique.  We
shall steer away from Ibsen's new dramatic technique and
instead discuss the defense of Ibsenism as a new moral
philosophy.  Shaw himself has been called one of the men
"who summon their generation to act by a new and higher
standard."  He made Ibsen his hero because Ibsen championed
the view that Shaw made the basis for many of his own plays:

> By "morals" (or "ideals") Shaw means conven-
> tional, current standards.  Because these stand-
> ards are universal and inherited from the past,
> they often do not fit particular situations and
> present-day societies.  Therefore good men--like
> some of Ibsen's characters--often choose to act
> "immorally," contrary to accepted morality.[15]

To Shaw, Ibsen became the first of the two types of
pioneers classified by Shaw in The Quintessence of Ibsenism.
This type of pioneer asserts "that it is right to do something hitherto regarded as infamous."  Ibsen felt that it
was right to think first of building himself and secondly

---

[14]Quoted in Shaw, Quintessence, pp. 91-93.
[15]Reuben A. Brower, "George Bernard Shaw," in Major
British Writers, ed. G. B. Harrison  (New York, 1959), II,
687.

-8-

of building the institutions of society.  To Shaw, this change explained the unkindly reception of Ibsen's new thoughts in England:  "So much easier is it to declare the right wrong than the wrong right. . . . a guilty society can more readily be persuaded that any apparently innocent act is guilty than that any apparently guilty act is innocent."[16]  Shaw seems to feel that Ibsen would have had more success telling people it was wrong to work on Monday than he would have had saying it was right to work on Sunday. Men could not accept the idea that the obligation of self-sacrifice could be removed from them--that it would be all right for them to consider a duty toward themselves first.

Shaw complained of the difficulty of finding "accurate terms" for Ibsen's new "realist morality."  To Shaw, it was Ibsen's thesis that "the real slavery of today is slavery to ideals of goodness."  Ibsen had devoted himself to showing that "the spirit of man is constantly outgrowing the ideals," and that "thoughtless conformity" to them is constantly producing tragic results.  Among those "ridden by current ideals," Ibsens plays were bound to be denounced as immoral. But, Shaw concluded,

---

[16]Shaw, pp. 23-25.

-9-

> There can be no question as to the effect
> likely to be produced on an individual by
> his conversion from the ordinary acceptance
> of current ideals as safe standards of conduct,
> to the vigilant openmindedness of Ibsen.   It
> must at once greatly deepen the sense of moral
> responsibility.[17]

Ibsen himself knew well and satirized in his plays the

moralists who inveighed against "the undermining of family

life" and the "defiance of the most solemn truths."   In

Ghosts, Pastor Manders, who represents a timid regard for

convention, warns people against books that he vaguely

associates with "intellectual progress"--and that he has

not read.   Rörlund, the schoolmaster in The Pillars of the

Community, sums up the position of the guardians of con-

ventional morality when he says:

> Our business is to keep society pure . . . to keep
> out all these experimental notions that an impatient
> age wants to force on us.[18]

Ironically, Rörlund provides a moral façade for "practical

men of affairs" like the ship owner Bernick.   Bernick, who

talks about his "deep-rooted sense of decency," has aban-

doned the woman he loved in order to marry a wealthy girl

---

[17]Shaw, pp. 147-149, 152, 154.
[18]Ibsen, Three Plays, pp. 27-28.

-10-

and save the family business.  He has abandoned to need and shame a married woman with whom he has had a secret affair. He has saved his own reputation in the community at the expense of having a younger friend blackened as a libertine and a thief.  Bernick's defense of his conduct is that he lives in a community in which "a youthful indiscretion is never wiped out."  The "community itself forces us into crooked ways."[19]  But Ibsen's heroes are people who rebel against the "tyranny of custom and convention"; who hold that "the spirit of truth and the spirit of freedom" are the "true pillars of the community."[20]

Ibsen was not intimidated by the controversy caused by his plays.  In a letter to a friend he wrote in 1881, he said:  "Ghosts will probably cause alarm in some circles. . . . If it didn't do that, there would have been no need to write it."  In a letter written a year later, he said: "That my new play would produce a howl from the camp of those 'men of stagnation' was something I was quite prepared for." Shortly afterward, he summed up his faith in the future in a letter that said in part:

---

[19] Three Plays, pp. 48, 97-98.
[20] Three Plays, pp. 116, 137.

-11-

> In time, and not before very long at that,
> the good people up home will get into their
> heads some understanding of Ghosts. But all
> those desiccated, decrepit individuals who
> pounced on this work, they will come in for
> devastating criticism in the literary histories
> of the future. People will be able to sniff
> out the nameless snipers and thugs who directed
> their dirty missiles at me from their ambush in
> Professor Goos's mouldy rag and other similar
> places. My book holds the future. Yon crowd
> that roared about it haven't even any proper
> contact with their own genuinely vital age.[21]

It was Ibsen's assertion of man's duty to himself,
against the tradition of conformity to custom and convention, that was the main grounds of significant controversy
over Ibsen's works. In presenting this view in his plays,
as a modern critic says, "Ibsen established realism as the
ruling principle of modern drama." Problems of the day had
been aired on the stage before, "but nobody before Ibsen
had treated them without equivocation or without stressing
secondary matters while ignoring primary ones." Because
he was the first, "Henrik Ibsen . . . has long held the
unofficial title of 'father of the modern drama.'"[22]

---

[21]Quoted in Henrik Ibsen, Ghosts, trans. Kai Jurgensen
and Robert Schenkkan (New York, 1965), pp. 126, 129-130.
[22]John Gassner, Introduction to Four Great Plays,
pp. vii-viii.

-12-

BIBLIOGRAPHY

Brandes, Georg. Creative Spirits of the Nineteenth Century, trans. Rasmus B. Anderson. New York: Thomas Y. Crowell Company, 1923.

Brower, Reuben A. "George Bernard Shaw," in Major British Writers, ed. G. B. Harrison. 2 vols. New York: Harcourt, Brace, and Company, 1959.

"Drama." Encyclopaedia Britannica, 1958, VII, 576-616.

Goodwin, Michael, ed. Nineteenth-Century Opinion: An Anthology (1877-1901). Hammondsworth, Middlesex: Penguin Books, 1951.

Granville-Barker, Harley. "When Ibsen Split the English Stage in Two," The Literary Digest, IIIC (April 28, 1928), 24-25.

Ibsen, Henrik. Four Great Plays by Ibsen. New York: E. P. Dutton & Co., 1959.

------. Ghosts, trans. Kai Jurgensen and Robert Schenkkan. New York: Avon Books, 1965.

------. Three Plays, trans. Una Ellis-Fermor. Hammondsworth, Middlesex: Penguin Books, 1950.

"Ibsen, Henrik Johan." Encyclopaedia Britannica, 1958, XII, 37-41.

"Inside Views of Ibsen in the Nineties," The Literary Digest, IIIC (May 12, 1928), 24.

"A Retrospective Eye on Ibsen," Theatre Arts Monthly, XII (March 1928), 199-211.

Shaw, Bernard. The Quintessence of Ibsenism, 3rd ed. New York: Hill and Wang, 1957.

Walkley, A. B. "Ibsen in England," The Living Age, XII (September 21, 1901), 790.

# 9

# GLOSSARY OF USAGE

NOTE: The following glossary reviews the status of words, word forms, and constructions that are frequently criticized as careless, illogical, excessively informal, or otherwise restricted in appropriateness and effectiveness. The glossary is limited to information that goes beyond the scope of the ordinary dictionary entry or that tends to be lost in the wealth of other information a dictionary provides.[1]

**a, an**.   The *a* should appear only before words that begin with a consonant when pronounced: *a desk, a chair, a house, a year, a C, a university.* The *an* should appear before words that begin with a vowel when pronounced (though, in writing, the first letter may be a consonant): *an eye, an essay question, an honest man, an A, an M, an uninformed reader.* In the latter position, *a* is nonstandard.

**above, above-mentioned, aforementioned, aforesaid**.   Avoid the use of *above, above-mentioned, aforementioned,* and the like, to refer to something previously mentioned. These phrases suggest the wooden, bureaucratic style of some business letters, many government publications, and most legal documents. Use a less mechanical, less obtrusive expression like

[1] For confusing words often included in a Glossary of Usage, see SP 2c; for a list of idiomatic prepositions, see D 1e.

*this point, this fact, these considerations.* If a *this* would not be clear, restate or summarize the point to which you wish to refer:

**allusion, illusion.** An "allusion" is a hint or indirect reference (to call an athlete a "Goliath" is to use a Biblical allusion). An "illusion" is a deceptive sense impression or a mistaken belief. When an illusion is serious and persistent enough, it may become a "delusion."

**amount, number.** *Amount* is sometimes used loosely instead of *number* in reference to things counted individually and as separate units.

Satisfactory:   A large number [not *amount*] of people were waiting.

Satisfactory:   The *number* [not *amount*] of unsold cars on dealers' lots was growing steadily.

***and* and *but* at the beginning of a sentence.** When *and* and *but* are used at the beginning of a sentence, or at the beginning of a paragraph, they have the effect of partly canceling out the pause signaled by the period or by the paragraph break. They can therefore suggest a sudden or an important afterthought. But many modern writers start sentences with *and* or *but* merely to avoid heavier, more formal connectives like *moreover, furthermore, however,* and *nevertheless.*

**and/or.** *And/or* is an awkward combination sometimes necessary in commercial or official documents. Its use in ordinary expository prose is an annoying mannerism.

**angle, approach, slant.** *Angle, approach,* and *slant* are currently overused as synonyms for "attitude," "point of view," "position," or "procedure."

**apt, liable, prone.** In informal speech and writing, *apt, liable,* and *prone* all appear in the sense of "likely." In formal usage, *apt* suggests that something is likely because of someone's aptitude ("He is apt to become a successful artist"); *liable* suggests that what is likely is burdensome or undesirable ("He is liable to break his leg"); *prone* suggests that something is almost inevitable because of strong habit or predisposition ("He is prone to suspect others").

**as**.    *As* as a substitute for *that* or *whether* ("I don't know *as* I can come") or as a substitute for *who* ("Those *as* knew her avoided her") is nonstandard. As a substitute for *because* or *while*, *as* is often criticized as ambiguous, unemphatic, or overused:

> *As* [better: "because"] we had no money, we gave him a check.

**attenuate, extenuate**.    Both *attenuate* and *extenuate* basically mean "to thin out." *Extenuate* is the legal term: "Extenuating circumstances" make a crime seem less serious or contemptible than it originally appeared.

**attribute, contribute**.    *Contribute* means "to give one's share" or "to have a share" in something; *attribute* means "to trace or ascribe something to a cause or source" ("He *attributed* the crossing of the letters in the mail to the intervention of a supernatural power").

**being as, being that**.    As substitutes for *because* or *since*, *being as* and *being that* ("*being that* I was ill") are nonstandard.

**between, among**.    *Between* is historically related to *twain*, which in turn is a variant of *two*. As a result, grammarians have often restricted *between* to references to two of a kind (distinguish *between* right and wrong) and required *among* in references to more than two (distinguish *among* different shades of color). *Between* is also appropriate when more than two things can be considered in pairs of two:

> He had sand *between* his toes.
> Bilateral trade agreements exist *between* many European countries.

Indiscriminate substitution of *between* for *among* invites avoidable criticism.

**blame for, blame on**.   There are two idiomatic uses of the word *blame:* "He blamed the passenger *for* the accident" and "He blamed the accident *on* the passenger." The first of these is preferred in formal English.

**calculate, reckon, expect, guess**.   In formal written English, *calculate* and *reckon* usually imply computing or systematic reasoning; *expect* implies expectation or anticipation; *guess* implies conjecture. In the sense of "think," "suppose," or "consider," these verbs are colloquial or dialectal.

***can* and *may***.   Formal English uses *can* in the sense of "be able to" or "be capable of," *may* to indicate permission. The use of *can* to indicate permission, increasingly common in speech and writing, is generally considered informal:

> **Formal:**   You *may* (have my permission to) take as much as you *can* (are able to) eat.
> **Informal:**   *Can* I speak to you for a minute?

**cannot help but**.   Although occasionally found in writing, *cannot help but* is widely criticized as an illogical or confused variant of *cannot help:*

> **Satisfactory:**   I *cannot help* wishing that I had never met you.
> **Satisfactory:**   I *cannot but* wish that I had never met you.

**childish, childlike**.   "Childish gesture" and "childlike gesture" both remind us of children; but the former suggests silliness or immaturity, the latter endearing innocence.

**compare with, compare to**.   We compare two cities *with* each other to see what they have in common, but we compare a city *to* an anthill to show what a city is like.

**continual, continuous**.   To be "continuous," something must extend without interruption in space or in time. People may keep up a "continual" conversation, interrupted because they have to pause for breath.

**couple of**. In formal writing, *couple* refers to two of a kind, a pair. Used in the sense of "several" or "a few," it is colloquial. Used before a plural noun without a connecting *of*, it is nonstandard.

**Colloquial:** We had to wait *a couple of* minutes.
**Nonstandard:** We had only *a couple* dollars left.

**credible, credulous, creditable**. Stories may be credible or incredible; the people who read them may be credulous or incredulous. An act that does someone credit is a creditable act.

**cute, great, lovely, wonderful, swell**. Words like *cute, great, lovely,* and *wonderful* so often express thoughtless or insincere praise that their use in formal writing can suggest immaturity. *Cute* is colloquial. *Swell* is slang.

**different than**. *Different from* is characteristic of formal written English. Nevertheless, *different than,* widely used in speech, is becoming acceptable in writing ("Life in cadet school for Major Major was no *different than* life had been for him all along."—Joseph Heller, *Catch-22*). Recent writers on usage point out that *different than* is the more economical way of introducing a clause:

**Economical:** We tried a different method *than* we had used last year.
**Less Economical:** We tried a different method *from the one* we had used last year.

**disinterested, uninterested**. In formal writing, *disinterested* usually means "unswayed by personal, selfish interest" or "impartial." The word is used especially to indicate the absence of financial interest or personal ambition ("We were sure he would be a *disinterested* judge.") *Disinterested* used in the sense of "uninterested" or "indifferent" is objectionable to many readers.

*do* **form for emphasis**.   Verb forms with *do, does,* or *did* can serve as emphatic variants of the simple present and the simple past: "She may not wear the latest fashions, but she *does* know how to cook." In student writing, the emphatic *do* is sometimes overused:

> **Overdone:**   I really *did appreciate* the teacher's help an awful lot.
> **Better:**   I *appreciated* the teacher's help.

**double comparative, double superlative**.   Short adjectives usually form the comparative by adding the suffix *er* (*cheaper*), the superlative by adding the suffix *est* (*cheapest*). Long adjectives, and adverbs ending in *ly*, usually employ the intensifiers *more* and *most* instead (*more expensive, most expensive; more carefully, most carefully*). Forms using both the suffix and the intensifier are nonstandard (*more cheaper, most cheapest*).

**double negative**.   Double and triple negatives—the use of additional negative words to reinforce a negation already expressed—are nonstandard: "I *didn't* do *nothing*." "*Nobody* comes to see me *no more*."

*due to* **as a preposition**.   *Due to* is generally accepted as an adjective: "His absence was *due to* ill health." "His absence, *due to* ill health, upset our schedule." As a preposition meaning "because of," *due to* is often criticized:

> **Objectionable:**   He cancéled his lecture *due to* ill health.
> **Safe:**   He canceled his lecture *because of* ill health.

**each other, one another**.   Conservative writers distinguish between *each other* (referring to two persons or things) and *one another* (referring to more than two).

**enthuse**.   *Enthuse* is a "back formation" from the noun *enthusiasm* and is used in colloquial English as a convenient shortcut for "become enthusiastic" and "move to enthusiasm." Similar back formations, like *reminisce* from *reminiscence*, have become generally acceptable. *Enthuse* still has a long way to go.

**etc.** *Etc.*, the Latin abbreviation for "and so on" or "and the like," often serves as a vague substitute for additional details, examples, or illustrations. Furthermore, *ect.* is a common misspelling; "and etc." and "such as . . . etc." are redundant and unnecessarily reveal the writer's ignorance of Latin.

**farther, further; all the farther.** A traditional rule required *farther* in references to space and distance ("We traveled *farther* than we had expected"), *further* in references to degree and quantity ("We discussed it *further* at our next meeting") and in the sense of "additional" ("without *further* delay"). *Further* is now widely accepted as appropriate in all three senses.

*All the farther* in the sense of "as far as" ("This is *all the farther* we go") is variously classified as colloquial, nonstandard, or dialectal.

**fortuitous, fortunate.** "Fortuitous" changes are accidental, unplanned developments that are not always fortunate.

**full, fulsome.** *Fulsome*, except when used by people who are confused by its similarity with *full*, means "offensive," or "disgusting." "Fulsome praise" is offensively exaggerated or insincere.

**gentleman, lady, female.** In nineteenth-century, and especially British, use, *gentleman* and *lady* identified people whose manners and social rank set them apart from the uneducated. Now both terms are usually used as polite equivalents of the blunter *man* and *woman*. Since they suggest refinement, they may sound pretentious when used in unrefined situations. *Female* is biological and impersonal; it is often condescending.

**get, got, gotten.** The verb *get* is used in many idiomatic expressions. Some of these are colloquial:

> *have got* (for "own," "possess," "have available")
> I *have got* ten dollars; she *has got* blue eyes; you *have got* ten minutes.

*have got to* (for "have to," "must," "be obliged")
I *have got to* leave now; we *have got to* think of our customers.

*get to* (for "succeed")
I finally *got to* see him.

*get* (for "understand")
*Get* it?

*get* (for "arrest," "hit," "kill")
The police finally *got* him.

*get* (for "puzzle," "irritate," "annoy")
What really *gets* me is that he never announces his tests.

Some grammarians commend the use of *get* in sentences like "He *got hit* by a truck" as an emphatic and unambiguous alternative to the ordinary passive, formed with *be, am, was, were* ("He *was hit* by a truck"). This use of *got* is still widely considered informal.

In American English, *have gotten* is an acceptable alternative to *have got,* except when the latter means *have* or *have to.*

**hadn't ought to.**   In formal English, *ought,* unlike some other auxiliaries, has no form for the past tense. *Hadn't ought* is informal; *had ought* nonstandard.

| | |
|---|---|
| Informal: | You *hadn't ought* to ask him. |
| Formal: | You *ought not to have* asked him. |

**hopefully.**   When used instead of expressions like "I hope" or "let us hope," *hopefully* is considered illogical by conservative readers.

| | |
|---|---|
| Informal: | *Hopefully,* the forms will be ready by Monday. |
| Formal: | *I hope* the forms will be ready by Monday. |

**human, humane.**   Not every human being is "humane"— that is, kind, compassionate, sensitive, or refined.

**if, whether.**   Conservative readers object to *if* when used to express doubt or uncertainty after such verbs as *ask, don't* *know, wonder, doubt.* The more formal connective is *whether:* "I doubt *whether* his support would do much good."

**in, into.** Formal writing often requires *into* rather than *in* to indicate direction: "He came *into* [not *in*] the room."

**in terms of.** A vague all-purpose connective frequent in jargon: "What have you seen lately *in terms of* new plays?"

> **Jargon:** *Virtue* originally meant "manliness" *in terms of* [better: "in the sense of"] warlike prowess or fortitude.

**infer, imply.** In formal usage, *imply* means to "indicate or suggest a certain conclusion"; *infer* means "to draw a conclusion on the basis of what has been indicated or suggested." A statement can have various implications, which may lead to inferences on the part of the reader.

**irregardless.** Used instead of *regardless, irregardless* is often heard in educated speech but is widely considered nonstandard.

**it's me, it is I.** Traditional grammarians required *it is I* on the grounds that the linking verb *is* equates the pronoun *I* with the subject *it* and thus makes necessary the use of the subject form. Modern grammarians accept *it is me* on the grounds that usual English word order (he hit *me*; she asked *me*) makes the object form natural. *It's me* is now freely used in informal speech; other pronouns (*us, him, her*) are still occasionally criticized as uneducated usage.

> **Informal:** I thought it was *him*. It could have been *us*.

**judicial, judicious.** A "judicial" decision is a decision reached by a judge or by a court. A "judicious" decision shows sound judgment. Not every judicial decision is judicious.

**later, latter.** "Although both Alfred and Francis were

supposed to arrive at eight, the former came earlier, the *latter later*."

**learn, teach.** In standard English, the teacher *teaches* (rather than *learns*) the learner; the learner is *taught* (rather than *learned*) by the teacher.

**leave, let.** In formal usage, *leave* does not mean "allow" or "permit"; you do not "leave" somebody do something. Nor does *leave* take the place of *let* in suggestions like "Let us call a meeting."

**less, fewer.** *Less* is often used interchangeably with *fewer* before plural nouns. This use of *less* was once widely condemned. The safe practice is to use *less* in references to extent, amount, degree (*less* friction, *less* money, *less* heat) but not in references to number (*fewer* people, *fewer* homes, *fewer* requirements).

***like* as a connective.** In informal speech, *like* is widely used as a connective replacing *as* or *as if* at the beginning of a clause:

| Informal: | Do *like* I tell you. |
| Formal: | Do *as* I tell you. |

| Informal: | The patient felt *like* he had slept for days. |
| Formal: | The patient felt *as if* [or *as though*] he had slept for days. |

Note that *like* is acceptable in formal usage as a preposition: "The girl looked *like* her mother."

**luxuriant, luxurious.** A "luxurious" house may be surrounded by "luxuriant"—that is, profusely growing—vegetation.

**moral, morale.** We talk about the "moral" of a story but about the "morale" of troops. People with good morale are not necessarily very moral, and vice versa.

**most, almost.** *Most* is informal when used in the sense of "almost" or "nearly": "*Most* everybody was there." "Mrs. Jones considers herself an authority on *most* any subject."

**on account of.** Nonstandard as a substitute for *because*.

Nonstandard: Once she is married, a teacher is likely to stop teaching *on account of* [should be "because"] she will have to take care of her own children.

**plan on.** In formal usage, substitute *plan to.*

Informal: My father had always *planned on* him taking over the farm as he grew older.

Formal: My father had always *planned to* have him take over the farm.

**possessives with verbal nouns.** A traditional rule requires that a verbal noun (gerund) be preceded by a possessive in sentences like the following:

Formal: He mentioned *John's winning* a scholarship.

Formal: I am looking forward to *your mother's staying* with us.

This rule is widely observed in formal writing. In informal speech and writing, the plain form is more common:

Informal: Imagine *John winning* a scholarship!

**practicable, practical.** A "practicable" plan seems capable of being put into practice. A "practical" plan, when put into practice, is workable or effective. Unlike things, people can be practical but not practicable.

**preposition at the end of a sentence.** Teachers no longer tell students not to end a sentence with a preposition. The preposition that ends a sentence is idiomatic, natural English, though more frequent in informal than in formal use.

Idiomatic: I don't remember what we talked *about.*

Idiomatic: She found her mother-in-law hard to live *with.*

Idiomatic: You know very well what I hired you *for.*

Note, however, that placing a comparatively unimportant word at the end of a sentence can make a sentence sound unemphatic:

**Emphatic:**    Let us not betray the ideals *for* which these men died.
**Emphatic:**    Do not ask *for* whom the bell tolls.

**prepositions often criticized.**    *Inside of* (for *inside*), *outside of* (for *outside*), and *at about* (for *about*) are redundant.

*Back of* for *behind* (*back of* the house), *inside of* for *within* (*inside of* three hours), *off of* for *off* (get *off of* the table), *outside of* for *besides* or *except* (no one *outside of* my friends), and *over with* for *over* (it's *over with*) are colloquial.

*As to, as regards,* and *in regard to* are generally acceptable, but they can seem heavy-handed and bureaucratic when used as indiscriminate substitutes for briefer or more precise prepositions.

**Awkward:**    I questioned him *as to* the nature of his injury.
**Preferable:**    I questioned him *about* his injury.

*As to whether, in terms of,* and *on the basis of* flourish in all varieties of jargon.

*Per* (a dollar *per* day), *as per* (*as per* your request), and *plus* (quality *plus* service) are common in business and newspaper English but inappropriate in a noncommercial context.

**provided, provided that, providing.**    *Provided, provided that,* and *providing* are interchangeable in a sentence like "He will withdraw his complaint, *provided* you apologize." However, only *provided* has consistently escaped criticism and is therefore the safest form to use.

**reason is because, reason why.**    In informal speech, *the reason . . . is because* often takes the place of the more formal *the reason . . . is that.* The former construction is often criticized as redundant, since *because* repeats the idea of cause already expressed in the word *reason.* Either construction can make a sentence unnecessarily awkward.

| | |
|---|---|
| **Informal:** | *The reason* that the majority rules *is because* it is strongest. |
| **Formal:** | *The reason* that the majority rules *is that* it is strongest. |
| **Less Awkward:** | The majority rules *because* it is strongest. |

*Reason why,* though equally open to the charge of redundancy, is less widely criticized.

**respectfully**, **respectively**.    *Respectfully* means "full of respect"; *respectively* means "with respect or reference to each of several things in the order in which they were mentioned" ("*Un* and *deux* mean one and two respectively").

**shall**, **will**.    In current American usage, *will* usually indicates simply that something is going to happen:

> I *will* ask him tomorrow.
> You *will* find it on your desk.
> Mr. Smith *will* inform you of our plans.

The more emphatic *shall* often indicates that something is going to happen as the result of strong determination, definite obligation, or authoritative command:

> I *shall* return.
> We *shall* do our best.
> Wages of common laborers *shall* not exceed twenty dollars a day.

*Shall* is also common in questions that invite the listener's approval or consent:

> *Shall* I wait for you?
> *Shall* we dance?

Formal English used to reverse the relationship between *will* and *shall* in the first person; that is, after *I* and *we* but not after *you, he,* or *they.* "I *shall* see him tomorrow" then expressed simple, unemphatic future; "I *will* not yield" expressed determination. Questions used the form expected in the answer: "*Shall* you see him tomorrow?" Current handbooks of grammar no longer require the observance of this convention.

**should**, **would**.    In many uses, *should* and *would* are parallel to *shall* and *will*. "I *would* help you if I could" is parallel to "I *will* help you"; the formal alternative, "I *should* help you if I could," is parallel to "I *shall* help you." However, both *should* and *would* are also used with distinctive meanings of their own. *Should* may express obligation ("I *should* study more"), probability ("I *should* be able to finish it tonight"), or a hypothetical condition ("If he *should* resist, call me for help"). *Would* may express customary action ("He *would* listen patiently to my excuses").

**split infinitives**.    Occasionally a modifier breaks up an infinitive; that is, a verbal formed with *to* (*to come, to promise, to have written*). The resulting split infinitive has long been idiomatic English and occurs in the work of distinguished writers. The traditional rule against it is now all but obsolete. Note, however, that a split infinitive can be awkward, especially if the modifier intervening after *to* consists of more than one word:

> **Awkward:**    He ordered us *to* with all possible speed *return* to our stations.
> **Better:**    He ordered us *to return* to our stations with all possible speed.

The words that most frequently split infinitives are overused intensifiers like *actually, definitely, literally, really,* and *virtually.* Omitting these altogether often improves the sentence:

> We expect the public *to* [literally] *overwhelm* us with orders.
> Education may be able *to* [virtually] *eliminate* race prejudice.

**superlative in reference to two**.    In informal speech and writing, the superlative rather than the comparative frequently occurs in comparisons between only two things. This use of the superlative is widely considered illogical and generally labeled inappropriate to formal usage.

> **Informal:**    Which of the two candidates is the *best* speaker?
> **Formal:**    Which of the two candidates is the *better* speaker?

*gl*

**take and**, **try and**, **up and**.   *Take and* (in "I'd *take and* prune those roses") and *up and* (in "He *up and* died") are dialectal. *Try and* for *try to* ("I'd *try and* change his mind") is colloquial.

**these kind**.   Agreement requires "*this kind* of car" or "*these kinds* of fish." "*These kind* of cars" and "*those kind* of cars" are informal.

**titles: *Dr.*, *Prof.*, *Reverend*.**   In references to holders of academic degrees or titles, *Dr. Smith* and *Professor Brown* are courteous and correct. *Professor* is sometimes abbreviated when it precedes the full name: *Prof. Paul F. Brown.* In references to a clergyman, *Reverend* is usually preceded by *the* and followed by the first name, by initials, or by *Mr.* (*the Reverend William Carper; the Reverend W. F. Carper; the Reverend Mr. Carper*).

**too**.   The use of *too* in expressions like "He isn't *too* well off" is often condemned as vague or overused.

**type**, **type of**, **-type**.   The practice of omitting the *of* in expressions like "this *type* of plane" is colloquial. *Type* is increasingly used as a suffix to turn nouns into adjectives: "an escape-type novel," "a drama-type program." Such combinations strike many readers as barbarisms, foreign to idiomatic, natural English. Often they are used to turn simple ideas into fuzzy, wordy phrases: "A subsidy-type payment" says no more than "subsidy."

**unique**, **perfect**, **equal**.   It is often argued that one thing cannot be *more unique, more perfect,* or *more equal* than another; either it is unique or it isn't. Formal English therefore often substitutes *more nearly unique, more nearly perfect, more nearly equal.*

**up**.   *Up* is often criticized as redundant in expressions like *finish up, heat up, hurry up, rise up,* or *sober up.* In other expressions it modifies meaning or adds emphasis: *buy up, clean* *up, dress up, speak up, use up.* Most of these combinations have a colloquial flavor. *Beat up* is slang.

**used to, didn't use to, used to could.**    *Used to* in questions or negative statements with *did* is informal and only occasionally seen in print ("the strident . . . anti-police slogans which *didn't use to* be part of the hippie mode"—*National Review*).

| | |
|---|---|
| **Informal:** | She *didn't use to* smoke. |
| **Formal:** | She *used not to* smoke. |

*Used to could* is nonstandard for *used to be able.*

***very* and *much*.**    Formal usage prefers *much* or *greatly* to *very* before a verbal like *surprised* or *embarrassed* (past participle) if the verbal idea is still strong; that is, if the verbal has not yet become an ordinary adjective with little suggestion of action or process:

| Sometimes Criticized | Safe |
|---|---|
| *very* surprised | *much* surprised |
| *very* embarrassed | *greatly* embarrassed |
| *very* astonished | *very much* astonished |

**where, where at, where to.**    In formal English, *where* takes the place of *where to* ("*Where* was it sent?") and *where at* ("*Where* is he?"). Both *where to* and *where at* are generally condemned as redundant.

*Where* used instead of *that* ("I read in the paper *where* a boy was killed") is colloquial.

**-wise.**    The practice of converting a noun into an adverb by tacking on *-wise* is characteristic of business or advertising jargon. Use *grammatically* for *grammar-wise*, *linguistically* for *language-wise.*

**without.**    *Without* is nonstandard when used as a connective introducing a clause.

**Nonstandard:**     The landlord won't let me stay *without* I pay the rent.

**Standard:**     The landlord won't let me stay *unless* I pay the rent.

***you* with indefinite reference**.   Formal writing generally restricts *you* to the meaning of "you, the reader." Much informal writing uses *you* with indefinite reference to refer to people in general; formal writing would substitute *one:*

**Informal:**     In ancient Rome, *you* had to be a patrician to be able to vote.

**Formal:**     In ancient Rome, *one* had to be a patrician to be able to vote.

# 10

# GRAMMATICAL TERMS

NOTE: Use the index to locate fuller discussion of many of the grammatical terms listed in this glossary.

**absolute construction**. A word or phrase that is grammatically independent of the rest of the sentence. Typically, a verbal or verbal phrase: "*The guests having departed,* Arvin locked the door."

**active**. See VOICE.

**adjective**. A class of words that can point out a quality of a noun (or noun equivalent). They occur characteristically as modifiers of nouns ("the *happy* child") and as predicate adjectives ("The child was *happy*"). They normally have distinctive forms for use in comparisons (*happier, happiest; more reasonable, most reasonable*).

**adjective clause**. A dependent clause serving an adjective function: "The man *who had startled us* apologized."

**adverb**. A class of words used to modify verbs, adjectives, other adverbs, or a sentence as a whole:

He ran *quickly.*
He was *strangely* silent.
He sang *moderately* well.
*Surprisingly*, he did not answer.

Many adverbs show the distinctive *-ly* ending.

**adverbial clause**.    A dependent clause serving an adverbial function: "We left *after the rain had stopped.*" "*When the bell had ceased to ring,* I opened the door."

**agreement**.    Correspondence, mainly in number, between grammatically related elements. Use of matching forms of a subject and its verb (the *dog barks*—the *dogs bark*); choice of a pronoun matching its antecedent ("*Each* member must be aware of *his* responsibility").

**antecedent**.    The noun (or equivalent) for which a pronoun substitutes: "*Aunt Hertha* fell sick soon after *she* arrived."

**appositive**.    A noun (or equivalent) placed as a modifier next to—usually after—another noun: "Mr. Brown, *the registrar*, proved most helpful."

**articles**.    *A* and *an* (the **indefinite** articles) and *the* (the **definite** article), used as noun markers: *a* book, *an* honest man, *the* door.

**auxiliaries**.    "Helping" verbs used in forming complete verbs: *be* (*am, are, was,* etc.), *have, shall* (*should*), *will* (*would*), *can* (*could*), *may* (*might*), *must, ought.*

**case**.    Inflected forms of nouns and pronouns, signaling certain grammatical relationships within a sentence: the **possessive** of nouns (*George's* friend), the **subject forms** and **object forms** of pronouns (*I–me, he–him,* etc.).

**clause**.    A subject-predicate unit that may combine with other such units in a sentence. **Independent** clauses are grammatically self-contained and can be punctuated as complete sentences:

> *I think; therefore, I am.*
> *I think. Therefore, I am.*

**Dependent** clauses are grammatically subordinate to an independent clause (main clause):

> Arvin had a dog, *which barked all night.*
> *After the rain stopped,* we went home.

See also ADJECTIVE CLAUSE, ADVERBIAL CLAUSE, NOUN CLAUSE.

**collective noun.**    A group noun that is singular in form but may require a plural verb:

> **Singular:**    The *jury votes* tomorrow. (thought of as a unit)
> **Plural:**    The *jury are* out to lunch. (thought of as individuals)

**comparative.**    The form of adjectives and adverbs that is used to indicate higher degree: "Blood is *thicker* than water."

**complement.**    A sentence element completing the predication of the verb. The complements of action verbs are called **objects**:

> Arvin called *the sheriff* (**direct** object).
> She wrote *my father* (**indirect** object) *a letter* (**direct** object).

The complement of a linking verb is a noun or adjective describing the subject (**subjective complement**):

> Her father was *a businessman* (**predicate noun**).
> The girl looked *pale* (**predicate adjective**).

After some verbs, an object is followed by a description of the object (**objective complement**):

> The editorial called the project *a failure.*
> Arvin labeled the charges *ridiculous.*

**conjunction.** See CONNECTIVES.

**conjunctive adverb.** See CONNECTIVES.

**connectives.** Words that connect sentence elements or clauses: **coordinating connectives** (*and, but, for, or, nor*); **subordinating connectives** (*if, when, because, though, whereas*); **adverbial connectives** (*however, therefore, consequently*).

**coordinate adjectives.** Two or more adjectives describing different qualities of the same noun, with a comma taking the place of *and:* "a *noisy, unruly* crowd."

**correlatives.** Pairs of connectives coordinating sentence elements or clauses: *either . . . or, neither . . . nor, not only . . . but also, whether . . . or.*

**determiners.** Noun markers including **articles** (*a, an, the*), **demonstrative pronouns** (*this, these; that, those*), and **possessive pronouns** (*my, your, his, her, its, our, their*).

**elliptical constructions.** Constructions in which missing elements can be supplied to facilitate grammatical analysis:

> The paintings [*that*] he collected filled a large room.
> When [*she was*] interviewed, the actress denied rumors of an impending engagement.

**expletives.** The *it* and *there* used as mere introductory words in *it-is, there-is, there-are* sentences.

**finite verb.** A term used to distinguish a complete verb from a verbal, which cannot by itself function as a predicate.

**function words.** Words whose major function is to establish grammatical relationships within a sentence: articles, connectives, prepositions.

**gender**.   The quality of nouns and pronouns that determines choice between *he, she,* or *it;* between *actor* and *actress, alumnus* and *alumna, fiancé* and *fiancée.*

**gerund**.   See VERBAL.

**idiom**.   An expression that does not conform to general grammatical patterns but is established by usage as the habitual way of conveying a given meaning: *bear in mind, have a mind to, keep in mind.*

**infinitive**.   See VERBAL.

**inflection**.   Changes in the form of words to reflect changes in grammatical relationships: the plural *-s* of nouns; the *-s, -ed,* or *-ing* of verbs; the *-er* or *-est* of adjectives.

**intensifier**.   Words that modify adjectives or adverbs and express degree; also called **intensive adverbs**: *very* hot, *quite* calm, *rather* young.

**interjection**.   A grammatically independent element used to express attitude or emotion: *ah, oh, ouch,* etc.

**kernel sentences**.   The minimum sentences from which more complicated structures are derived in transformational grammar. They are the **source sentences** from which actual sentences are generated by successive transformations.

**linking verb**.   See VERB.

**modifier**.   A word, phrase, or clause that develops or restricts the meaning of another sentence element or the sentence as a whole (see ADJECTIVE, ADVERB). **Restrictive** modifiers contribute to identification and need no punctuation; **nonrestrictive** modifiers provide additional information not essential to identification and are set off, normally by commas:

**Restrictive:**      The man *who returned my wallet* was a complete stranger.

**Nonrestrictive:**   Mr. Norton, *who found my wallet,* is an old friend.

**mood.**   The classification of verb forms as **indicative** (plain or factual: "I am ready"); **imperative** (request or command: "Be quiet"); and **subjunctive** (hypothetical or contrary to fact: "I wish he were here!").

**noun.**   A class of words that name or classify people, animals, things, ideas. They occur typically as subjects of clauses or as objects of verbs and prepositions. Their appearance is often signaled by noun markers like the **articles** (*a, an, the*). Many nouns add *-s* to the plain form to form the plural: *dogs, cars, houses, colleges.*

**noun clause.**   A dependent clause taking the place of a noun: "*That he was late* does not surprise me."

**noun equivalent.**   A sentence element (pronoun, infinitive, gerund, noun clause) that is grammatically equivalent to a noun.

**number.**   Choice of appropriate forms to express **singular** (one of a kind) or **plural** (more than one).

**object.**   See COMPLEMENT.

**object form.**   See CASE.

**participle.**   See VERBAL.

**passive.**   See VOICE.

**past.**   See TENSE.

**perfect.**   See TENSE.

**person**.    Choice of appropriate forms to express the person speaking (**first person**: *I know, we know*); the person spoken to (**second person**: *you know*); or the person spoken about (**third person**: *he knows, they know*).

**phrase**.    A group of related words, typically a preposition or a verbal accompanied by its object or other related material.

| | |
|---|---|
| **Prepositional Phrase:** | I rene sat *at the window.* |
| **Verbal Phrase:** | Father gave up *smoking cigars.* |

**predicate**.    The second basic element of the typical written sentence, making an assertion about the subject. The predicate consists of a complete (finite) verb and its possible complements and modifiers.

**preposition**.    A class of words that relate a noun (or equivalent) to the rest of the sentence: "Arvin left *after* dark."

**present**.    See TENSE.

**principal parts**.    The basic forms of a verb: simple present (*know*), simple past (*knew*), past participle (*known*).

**progressive construction**.    Verb form expressing action in progress: "Fred *was lighting* a cigarette."

**pronoun**.    A class of words taking the place of nouns; classified as **personal** (*I, you, he*), **possessive** (*my, your, his*), **reflexive** or **intensive** (*myself, yourself, himself*), **demonstrative** (*this, that*), **relative** (*who, which, that*), **interrogative** (*who, which, what*), and **indefinite** (*one, anyone, everyone*). See also CASE.

**relative clause**.    A dependent clause related to the main clause by a relative pronoun: "The article *that I mentioned* begins on page 5."

**restrictive**.    See MODIFIER.

**sentence**.　A grammatically complete and self-contained unit of thought or expression, set off from other such units by end punctuation. The typical written sentence contains at least a subject and a predicate ("Birds sing"). The most common exception is the subjectless request or command, in which the subject is said to be understood ("Show him in").

Sentences combining two or more independent clauses are called **compound**. Sentences combining an independent and one or more dependent clauses are called **complex**. A combination of the two types is called **compound-complex**.

| | |
|---|---|
| Compound: | He hummed, and she sang. |
| Complex: | He hummed when she sang. |
| Compound-Complex: | When they heard the news, he hummed and she sang. |

**source sentence**.　See KERNEL SENTENCE.

**subject**.　The first basic element of the typical written sentence, about which the predicate makes an assertion.

**subject form**.　See CASE.

**subjunctive**.　See MOOD.

**superlative**.　The form of adjectives and adverbs used to express highest degree: "Fred is the *fastest* runner on the team."

**tense**.　The system of verb forms expressing primarily different relationships in time:

| | | | |
|---|---|---|---|
| Present: | I know | Perfect: | I have known |
| Past: | I knew | Past Perfect: | I had known |
| Future: | I will (shall) know | Future Perfect: | I will (shall) have known |

**transformation**.　One of the successive steps by which more complicated structures are produced from simple ones in a transformational grammar. The reshuffling, addition, or deletion of grammatical elements needed, for instance, to turn present into past tense, active into passive voice, or an affirmative into a negative statement. See also KERNEL SENTENCE.

**transitive.**  See VERB.

**verb.**  A class of words that signal the performance of an action, the occurrence of an event, or the presence of a condition. Verbs appear in typical verb positions: "Let's *leave*." "The boys *left* the scene." They typically take an *-s* in the third person singular of the present tense (*asks, leaves, condones*). They use characteristic **auxiliaries** in forms consisting of more than one word (*have left, was asked, will be leaving*). **Action verbs** are modified by adverbs; **linking verbs** are followed by adjectives:

| Action Verb: | He *responded* quickly. |
| Linking Verb: | His response *seemed* quick. |

**Regular** verbs use the same form for the simple past and the past participle:

| Regular: | I *laughed* | I have *laughed* |
| Irregular: | I *knew* | I have *known* |

**Transitive** verbs normally require an object:

| Transitive: | He *raises* chickens. |
| Intransitive: | He *rises* early. |

See also TENSE, MOOD, VOICE.

**verbal.**  A form that is derived from a verb but does not by itself function as a predicate: **infinitive** (*to* form), **present participle** (*-ing* form used as an adjective), **gerund** (*-ing* form used as a verbal noun), **past participle** (*-ed* form in regular verbs, irregular in others). Verbals appear as noun equivalents, modifiers, and *parts* of verbs.

| Infinitive: | He liked *to dream*. |
| Present Participle: | Her *dreaming* look entranced him. |

| | |
|---|---|
| **Gerund:** | *Dreaming* got him nowhere. |
| **Past Participle:** | He had *dreamed* of childhood days. |

**voice.** The verb form that shows whether the subject is acting (**active**) or acted upon (**passive**):

| | |
|---|---|
| **Active:** | Eileen *feeds* the children. |
| **Passive:** | The children *are fed* by Eileen. |

# APPENDIX: LETTERS

*Make the appearance and style of your business letters suggest the qualities prized by business people: competence and efficiency.*

Correspondence creates special problems of manuscript form. In writing or answering a formal invitation, you will do well to follow forms suggested in a book of etiquette. In writing a personal letter, you may allow yourself considerable freedom, as long as you keep your handwriting legible and use presentable stationery. Between these extremes of formality and informality is the kind of letter that you may have to write to a teacher, to a college official, or to a future employer. In applying for a scholarship or for a job, you will do well to follow a conventional letter form.

## Format and Style

*Make sure your business letters are neat and consistent in format, clear and courteous in style.* The specimen letter on page 389 illustrates a format widely used in business correspondence. You may use it as a model for spacing, indention, and punctuation.

Notice the following possible variations:

(1) When you are not using the letterhead of a firm or

*809 East Victoria Street* • *Dominguez Hills, California 90247*

Heading ⟶ June 14, 19___

Institute for Better Business Writing, Inc.
1000 University Way
Los Angeles, California    90025    ⟵ Inside Address

Gentlemen: ⟵ Salutation

I was happy to receive your request for information
regarding business letter formats.

The format of this letter is the one most frequently
used in business.  It's called the block format.
With the exception of the heading and the signature
block, all its elements begin at the left hand margin,
even the first word of each paragraph.  The body of
the letter is single-spaced, with double spacing
between paragraphs.

Body

Secretaries generally like the block format better
than the older indented formats.  It has a clean and
precise appearance, and is quicker to type -- no
fiddling around with indentations.

There are other formats in use, but the block format
seems to have the widest appeal.  You won't go wrong
adopting it for all your official correspondence.

Signature Block

   complimentary close
   signature
   signature identification

Sincerely yours,

*Walter Wells*

Walter Wells
Department of English

WW:mea ⟵ IEC Block
   cc:   Dean Howard Brody

    initials (of author and typist)
    enclosures (if any)
    carbon copies

institution, type in *your address* above the date, as follows:

138 South Third Street
San Jose, California   95126
January 12, 1968

Mr. Ralph J. Clark, Jr.
Personnel Manager
San Rafael Independent-Journal
185 Washington Street
San Rafael, California

Dear Mr. Clark:

(2) A *married woman* should put (*Mrs.*) in front of her typed name.

Try to write clearly and naturally; do not adopt a special business jargon when you write a business letter. Avoid especially the following: a *stodgy*, old-fashioned businessese ("wish to advise that," "beg to acknowledge," "am in receipt of," "pursuant to," "the aforementioned"); a *breezy* "shirtsleeve" English ("give it the old college try," "fight tooth and nail," "give them a run for their money").

## The Letter of Application

*Make your letter of application suggest competence, confidence, and a genuine interest in the position for which you apply.* Employers look for employees who will prove an asset to their organization and who are at the same time good to work with and good to know. They shy away from applicants who seem to promise problems, trouble, complexes, or an overinflated ego. Remember the following advice:

(1) If possible, be *specific* about the position for which you apply. Introduce the letter by mentioning the advertisement or the person that informed you of the vacancy (but do not mention leads that smack of the "grapevine").

(2) Stress *previous training* and practical experience that you can show to be relevant to the job. Give a factual tone to the account of your qualifications, while at the same time presenting them to advantage.

(3) Give your letter *character*. Establish your identity. Many job applications look very much the same, and the anonymous, average applicant has little chance to be remembered—and to be preferred. If you have strong positive convictions about the work of the organization to which you apply, state them in a paragraph or two. If you have some serious thoughts about the role of business in a free society, hazard them.

(4) If you list *references,* obtain prior permission from those whose names you use. Common sense suggests that you quietly drop from your list the name of any teacher or former employer who shows little enthusiasm when you tell him about your plans.

(5) If the account of your qualifications is extensive, put it on a separate "data sheet," or *résumé.*

Study the sample letters on pages 392–394:[1]

## Exercises

**A.** Find a project or recent development that merits publicity or support. Write a letter about it to the editors of a newspaper or magazine, to a legislator, or to a responsible official. Observe conventional letter form.

**B.** Write a letter of application for a position in which you have at one time or another taken an interest. State the qualifications that you might have by the time you are ready to apply for the position in earnest.

[1] The sample letters in this section are adapted from Walter Wells, *Communications in Business* (Belmont, California: Wadsworth Publishing Company, 1968).

Dear Mr. Clark:

In answer to your advertisement, I wish to apply for a post as a general reporter. My credentials are that I am a journalism major, and I have had some practical experience of working for a newspaper.

On February 1, I shall graduate from San Jose State College. While getting a degree, I have taken a broad range of courses, representing all areas of editing and reporting. Also, I have been a general reporter for the Spartan Daily for two years and a feature editor for one year. Last summer I worked for thirteen weeks on the Santa Clara Journal, as an "intern" sponsored by the Journalism Department of my college. I did general reporting and some photography.

The following gentlemen have agreed to supply references:

> Dr. John Williams
> Department of Journalism
> San Jose State College
> San Jose, California
>
> Mr. Thomas Bigelow
> General Manager
> Santa Clara Journal
> Santa Clara, California
>
> Mr. Richard H. James
> Editor
> Los Angeles Examiner
> Los Angeles, California

I am prepared to be interviewed when you find it convenient.

> Yours truly,
>
> *Gerald P. Johnson*
>
> Gerald P. Johnson

Mr. Daniel Levin, Attorney at Law
Peale, Corman, Bishop, Levin & Dilworthy
80 Lomita Canyon Boulevard, Suite 7630
Beverly Hills, California    92025

Dear Mr. Levin:

Edith Winters informs me of an opening in your secretarial staff, a position for which I should very much
like to become a candidate.

I understand that you need a legal secretary with a
rapid stenographic skill and the ability to handle a
large volume of correspondence. Along with my degree
in legal stenography from Foothill Junior College, I
have four years of secretarial experience in retail
dry goods and in insurance. My shorthand speed is
145 words per minute. On my present job, I handle
between forty and sixty letters every day. Both at
Foothill and on the job, I have had training sufficient to prepare me to handle routine letters without
supervision.

My present job at Southwestern Life & Indemnity has
been quite satisfactory, but, having taken my degree
recently, I seek the further challenges and rewards
of a top-flight legal firm. Miss Winters' enthusiasm
for her work assures me that I would like the job. I
hope the enclosed résumé will help interest the firm in
me.

I can be in Los Angeles for an interview any afternoon
convenient for you. May I look forward to speaking
with you about the position you have available?

                    Yours sincerely,

                    *Laura Edmondson*

                    Laura Edmondson

ADAM PIERCE

Demmler Hall
Valhalla University
Kent, Ohio    26780
613 KE 8 7600

Age:  23
Ht:  6-1  Wt:  170
Single
Willing to relocate

## Education

B.S. in Industrial Engineering, Valhalla University,
June 1969; top 10% of class, with special course
work in statistics, motivational psychology,
business law, and communications.

Won U.S. Paint Company Scholarship 1968
Member of Industrial Relations Club
Elected Secretary of the Student Council
On Dean's Honor Roll since 1966

Also attended Colfax College, Colfax, Indiana, 1964-65

## Experience

Staff Supervisor, Cleveland Boys' Club Camp, Kiowa, Ohio,
summer 1968; responsible for housing, activities
scheduling and occasional discipline of fourteen
counselors and 110 campers.

Camp Counselor, Cleveland Boys' Club Camp, Kiowa, Ohio,
summers of 1966 and 1967.

## Personal Interests

Politics, world affairs, camping, chess, junior chamber
of commerce member, and volunteer hospital worker.

## Military Service

Served six months' active duty, U.S. Army, Fort Dix,
New Jersey, Oct. 1965 to April 1966.  Presently
on reserve duty, attending one weekend meeting
per month.

## References

Will gladly be provided upon request.

# INDEX

**395**